The PMP® Exam

HOW TO PASS ON YOUR FIRST TRY

5th Edition

ANDY CROWE, PMP

Velociteach

Velociteach is a Global Registered Education Provider with the Project Management Institute.

All inquiries should be addressed to (e-mail): info@velociteach.com

First Edition, May, 2003
Second Edition, June, 2004
Third Edition, October, 2005,
Fourth Edition, April, 2009
Fifth Edition, First printing: May, 2013
    Second printing, August, 2013
    Third printing, September, 2013
    Fourth printing, November, 2013
    Fifth printing, April, 2014

International Standard Book No. ISBN-13: 978-0-9827608-5-7
          ISBN-10: 0-9827608-5-7

ATTENTION CORPORATIONS, UNIVERSITIES, COLLEGES, AND PROFESSIONAL ORGANIZATIONS. Quantity discounts are available on bulk purchases of this book. For information, please contact info@velociteach.com.

To Clint, Kyle, and Anne.

Also by Andy Crowe

Available on Amazon.com in print and Kindle editions.

Contents

Foreword

This is the 5th edition of **The PMP exam: How to Pass on Your First Try**. This represents a significant update over the 4th edition, with new content, 50 new questions, over 100 new glossary terms, and a new, cleaner layout. Over 100,000 copies of this book have been sold now, preparing people from all over the world to pass the PMP Exam.

The PMP exam is particularly infamous. It is loaded with difficult questions and terminology that test both your knowledge and your ability to apply it in tough situations. Before you panic, however, rest assured that this book works, and it works well. Studying for PMP certification takes a significant amount of commitment and effort, but knowing what to study should be effortless. That's where this book comes in!

The processes are not arbitrary. They are derived from a compilation of generally accepted best practices, industry knowledge, and wisdom that has taken decades to evolve into its current form. Those who pass the exam without truly understanding the driving philosophy and reasons behind the material are doing themselves and the project management profession a great disservice.

Several resources exist for PMP exam preparation, so why should this be the one volume you use? Because it's designed from page one to be better. It is clearly organized and presents the material in an easily understandable format without insulting the reader's intelligence. Every process, input, tool and technique, and output is clearly explained, and the reasons underlying each are addressed. There is also a glossary of terms in the back that is an excellent reference by itself. Combined with the online companion website, insite.velociteach.com, you'll find more than enough to help you pass the PMP exam!

I believe you will find this end result to be the most complete, concise, and up to date study resource for the PMP exam.

Here's to your success!

ANDY CROWE, PMP, PgMP, PMI-ACP

About the Author

Andy Crowe, PMP, PgMP, PMI-ACP speaks, writes, and researches prolifically on project management. In addition to this book, he has authored _Alpha Project Managers: What The Top 2% Know that Everyone Else Does Not_. and _The PMI-ACP Exam: How To Pass On Your First Try_. Crowe is founder and CEO of Velociteach, a company passionate about the dissemination of best practices in project management, headquartered in Kennesaw, GA. He spends much of his time writing in the Blue Ridge Mountains.

Stay Current

Get updates from Andy on Twitter at _twitter.com/andycrowe_ and from Velociteach at _twitter.com/velociteach._

Ask exam-related questions, participate in discussions, and stay on top of trends and best practices in project management by communicating with Andy and the Velociteach team via their project management blog at _savvypm.velociteach.com_.

Get exam tips, free content, and special offers by liking this book at _facebook.com/PMPExam_

About Velociteach

Velociteach, a Kennesaw, GA company, is one of the US Chamber of Commerce's top 100 small businesses for 2013 and the Project Management Institute's Continuing Professional Education Provider of the Year for 2012. As a Global Registered Education Provider (R.E.P.), Velociteach offers training around the world, teaching certification and advanced project management theory and practice.

Velociteach offers live classroom, distance, and e-learning courses around the world. Full details on this and other course offerings are available online at www.velociteach.com.

Introduction

The best part of my job has to be hearing from people who bought this book, took an online class, or attended one of our project management boot camps. Practically every day I get email from someone who passed the PMP exam, and it always brightens my day. I read them all, and I try to respond to each of them. Being on the receiving end of hundreds of thank you letters each year is incredibly rewarding and also quite humbling.

I wrote the first edition of this book in 2002, and I have worked on it constantly since then to keep it accurate and relevant. It is a labor of love.

The 5th edition is packed with new content, more questions, more diagrams, and nearly 100 new glossary terms than the 4th edition had. The questions that were added were carefully crafted to be compatible with the 2013 exam changes. Those who are familiar with earlier editions should find this edition to be an upgrade in virtually every way.

There is an old saying, "If it were easy, everyone would do it." Among the many certifications available today, the PMP stands out as the most prestigious, in part because it is considered highly difficult to attain.

This book will cut down on the difficulty factors and demystify the material. In the following chapters, you will find exactly what you need to study for the test, how to learn it, how to apply it, and why it is important. *The PMP Exam: How to Pass on Your First Try* is a complete resource to help you prepare fully for the PMP certification exam.

In order to get the most from your efforts, you should read the material in this book, practice the examples, and then take and re-take the sample exam, reading the explanations that accompany each question. Additionally, Chapter 14 was written to help you know when you are ready to take the exam.

All in all, you should find your preparation for PMP certification a highly rewarding experience. Aside from the financial and career benefits that accompany it, PMP certification is a very worthy goal. The PMP is one of the most fungible certifications you can earn, recognized by nearly every industry and in over 120 countries around the world.

Conventions Used in this Book

The 5th edition of <u>The PMP Exam: How to Pass on Your First Try</u> is structured differently than other exam preparation materials. Some of the key features that will help you get the most from this book are listed below:

- Instead of making the book gender neutral (he/she), the masculine pronoun was generally used. Writers struggle with the best way to do this, as there is no gender-neutral singular pronoun in English ("their" is not a grammatically correct substitute for "his" or "her", nor is "they" a grammatically correct substitute for "he" or "she"). The use of this convention was not intended to diminish the role of female project managers. Rather, this choice was made to improve the readability of the book.

- In order to create a comprehensive reference, every process, input, tool and technique, and output is included, but to help you prioritize your study, key information for the exam is designated by a symbol next to topics of particular importance.

- There is a structure and priority to the material. The book will guide you, and by the time you have read a chapter or two and taken a couple of the quizzes, you will start to understand. By studying the right information with the proper emphasis, you can be confident of passing. You will also find many topics not even mentioned in the PMBOK® Guide expanded on quite heavily in this book. These come from recognized sources and volumes on which the exam relies.

- The philosophy behind each knowledge area and many of the sub-topics is explained. Because several questions on the PMP Exam require you to apply the information instead of simply regurgitating it, you must understand "why" the information is structured the way it is, instead of merely memorizing it.

- A large portion of the PMP Exam relies on understanding key terms related to project management. Many test-takers go wrong by relying on their own experiences to interpret terminology instead of understanding PMI's definitions. PMI's use of a term or concept may be very different than that of someone who has not had exposure to PMI's philosophy. Key terms are given special attention where necessary to help readers become acquainted with PMI's usage of project management terms and concepts.

- The decision was made to omit the word "project" in literally thousands of instances, believing that its inclusion did not make the material easier to understand, nor would its omission result in a lower exam score; however, for those of you who take offense at this (and you know who you are), the author offers this small consolation: "project, project."

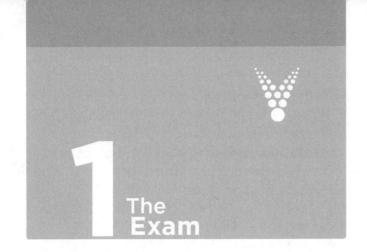

1 The Exam

Difficulty	Memorization	Exam Importance
LOW	HIGH	HIGH

This chapter will explore the PMP certification exam, what it is like, and the material it covers. It will clarify exactly what the test is, how it is structured, and an overview of the contents. Specific strategies on how to pass the exam will be discussed in Chapter 14 – How to Pass the PMP on Your First Try.

What the Exam Tests

Before we discuss what the PMP certification exam does test, let's clear up a few misconceptions about the exam.

The PMP certification exam *does not* test:

- Your project management experience or competence
- Your common sense
- Your knowledge of industry practices
- Your knowledge of how to use software tools
- What you learned in management school
- Your intelligence

The PMP certification exam *does* test:

- Your knowledge of PMI's processes
- Your understanding of the many terms that are used to describe the processes
- Your ability to apply those processes in a variety of situations
- Your ability to apply key formulas to scheduling, costing, estimating, and other problems

A Passing Grade

Not to scare you right away, but the cold, hard truth is that many who take the PMP Exam do not pass. Those who do not pass come from a broad cross-section of people, ranging from those who have approached the exam with extensive preparation, including books and training classes, to those who have barely expended any effort. By using this book, you are tilting the scales decidedly in your favor!

The exam is pass/fail, and to pass the PMP Exam, you have to answer at least 106 questions correctly out of the 175 graded questions on the test (more on graded questions later). That translates to 61%, and if your first reaction to the 61% mark is that it does not sound very impressive, consider that the 2013 exam revision is tougher than the one many people took in years past. 61% is a great score, and each year, tens of thousands of project managers do not pass.

Some people find it very difficult to understand why they cannot study and make a perfect score on the PMP. It is a good thing to want to do well on the exam, but considering the incredible breadth of material, simply passing it is a terrific accomplishment! Experts disagree over some of the questions, and there will be some that you will feel absolutely certain you got right that you likely missed. This has more to do with the way the questions are constructed and worded than it does with the study effort you put in, your intellectual powers, or your test-taking abilities.

Your goal in taking the PMP should be to do your absolute best and to make sure that your best effort falls within PMI's passing score limits.

The Exam Material

Your PMP Exam will be made up of exactly 200 questions, covering a broad variety of material, but only 175 of those questions will count

Question Allocation on the PMP Exam

Process Group	Number of Questions	% of Exam
Initiating	23	13%
Planning	42	24%
Executing	52	30%
Monitoring and Controlling	44	25%
Closing	14	8%
Total Graded Questions	175	100%

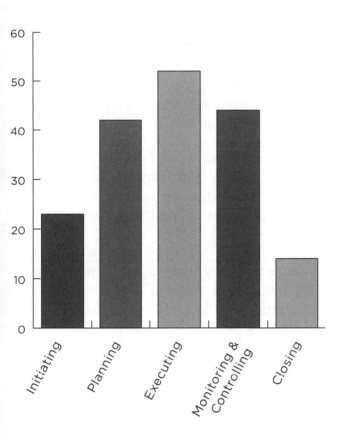

toward your score. The other 25 questions are considered experimental questions that PMI is evaluating for use on future exams. The good news is that these 25 questions do not count toward your grade. The bad news is that you will never know which questions count and which do not since they are scattered randomly throughout the exam.

PMI does provide some guidelines as to how the material will be presented. The exam was significantly updated July 31, 2013, and the updated material and questions are allocated as shown in the table on the previous page.

The terms used here - initiating, planning, executing, monitoring and controlling, closing, and professional and social responsibility - will be explained in Chapter 3 – Process Framework.

This fact shocks many people preparing for the exam, but the **PMBOK Guide (pronounced "pim-bock"), which stands for a Guide to the Project Management Body of Knowledge, is not a single study source for the PMP Exam.** The PMBOK Guide does provide an excellent definition and presentation of the overall processes, but it does not give you much help in knowing how that material will translate to the exam. Many of those who do not pass the PMP Exam tried to use the PMBOK Guide as their study guide and were surprised that there were questions, terms, and concepts on the exam that were not in the PMBOK Guide.

The Exam

Getting to the Test (Application)

It is highly recommended that you join the Project Management Institute prior to signing up to take the test. At publication time, the new member fee was $139.00 ($129.00 membership + $10.00 new member activation fee). Application may be made online at www.pmi.org, or you may obtain an application from PMI by calling (610) 356-4600.

After joining PMI, you will receive a membership number that you can use to receive a $150.00 discount on the exam's non-member fee, so you instantly save money by joining. The Examination Fee will be $405.00 for a member in good standing. If you elect not to join PMI, it will cost $555.00 to apply to take the test.

In addition to the financial advantage, there are many other benefits that come with joining PMI, including a subscription to PMI's publications, PM Network and PM Today; discounts on books and PMI-sponsored events; and access to a wealth of information in the field of project management.

When you get ready to apply for eligibility for PMP certification, you can apply online or use printed forms. If at all possible, you should apply online. Depending on the time of year, wait times have been known to stretch out for weeks when using printed forms through the mail, while online applicants usually report turnaround times within one

Requirements to Apply with a College Diploma

- A University Degree
- 4,500 hours of project management experience
- 35 hours of project management education

Requirements to Apply without a College Diploma

- A High school diploma or equivalent
- 7,500 hours of project management experience
- 35 hours of project management education (note that the online class included on the keycard in the back of this book can provide you with eight of those contact hours).

to two weeks. The length of time can vary, depending on the volume of applications that PMI is processing. In any case, **you must have your letter of eligibility from PMI to sit for the PMP certification exam.**

To be eligible for PMP certification, you will need to demonstrate that you meet certain minimum criteria. The current qualifications that PMI requires are summarized in the table on the previous page.

In short, if you hold a university degree, you should apply under the first category. If not, you should apply under the second. See PMI's official guide, available online at www.pmi.org, for more details on this point.

Ongoing Education

PMPs are expected to demonstrate not only knowledge and experience but also their ongoing commitment to the field of project management. To promote such commitment, PMI requires that all PMPs maintain their certification status by completing at least 60 Professional Development Units (PDUs) every 36 months. The requirements for PDUs are defined in further detail in the PMI Continuing Certification Requirements Program Handbook given to all PMPs, and these requirements are similar in nature to requirements that legal, medical, and other professions have adopted. In order to maintain the value of this certification, PMI requires its PMPs to maintain a project management focus and a continued commitment to the field of project management.

The Testing Environment

The PMP certification exam is administered in a formal environment. There is no talking during the exam, and you cannot bring notes, books, paper, cell phones, PDAs, or many types of calculators into the examination room with you. The PMP is considered a "high-stakes" or "high-security" exam and is very carefully monitored. Test-takers are constantly observed by the test proctor and are under recorded video and audio surveillance. This can be distracting as well as unnerving, so it is important to be mentally prepared as you walk into the exam.

The test is delivered on a Windows-based PC that runs a secure, proprietary testing application. The computer setup is very straightforward, with a mouse and keyboard and a simple graphical user interface used to display the test. PMI can arrange special accommodations for those test takers who have special physical needs.

The Exam

To get a feel for how the real PMP Exam looks and feels, use the key found in the back cover of this book to gain access to *insite.velociteach.com* for simulated PMP Exams and other content.

Recently, PMI has also made provision for certain test-takers who do not live near a testing center to take a paper version of the exam. While this book focuses on the computerized version of the exam, the content of both versions of the exam is identical, and your preparation should not be any different. More information on the paper-based exam may be found online at *www.pmi.org.*

The exam ends either when your 4-hour time limit has been reached (more on this in a moment) or when you choose to end the exam. Once the exam is over, you will know your score within a few seconds, and those results are electronically transmitted to PMI. If you passed, you are immediately a "PMP," and you may start using that designation after your name. PMI will mail you all of the official information, including your PMP lapel pin and certificate, within a few weeks. If you did not pass, you may take the exam up to three times in a calendar year. If you do not pass on your third attempt, you must wait one year from your last attempt to reapply.

The Time Limit

Taking a test while the clock is ticking can be unnerving. The PMP Exam is a long exam, but you are given a significant block of time to complete the test. From the time you begin the exam, you will have 240 minutes (4 hours) to finish. For most people, this is enough time to take the test and review the answers. The allocation works out to 72 seconds per question if no breaks are taken. While a few of the more complicated questions will certainly require more than 72 seconds, most will take much less time.

The subject of time management for the exam, along with a suggested strategy for managing your time, is covered later in Chapter 14 - How to Pass the PMP on the First Try.

Question Format

Exam questions are given in a multiple choice format, with four possible answers, marked A, B, C, and D, and only one of those four answers is correct. Unlike in some exams, there is no penalty for guessing, so it is to your advantage to answer every question on the PMP Exam, leaving none of them blank.

Many of the questions are quite short in format; however, the PMP Exam is famous (or infamous) for its long, winding questions that are difficult to decipher. To help you prepare, you will see different question styles represented in this book. Going through all the sample questions provided in this volume is an excellent way to prepare for the types of questions you will encounter on the actual exam.

2 Foundational Terms and Concepts

Difficulty	Memorization	Exam Importance
MEDIUM	MEDIUM	HIGH

What is a project? How is it different from operations or a program? What is a project manager, and how do different organizational structures change the role and power of a project manager? Here is the place you need to begin in order to prepare for the exam. Before you can understand this approach to project management, you need a solid overview of these and other topics.

While much of the rest of this book is focused on PMI's 47 processes, inputs, tools, techniques, outputs, and formulas, this chapter lays the foundation upon which those knowledge areas are built. The rest of the book will make more sense after you understand this chapter.

Philosophy

PMI's philosophy of project management does not disconnect projects from the organizations that carry them out. Every project has a context and is heavily influenced by the type of organization in which the project is performed.

Every organization, and every project varies, so it is understandable that stakeholders within those projects will play different roles. An effective project manager must identify the different types of project stakeholders (such as customers, the project sponsor, and senior management), understand their needs, and help them work together to create common and realistic goals that will lead to a successful outcome.

Importance

Because this chapter is foundational, it is highly important. There will be many questions on the PMP Exam that test your understanding of a project manager, stakeholder, and sponsor. You must also be able to identify the different types of organizations, and to recognize a project as compared to other types of related endeavors. Spend time making certain you understand these terms and definitions.

Preparation

The volume of material here is significant, and much of the information is marked as important. Test preparation should be focused on memorization of the terms and your ability to apply them. Word for word memorization is not essential, but a solid understanding is.

Essential Terms

We'll begin preparation for the PMP Exam by cementing your understanding of the following terms:

 *Process*

Kev Fact

Processes are encountered regularly when studying for the PMP Exam. For purposes of the test, think of a process as a package of inputs, tools, and outputs used together to do something necessary and valuable for the project. For instance, Develop Schedule is the process in which the project schedule is created. Identify Risks is

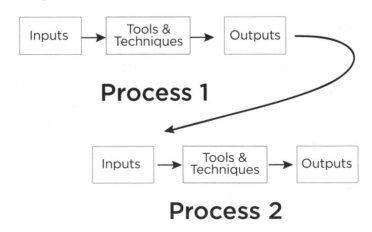

A diagram showing interactions between processes

the process in which the list of risks is created, etc. There are 47 unique processes you will need to understand for the exam, all of which are covered in this book.

As the preceding diagram illustrates, the outputs from one process are often used as inputs into one or more processes. Later in this chapter some of the most common inputs, tools, techniques, and outputs are covered.

Every process may be performed more than one time on a single project and even within a single phase (don't worry, phases are covered next). For instance, just because you have created the project schedule, it does not mean that you will not revisit the process of Develop Schedule if a piece of scope functionality is added or subtracted. You may actually perform that process multiple times. This holds true for all 47 processes in this book, and it is important not to think about them as happening sequentially or discretely. Many processes may be performed in parallel with other processes and revisited often.

Phases

Kev Fact

Many organizations use project methodologies that define project phases. These phases may have names like "requirements gathering," "design," "construction," "testing," and "implementation." Each phase of a project produces one or more deliverables.

One of the major problems test-takers have when encountering this material is to understand that all of the processes covered here may take place within each phase of the project. In other words, if your organization's methodology specifies a phase for product design, some or all of the 47 processes (described in chapters 4-13 of this book) may take place in that phase alone, only to be repeated in the subsequent project phases. Keep this fact in mind while reading the remaining chapters.

It is important to understand that there are not prescribed phases for you to use on your project. Instead, processes are defined that will fit into your project methodology.

The example below shows how deliverables are usually associated with each phase. The deliverables are reviewed to determine whether the project should continue. This decision point is known as an exit gate or a kill point, and the decision on whether to proceed with the project is usually made by a person external to the project.

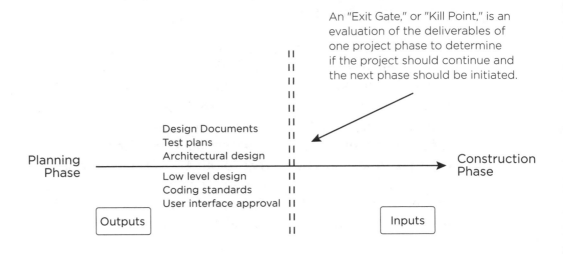

An "Exit Gate," or "Kill Point," is an evaluation of the deliverables of one project phase to determine if the project should continue and the next phase should be initiated.

Planning Phase — Design Documents, Test plans, Architectural design, Low level design, Coding standards, User interface approval — Construction Phase

Outputs   Inputs

Project

Kev Fact

As you might guess, the definition of the word "project" is important for the exam. A project is a temporary (finite) group of related tasks undertaken to create a unique product, service, or result. You may encounter a question on the exam that describes a situation and asks you whether that situation represents a project. If you see such a question, remember that you are looking for the following characteristics:

- A project is time-limited (it has a definite beginning and end).
- A project is unique (it has not been attempted before by this organization).
- A project is undertaken for a purpose (it will yield a specific product, service, or result).

Program

Kev Fact

A program is a larger effort than a project, because it is a group of related projects coordinated together. Programs may also include

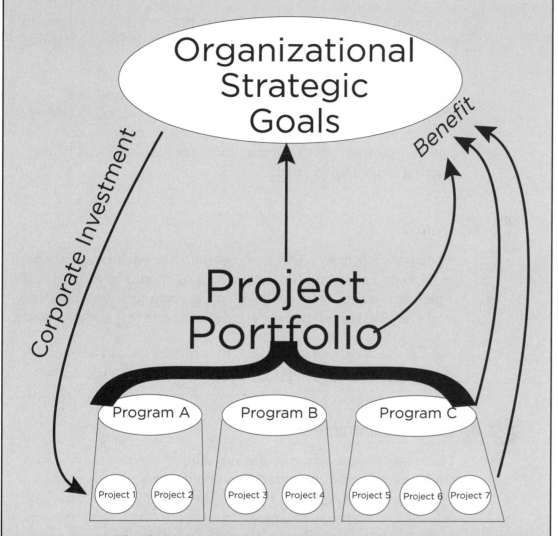

As the above diagram illustrates, companies set strategic goals for the entire organization. A company's project portfolio represents all of the project and program investments they make.

Programs represent a group of projects managed together in order to gain efficiencies on cost, time, technology, etc. For instance, by managing three related technology projects as a program, an organization might be able to save time and money by developing several common components only once and leveraging them across all of the projects that use those components.

Project management is the application of resources, time, and expertise to meet the project requirements. Project management usually applies to individual projects.

Essential Terms

operations. Organizations often group projects into programs in order to realize some benefit that could not be achieved if those projects were not undertaken in concert.

For example, building a new airport might be viewed as a program, made up of numerous component projects, and this program would certainly take the ongoing operations into consideration in order to make things run smoothly and to keep ongoing costs under control.

Portfolio

Key Fact

A company's project portfolio represents the entire investment in projects and programs. Project portfolios should be aligned to the organization's strategic goals. In fact, an organization's portfolio might be considered the truest indicator of its real strategic goals.

Ideally, the benefit of all project investments should be expressed in how they meet or support the organization's strategic goals.

Progressive Elaboration

Key Fact

The term "progressive elaboration" simply means that you do not know all of the characteristics about a product when you begin the project. Instead, they may be revisited often and refined. For instance, you may gather some of the requirements, perform preliminary design, take the results to the stakeholders for feedback, and then return to gather more requirements. The characteristics of the product emerge over time, or "progressively."

Project Management

Key Fact

Project management is using skills, knowledge, and resources to satisfy project requirements.

Success

Key Fact

The definition of project success is delivering the project within the set boundaries of scope, cost, schedule, quality, and risk.

Kev Fact

Historical Information

Historical information is found many places on the exam, usually under the umbrella heading of "organizational process assets." Historical information is found in the records that have been kept on previous projects. These records can be used to help benchmark the current project. They may show what resources were previously used and what lessons were learned. More than anything, historical information is used to help predict trends for the current project and to evaluate the project's feasibility.

Because PMI advocates constant improvement and continuous learning, historical records are extremely important in project management, and they are used heavily during planning activities. They can provide useful metrics, be used to validate assumptions, and help prevent repeated mistakes.

The term "historical information" is as old as project management itself, but as was alluded to earlier, the term has recently given way to the more comprehensive "organizational process assets," covered later in this chapter. You may well see historical information pop up on the exam, but know that it now fits neatly under the broader heading of organizational process assets. That is because any historical information you have is actually an asset for the organization to use on future projects.

Kev Fact

Baseline

The term baseline is used for certain plans: scope, time, cost, and for the project plan itself. The baseline is simply the original plan plus any approved changes. Many people who take the exam do not understand that the baseline includes all approved changes. Baselines are used as tools to measure how performance deviates from the plan, so if the plan changes, and once that change is approved, the new plan becomes the baseline. This is an important concept.

Suppose you were running a one mile race, and you considered that distance as your baseline. Your plan was to run at the healthy pace of seven minutes per mile. Now suppose that the race length was changed to a three mile race. You ran the race and still finished in a very respectable 25 minutes. Would you want your progress measured against the original distance or the updated one? If you did not update your baseline to three miles, your pace of 25 minutes against the original distance of one mile would not be very impressive at all. Your performance measurements would only be meaningful if you had an accurate baseline.

Remember that your project's baseline is defined as the original plan plus all approved changes. Even though the baseline changes as the plan changes, it is a good idea to keep records that show how the plan has progressed and changed over time.

Key Fact

Lessons Learned

The key word for you to remember when you think of lessons learned is "variances." Lessons learned are gathered at the end of each phase or at the end of the project, and they focus on variances between the plan and the results. The goal is to detail what lessons were learned that should be shared with future projects. Lessons learned from past projects are another organizational process asset, which is an input into many planning processes. It is important that lessons learned put a special emphasis on what was planned to happen, what actually happened, and what you would have done differently in order to avoid any variances.

Key Fact ## Regulation

A regulation is an official document that provides guidelines that must be followed. Compliance with a regulation is mandatory (e.g., in the United States, wheelchair ramps are required for many streets and buildings). Regulations are issued by government agencies or another official organization.

Key Fact ## Standard

A standard is a document approved by a recognized body that provides guidelines. Compliance with a standard is not mandatory but may be helpful. For example, the size of copy paper is standardized, and it would probably be a very good idea for paper manufacturers to follow the standard, but there is

Essential Terms

not a law in most countries requiring that copy paper be made the standard size. The PMBOK Guide provides a standard for project management.

System

There are several instances of "systems" in this book. A system incorporates all the formal procedures and tools put in place to manage something. The term "system" does not refer only to computer systems, but to procedures, checks and balances, processes, forms, software, etc. For instance, the project management information system (discussed in Chapter 4 – Project Integration Management), may include a combination of high-tech and low-tech tools such as computer systems, paper forms, policies and procedures, meetings, etc.

Project Roles

Another area of study regarding the project context is that of the roles and responsibilities found on projects. You should be familiar with the following terms related to project roles:

Project Manager

The project manager is the person ultimately responsible for the outcome of the project. The project manager is:

- Formally empowered to use organizational resources
- In control of the project
- Authorized to spend the project's budget
- Authorized to make decisions for the project

Project managers are typically found in a matrix or projectized organization (more about types of organizations shortly). If they do exist in a functional organization, they will often be only part-time and will have significantly less authority than project managers in other types of organizations.

Because the project manager is in charge of the project, most of the project's problems and responsibilities belong to him or her. It is typically a bad idea for the project manager to escalate a problem to someone else. The responsibility to manage the project rests with the project manager, and that includes fixing problems.

Project Coordinator

Kev Fact

In some organizations, project managers do not exist. Instead, these organizations use the role of a project coordinator. The project coordinator is significantly weaker than a project manager. This person may not be allowed to make budget decisions or overall project decisions, but they may have some authority to reassign resources. Project coordinators are usually found in weak matrix or functional organizations.

Project Expeditor

Kev Fact

The weakest of the three project management roles, an expeditor is a staff assistant who has little or no formal authority. This person reports to the executive who ultimately has responsibility for the project. The expeditor's primary responsibility lies in making sure things arrive on time and that tasks are completed on time. An expeditor is usually found in a functional organization, and this role may be only part-time in many organizations.

Senior Management

Kev Fact

For the exam, you can think of senior management as anyone more senior than the project manager. Senior management's role on the project is to help prioritize projects and make sure the project manager has the proper authority and access to resources. Senior management issues strategic plans and goals and makes sure that the company's projects are aligned with them. Additionally, senior management may be called upon to resolve conflicts within the organization.

Functional Manager

Kev Fact

The functional manager is the departmental manager in most organizational structures, such as the manager of engineering, director of marketing, or information technology manager. The functional manager usually "owns" the resources that are loaned to the project, and has human resources responsibilities for them. Additionally, he may be asked to approve the overall project plan. Functional managers can be a rich source of expertise and information available to the project manager and can make a valuable contribution to the project. Be aware that functional managers are the most likely persons with whom project managers experience conflict on a project.

Kev Fact

Stakeholder

Stakeholders are individuals who are involved in the project or whose interests may be positively or negatively affected as a result of the execution or completion of the project. They may exert influence over the project and its results. This definition can be very broad, and it can include a vast number of people! Often when the term "stakeholders" appears on the exam, it may be referring to the key stakeholders who are identified as the most important or influential ones on the project.

Kev Fact

Sponsor

The sponsor is the person paying for the project. He may be internal or external to the company. In some organizations the sponsor is called the project champion. Also, the sponsor and the customer may be the same person, although the usual distinction is that the sponsor is internal to the performing organization and the customer is external.

The sponsor may provide valuable input on the project, such as due dates and other milestones, important product features, and constraints and assumptions. If a serious conflict arises between the project manager and the customer, the sponsor may be called in to help work with the customer and resolve the dispute.

Kev Fact

Project Office (also referred to as Project Management Office or PMO)

This term refers to a department that can support project managers with methodologies, tools, training, etc., or even ultimately control all of the organization's projects. Usually the project office serves in a supporting role, defining standards, providing best practices, and auditing projects for conformance.

Project Roles

Program Manager

As the title suggests, program managers are responsible for programs. A program is multiple coordinated projects, and the program manager manages these at a higher level than the project manager does. For instance, the project manager may be responsible for the daily management of a given project, while the program manager is responsible for coordinating several projects at once in order to achieve a common goal. For the exam, you should think of it this way: you (the project manager) manage the details of a project and report status and other relevant information to the program manager.

Project Context

Another major area of study for the PMP Exam is the concept of a project context, which is the organizational environment where the project is carried out. A large part of the project context is determined by the organization's structure or type of organization.

Types of Organizations

The type of organization that undertakes a project will have an impact on the way the project is managed and even its ultimate success. There are three major types of organizations: functional organizations, projectized organizations, and a blend of those two called matrix organizations. Furthermore, matrix organizations can be characterized as weak, balanced, or strong.

The chart that follows summarizes essential information regarding these three types of organizations. You should be very familiar with this information before taking the exam, as you may see several questions that describe a project or situation and require you to identify what type of organization is involved.

Organizational Structures

Type	Description	Who is in Charge?	Benefits	Drawbacks
Functional	Very common organizational structure where team members work for a department, such as engineering or accounting, but may be loaned to a project from time to time. The project manager has low influence or power and could even be part time.	Functional (department) manager	• Deeper company expertise by function. • High degree of professional specialization. • Defined career paths for the team.	• Project manager is weak. • Projects are prioritized lower. • Resources are often not dedicated to a project.
Projectized	The organization is structured according to projects instead of functional departments. The project manager is both the manager of the project and of the people. He is highly empowered and has the highest level of control. It is more commonly found in consulting environments.	Project manager	• Project manager has complete authority. • Project communication is easiest since everyone is on a single team. • Loyalty is strong, to both the team and the project. • Contention for resources does not exist.	• Team members only belong to a project – not to a functional area. • Team members "work themselves out of a job" – they may have nowhere to go when the project is over. • Professional growth and development can be difficult.
Matrix	A hybrid organization where individuals have both a functional manager for human resources and a project manager for projects. In a strong matrix, the project manager carries more weight. In a weak matrix, the functional manager has more authority. In a balanced matrix, the power is shared evenly between the functional and project managers.	Power shared between project manager and functional manager	Can be the "best of both worlds." Project managers can gain the deep expertise of a functional organization while still being empowered to manage the resources on the project.	• Higher overhead due to duplication of effort on some tasks. • Resources report to a functional manager and they have a "dotted line" to a project manager, sometimes causing conflict and confusion. • High possibility for contention between project managers and functional managers. • Because resources do not report to the project manager, they may be less loyal to him or her.
Composite	An organization that has more than one type of reporting structure. Many larger organizations have both functional and projectized structures across the enterprise.	Varies according to the group that contains the project	May include any of the benefits from other organizational structures.	Added organizational types may introduce more complexity.

Organizational Structures

Project Manager's Power

Kev Fact

Once you are comfortable in your understanding of types of organizations and the roles that different stakeholders play in a project, you can see that the organizational context in which a project is carried out will have a great deal of influence on that project. One way that the type of organization affects the project manager in particular is in how much power he or she has. The chart below illustrates the relationship between a project manager's level of empowerment and the type of organization in which he works.

The Project Manager's Power by Organization Type

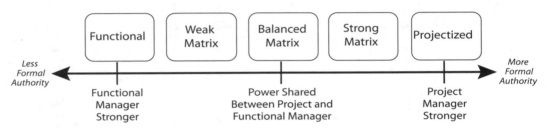

Project Manager's Management Skills

Kev Fact

The practice of project management overlaps many other disciplines. Since most projects are performed within an organization, there are other management skills that make up the foundation of project management. These skills will probably have a significant effect on projects. The project manager should have experience in:

Leading

Setting direction, aligning people to that direction, motivating them, and inspiring them to commit.

Communicating

Exchanging information clearly and correctly. Although communication skills are not emphasized on the exam, they are important to the project manager and critical to the success of the project.

Negotiating

Working to reach a mutual agreement. Negotiations may happen with groups or individuals inside and outside the organization. The goal of negotiating is to create a win-win outcome that is sustainable for all parties.

Problem Solving

Defining the problem and dealing with the factors that contribute to or cause the problem. Problem solving is such an important and favored skill for the project manager that if you see it as one of the choices on the exam, you should give it very careful consideration (i.e., it is quite likely the correct answer).

Influencing

Accomplishing something without necessarily having formal power. Influencing the organization requires a keen understanding of the way the organization is structured, both formally and informally.

Project Governance

Oftentimes there is a group within the organization or outside of the organization that looks at how the project work is being performed to ensure that it is being done the right way. This typically takes place throughout the entire project life cycle.

Project governance may be used to define processes used across the project and to rate the project manager's performance.

Project Life Cycle

The project life cycle is simply a representation of the phases that a project typically goes through. These phases are general, but they are representative of the common flow of activities on a project.

Project Manager's Skills

The six phases represented at the bottom of the following graphic describe the way in which a project typically progresses. It should be noted, however, that this depiction is very general, and different phases and phase names are used by different industries and projects.

The image also shows some other facts about the project life cycle that often appear on the PMP Exam in the form of questions. These questions typically focus on the fact that resource and cost levels rise early in the project and drop over time, or how risk and stakeholders' ability to influence the project is highest early in the project and decreases as the project progresses.

Project Life Cycle

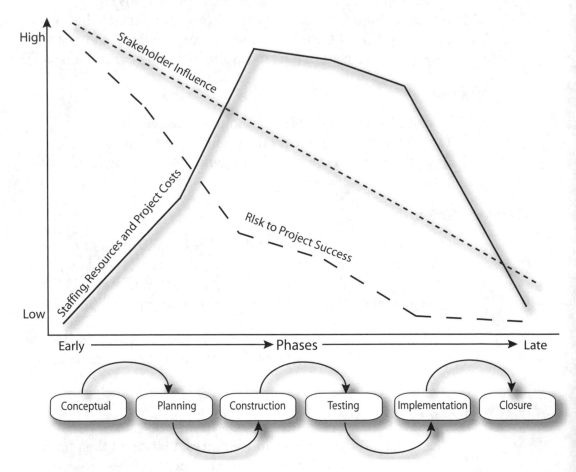

The Triple Constraint

Kev Fact

Another fundamental topic in project management is commonly referred to as "the triple constraint." It is based on the realization that while changes do occur during a project, they do not happen in a vacuum. When the scope of a project is changed, time and cost are also affected. Of course, the same is true when changes are made to cost or time. Those changes will have some impact on the other two areas.

As many different types of changes will be requested in most projects, it is essential in project management to be mindful of the triple constraint and to help keep others aware of it. The project manager should not simply accept all changes or change requests as valid; rather, the project manager should evaluate how those changes affect the other aspects of the project.

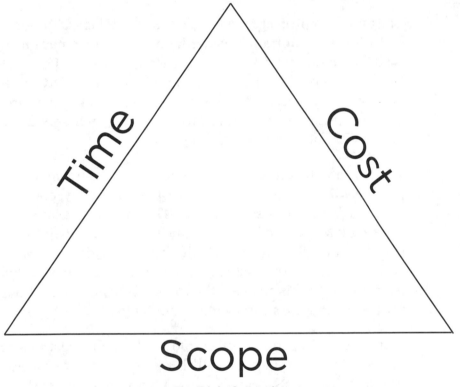

The Triple Constraint

The triple constraint, or as some know it, the iron triangle, is simply the concept that scope, time, and cost are closely interrelated. Just as you cannot modify one side of a triangle without changing one or both of the other lengths, you cannot simply change one part of the triple constraint without affecting other parts.

However common a practice it may be in some organizations to slash a budget without revisiting the scope or the schedule, the project manager should not simply accept these mandates. The triple constraint is in place whether or not the organization recognizes and accepts it.

Kev Fact

Project Management Methodology

The topic of a project management methodology is important. In fact, it's very important because it underscores something that is vital to understand as you prepare for the exam. The PMBOK Guide does not describe a methodology. The PMBOK Guide describes 47 processes used to manage a project. These processes are used by an organization's project management methodology, but they are not the methodology.

To illustrate the difference between the 47 project management processes and a project management methodology, consider the analogy of two baseball teams. The Atlanta Braves and the New York Mets both have the same set of rules when they play, but they likely have very different strategies of how they will capitalize on those strengths and use those rules to their advantages. In this analogy, the rules would equate to the processes, and the strategy to methodology.

Different organizations will employ different project management methodologies, while they will all adhere to the 47 processes. And just as a team's strategy may be more nuanced and rich than the simple rules on which it is based, an organization's methodology may be a very rich and detailed implementation of the project management processes.

Kev Fact

Work Authorization System (WAS)

This concept is very important, even though it is not a formal part of any process. The Work Authorization System (WAS) is part of the overall project management information system (PMIS). The WAS is used to ensure that work gets performed at the right time and in the right sequence. It may be an informal e-mail sent by the project manager to a functional manager or a formal system used to get an assigned resource released to complete scheduled work.

Common Inputs, Tools, Techniques, and Outputs

Throughout this book, several inputs, tools and techniques, and outputs of the 47 project management processes are referenced repeatedly. Since there are 618 inputs, tools and techniques, and outputs, the decision was made to discuss several of these in the following paragraphs rather than repeat them time and again throughout the book. This section should serve as a reference as you encounter them, and spending extra time here should help improve your overall understanding of the material.

In fact, this section is so important that you should read it now, and then come back to reread it after you have read chapters 4–13.

Common Inputs

Kev Fact

Enterprise Environmental Factors

This input can cover a lot of ground, and it appears as an input into many planning processes. In fact, it is used so frequently that you may be tempted to just skim right over it, but be careful! Enterprise environmental factors are important to your understanding of the exam material, and you should make sure you have a solid grasp of why they are used so commonly.

Consider the things that impact your project that are not part of the project itself. Just a few of these include:

- Your company's organizational structure
- The corporate culture
- Your organization's values and work ethic

Common Inputs

- Laws and regulations where the work is being performed or where the product will be used
- The characteristics of your project's stakeholders (e.g. their expectations and willingness to accept risk)
- The overall state of the marketplace for your project
- Your organization's infrastructure
- The stakeholder or organization's appetite for risk

In fact, enterprise environmental factors can be anything external to your project that affects your project. That is why it is so important to consider these factors when planning your project and to explore how they will influence your project.

Key Fact

Organizational Process Assets

What information, tools, documents, or knowledge does your organization possess that could help you plan for your project? Some of these might be quite obvious, such as the project plan from a previous, similar project performed by your organization, while some may be more difficult to grasp at first, such as company policy. Consider, however, that both of these assets will help you as you plan. For instance, company policy adds structure and lets you know the limits your project can safely operate within, so you do not have to waste time or resources discovering these on your own. Organizational process assets are typically divided into the categories of processes, procedures, and corporate knowledge.

A few examples of organizational process assets are:

- Templates for common project documents
- Examples from a previous project plan
- Organizational policies, procedures, and guidelines for any area (risk, financial, reporting, change control, etc.)
- Software tools
- Databases of project information
- Estimating data for budget or schedule components
- Historical information
- Lessons learned
- Knowledge bases
- Special corporate competencies

Anything that your organization owns or has developed that can help you on a current or future project may be considered an organizational process asset, and part of your job on the project is to contribute to these assets wherever possible on your project.

Project Documents

This concept is so vague as to be difficult to exploit on the exam. Project documents are very frequently brought into processes as an input, and these may be any documentation the project produces or ones that influence the project (such as agreements or standards).

Key Fact

Project Management Plan

The project management plan is one of the most important documents discussed in this book. It may be thought of as the culmination of all the planning processes. It is crucial that you understand what it is, where it comes from, and how it is used.

For the purpose of the exam, the definition of the project management plan is a single approved document that guides execution, monitoring and control, and closure. The use of the word "single" in this definition is a bit unusual, since the project management plan is actually made up of several documents; however, once these component documents become approved as the project management plan, they become fused together as one document. Don't assume that the project management plan is always overly formal or detailed. The project management plan should be appropriate for the project. That means that it may be documented at a summary level, or it may be very detailed.

Common Inputs

Following is a list of the components that make up the project management plan. The project management plan is covered in more detail in Chapter 4 - Integration Management under Develop Project Management Plan. Additionally, each of these components is covered in later chapters of this book.

- Scope management plan
- Requirements management plan
- Schedule management plan
- Cost management plan
- Quality management plan
- Process improvement plan
- Human resource management plan
- Communications management plan
- Risk management plan
- Procurement management plan
- Stakeholder management plan

Common Tools

Key Fact *Analytical Techniques*

A common set of techniques used to understand root causes or to forecast scenarios. Analytical techniques may include any type of structured or unstructured analysis.

Key Fact *Expert Judgment*

The tool of expert judgment is used time and again throughout this material. The tool is exactly what it sounds like, and the reason it is so common is that it can be used whenever the project team and the project manager do not have sufficient expertise. You do not need to worry about whether the experts come from inside the organization or outside, whether they are paid consultants or offer free advice. The most important things to remember for the exam are that this tool is highly favored and is very commonly found on planning processes.

Facilitation Techniques

Facilitators are designed to help groups resolve issues and to reach consensus. While the project manager is in charge of the project, he or she will not be in charge of every group of stakeholders. The art of facilitation becomes an important technique and an important skill for the project manager.

Group Decision-Making Techniques

Group decision-making techniques, for purposes of the exam, generally includes **Consensus** (everyone agrees to support the group's decision), **Unanimity** (everyone has to agree), **Majority** (over 50% have to agree), **Plurality**, (the largest group of votes wins, but 50%+ is not required), **Dictatorship** (the person in charge makes the decision and everyone else follows). The technique of dictatorship is not favored on the exam.

Meetings

Like it or not, meetings play an important part in the management of a project, and this tool appears frequently in the 47 processes. These meetings may be colocated or virtual in nature, and they are almost unrestricted in terms of what is discussed and who attends.

Project Management Information System

The Project Management Information System (PMIS) is another important tool to know for the exam. It is an automated system to support the project manager by optimizing the schedule and helping collect and distribute information. It is your system that helps you produce and keep track of the documents and deliverables. For example, a PMIS might help your organization produce the project charter by having you fill in a few fields on a computer screen. It might then create the project charter and set up a project billing code with accounting. While the PMIS usually consists primarily of software, it will often interface with manual systems.

Common Tools

Another important element of the PMIS is that it will contain the configuration management system, which also contains a change control system.

The point of a configuration management system is to manage different configurations of a product. Typically, a product will be baselined at a point, and different configurations, versions, products, or branches, are managed from that point.

For example, a software company may create a base package that must be implemented for each customer. The configuration management system is used to ensure that new base functionality does not break existing custom features and that changes are evaluated across all relevant versions of the product.

The PMIS is sometimes considered to be an enterprise environmental factor, since it is part of the environment in which the project is performed.

Common Outputs

The next three items (Work Performance Data, Work Performance Information, and Work Performance Reports) are very similar, and they commonly appear as inputs or outputs. The important thing is to understand what they are and how they are used.

Work Performance Data

Work performance data is simply the raw data with no additional analysis applied. It most often shows up as an output from processes where the work is being executed. The data, by itself, is not in an overly useful form.

Work Performance Information

Work performance information is different from the aforementioned "Work performance data" in that it has been analyzed and processed. If you are dealing with a summary figure, a percentage, or another useful statistic, you are likely looking at work performance information.

Work Performance Reports

Work performance reports are the work performance information compiled into the format of a presentation or report. Work performance reports typically accompany formal recommendations, decisions, or conclusions about the project.

Change Requests

As work is performed, it is common for changes to be requested. These changes can take on many forms. For instance, there may be change requests to increase the scope of the project or to cut it down in size. There may be change requests to deliver the product earlier or later, to increase or decrease the budget, or to alter the quality standards.

The point to this is that these change requests are frequent as work is executed, or monitored and controlled. Like the previous example, all requested changes are brought into the process of Perform Integrated Change Control where they will be evaluated for impact on the whole project and ultimately approved or rejected. Approved change requests often modify the project management plan and components such as the schedule, cost, and scope baselines.

Change requests are typically related to corrective action (any change to bring future results in line with the plan), preventive action (changes made to avoid the occurrence of a problem), or defect repair.

Updates (All Categories)

Updates as process outputs occur so often that it makes it very difficult for the test taker to keep it all straight. For purposes of the exam, know that updates to plans come out of planning, executing, and monitoring and controlling processes. Most of these are common sense, and rather than take up valuable brain space explaining each individual one, the concept is addressed here and referenced throughout the book.

Common Outputs

3 Process Framework

Difficulty	Memorization	Exam Importance
LOW	HIGH	HIGH

The process framework is the structure on which all of the material in this book is built. All of the processes are organized into ten knowledge areas and based on five foundational process groups:

1. Initiating
2. Planning
3. Executing
4. Monitoring and Controlling
5. Closing

Each of the 47 processes performed as part of a project can be categorized into one of these process groups. Additionally, every question you will see on the exam will tie back to one of these five groups.

This chapter describes what processes, knowledge areas, and process groups are, explains how they are structured, and provides an overview of the project management framework.

Importance

This chapter is essential to your understanding of how this material is organized and structured. Do not be discouraged if you find the material somewhat confusing at first. The more you read and study from this book, the better you will understand these terms and how they are applied.

Essential Terms

Preparation

There is significant memorization that accompanies this chapter. You need to understand these terms and the overall organization of this material. This chapter contains only a little that will actually show up on the exam, but it has to be mastered before chapters 4 – 13 can be fully comprehended.

Essential Terms

The essential information here builds on what you learned in the previous chapter by adding a few more important terms. It is not necessary to memorize all the definitions, but make sure that you do understand them. They are foundational to the rest of the book and highly important for the exam.

Processes

The term "process" is one of the most important and frequently used terms you will encounter when studying for the PMP Exam. Processes are composed of three elements: inputs, tools and techniques, and outputs.

The different inputs, tools and techniques, and outputs are combined to form processes, which are performed for a specific purpose. For instance, Develop Schedule is a process, and as its name implies, it is performed to develop the project schedule. Identify Risks is another process, with different inputs, tools and techniques, and outputs, where (you guessed it) you identify the risks which could affect the project. There are 47 unique processes, and you will need to be familiar with all of them.

Inputs

The inputs are the starting points for the processes. Just as ingredients are the building blocks for recipes, there are specific and unique inputs into each project management process that are used as building blocks for that process. You might think of inputs as your raw materials. They are what we will use to get things done.

Tools and Techniques

Tools and techniques are the actions or methods that are used to transform inputs into outputs. Tools can be many things, such as software, which can be used as a tool to help plan the project and analyze the schedule. Techniques are methods, such as flowcharting, which help us to frame, approach, and solve the problem. We combine tools and techniques since they are both used to solve problems and create outputs.

Outputs

Every process contains at least one output. The outputs are the ends of our efforts. The output may be a document, a product, a service, or a result. Usually the outputs from one process are used as inputs to other processes or as part of a broader deliverable, such as the project plan.

Knowledge Areas

The knowledge areas in this material have been organized into ten groups. Each of the 47 project management processes fits into one of these ten knowledge areas. They are:

1. Integration Management (covered in chapter 4)
2. Scope Management (covered in chapter 5)
3. Time Management (covered in chapter 6)
4. Cost Management (covered in chapter 7)
5. Quality Management (covered in chapter 8)
6. Human Resource Management (covered in chapter 9)
7. Communications Management (covered in chapter 10)
8. Risk Management (covered in chapter 11)
9. Procurement Management (covered in chapter 12)
10. Stakeholder Management (covered in chapter 13)

Each of the knowledge areas listed above has a chapter dedicated to it.

Process Groups

The project management processes defined and described here are not only presented according to the ten different knowledge areas; they are also arranged according to process groups. The same 47 processes that are included in the ten knowledge areas are organized into the five process groups.

Knowledge Areas

The five process groups are:

1. **Initiating** - processes that begin the project
2. **Planning** - processes that create the plans that will govern the work
3. **Executing** - processes that execute the plans and produce work
4. **Monitoring and Controlling** - processes that compare the results to the plan and make adjustments for future work
5. **Closing** - processes that complete the project or a phase or component of a project or procurement, create records, and archive information

Every process that takes place on the project also fits into one of those five groups.

Think of process groups as categories for processes. They tell what kind of process it is. The diagram below may help you to understand the process groups by giving you some verbs most commonly associated with each one. You will notice some overlap between the groups, and this mirrors the fact that there is occasionally some overlap between processes. When learning each process, it is important that you understand the group to which it belongs.

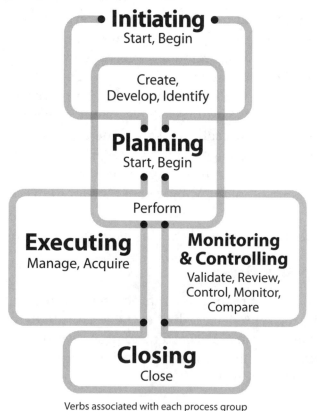

Verbs associated with each process group

Process Groups

Organization

As hinted at in the previous paragraphs, each process has two homes. It fits into a process group *and* a knowledge area. As the chapters in this book are aligned to knowledge areas, you will be able to see how processes are associated with different knowledge areas.

Understanding the Flow

Do not fall into the trap of thinking that the first step is to do the processes in initiation, the second step is to do the processes in planning, and so on. Although projects may flow very roughly that way, you need to understand that the scope of a project is "progressively elaborated," which means that some processes are performed iteratively. Some planning must take place, then some executing, then some controlling. Further planning may be performed, further executing, and so on. The five process groups are by no means completely linear. More importantly, a process may be repeated multiple times throughout a project's life cycle.

Perhaps one of the biggest misconceptions people have of this material is believing that these process groups are the same thing as project phases. Understand that all 47 processes could be performed one or more times in each project phase.

Organization and Flow

Process Group 1 - Initiating

Integration	Scope	Time	Cost	Quality	HR	Communications	Risk	Procurement	Stakeholder
✓									✓

Initiating

Develop Project Charter

Identify Stakeholders

The Initiating Process Group is one of the simpler groups in that it is made up of only two processes: Develop Project Charter and Identify Stakeholders. These two processes are described in further detail in Chapter 4 – Integration Management, and Chapter 13 – Stakeholder Management. This is the process group that gets the project officially authorized and underway.

The way in which a project is initiated, or begun, can make a tremendous difference in the success of subsequent processes and activities.

Although many processes may not be performed in a strict order, the initiating process should be performed first or at least very early on. In initiation, the project or phase is formally begun, the project manager is named, and the stakeholder register is produced.

If a project is not initiated properly, the end results could range from a lessened authority for the project manager to unclear goals or uncertainty as to why the project was being performed.

A project that is initiated properly would have the business need clearly defined and would include a clear direction for the scope as well as information on why this project was chosen over other possibilities, along with a list of the project's stakeholders.

Initiation may be performed more than once during a single project. If the project is being performed in phases, each phase could require its own separate initiation, depending on the company's methodology, funding, and other influencing factors. There is a reason why this might be advantageous. On a longer or riskier project, requiring initiation to take place on each phase could help to ensure that the project maintains its focus and that the business reasons it was undertaken are still valid.

Process Group 2 - Planning

Integration	Scope	Time	Cost	Quality	HR	Communications	Risk	Procurement	Stakeholder
✓	✓	✓	✓	✓	✓	✓	✓	✓	✓

PLANNING

Develop Project Mgt. Plan

Plan Scope Management

Collect Requirements

Define Scope

Create WBS

Plan Schedule Management

Define Activities

Sequence Activities

Estimate Activity Resources

Estimate Activity Durations

Develop Schedule

Plan Cost Management

Estimate Costs

Determine Budget

Plan Quality Management

Plan Human Resource Managment

Plan Communications Management

Plan Risk Management

Identify Risks

Perform Qualitative Risk Analysis

Perform Quantitative Risk Analysis

Plan Risk Responses

Plan Procurement Management

Plan Stakeholder Management

Planning is the largest process group because it has the most processes, but do not make the leap that it also involves the most work. Although this is not a hard and fast rule, most projects will perform the most work and use the most project resources during the executing processes.

Project planning is extremely important, both in real life and on the PMP Exam. The processes from planning touch every one of the knowledge areas! You should be familiar with the 24 processes that make up project planning as shown in the graphic on the left of this page.

The order in which the planning processes are performed is primarily determined by how the outputs of those planning processes are used. The outputs of one process are often used as inputs into a subsequent planning process. This dictates a general order in which they must take place. For instance, the project scope statement (created during Define Scope) is used as an input to feed the work breakdown structure (created during the Create WBS process). The work breakdown structure is then used as an input to create the activity list (created during Define Activities). You may, for example, encounter a question similar to the one below:

What is the correct sequence for the following activities?

A. Create project scope statement. Create work breakdown structure. Create activity list.

B. Create project scope statement. Create activity list. Create work breakdown structure.

C. Create work breakdown structure. Create project scope statement. Create activity list.

D. Create activity list. Create project scope structure. Create work breakdown structure.

Planning Processes

In this example, the correct sequence is represented by choice 'A'. This question requires an understanding of concepts introduced throughout this chapter, such as how scope items (the work breakdown structure) are created first, time-related planning processes (the activity durations) are performed second, and cost planning processes (the budget baseline) are performed third.

Planning Processes

Process Group 3 - Executing

Integration	Scope	Time	Cost	Quality	HR	Communications	Risk	Procurement	Stakeholder
✓				✓	✓	✓		✓	✓

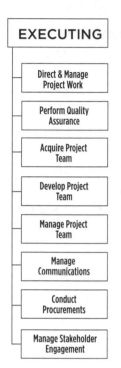

EXECUTING

- Direct & Manage Project Work
- Perform Quality Assurance
- Acquire Project Team
- Develop Project Team
- Manage Project Team
- Manage Communications
- Conduct Procurements
- Manage Stakeholder Engagement

As alluded to earlier, executing processes typically involve the most work. You do not need to memorize a list of executing processes like the one for planning, but you should know that the executing process group is where the work actually gets carried out. In this group of processes, parts are built, planes are assembled, code is created, documents are distributed, and houses are constructed. Other elements are also included here, such as procurement and team development. These all happen during the executing processes.

Some of the processes in the executing process group are intuitive, such as Direct and Manage Project Work. Others, such as Perform Quality Assurance and Manage Communications, often catch test-takers by surprise because they had different preconceptions of what was involved.

As chapter 1 disclosed, there are currently 52 questions on the exam covering these eight processes, so it is important to learn them well. The key to understanding the executing processes is remembering that you are carrying out the plan.

Executing Processes

Process Group 4 - Monitoring and Controlling

Integration	Scope	Time	Cost	Quality	HR	Communications	Risk	Procurement	Stakeholder
✓	✓	✓	✓	✓		✓	✓	✓	✓

Monitoring & Controlling

- Monitor & Control Project Work
- Perf. Integrated Change Control
- Validate Scope
- Control Scope
- Control Schedule
- Control Costs
- Control Quality
- Control Communications
- Control Risks
- Control Procurements
- Contr. Stakeholder Engagement

Monitoring and controlling processes are some of the more interesting processes. These processes touch every knowledge area except for human resources. (Typically human resource monitoring and controlling activities would be handled by the functional manager). Activities that relate to monitoring and controlling simply ensure that the plan is working. If it is not, adjustments should be made to correct future results. In monitoring and controlling processes, things are measured, inspected, reviewed, compared, monitored, verified, and reported. If you see one of those key words on a question, there is a good chance it is related to a monitoring and controlling process.

Planning processes are easy enough to grasp for most people. Executing processes are simply carrying out the plan, and monitoring and controlling processes are taking the results from the executing processes and comparing them against the plan. If there is a difference between the plan and the results, corrective action is taken, either to change the plan or to change the way in which it is being executed (or both) in order to ensure that the work results line up with the plan.

Monitoring and controlling processes present another rich area for exam questions. There will be 44 questions on the PMP Exam, covering the eleven processes in this group.

Keep in mind that monitoring and controlling processes look backward over previous work results and the plan, but corrective actions, which often result from these processes, are forward-looking. In other words, monitoring and controlling is about influencing future results and not so much about fixing past mistakes. It is very important that you understand the previous statement for the exam. That concept is reinforced throughout the next several chapters.

Monitoring & Controlling Processes

Process Group 5 - Closing

Integration	Scope	Time	Cost	Quality	HR	Communications	Risk	Procurement	Stakeholder
✓								✓	

Closing

- Close Project or Phase
- Close Procurements

The project does not end with customer acceptance. After the product has been verified against the scope and delivered to the customer's satisfaction, any contracts must be closed out (Close Procurements), and the project records must be updated, the team must be released, and the project archives and lessons learned need to be updated (Close Project or Phase).

These processes need to be considered as part of the project since the files, lessons learned, and archives will be used to help plan future projects.

Although there are only two processes in the Closing Process Group, the 14 questions about them make up 8% of the exam. You would do well to build a thorough understanding of what they are, how they work, and how they relate to the other processes.

If you find that you need more help in understanding the content of this chapter, read through it a couple of times before you go on. You may also want to read through Chapter 3 of the PMBOK Guide after you have read this chapter. It will be much easier to comprehend once you have an understanding of its underlying structure.

Closing Processes

The 47 Processes of Project Management

Process Group / Knowledge Area	Initiating	Planning	Executing	Monitoring & Controlling	Closing
Integration	Develop Project Charter	Develop Project Management Plan	Direct & Manage Project Work	Monitor & Control Project Work Perform Integrated Change Control	Close Project or Phase
Scope		Plan Scope Management Collect Requirements Define Scope Create WBS		Validate Scope Control Scope	
Time		Plan Schedule Management Define Activities Sequence Activities Estimate Activity Resources Estimate Activity Durations Develop Schedule		Control Schedule	
Cost		Plan Cost Management Estimate Costs Determine Budget		Control Costs	
Quality		Plan Quality Management	Perform Quality Assurance	Control Quality	
Human Resource		Plan Human Resource Management	Acquire Project Team Develop Project Team Manage Project Team		
Communications		Plan Communications Management	Manage Communications	Control Communications	
Risk		Plan Risk Management Identify Risks Perform Qualitative Risk Analysis Perform Quantitative Risk Analysis Plan Risk Responses		Control Risks	
Procurement		Plan Procurement Management	Conduct Procurements	Control Procurements	Close Procurements
Stakeholder	Identify Stakeholders	Plan Stakeholder Management	Manage Stakeholder Engagement	Control Stakeholder Engagement	

The Processes of
Project Management

4 Integration Management

Difficulty	Memorization	Exam Importance
HIGH	MEDIUM	HIGH

When you look at a project, do you see the forest or the trees? In other words, do you look at the big picture, focusing on the deliverables, or the smaller and more numerous tasks that must be performed in order to complete the project?

When it comes to the processes of project management, most of it is made up of trees; however, Project Integration Management represents the whole forest. It focuses on the larger, macro things that must be performed in order for the project to work. Whereas much of this material is organized into smaller processes that produce a plan or update a document, the processes of integration are larger and more substantial.

Integration management is the practice of making certain that every part of the project is coordinated. In integration

The processes of Project Integration Management with their primary outputs

Integration Management

Develop Project Charter
Project Charter

Develop Project Management Plan
Project Management Plan

Direct and Manage Project Work
Deliverables

Monitor and Control Project Work
Work Performance Reports
Change Requests

Perform Integrated Change Control
Approved Change Requests
Change Log

Close Project or Phase
Final Product Transition

management, the project is started, the project manager assembles the project plan, executes the plan, and verifies the results of the work, and then the project is closed. At the same time, the project manager must prioritize different objectives that are competing for time and resources and also keep the team focused on completing the work.

This chapter focuses on six integration management processes and how they fit together and interact with each other.

Philosophy

Integration management takes a high-level view of the project from start to finish. The reason that the word "integration" is used is that changes made in any one area of the project must be integrated into the rest of the project. For instance, the human body's various systems are tightly integrated. What you eat and drink can affect how you sleep, and how much sleep you get can affect your ability to function in other areas. When viewing your physical health, it is wise to look across your diet, exercise, sleep, stress, etc., since changes or improvements in one area will probably trickle into others.

Integration management is similar. Changes are not made in a vacuum, and while that is true for most of the processes in this book, it is especially true among the processes covered in this chapter.

The philosophy behind integration management is twofold:

1. During the executing processes of the project, decision-making can be a chaotic and messy event, and the team should be buffered from as much of this clamor as possible. This is in contrast to the planning processes where you want the team to be more involved. You do not want to call a team meeting during execution every time a problem arises. Instead, the project manager should make decisions and keep the team focused on executing the work packages.

2. The processes that make up project management are not discrete. That is, they do not always proceed from start to finish and then move on to the next process. It would be wonderful if the scope were defined and finished and then went to execution without ever

needing to be revisited; however, that is not the way things typically work. Even the most rigorously-managed projects will revisit processes across the spectrum of planning, execution, and control. This is similar to the way a musician in a symphony will tune an instrument at the beginning of a concert but will likely retune and make small adjustments multiple times throughout the performance. Variables change over time, and when they do, a plan or the way in which a project is being carried out needs to be updated.

Importance

The importance of this section is high; you should expect several questions on the exam that relate directly to this chapter.

Preparation

The difficulty factor of this material is considered high primarily because there is so much information to understand. In earlier versions of the exam, integration management was not considered to be overly difficult, but much of the material that was in other knowledge areas has been moved into integration management. While the material may not present as much technical difficulty as other areas such as time, quality, or cost, it may be new to many project managers and thus present a challenge. This chapter will guide you on where to spend most of your time and how to focus your study effort.

Integration Management Processes

There are six processes in the integration management knowledge area. These are: Develop Project Charter, Develop Project Management Plan, Direct and Manage Project Work, Monitor and Control Project Work, Perform Integrated Change Control, and Close Project or Phase. Below are the breakouts that show to which process group each item belongs:

Process Group	Integration Management Process
Initiating	Develop Project Charter
Planning	Develop Project Mgt Plan
Executing	Direct and Manage Project Work
Monitoring & Controlling	Monitor & Control Project Work, Perform Integrated Change Control
Closing	Close Project or Phase

In the knowledge area of integration management, it is also essential that you know the main outputs that are produced during each process. The different key outputs that are created in each process are summarized in the chart below.

Process	Key Outputs
Develop Project Charter	Project Charter
Develop Project Management Plan	Project Management Plan
Direct and Manage Project Work	Deliverables Work Performance Data Change Requests
Monitor & Control Project Work	Change Requests Work Performance Reports
Perform Integrated Change Control	Approved Change Requests Change Log
Close Project or Phase	Final Product, Service, or Result Transition

Integration Management Processes

Develop Project Charter

Initiating

What it is:

> The charter is the document that officially starts the project, and this is the process that creates it. Expect the charter to have an important role on the exam.

Why it is important:

> The charter is one of the most important documents on a project because it is essential for creating the project. If you don't have a charter, you don't have an official project. As you will see later in this section, the lack of a charter can cause problems for the project manager that may not manifest themselves until much later.

When it is performed:

> This process is one of the first ones performed. It is common for some pre-planning to take place on a project before it becomes official, but it will not be a real project until the charter is issued.

How it works:

Inputs

Kev Fact

Project Statement of Work

> The statement of work (SOW) is a written description of the project's product, service, or result. This will be supplied by the customer; however, if the customer is your own organization, the project's sponsor should supply this.

> If the project is for an external customer, the SOW will typically be attached to the procurement documents and the contract.

> The essential elements of the SOW are that it includes what is to be done, the business reason for doing it, and how the project supports the organization's strategy.

Key Fact

Business Case

The business case explains why this project is being undertaken, the problem it will solve, and the benefit cost analysis.

Projects may be undertaken for several reasons, which should be explained in the business case:

Market demand

A common scenario is for a business to identify a market need that they can satisfy through a project.

Business need

If senior management is in need of a new reporting tool to allow them to analyze trends, it might be rational to initiate a project to accomplish this.

Customer request

A customer paying for a new project is the most common scenario for projects being initiated.

Technological advance

New technological discoveries make new products and services possible. The auto industry is just one example of how new advances in battery technology have made their ways into cars and trucks around the world. Each of these projects was begun because of a technological advance.

Legal requirement

New laws or a new interpretation of an existing law will often give rise to the need to initiate a project.

Ecological impact

Some companies are undertaking projects to reduce their carbon footprint or ecological impact. This is considered to be a valid reason to begin a project.

Social need

As an example of addressing social needs, numerous organizations are springing up to bring entrepreneurship to some of the most impoverished regions on earth. Many of these goals are also largely accomplished through projects.

Kev Fact

Project Selection Methods

Companies select projects using a variety of methods. The most common methods seek to quantify the monetary benefits and expected costs that will result from a project and compare them to other potential projects to select the ones which are most feasible and desirable. Such methods are called "benefit measurement methods."

Other methods apply calculus to solve for maximizations using constrained optimization. Constrained optimization methods are mathematical and use a variety of programming methods. If you see the terms linear programming, or non-linear programming, on the exam, you'll know they refer to a type of constrained optimization method and that the question is referring to techniques of project selection. You should not need to know how to calculate values for constrained optimization or linear programming for the exam, but you do need to know that they are project selection methods.

The following are additional terms in the fields of economics, finance, managerial accounting, and cost accounting that are sometimes used as tools for project selection. These are not listed in the PMBOK Guide, but they may show up on the exam. It is not necessary to memorize these definitions word for word; however, it is important to understand what they are and how they are used.

Benefit Cost Ratio (BCR)

The BCR is the ratio of benefits to costs. For example, if you expect a construction project to cost $1,000,000, and you expect to be able to sell that completed building for $1,500,000, then your BCR is $1,500,000 ÷ $1,000,000 = 1.5 to 1.

In other words, you get $1.50 of benefit for every $1.00 of cost. A ratio of greater than 1 indicates that the benefits are greater than the costs.

Develop Project Charter

Economic Value Add (EVA)

When you look at the value of a project, it is sometimes easy to lose sight of the big picture of adding value to shareholders. Economic Value Add, also called EVA, looks at how much value a project has truly created for its shareholders. It does more than simply look at the net profits. It also looks at the opportunity costs. By taking all of the capital costs into account, EVA can effectively show how much wealth was created (or lost) over a period of time. It takes into account the fact that there are opportunity costs to every financial expenditure, and that if a project does not make more money than those opportunity costs, it has not truly added economic value to the organization.

To calculate EVA, start with the after-tax profits of the project. Then subtract out the capital invested in that project multiplied by how much that capital cost.

For example, company XYZ invested $175,000 in a project, and that project returned a net profit of $10,000 in the first year of operation. Accountants would probably celebrate the net profit, but what does the EVA tell us about shareholder value? First, we need to determine the real cost of that capital. In this case, we will estimate 6%, since the organization could have invested that same $175,000 and earned a 6% return. When we calculate EVA, we apply the following formula:

After tax profit – (capital expenditures * cost of capital),
or $10,000 – ($175,000 × .06) = –$500.
Even though the project returned an accounting net profit, it would have been better for XYZ to bank the money instead. In other words, XYZ actually passed up $500 as far as EVA is concerned, since they would have earned $10,500 in interest if they had invested in the bank instead of the project.

Internal Rate of Return (IRR)

IRR, or "Internal Rate of Return," is a finance term used to express a project's returns as an interest rate. In other words, if this project were an interest rate, what would it be? Do not worry about the formula for the exam, but you should understand that just like the interest rate on a savings account, bigger is better when looking at IRR.

Net Present Value (NPV)

See Present Value definition below for an explanation of Net Present Value (NPV) and Present Value (PV).

Opportunity Cost

Based on the theory that a dollar can only be invested in one place at a time, opportunity cost asks "what is the cost of the other opportunities that were passed up by investing our money in this project?" For project selection purposes, the smaller the opportunity cost, the better, because it is not desirable to miss out on a great opportunity.

Payback Period

The payback period is how long it will take to recoup an investment in a project. If someone owed you $100, you would prefer that they pay it to you immediately rather than paying you $25 per month for 4 months. As you want to recoup your investment as quickly as possible in order to free that money up for another investment opportunity, a shorter payback period is always better than a longer one, all other things being equal.

Present Value (PV) and Net Present Value (NPV)

PV is based on the "time value of money" economic theory that a dollar today is worth more than a dollar tomorrow. If a project is expected to produce 3 annual payments of $100,000, then the present value (how much those payments are worth right now) is going to be less than $300,000. The reason for this is that you will not get your entire $300,000 until the 3rd year, but if you took $300,000 cash and put it in the bank right now, you would end up with more than $300,000 in 3 years.

PV is a way to take time out of the equation and evaluate how much a project is worth right now. It is important to understand that with PV, bigger is better.

Net Present Value (NPV) is the same as Present Value except that you also factor in your costs. For example, you have constructed a building with a PV of $500,000, but it cost you $350,000. In this case, your NPV would be
$500,000 − $350,000 = $150,000.

Remember that a bigger PV or NPV makes a project more attractive, and that NPV calculations have already factored in the cost of the project.

Develop Project Charter

Return On Investment (ROI)

Return On Investment is a percentage that shows what return you make by investing in something. Suppose, for example, that a company invests in a project that costs $200,000. The benefits of doing the project save the company $230,000 in the first year alone. In this case, the ROI would be calculated as the (benefit − cost) ÷ cost, or $30,000 ÷ $200,000 = 15%.

Note that you should not worry about memorizing this calculation for the exam, but you do need to understand that for ROI, bigger is better.

Return on Invested Capital (ROIC)

The measure of ROIC looks at how an organization uses the money invested in a project, and it is expressed as a percentage. It asks "for every dollar of cash I invest in a project, how much should I expect (or did I earn) in return?" This invested money could be cash on hand or cash that was borrowed. For the purposes of project management, the calculation is fairly simple.

Use the formula:

ROIC = Net Income (after tax) from Project ÷ Total Capital Invested in the project

For example, Fictional Enterprises invested $250,000 in a project that generated $60,000 top line revenue in its first year, with $20,000 in operational costs and a tax liability of $8,750. To calculate the ROIC, first calculate the after tax profits by subtracting the costs from the revenue.

This is: $60,000 − $20,000 − $8,750 = $31,250.

Now apply the ROIC formula as follows:

ROIC = $31,250 ÷ $250,000 = 12.5%

This means that Fictional's project is returning 12.5% annually on the cash it invested to perform the project.

Agreements

In this case, the word "agreement" is synonymous with a contract. Not all projects are performed under contract, so this input may or may not be relevant. When a project is performed under contract for another organization, it is common for the contract to be signed prior to the project beginning. As we are ready to start the project and create the charter, the contract provides an essential input.

Enterprise Environ. Factors — See Ch. 2, Common Inputs

Organizational Process Assets — See Ch. 2, Common Inputs

Tools

Expert Judgment — See Ch. 2, Common Tools

Facilitation Techniques — See Ch. 2, Common Tools

Outputs

Kev Fact

Project Charter

Once an organization has selected a project or a contract is signed to perform a project, the project charter must be created. Following are the key facts you need to remember about the project charter.

The Project Charter

- It is created during the Develop Project Charter process.
- It is created based on some need, and it should explain that need.
- It is signed by the performing organization's senior management.
- It names the project manager and gives him the authority to spend money and to allocate resources.
- It should include the high-level project requirements.
- It should include a high-level milestone view of the project schedule.
- It is a high-level document that does not include project details; the specifics of project activities will be developed later.
- It includes a summary-level preliminary project budget.

Planning

Develop Project Management Plan

What it is:

When many people think of a project plan, they mistakenly think only of a Gantt chart or a schedule. Many project managers who have carried this misconception into the PMP Exam have been chewed up and spit out by the test! As you will see in this section, the project management plan is a very important document that guides the project's execution and control, and it is much more than a schedule chart.

Why it is important:

This one should be easy. The project plan guides your work on the project. It specifies the who, what, when, where, and how. This document is used repeatedly throughout this book, so a solid understanding of it will pay dividends throughout your study.

When it is performed:

When the process of Develop Project Management Plan is performed is an interesting point since the project management plan is not developed all at once. This plan is progressively elaborated, meaning that it is developed, refined, revisited, and updated. Ultimately, it represents a compendium of the other major planning outputs, so it will need to be assembled after the component plans have been created.

How it works:

Inputs

Project Charter — See Develop Project Charter, Outputs

Outputs from Processes

The project plan represents 16 component plans, fused together. These plans are described in the outputs section of this process in more detail.

Enterprise Environ. Factors — See Ch. 2, Common Inputs

Organizational Process Assets — See Ch. 2, Common Inputs

Tools

Expert Judgment — See Ch. 2, Common Tools

Facilitation Techniques — See Ch. 2, Common Tools

Outputs

Key Fact

Project Management Plan

The project management plan is the sole output of this process, and it is one of the most important outputs from any process.

To understand the project management plan, consider its definition. The project plan is "a formal, approved document that defines how the project is managed, executed, and controlled. It may be summary or detailed and may be composed of one or more subsidiary management plans and other planning documents."

The keys to understanding this are broken out below:

1. The project management plan is formal. It is important to think of the project management plan as a formal, written piece of communication.

2. The project management plan is a single document. It is not 16 separate plans. Once those separate documents are approved as the project plan, they become a single document.

3. The project management plan is approved. In other words, there is a point in time at which it officially becomes the project plan. Who approves it is going to differ based on the organizational structure and other factors, but typically it would be:

- The project manager
- The project sponsor
- The functional managers who are providing resources for the project
- The team

It is also important to understand that we do not typically think of the customer or senior management as approving the project plan. The customer will sign a contract, but will often leave the inner workings to the performing organization (ideally, anyway). The organization's senior management usually cannot get down to the level of reviewing every component document and approving the project plan, and especially not for each and every project.

Once the project plan is approved, it is not changed on a whim. There is some process in place for making changes and updates to it.

4. The project management plan defines how the project is managed, executed, and controlled. This means that the document provides the guidance on how the bulk of the project will be conducted.

5. The project management plan may be summary or detailed. Even though this wording is in the definition, for the exam you will do much better to think of the project management plan as always being detailed!

The project management plan is made up of several components, which you may think of as chapters in the overall plan. More formal and mission-critical projects will have longer and more formal components. On actual projects, not every project management plan will contain every one of the 16 components shown in the graphic, but you should be familiar with the components illustrated before taking the exam.

Components of the Project Management Plan

- Scope Baseline
- Schedule Baseline
- Cost Baseline
- Scope Management Plan
- Requirements Management Plan
- Schedule Management Plan
- Cost Management Plan
- Quality Management Plan
- Process Improvement Plan
- Human Resource Plan
- Communications Management Plan
- Risk Management Plan
- Procurement Management Plan
- Stakeholder Management Plan
- Change Management Plan
- Configuration Management Plan

Develop Project Plan

Another important thing to note about the project management plan is that most of its components are developed in other processes. For instance, the project risk management plan is developed in Plan Risk Management.

Component of the Project Plan	Process Where Created
Scope Baseline	Create WBS
Schedule Baseline	Develop Schedule
Cost Baseline	Determine Budget
Scope Management Plan	Plan Scope Management
Requirements Management Plan	Plan Scope Management
Schedule Management Plan	Plan Schedule Management
Cost Management Plan	Plan Cost Management
Quality Management Plan	Plan Quality Management
Process Improvement Plan	Plan Quality Management
Human Resource Plan	Plan Human Resource Management
Communication Management Plan	Plan Communications Management
Risk Management Plan	Plan Risk Management
Procurement Management Plan	Plan Procurement Management
Stakeholder Management Plan	Plan Stakeholder Management
Change Management Plan	Develop Project Management Plan
Configuration Management Plan	Develop Project Management Plan

Develop Project Plan

Executing

Direct and Manage Project Work

What it is:

When learning the processes of project management, it is easy to walk away with the impression that the project manager must spend most of his or her time planning. Thankfully, however, that is not the case. Most of a project's time, cost, and resources are expended right here in the Direct and Manage Project Work process. This is where things get done!

In Direct and Manage Project Work, the team is executing the work packages and creating the project deliverables.

Why it is important:

The Direct and Manage Project Work process is where roads get built, software applications get written, buildings are constructed, and products roll off the assembly line.

When it is performed:

This process is difficult to put a time frame on, and it is important that you understand why that is true. People mistakenly think about project management as occurring linearly. That is, you plan, you execute, you monitor and control, and then you close, in that order. However, that is not the way most projects are performed.

On a real project, you may do some planning, some execution, and then monitor and control, only to return to more planning, more execution, and more monitoring and controlling. In reality, you may repeat this cycle numerous times.

Therefore, when looking at the process of Direct and Manage Project Work, you should not think of it as a single occurrence, but understand that it occurs any time you are following the project management plan to create project deliverables.

Direct and Manage Project Work

How it works:

Inputs

Key Fact

Project Management Plan

Remember that the project management plan guides the management, execution, and monitoring and controlling of the project. In this process, we are primarily concerned with the execution of the project plan; therefore, it is the essential input into this process. See the preceding process, Develop Project Management Plan, for more details on the project management plan.

Approved Change Requests — See Ch. 2, Common Outputs

Enterprise Environmental Factors — See Ch. 2, Common Inputs

Organizational Process Assets — See Ch. 2, Common Inputs

Tools

Expert Judgment — See Ch. 2, Common Tools

Project Mgt Information System — See Ch. 2, Common Tools

Meetings— See Ch. 2, Common Tools

Outputs

Key Fact

Deliverables

This is arguably the most important output in the entire book! A deliverable is any product, service, or result that must be completed in order to finish the project. Some projects also must develop capabilities in order to finish a project, and these may be deliverables as well. For instance, a project may need to develop a new manufacturing technique before it can create a product. In that case, the capability that the team develops could be considered a deliverable. It is also important to understand what happens to the deliverables that are created. They flow through the processes of Control Quality and Validate Scope until they meet specifications for completeness and correctness.

Kev Fact

Work Performance Data

If the deliverables are the most important output of this process, this one is the second most important. It isn't only the deliverables that flow out of this process, but also the data about how those deliverables are being produced.

Keep in mind that work performance data is eventually converted into work performance information after it has been analyzed and understood. The data collected here is raw and unprocessed at this point.

Change Requests — See Ch. 2, Common Outputs

Project Mgt. Plan Updates — See Ch. 2, Common Outputs

Project Documents Updates — See Ch. 2, Common Outputs

Direct and Manage Project Work

Monitor and Control Project Work

What it is:

The process of Monitor and Control Project Work takes a look at all of the work that is being performed on a project and makes sure that the deliverables and the way in which they are being produced are in line with the project plan.

You will notice that most of the inputs, tools, and outputs to this process are common ones. You should focus your study on the process itself and not so much on the components. Monitor and Control Project Work is important because it is another macro integration process. It looks at how the overall project is progressing and takes corrective action as needed through change requests. For instance, if the overall project is late, you might decide to trim the scope for the first release. Conversely, if you are significantly ahead of schedule, you might change the number of resources you are using. Both of these would be examples of the kinds of activities involved in Monitor and Control Project Work. The project manager makes large, macro decisions about the project based on how things have been progressing and how they are forecasted to continue.

Why it is important:

All monitoring and controlling processes fulfill a sort of oversight role on the project. They compare the work results to the plan and make whatever adjustments are necessary to ensure that the two match. Any necessary changes in the work or the plan are identified and made in this process.

They also monitor all project information to ensure that risks are being identified and managed properly and to make sure that performance is on track.

When it is performed:

Monitor and Control Project Work is closely tied to the previous process, Direct and Manage Project Work, and it takes place as long as there is work on the project to be carried out.

How it works:

Inputs

Project Management Plan — See Ch. 2, Common Inputs

Key Fact

Schedule Forecasts

Schedule forecasts, like cost forecasts are used as part of earned value calculations (covered in chapter 7), and this process is often where the progress is measured against the plan and corrective action is taken as needed.

Cost Forecasts

Cost forecasts are brought into this process to measure how costs are stacking up against the plan. Earned value calculations are performed against the schedule (see the previous input) and the budget, and corrective action is taken when appropriate.

Validated Changes

When changes are approved and made, they need to be brought back into this process to make sure they were executed and rolled out properly.

Work Performance Information — See Ch. 2, Common Inputs

Enterprise Environ. Factors — See Ch. 2, Common Inputs

Organizational Process Assets — See Ch. 2, Common Inputs

Tools

Expert Judgment — See Ch. 2, Common Tools

Analytical Techniques

There is a saying that "nothing speaks louder than data." In this case, analysis is used to look at the data and spot trends, determine root cause, to analyze buffers, and to ensure that the project is operating within performance and risk tolerances.

PM Information System — See Ch. 2, Common Tools

Meetings — See Ch. 2, Common Tools

Outputs

Change Requests — See Ch. 2, Common Outputs

Kev Fact

Work Performance Reports

Notice that the work performance information is an input into this process, and these reports come out. They are used to create awareness and to help with decision-making.

Project Mgt. Plan Updates— See Ch. 2, Common Outputs

Project Documents Updates— See Ch. 2, Common Outputs

Monitor and Control
Project Work

Monitoring & Controlling

Perform Integrated Change Control

What it is:

Some processes are more important than others for the exam, and this one qualifies as one of the most important.

Every change to the project, whether requested or not, needs to be processed through Perform Integrated Change Control. It is in this process where you assess the change's impact on the project.

Why it is important:

Perform Integrated Change Control brings together (i.e., integrates) all of the other monitoring and controlling processes. When a change occurs in one area, it is evaluated for its impact across the entire project.

For example, suppose you came in to work one morning and found that a new legal requirement meant that the quality of your project's product needed to be improved. Would you only look at the quality processes on the project? No. After understanding the quality impact of this change, you would likely need to evaluate the impact on the scope of the project, the activity duration estimates, the overall schedule, the budget estimates, the project risks, contract and supplier issues, etc. In other words, you would need to integrate this change throughout every area of the project.

One way in which Perform Integrated Change Control differs from the previous process, Monitor and Control Project Work, is that Perform Integrated Change Control is primarily focused on managing change to the project's scope, while Monitor and Control Project Work is primarily focused on managing the way that scope is executed. For example, consider a new construction project for a hospital. If a change request were submitted that added a new wing to the hospital building, then that change request would be evaluated through Perform Integrated Change Control to understand its impact on the whole project. If, however, the project team members were performing slower than planned, that would be factored into Monitor and Control Project Work, and corrective action would be taken to ensure that the plan and the execution lined up. Even though both are controlling processes, each has a different focus.

Perform Integrated Change Control (sidebar)

When it is performed:

Like the processes Direct and Manage Project Work and Monitor and Control Project Work, Perform Integrated Change Control takes place as long as there is work on the project to be performed.

How it works:

Inputs

Project Management Plan — See Ch. 2, Common Inputs

Work Performance Reports — See Ch. 2, Common Outputs

Change Requests— See Ch. 2, Common Outputs

Enterprise Environmental Factors — See Ch. 2, Common Inputs

Organizational Process Assets — See Ch. 2, Common Inputs

Key Fact

Tools

Expert Judgment — See Ch. 2, Common Tools

Meetings

The change control board is a formally constituted committee responsible for reviewing changes and change requests. The level of authority of a change control board varies among projects and organizations; however, its level of authority should be spelled out in the project management plan. The change control meetings are the forums for formally evaluating these changes.

Change Control Tools

Tools here are used to manage the flow of information for the Change Control Board. The number of tasks and the associated workflow may become difficult to manage without some type of system in place.

Outputs

Approved Change Requests

All formally requested changes must be approved or rejected. The approved change requests are channeled back into Direct and Manage Project Work.

Change Log

The change log is the central place to keep track of all changes and change requests that occur on a project. They are documented here and are communicated to the stakeholders.

Project Management Plan Updates — See Ch. 2, Common Outputs

Project Documents Updates — See Ch. 2, Common Outputs

Close Project or Phase

What it is:

One of the key attributes of a project is that it is temporary. This means that every project eventually comes to an end, and that is exactly where this process comes into play.

Close Project or Phase is all about shutting the project down properly. This includes creating the necessary documentation and archives, capturing the lessons learned, ensuring that the contract is properly closed, and updating all organizational process assets.

Why it is important:

Projects that skip this process often are left open, limping along for months without official closure. Taking the time to do this step, and to do it properly, will ensure that the project is closed as neatly and as permanently as possible and that records are properly created and archived. These records become organizational process assets for use on future projects the organization undertakes.

When it is performed:

By looking at the name of this process, you can probably deduce that it is performed at the very end of the project or at the end of each phase. Projects that have six phases would likely perform this process seven times (once after each phase, and once for the project as a whole). In real practice, you might well perform some of the activities in this process before the project or phase ends, but for the exam, think of it as taking place at the end of the project or phase.

How it works:

Inputs

Project Management Plan — See Ch. 2, Common Inputs

Accepted Deliverables — See Direct and Manage Project Work - Outputs

Organizational Process Assets — See Ch. 2, Common Inputs

Tools

Expert Judgment — See Ch. 2, Common Tools

Analytical Techniques — See Ch. 2, Common Tools

Meetings — See Ch. 2, Common Tools

Key Fact

Outputs

Final Product, Service, or Result Transition

This output represents not so much the product itself, but the acceptance and handover of responsibility to the receiving party (e.g., the customer, operations, support group, or another company). The transition implies that the product has been accepted and is ready for this handover.

Organizational Process Assets Updates

In the course of a project, information will be gleaned, tools will be purchased or built, knowledge and experience will be gained, and documents (some of which may be reused one day) will be created. All of this should be updated as an organizational process asset and delivered to the appropriate group or individual(s) responsible for maintaining them. Often this will be the project management office.

Close Project
or Phase

Integration Management
QUESTIONS

1. **Producing a project plan may BEST be described as:**

   A. Creating a network logic diagram that identifies the critical path.

   B. Using a software tool to track schedule, cost, and resources.

   C. Creating a document that guides project plan execution.

   D. Creating a plan that contains the entire product scope.

2. **Project management plan updates are NOT an output of:**

   A. Perform Integrated Change Control.

   B. Develop Project Management Plan.

   C. Direct and Manage Project Work.

   D. Monitor and Control Project Work.

3. **You are meeting with a new project manager who has taken over a project that is in the middle of executing. The previous project manager has left the company and the new project manager is upset that change requests are streaming in from numerous sources including his boss, the customer, and various stakeholders. The project manager is not even aware of how to process all of these incoming change requests. Where would you refer him?**

   A. Project scope statement.

   B. Project management plan.

   C. The previous project manager.

   D. Project charter.

4. **Centurion Corporation has initiated a new project to modernize their human resources records and to bring them into compliance. A manager at Centurion is drafting the project charter for review. Which of the following would be the most important item that she would need in order to complete this task and why?**

   A.   Managerial approval to proceed, because it may affect whether or not the project moves forward.

   B.   A scope statement, because it will set the parameters for the product scope.

   C.   A scope statement, because it will set the parameters for the project scope.

   D.   A business case, because it explains the justification for the project.

5. **The project charter is:**

   A.   Developed before the project statement of work, and after the project management plan.

   B.   Developed after the project statement of work, and before the project management plan.

   C.   Developed before the contract, and after the project management plan.

   D.   Developed before the contract, and before the project management plan.

6. **The project management information system would likely include all of the following EXCEPT:**

   A.   A scheduling tool.

   B.   An information distribution system.

   C.   A system for collecting information from team members.

   D.   A system for identifying stakeholders.

7. **A defect in the product was brought to the project manager's attention, and now the project team is engaged in repairing it. Which project management process would be the most applicable to this?**

    A. Perform Integrated Change Control.

    B. Monitor and Control Project Work.

    C. Direct and Manage Project Work.

    D. Close Project or Phase.

8. **If you are creating a single document to guide project execution, monitoring and control, and closure, you are creating:**

    A. The execution plan.

    B. The project management plan.

    C. The integration plan.

    D. The project framework.

9. **Change control meetings are held as part of which process?**

    A. Direct and Manage Project Work.

    B. Monitor and Control Project Work.

    C. Perform Integrated Change Control.

    D. Evaluate Requested Changes.

10. **Which of the following statements is NOT true regarding the project charter?**

    A. The project charter justifies why the project is being undertaken.

    B. The project charter assigns the project manager.

    C. The project charter specifies any high-level schedule milestones.

    D. The project charter specifies what type of contract will be used.

11. **Which of the following represents the project manager's responsibility regarding change on a project?**

    A. Influence the factors that cause project change.

    B. Ensure all changes are communicated to the change control board.

    C. Deny change wherever possible.

    D. Prioritize change below results.

12. **The project management plan is made up of:**

   A.   The other planning outputs.

   B.   The other planning outputs, tools, and techniques.

   C.   The aggregate outputs of approved software tools.

   D.   The business case, key value justifications, and the GANTT chart.

13. **When changes are approved and made to the project, they should be:**

   A.   Tracked against the project baseline.

   B.   Incorporated into the project baseline.

   C.   Included as an addendum to the project plan.

   D.   Approved by someone other than the project manager.

14. **Which statement about the project statement of work is true?**

   A.   The project statement of work is generally used to define the business case for the project.

   B.   The project statement of work is generally created only when one or more portions of the project are being procured from outside the organization.

   C.   The project statement of work is generally created before the project is formally initiated.

   D.   The project statement of work is generally considered to be an enterprise environmental factor.

15. **Work performance information is used for all of the following reasons EXCEPT:**

   A.   It provides information on resource utilization.

   B.   It provides information on which activities have started.

   C.   It shows what costs have been incurred.

   D.   It is used to help identify defects.

16. **You are a project manager, and your team is executing the work packages to produce a medical records archive and retrieval system. Two of the project's customers have just asked for changes that each says should be the number one priority. What would be the BEST thing to do?**

    A. Have the project team meet with the customers to decide which would be easiest and prioritize that one first.

    B. Assign someone from the team to prioritize the changes.

    C. Prioritize the changes without involving the team.

    D. Deny both changes since you are in project execution.

17. **The program manager is asking why your project is scheduled to take sixteen months. He claims that previous projects in the organization were able to be completed in less than half of that time. What would be the BEST thing to do?**

    A. Look for historical information on the previous projects to understand them better.

    B. Refer the program manager to the schedule management plan.

    C. Refer the program manager to the project management plan.

    D. Explain to the program manager that estimates should always err on the side of being too large.

18. **You work for a defense contractor on a project that is not considered to be strategic for the company. Although the project is not the company's top priority, you have managed to secure many of the company's top resources to work on your project. At today's company meeting, you find out that your organization has won a very large, strategic project. What should you do FIRST?**

    A. Contact management to find out if you can be transferred to this project because it is strategic to the company.

    B. Contact management to find out how this new project will affect your project.

    C. Hold a team meeting and explain that since the resources have been allocated to your project, they are not eligible to go to the new project.

    D. Fast track your project to accelerate its completion date.

19. **Each time that the project sponsor requests a change to the project, the project manager calls a meeting of the change control board. Which of the following is TRUE?**

    A. This represents a collaborative style of management.

    B. This represents withdrawal by the project manager.

    C. This represents Perform Integrated Change Control.

    D. This represents the lack of a project management information system.

20. **Alex has received an inquiry from a functional manager about how the team is performing. In reality, the team's productivity has been lagging for the past two months, but Alex is confident that this problem can be solved. Which process would most likely produce the information the functional manager has requested?**

    A. Direct and Manage Project Work.

    B. Monitor and Control Project Work.

    C. Report Performance.

    D. Integrated Change Control.

21. **Your organization has a policy that any project changes that increase the project's budget by more than 1.5% must be signed off by the project office. You have a change that was requested by the customer that will increase the budget by 3%; however, the customer has offered to pay for all of this change and does not want to slow it down. Which option represents the BEST choice?**

    A. Approve the change yourself and take it to the project office after the work is underway.

    B. Ask the customer to take the change to the project office and explain the situation.

    C. Do not allow the change since it increases the budget by over 1.5%.

    D. Take the change to the project office.

22. **The person or group responsible for evaluating change on a project is:**

    A.   The change control board.

    B.   The sponsor.

    C.   The project team.

    D.   The program manager.

23. **The output of the Direct and Manage Project Work process is:**

    A.   The work packages.

    B.   The project management information system.

    C.   The deliverables.

    D.   The work breakdown structure.

24. **Two projects are being considered by the project office, Project Clarity, and Project New Scale. The Chief Project Officer is planning to evaluate the projected Return On Investment Capital for both projects. In order to do that, what information would be most helpful?**

    A.   The total projected capital investment and net income.

    B.   The total projected benefit and cost.

    C.   The total projected capital expenditures and cost of capital.

    D.   The total projected return on investment, the cost of capital, and the current interest rate.

25. **Which component of the project management plan is created in Develop Project Management Plan?**

    A.   Change Management Plan.

    B.   Requirements Management Plan.

    C.   Process Improvement Plan.

    D.   Stakeholder Management Plan.

Answers to
Integration Management Questions

1.   **C.** The project plan is a single, approved plan that drives execution, monitoring and control, and closure. Note that the definition in answer 'C' was not perfect, but it was the best choice. 'A' is incorrect since it is only a part of planning. 'B' is incorrect because that will not make up the entire project plan. 'D' is incorrect since scope may or may not be a part of the project plan, but it does not make up all of it.

2.   **B.** The project management plan is created in Develop Project Management Plan. It, along with other plans, is updated in the other processes listed.

3.   **B.** The project management plan would contain the methods for processing changes to the project.

4.   **D.** The business case is a formal input to the process of Develop Project Charter, where the charter is created, making this the best choice. The business case provides the reasons why the project needed to be initiated. 'A' is not a very good choice here because the charter, which is being created here, represents managerial approval, so that would not be needed to complete this task. Rather, that would be an outcome of this task. Both 'B' and 'C' are not good choices, because the scope statement is an output that is created later.

5.   **B.** Questions like this will be on the exam, and in order to answer them, you have to understand the rough order in which the deliverables are produced and processes are conducted. In this case, the typical order among the items listed is project statement of work, contract, project charter, and project management plan. If you analyze the inputs and outputs used by the integration processes, you will gain a better understanding of this order.

6.   **D.** The project management information system (PMIS) is covered in Chapter 2 – Foundational Terms and Concepts. The PMIS is an automated system to support the project manager by optimizing the schedule and helping collect and distribute information. 'D' would not be a function of the PMIS. It is generally a manual process performed by the project manager and the team.

7.   **C.** Direct and Manage Project Work is the only process in the list where defects are repaired. Approved change requests are an input, and deliverables are an output.

8.   **B.** This is the definition of the project management plan.

9.   **C.** As you think about this one, ask yourself which process group would use a tool like change control meetings. The answer to that question is "monitoring and controlling." Now, you can immediately narrow it down to two processes represented in answers 'B' and 'C'. Keep the flow of these processes in mind. Change requests flow out of Monitor and Control Project Work and into Perform Integrated Change Control, where they are evaluated in meetings. Answer 'D' may sound great, but it is not the name of a real process.

10. **D.** The project charter does not specify anything about contracts. A contract with your customer would have been an input into the Develop Project Charter process, and any contracts you may use during procurement won't be identified until later in the project. 'A' is incorrect because the project charter does specify why the project is being undertaken and often even includes a business case. 'B' is incorrect because the project charter is the place where the project manager is named. 'C' is incorrect because the project charter specifies any known schedule milestones and a summary level budget.

11. **A.** The project manager must be proactive and influence the factors that cause change. This is one of the key tenets of monitoring and controlling processes in general and Perform Integrated Change Control in particular.

12. **A.** The project management plan consists of many things, but the only one from this list that matches is the outputs from the other planning processes, such as risk, cost, time, quality, etc. 'B' is incorrect because the other tools and techniques do not form part of the project plan.

13. **B.** Did this one fool you? Approved changes that are made to the project get factored back into the baseline. Many people incorrectly choose 'A', but the purpose of the baseline is NOT to measure approved change, but to measure deviation.

14. **C.** The project statement of work is an input into the process Develop Project Charter, which formally kicks off the project. That means that the charter is created before there is even an official project. 'A' is incorrect since any of the methods of benefit measure or other contents of the business case do not rely on the project scope statement. 'B' is not a good answer because you need the project scope statement whether the project is being performed by the internal team or by someone else. 'D' is incorrect since the statement of work could be considered to be an organizational process asset, but enterprise environmental factors are more about the climate that affects the project, which is not descriptive of the project statement of work.

15. **D.** The work performance information is all about how the work is being performed, but it is not used in identifying defects. 'A' is incorrect because it does provide detail on what resources have been used and when. 'B' is incorrect because it provides information on which activities have been started and what their status is. 'C' is incorrect because it provides information on what costs were authorized and what costs have been incurred.

16. **C.** Prioritizing the changes is the job of the project manager. 'A' is wrong because you do not want to distract the team at this point – they should be doing the work. 'B' is wrong because it is the project manager's responsibility to help prioritize competing demands. 'D' is incorrect, because changes cannot automatically be denied simply because you are in execution.

17. **A.** Historical information (an organizational process asset) was covered in Chapter 2 – Foundational Terms and Concepts, and it may provide an excellent justification for why your project is taking sixteen months, or perhaps it will show you how someone else accomplished the same type of work in less time.

Either way, it provides a great benchmark for you to factor in to your project. 'B' is incorrect since the schedule management plan only tells how the schedule will be managed. 'C' is incorrect because **the project plan will not specifically** address the program manager's concern about why the project is taking longer than he expects. 'D' is wrong because estimates should be accurate with a reserve added on top as may be appropriate.

18. **B.** Always evaluate things thoroughly before you act! You need to know if your project is going to be affected before taking action. Many people incorrectly choose 'D', but fast tracking the schedule increases risk, and that would not be necessary or appropriate until you fully understood the situation.

19. **C.** Change control boards meet to evaluate change requests. They do this during the process of Perform Integrated Change Control.

20. **'B'** Monitor and Control Project work is the correct answer, since its main function is to produce the work performance reports, and these explain how the team is performing against the plan. 'C' is not a real process (interestingly it used to be, but it is has been phased out).

21. **D.** As discussed in Chapter 2 – Foundational Terms and Concepts, organizational policies must be followed. None of the other options presents an acceptable alternative. Choice 'B' would be asking the customer to do the project manager's job.

22. **A.** The change control board is responsible for evaluating changes to the project.

23. **C.** The deliverables are the key output of Direct and Manage Project Work.

24. **A.** The formula for Return On Investment Capital (ROIC) is Net Income / the Total Capital Investment. This makes 'A' the best choice.

25. **A.** The change management plan and the configuration management plan are created in the process of Develop Project Management Plan. 'B', 'C', and 'D' are all created elsewhere and are brought into this process to be compiled into the project management plan

5 Scope Management

Difficulty	Memorization	Exam Importance
HIGH	MEDIUM	HIGH

The processes of Project Scope Management with their primary outputs

Scope Management

Plan Scope Management
Scope Management Plan
Requirements Management Plan

Collect Requirements
Requirements Documentation

Define Scope
Project Scope Statement

Create WBS
Scope Baseline

Validate Scope
Accepted Deliverables

Control Scope
Work Performance Info
Change Requests

A solid grasp of project scope management is foundational to your understanding of the material on the PMP Exam. While no topic in this book is particularly easy, scope management presents fewer difficulties than most other areas of the test. Most people find scope management to be more intuitive than other areas, since it has no complex formulas to memorize and no particularly difficult theories. Instead, scope management is a presentation of logical processes to understand requirements, define, break down, and control the scope of the project, and verify that the product was completed correctly.

Philosophy

The philosophy behind this presentation of scope management can be condensed down to these two statements:

1. The project manager should always be in control of the scope through rigid management of the requirements, details, and processes.

2. Scope changes should be handled in a structured, procedural, and controlled manner.

It is important to begin with the end in mind when it comes to scope management so that each requirement is documented with the acceptance criteria included. Good scope management focuses on making sure that the scope is well defined and clearly communicated and that the project is carefully managed to limit unnecessary changes. The work is closely monitored to ensure that when change does happen on the project, it is evaluated, captured, and documented. Project managers should also work proactively to identify and influence the factors that cause change.

The overall goals of scope management are to define the need, to set stakeholder expectations, to deliver to the expectations, to manage changes, and to minimize surprises so that the product will ultimately be accepted.

Importance

The topic of scope is very important on the exam. When we refer to the project "scope," we are referring to the work needed to successfully complete the project and only that work. Many companies have a culture in which they try to exceed customer expectations by delivering more than was agreed upon; this practice, often referred to as "gold plating," increases risk and uncertainty and may inject a host of potential problems into the project.

Preparation

While this section requires less actual memorization than some other knowledge areas, many of the test questions can be very tricky, requiring a solid and thorough understanding of the theories and practices of scope management.

Scope Management Processes

As a starting point, you should understand that the knowledge area of scope management consists of the following elements:

- Planning the overall scope-related efforts
- Gathering the requirements for the product and the project
- Defining and documenting the deliverables that are a part of the product and the project (the scope)
- Creating the work breakdown structure (WBS) and baselining the scope

- Checking the work being done against the scope to ensure that it is complete and correct
- Ensuring that all of what is "in scope" and only what is "in scope" is completed and that changes are properly managed

There are six processes in the scope management knowledge area. These are Plan Scope Management, Collect Requirements, Define Scope, Create Work Breakdown Structure, Validate Scope, and Control Scope. Below are the breakouts that show to which process group each item belongs:

PROCESS GROUP	SCOPE MANAGEMENT PROCESS
Initiating	(none)
Planning	Plan Scope Management, Collect Requirements, Define Scope, Create WBS
Executing	(none)
Monitoring & Controlling	Validate Scope, Control Scope
Closing	(none)

In the knowledge area of scope management, it is also essential that you know the main outputs that are produced during each process. The different key outputs that are created in each process are summarized in the chart below.

PROCESS	KEY OUTPUTS
Plan Scope Management	Scope Management Plan Requirements Management Plan
Collect Requirements	Requirements Documentation, Requirements Traceability Matrix
Define Scope	Project Scope Statement
Create WBS	Scope Baseline
Validate Scope	Accepted Deliverables
Control Scope	(Scope) Change Requests

Planning

Plan Scope Management

What it is:

Plan Scope Management is a process that looks at the other (subsequent) five scope processes and plans the approach as to how they will be carried out.

Why it is important:

This process has a very significant impact on the success of the project since the requirements are the primary means of understanding and managing stakeholder expectations. Also schedule, budget, quality specifications, risk factors, and resource planning (discussed in later chapters) will tie back to the work done here.

When it is performed:

This process is a bit unusual in that it appears to be part of a loop. One of the outputs of Plan Scope Management is the Scope Management Plan, but the Scope Management Plan is part of the Project Management Plan, which is an input into Plan Scope Management. To understand this, consider that this process has several parts that are developed together. The unfinished Project Management Plan is brought in, and the Scope Management Plan is produced.

How it works:

Inputs

Project Management Plan

The project management plan, although unfinished at this point, is brought in to help determine how the scope will be gathered, defined, broken down, validated, and managed.

Project Charter — See Ch. 4, Develop Project Charter

Enterprise Environ. Factors — See Ch. 2, Common Inputs

Organizational Process Assets — See Ch. 2, Common Inputs

Tools

Expert Judgment — See Ch. 2, Common Tools

Meetings — See Ch. 2, Common Tools

Outputs

Kev Fact

Scope Management Plan

The scope management plan is one of the 16 components of the project plan. It describes how the scope documents will be prepared and how the remaining scope processes will be carried out.

Kev Fact

Requirements Management Plan

The requirements management plan defines what activities the team will perform in order to gather and manage the project requirements. It is important to note that this document is only the plan for how the requirements will be managed and not the requirements themselves.

The requirements management plan is important because it shows how requirements will be gathered, how decisions will be made, how changes to the requirements will be handled, and how the requirements will be documented.

Once the requirements management plan is created, it is integrated into the overall project management plan.

Planning

Collect Requirements

What it is:

The process of Collect Requirements is about understanding what is needed to satisfy the stakeholders and creating a document to reflect that understanding. This is true for both the product and the project as a whole.

How much time and energy is invested in Collect Requirements will vary from project to project, depending on the needs.

Why it is important:

This process has a very significant impact on the success of the project since the requirements are the primary means of understanding and managing stakeholder expectations. Also, schedule, budget, quality specifications, risk factors, and resource planning will tie back to the requirements.

When it is performed:

This process typically takes place quite early in the project because of the impact requirements have on the rest of the project. Some methodologies, such as Rolling Wave, call for it to be repeated throughout much of the project life cycle.

The requirements will factor heavily into the project plan and should certainly be gathered and accurately documented before any execution takes place.

Develop Project Charter and Identify Stakeholders must be performed before it is possible to perform Collect Requirements.

How it works:

Inputs

Scope Management Plan

Even though the requirements management plan is brought into this process, the scope management plan also brings clarity to the types of requirements that the team will gather.

Requirements Management Plan

The requirements management plan describes how the requirements will be collected and documented.

Stakeholder Management Plan

The stakeholder management plan informs how deeply the stakeholders should be involved in the requirements process.

Project Charter

The charter is brought into Collect Requirements because it provides a high-level description of the project's product, service, or result. This description is used as guidance to help flesh out the requirements.

Key Fact

Stakeholder Register

The stakeholder register contains a list of all of the project stakeholders, and it is these stakeholders who can explain the requirements and the underlying needs. Since the requirements will be built to ultimately satisfy the stakeholders, it is important to involve the right stakeholders early in the project and to ensure that they have the appropriate voice on the project.

Tools

Interviews

Interviews are typically conducted by the project manager or business analyst with a subject matter expert. The subject matter expert can help explain what the product should contain and why it matters.

Focus Groups

Whereas interviews are generally conducted one-on-one, focus groups are conducted by someone on the project team who meets with a group of stakeholders to discuss their needs and requirements. Focus groups are intended to create a safe environment for stakeholders to discuss their expectations of the project.

Key Fact

Facilitated Workshops

The goal behind facilitated workshops is to co-locate all of the key stakeholders together and to elaborate the requirements. In order to have a successful facilitated workshop, it is essential to have a skilled facilitator. Problems can generally be dealt with in the sessions since all of the relevant people may already be there.

Examples of facilitated workshops are: Joint Application Development and Quality Function Deployment.

Key Fact

Group Creativity Techniques

Creativity is an important part of the requirements gathering process, and good project managers know the importance of creating an environment where people can safely process ideas. Some of the techniques that are most commonly associated with creativity are:

Brainstorming, where ideas are shared in a rapid-fire setting and are not discussed until everyone is out of ideas.

Nominal Group Technique, where brainstormed ideas are voted upon and sorted by priority.

Delphi Technique, a means of gathering expert judgment where the participants do not know who the others are and therefore are not able to influence each other's opinion. The Delphi Technique is designed to prevent groupthink and to find out a participant's real opinion.

Idea and Mind Mapping, a technique of diagramming ideas and creating meaningful associations in a graphical format. A mind map helps the team see meaningful associations among ideas.

Collect Requirements

Group Decision-Making Techniques

One of the more difficult aspects of a project manager's job can be to get various stakeholders to make a decision. There are numerous techniques that a project manager can use to help drive decisions forward. They include Unanimity, Majority, Consensus, Plurality, and Dictatorship. Each of these techniques is explained further in the glossary. It would be a good idea to pause here and look up each of those five terms before going further.

Kev Fact

Questionnaires and Surveys

This technique works well with large groups of people, allowing the team to gather opinions and requirements rapidly. Because the questionnaire or survey is generally in a standard format, aggregation and analysis is easier than with some other forms.

Observation

Also known as "job shadowing," observation is where a worker is studied as he performs his job. The goal is to understand how the worker performs and to capture any requirements that may not be evident through interviews or other methods.

Prototypes

Prototyping creates a model of the end product with which the user can interact. The advantage of a prototype is that the idea becomes tangible and can be used by people, allowing the project team to understand what works and does not work about the model. Prototypes receive varying degrees of emphasis, depending on the end product and on the project methodologies. They are especially friendly to the project management idea of progressive elaboration, which stresses that a deliverable can be revisited repeatedly before it is finalized.

Benchmarking

Benchmarking is all about looking outside of the project to understand best practices. These may come from other departments in the company or similar organizations within the same industry.

Context Diagrams

A context diagram is the generic term for a use case diagram which shows systems and the "actors" that interact with the system. Each actor may be a user or another system.

Document Analysis

This one is as simple as it sounds. Reading existing documentation is one way to gather requirements by understanding the requirements that currently exist.

Outputs

Requirements Documentation

This is simply a document that describes what needs to be performed and why each requirement is important on the project. The requirements documentation should include a description of:

- The root business problem being solved
- The source of the requirement
- The way each requirement addresses the problem
- How the business processes interact with the requirements
- Associated measurements for each requirement
- Business, legal, and ethical compliance
- Constraints and assumptions
- Anticipated impact of the requirement on others

Requirements Traceability Matrix

Once a requirement is collected, it is important to be able to identify the source. That is what this document does. The source could originate from a stakeholder or departmental request, a legal, contractual, or ethical need, an underlying requirement, or any number of other sources. The thing to remember here is that if a requirement is important enough to be documented, it is important to list the source here. The requirements traceability matrix can also include information about who owns the requirement, the status of the requirement, etc.

Planning

Define Scope

What it is:

At some point, every project must develop a clear understanding of the requirements to be executed, verified, and delivered. The scope of the project must be understood and documented in detail.

Why it is important:

The scope of the project is what ultimately drives the execution of the project, and Define Scope is the process where the project's requirements are more thoroughly understood and documented. The importance of this process is directly related to how important the requirements are. A large, mission-critical project will perform this process very thoroughly, while a smaller project, or one that is highly similar to a project that has been performed previously, will probably be less formal and detailed. Likewise, a project that has extremely high material costs (e.g., an offshore drilling platform) will likely spend more time and effort on Define Scope than a project with less risk of error.

When it is performed:

This process may be started as soon as the Collect Requirements process has been completed. Because projects are generally progressively elaborated, this process, along with the requirements, may be revisited many times throughout the life of the project; however, it is generally begun very early in the project life cycle.

Develop Project Charter, Identify Stakeholders, and Collect Requirements must be performed before it is possible to perform Define Scope.

How it works:

During the Define Scope process, the project manager refines the requirements collected earlier in the project by performing additional analysis, factoring in any approved changes, and adding

Define Scope

detail. The project scope statement, which is the output of this process, has detailed information about the project scope and requirements.

Inputs

Scope Management Plan

The scope management plan, one of the components of the project plan, describes how all of the scope activities will be managed, including this one.

Project Charter

The project charter is the organization document formally creating the project and outlining its goals. Since this process will be creating a detailed view of the scope, the project charter is needed. If the project charter does not exist, then the project manager should still capture the project's overall goals, a brief description of the scope, and the known constraints and assumptions before performing Define Scope.

Requirements Documentation

The stakeholder requirements provide the primary fuel for this process. Requirements define what the project has to do and the degree to which it must perform. The process of Define Scope then turns those requirements into a more detailed project scope statement.

Organizational Process Assets — See Ch. 2, Common Inputs

Tools

Expert Judgment

This tool involves having experts work with the project team to develop portions of the project scope statement. These are typically experts on the technical matters that need to be documented.

Product Analysis

Product analysis is a detailed analysis of the project's product, service, or result, with the intent of improving the project team's understanding of the product and helping to capture that understanding in the form of requirements. The tools that may be used in product analysis will vary among industries and organizations, but common ones include:

- Product breakdown
- Systems analysis
- Requirements analysis
- Systems engineering
- Value engineering
- Value analysis

Kev Fact

Alternatives Generation

The goal of alternatives generation is to make sure that the team is properly considering all options as they relate to the project's scope. Techniques to generate creative thought such as brainstorming are used most often for this.

Kev Fact

Facilitated Workshops

The tool of Facilitated Workshops, described in the tools of the Collect Requirements process, can help develop the understanding of the scope in more detail.

Outputs

Kev Fact

Project Scope Statement

The project scope statement is the document used to level-set among the project's stakeholders. The project scope statement contains many details pertaining to the project and product deliverables, including: the goals of the project, the product description, the requirements for the project, the constraints and assumptions, and the identified risks related to the scope. The objective criteria for accepting the product should also be included in the project scope statement.

Project Documents Updates

Many documents may be updated as the scope is elaborated and defined, including the stakeholder register, the requirements documentation, and the requirements traceability matrix. Other documents related to risk, estimates, and issues may be updated as well.

Define Scope

Create WBS

What it is:

This process probably gets the award for the most confusing name. You would think that Create WBS would be all about producing the work breakdown structure, but the WBS is not listed as one of its outputs. Actually, this process does create the WBS, but at the same time it combines it with two other documents to create the Scope Baseline. While the main product of this process is the work breakdown structure, the main output will be the Scope Baseline. You will learn more about what a baseline is when we get to that output.

Why it is important:

The work breakdown structure, or WBS, is one of the most important topics for the exam. The reason for its importance is tied to how it is used. After its creation, the WBS becomes a hub of information for the project, and arguably the most important component of the project plan. Risks, activities, costs, quality attributes, and procurement decisions all tie back to the WBS, and it is a primary tool for verifying and controlling the project's scope.

When it is performed:

Create WBS is typically performed early in the project, after the requirements have been collected and the scope has been defined, but before the bulk of the work is executed.

Develop Project Charter, Identify Stakeholders, Collect Requirements, and Define Scope must be performed before it is possible to perform Create WBS.

Create WBS

How it works:

Inputs

Scope Management Plan

There are multiple approaches a team can take to create the WBS and baseline the scope. The scope management plan describes which one the team will use on this project and how it will be carried out.

Project Scope Statement

The project scope statement describes the scope of the project in detail. It will be used in this process as a primary starting point from which to create the WBS.

Requirements Documentation

This output of the Collect Requirements process ties each requirement back to a specific business need or benefit, and like all planning documents, this one is often progressively elaborated.

Enterprise Environ. Factors — See Ch. 2, Common Inputs

Organizational Process Assets — See Ch. 2, Common Inputs

Organizational process assets can take on different meanings in different contexts. In the case of Create WBS, the most common assets would consist of methodologies that spell out how to create the work breakdown structure, software tools to create the graphical chart, WBS templates, and completed WBS examples from previously performed projects.

Tools

Kev Fact

Decomposition

The sole tool used in creating the WBS, decomposition, involves breaking down the project deliverables into progressively smaller components. In a WBS, the top layer is very general (perhaps as general as the deliverable or product name, or some even go so far as to make the top node the overall program), and each subsequent layer is more and more specific. The key to reading the WBS is to understand that every level is the detailed explanation of the level above it.

Create WBS

Decomposition may be thought of as being similar to the arcade game Asteroids™ from years ago. Large pieces are progressively broken down into smaller and smaller pieces.

So, how do you know when you have decomposed your WBS far enough? As you have probably realized, the nodes could be decomposed to ridiculously low levels, wasting time and actually making the project difficult to understand, manage, and change. There are many things to consider when deciding how far to decompose work, but three of the best questions to ask are:

1. Are your work packages small enough to be estimated for time and cost?
2. Are the project manager and the project team satisfied that the current level of detail provides enough information to proceed with subsequent project activities?
3. Is each work package small enough to be able to be assigned to a single person or group that can be accountable for the results?

If you can answer "yes" to those three questions, your work packages are probably decomposed far enough.

Expert Judgment — See Ch. 2, Common Tools

Outputs

Kev Fact

Scope Baseline

The scope baseline is an important output that includes the project scope statement, the WBS, and the WBS dictionary. Baselines are made up of the original plan plus all approved changes.

Project Scope Statement

A baseline (whether for scope, schedule, cost, or quality) is the original plan plus all approved changes. In this instance, the scope baseline represents the combination of the project scope statement, the WBS, and the WBS dictionary. When the scope baseline is created, it is placed under control, meaning that changes to the scope are made according to the scope management plan.

WBS

The writers of the current edition of the PMBOK Guide currently advocate that the work breakdown structure always be based on the project deliverables, rather than the tasks needed to create those deliverables, and that it be built from the top down.

The WBS is primarily constructed through decomposition, the practice of breaking down deliverables (product features, characteristics, or attributes) into progressively smaller pieces. This process continues until the deliverables are small enough to be considered work packages. A node may be considered a work package when it meets the following criteria:

- The work package cannot be easily decomposed any further
- The work package is small enough to be estimated for time (effort)
- The work package is small enough to be estimated for cost
- The work package may be assigned to a single person

If the node is being subcontracted outside of the performing organization, that node, regardless of size, may be considered a work package, and the subcontracting organization builds a "sub-WBS" from that node.

The resulting WBS is a graphical, hierarchical chart, logically organized from top to bottom. Each node on the WBS has a unique number used to locate and identify it.

Each level of the WBS is mutually exclusive and cumulatively exhaustive. This means that there are no gaps and no overlap in the work packages. No piece of scope is eliminated, and nothing is duplicated.

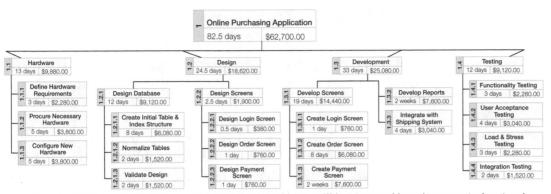

Sample WBS (cost and time estimates depicted here will be covered in subsequent chapters)

Elements of a Good Work Breakdown Structure (WBS):

- It must be detailed down to a low level. The lowest level consists of work packages that define every deliverable on the project.
- It is graphical, arranged like a pyramid, where each sub-level rolls up to the level above it.
- It numbers each element, and the numbering system should allow anyone who reads the WBS to find individual elements quickly and easily.
- It should provide sufficient detail to drive the subsequent phases of planning.
- It may often be borrowed from other projects in the organization as a starting point. These starting points are known as templates.
- It is thorough and complete. If an item is not in the WBS, it does not get delivered with the project.
- It is central to the project.
- The project team, and not just the project manager, creates the WBS. Developing the WBS can also be a means of team-building.
- It is an integration tool, allowing you to see where the individual pieces of work fit into the project as a whole.
- It helps define responsibilities for the team.
- It is a communication tool.

Create WBS

Create WBS

WBS Dictionary

The WBS dictionary is a document that details the contents of the WBS. Just as a language dictionary defines words, a WBS dictionary provides detailed information about the nodes on a WBS.

Because the WBS is graphical, there is a practical limit to how much information can be included in each node. The WBS dictionary solves this problem by capturing additional attributes about each work package in a different document that does not have the graphical constraints that the WBS does.

For each node in the WBS, the WBS dictionary might include the number of the node, the name of the node, the written requirements for the node, to whom it is assigned, and time, cost, and account information.

Project: Online Ordering Application	
Work Package ID: 1.1.3	
Work Package Name: Configure New Hardware	
Work Package Description: All new hardware should be configured, including any hardware settings and preparation such as formatting of storage. The correct operating system should be loaded, and the appropriate patches should be applied. Any security settings, including virus scanning software, should be applied. The hardware should be added to the company domain and should be compliant with all company policy regarding hardware and security.	
Assigned to: Lee Abbott	**Department:** I.T.
Date Assigned: 4/15/13	**Date Due:** 4/22/13
Estimated Cost: $3,800.00	**Accounting Code:** HMIT-0229

Sample WBS Dictionary Entry

Project Documents Updates

Through the process of creating the scope baseline and WBS, the understanding of the project often changes and improves. This change in understanding should be documented back in the appropriate place. For instance, if decomposition uncovered a missing requirement after validating that requirement with the stakeholders, the project manager should update the requirements documentation.

Create WBS

Monitoring & Controlling

Validate Scope

What it is:

Validate Scope is easily confused with other processes. Many people fall into the trap of thinking that this process involves verifying that the scope is documented accurately; however, this is not correct. Validate Scope is the process of ensuring that the product, service, or result of the project matches the documented scope.

In general, controlling processes compare the plan with the results to see where they differ and take the appropriate action. This fits Validate Scope very well since the product is compared with the scope to ensure they match.

Validate Scope has quite a few similarities to the process of Control Quality (covered in Chapter 8, Quality Management) in that they both inspect the product against the scope; however, there are some key differences between them.

- Validate Scope is often performed after Control Quality, although it is not unusual for them to be performed at the same time.

- Validate Scope is primarily concerned with completeness, while Control Quality is primarily concerned with correctness.

- Validate Scope is concerned with the acceptance of the product by the project manager, the sponsor, the customer, and others, while Control Quality is concerned with adherence to the quality specification.

    One more important note about Validate Scope is that if the project is canceled before completion, Validate Scope should be performed to document where the product was in relation to the scope at the point when the project ended.

Why it is important:

If the process of Validate Scope is successful, the product is accepted by the project manager, the customer, the sponsor, and sometimes by the functional managers and key stakeholders. This acceptance is a significant milestone in the life of the project.

Validate Scope

When it is performed:

This process would be performed after at least some of the product components have been delivered, although it may be performed several times throughout the life of the project. As mentioned above, Validate Scope is typically performed after Control Quality but can be performed at the same time. At a minimum, it would be performed late in the project life cycle as the product is delivered.

How it works:

Inputs

Project Management Plan

The project management plan contains the scope management plan and the scope baseline. These documents are useful because they provide the plan for how Validate Scope will be carried out and base original scope plus all approved changes.

Requirements Documentation

The requirements documentation provides all of the requirements for the product and the project that originated with the stakeholders. It provides useful source information when comparing the documentation with the product, service, or result.

Requirements Traceability Matrix

The requirements traceability matrix helps identify the source of each individual requirement. This can be useful when performing Validate Scope since it may be important to know which stakeholder requested the requirement and why.

Verified Deliverables

Validate Scope is all about comparing the deliverables with the documented scope to ensure that everything was completed. This comparison may be performed several times during the life of the project.

Work Performance Data

Sometimes a team can achieve the right outcome, but the path to get there was unacceptable. For instance, if the team delivered a good product but individuals averaged 90 hour work weeks to accomplish the work, it is likely not acceptable. Work Performance Data tells more about "how" the deliverables were created, which needs to be considered along with the product itself.

Tools

Inspection

Inspection involves a point-by-point review of the scope and the associated deliverable. For instance, a pre-occupancy walkthrough by a building inspector would be an example of the tool of inspection. User-acceptance testing of a software product could be another example where the tool of inspection was used to make sure the deliverables matched the documented scope.

Group Decision-Making Techniques — See Collect Requirements, Tools

Outputs

Accepted Deliverables

Acceptance of the deliverables is the primary output of the process of Validate Scope. This process is typically performed by the project manager, the sponsor, the customer, and the functional managers, and the result is a formal, written acceptance by the appropriate stakeholders.

Change Requests

Change requests are a normal result of an inspection. When the deliverables are inspected in-depth and compared with the documented scope, change requests will often result.

Work Performance Information

The WPI tells about how something was created, including whether it was on time, within budget, how the resources used compared with estimates, and other metrics of interest.

Project Documents Updates — See Ch. 2, Common Outputs

Control Scope

What it is:

Control Scope is a process that lives up to its name. This process is about maintaining control of the project by preventing scope change requests from overwhelming the project, and also about making certain that scope change requests are properly handled.

One of the more challenging concepts behind Control Scope can be that of resolving disputes. Although many disputes over project scope or product requirements are not simple, keep in mind that the customer's interests should always be weighed heavily. That does not mean that the customer is always right! Instead, it means that the customer is one of the most important stakeholders. All other things being equal, disputes should be resolved in favor of the customer.

Why it is important:

Anyone who has managed a project where scope change was a problem knows the importance of Control Scope. This process makes certain all change requests are processed, and also that any of the underlying causes of scope change requests are understood and managed. It is important not only to manage scope change requests, but also to prevent unnecessary ones.

When it is performed:

Control Scope is an ongoing process that begins as soon as the scope baseline is created. Until that point, the scope is not considered stable or complete enough to control; however, once the scope baseline is created, each scope change request must be carefully controlled and managed. Additionally, any time the work results are known to differ from the documented scope, this process should be performed, whether or not the scope change was requested in advance.

Control Scope

How it works:

Inputs

Project Management Plan

The project management plan contains the scope baseline and the scope management plan, and these are the most interesting components for Control Scope. This scope baseline consists of the WBS, the WBS dictionary and the project scope statement, and it is the documented source for what the project team is supposed to create. The scope baseline provides the baseline that the project manager will control. Other sections of the project management plan that are of interest here are the change management plan, the configuration management plan, and the requirements management plan.

Requirements Documentation

When a change request comes in, or when a change to the scope is detected, the requirements documentation should be consulted to understand and evaluate that change in light of the original requirement.

Requirements Traceability Matrix

This input is similar to the previous one in that it helps the project manager evaluate a change or a change request in light of the original requirement. The traceability matrix helps the project manager determine the source of the requirement so that the proper stakeholders can be consulted as necessary.

Kev Fact

Work Performance Data

This input is very similar in nature to the performance reports (discussed in chapter 10, Communications Management). It provides information on all aspects of the work completed as it relates to the project plan. Note here how the raw work performance data is an input and the more refined work performance information is the output.

Organizational Process Assets — See Ch. 2, Common Inputs

Tools

→ Variance Analysis

Variance analysis can be used to measure differences between what was defined in the scope baseline and what was created. Variance analysis can be particularly useful in the process of Control Scope as a way to investigate and understand the root causes behind these differences.

Outputs

→ *Work Performance Information*

An important part of all monitoring and controlling processes is understanding work performance data and how it differs from the plan.

Change Requests

As scope changes are made to the scope baseline, these must be factored into updates to the WBS. If the change represents a new piece of scope, the work must be decomposed in the WBS down to work package level and then brought into the other appropriate processes.

Project Management Plan Updates

The project management plan must be kept up to date throughout the life of the project. Any change in scope should be reflected in the project management plan, along with any other resulting changes in cost, schedule, risk, quality, procurement, etc.

Project Documents Updates — See Ch. 2, Common Outputs

Organizational Process Assets Updates

Any time corrective action is implemented, changes may need to be made to the organizational process assets. The reason behind this is that the change or corrective action may have demonstrated that the organizational process assets you used (e.g., a previous project scope management plan or an organizational policy) were not wholly adequate for this project and need to be updated for future projects.

Control Scope

Scope Management Questions

1. **Your project team is executing the work packages of your project when a serious disagreement regarding the interpretation of the scope is brought to your attention by two of your most trusted team members. How should this dispute be resolved?**

    A. The project team should decide on the resolution.

    B. The dispute should be resolved in favor of the customer.

    C. The dispute should be resolved in favor of senior management.

    D. The project manager should consult the project charter for guidance.

2. **Which of the following statements is FALSE regarding a work breakdown structure?**

    A. Activities should be arranged in the sequence they will be performed.

    B. Every item should have a unique identifier.

    C. The work breakdown structure represents 100% of the work that will be done on the project.

    D. Each level of a work breakdown structure provides progressively smaller representations.

3. **Mark has taken over a project that is beginning the construction phase of the product; however, he discovers that no work breakdown structure has been created. What choice represents the BEST course of action?**

    A. He should refuse to manage the project.

    B. He should stop construction until the work breakdown structure has been created.

    C. He should consult the WBS dictionary to determine whether sufficient detail exists to properly manage construction.

    D. He should document this to senior management and provide added oversight on the construction phase.

4. **The project has completed execution, and now it is time for the product of the project to be accepted. Who formally accepts the product?**

    A. The project team and the customer.

    B. The quality assurance team, senior management, and the project manager.

    C. The sponsor, key stakeholders, and the customer.

    D. The project manager, senior management, and the change control board.

5. **Creating the project scope statement is part of which process?**

    A. Project Scope Management.

    B. Collect Requirements.

    C. Define Scope.

    D. Validate Scope.

6. **The main point of Create WBS is to:**

    A. Decompose the scope of the product.

    B. Decompose the scope of the project.

    C. Create a baseline of the entire scope.

    D. Define all of the scope to be performed.

7. **The project scope statement should contain:**

    A. The work packages for the project.

    B. A high level description of the scope.

    C. The level of effort associated with each scope element.

    D. A detailed description of the scope.

8. **The most important part of Validate Scope is:**

    A. Gaining formal acceptance of the project deliverables from the customer.

    B. Checking the scope of the project against stakeholder expectations.

    C. Verifying that the project came in on time and on budget.

    D. Verifying that the product met the quality specifications.

9. **The organizational process assets would include all of the following except:**

   A.   Templates.

   B.   Financial control procedures.

   C.   Standardization guidelines.

   D.   The project management information system.

10. **Which of the following is NOT part of the scope baseline?**

   A.   The requirements documentation.

   B.   The project scope statement.

   C.   The work breakdown structure.

   D.   The WBS dictionary.

11. **You have taken over as project manager for a data warehouse project that is completing the design phase; however, change requests that affect the requirements are still pouring in from many sources, including your boss. Which of the following would have been MOST helpful in this situation?**

   A.   A project sponsor who is involved in the project.

   B.   A well-defined requirements management plan.

   C.   A change control board.

   D.   A change evaluation system.

12. **What is the function of the project sponsor?**

   A.   To help manage senior management expectations.

   B.   To be the primary interface with the customer.

   C.   To fund the project and formally accept the product.

   D.   To help exert control over the functional managers.

13. **The project manager and the customer on a project are meeting together to review the product of the project against the documented scope. Which tool would be MOST appropriate to use during this meeting?**

    A. Verification analysis.

    B. Inspection.

    C. Gap analysis.

    D. Feature review.

14. **A project team has a dedicated scoping phase for their project where all subject matter experts are meeting together with a trained facilitator. They have interviewed each person in the room to gather ideas for functionality and are now voting on them to put them in order of priority. This list will be used to feed requirements to the project team. The group's activities are an example of:**

    A. The Nominal Group Technique.

    B. Brainstorming.

    C. The Borda Method.

    D. Tuckman's Model.

15. **You have just assumed responsibility for a project that is in progress. While researching the project archives, you discover that the WBS dictionary was never created. Which of the following problems would LEAST likely be attributable to this?**

    A. Confusion about the meaning of specific work packages.

    B. Confusion about who is responsible for a specific work package.

    C. Confusion about which account to bill against for a specific work package.

    D. Confusion about how to change a specific work package.

16. **16. A team member makes a change to a software project without letting anyone else know. She assures you that it did not affect the schedule, and it significantly enhances the product. What should the project manager do FIRST?**

    A. Find out if the customer authorized this change.

    B. Submit the change to the change control board.

    C. Review the change to understand how it affects scope, cost, time, quality, risk, and customer satisfaction.

    D. Make sure the change is reflected in the requirements management plan.

17. **The product you have delivered has been reviewed carefully against the scope and is now being brought to the customer for formal acceptance. Which process is the project in?**

    A. Validate Scope.

    B. Audit Scope.

    C. Close Scope.

    D. Control Scope.

18. **You are working with stakeholders, using the Nominal Group Technique to help promote creativity. Which choice represents the MOST likely results of your work?**

    A. The requirements documentation and the project scope statement.

    B. The requirements documentation and the requirements traceability matrix.

    C. The work breakdown structure and the WBS dictionary.

    D. Accepted deliverables and change requests.

19. **Sara and Eric are two project managers having a discussion about which metrics to use to gauge project performance. They agree that benchmarking is a preferred approach, but Eric maintains that the best metrics should come from industry standards published by their industry group. Sara believes that they should benchmark within their own organization to see how well other departments are performing and base their own projections from those. In the context of their discussion, which of the following statements is true?**

A. Benchmarking is best performed against external companies to capture best practices from outside the organization.

B. Benchmarking is best performed against departments within the organization to compare against similar entities.

C. Benchmarking may look within the organization or outside the organization, based on the need.

D. Benchmarking should be only be used once operations have stabilized in order to gather reliable metrics.

20. **A large defense contractor to the government is facilitating an inspection of their project's product with their customer when the customer notices a feature that was not requested or documented. The project manager for the defense contractor points out that this feature adds significant value, but the customer is concerned that it may also introduce risk. Can the customer accept the product?**

A. Only if the new feature passes inspection.

B. No. The new feature has to be evaluated for its impact on the project.

C. No. The new feature is outside of the documented scope, and that is unacceptable.

D. Yes, as long as the product scope has been fulfilled.

21. **You are the project manager for a large construction project, and you identify two key areas where changing the scope of the product would deliver significantly higher value for the customer. Which of the following options is MOST correct?**

    A. Make the changes if they do not extend the cost and time line.

    B. Make the changes if they do not exceed the project charter.

    C. Discuss the changes with the customer.

    D. Complete the current project and create a new project for the changes.

22. **Which of the following activities is done FIRST?**

    A. Creation of the requirements documentation.

    B. Creation of the work breakdown structure.

    C. Creation of the activity list.

    D. Creation of the scope baseline.

23. **Which of the following statements is TRUE concerning functionality that is over and above the documented scope?**

    A. It should be channeled back through the change control board to ensure that it gets documented into the project scope.

    B. Additional functionality should be leveraged to exceed customer expectations.

    C. The final product should include all the functionality and only the functionality documented in the scope baseline.

    D. Additional functionality should be reviewed by the project manager for conformity to the product description.

24. **A project manager has been managing a project for six months and is nearing completion of the project; however, change requests are still pouring in. The project is ahead of schedule but over budget. Which of the following statements is TRUE?**

    A. The project manager should influence the factors that cause change.

    B. Changes should only be evaluated after the original scope baseline has been delivered and accepted.

    C. Changes introduced at this point in the project represent an unacceptable level of risk.

    D. Changes should be evaluated primarily on the basis of how much value they deliver to the customer.

25. **Complete the list of group decision-making techniques: Unanimity, Majority, Consensus, Plurality...**

    A. Agreement.

    B. Dictatorship.

    C. Solidarity.

    D. Coalition.

Answers to Scope Management Questions

1. **B.** In general, disagreements should be resolved in favor of the customer. In this case, the customer is the best choice of the four presented. 'A' is not a good choice because it is your job to keep the team focused on doing the work and out of meetings where they are arguing about the scope. Besides, the team brought you this problem, so their ability to resolve it is already in question. 'C' is incorrect because all things being equal, project disputes should be resolved in favor of the customer and not in favor of senior management. Since you don't have enough information to steer you toward senior management, resolving it in favor of the customer was the right choice here. 'D' is incorrect because the project charter is a very general and high-level document. As it is issued before either the scope statement or the work breakdown structure is created, it would be of little use in resolving an issue of scope dispute that occurred during execution.

2. **A.** You don't tackle activity sequencing as part of the work breakdown structure. That part comes later. The WBS has no particular sequence to it, not to mention that it is not decomposed to activity level. 'B' is incorrect since every WBS element does have a unique identifier. 'C' is incorrect since the WBS is the definitive source for all of the work to be done. Remember – if it isn't in the WBS, it isn't part of the project. Choice 'D' is incorrect because the WBS is arranged as a pyramid with the top being the most general, and the bottom being the most specific. The lowest level of the WBS would also be the smallest representation of work.

3. **B.** In this situation, you cannot simply skip the WBS, as you may be tempted to do. Mark should take time to create the WBS, which is usually not a lengthy process. 'A' may sound good, but in reality a PMP needs to be ready to work to solve most problems. You might refuse to manage a project if there is an ethical dilemma or a conflict of interest, but not in other circumstances. 'C' is incorrect since the WBS dictionary cannot be created properly unless the WBS was created first. If there is a WBS dictionary and no WBS, that would be a big red flag. 'D' is incorrect since merely documenting that there is a serious problem is not a solution. Additionally, providing more oversight would not solve the problem here. The real problem is that the WBS has not been created, and that will trickle down to more serious problems in the future of the project.

4.   **C.** The project manager verifies the product with the key stakeholders, the sponsor, and the customer.

5.   **C.** The project scope statement is created as part of the Define Scope process. You should have narrowed your guesses down to 'B' and 'C' quickly, since the project scope statement is a planning output, and 'B' and 'C' are the only two planning processes. 'A' is incorrect because it is the name of a knowledge area and not a process, and 'D' represents a monitoring and controlling process, which usually results in outputs such as change requests but never planning documents.

6.   **C.** The clue here is the words "main point" which would be found in the main output. The scope baseline represents three documents: the scope statement, the WBS, and the WBS dictionary, and this is the point of the process Create WBS. 'B' would be a better choice than 'A', but it is only a component of the scope baseline. 'D' would happen in the process Define Scope and not in Create WBS.

7.   **D.** The project scope statement needs to include a detailed description of the scope of work to be performed. Choice 'A' is incorrect as the WBS is created later as part of the Create WBS process. 'B' is tricky, but it is incorrect. The preliminary scope statement contains a high level description of the scope, but the project scope statement is detailed. 'C' is incorrect, because the level of effort is estimated after the scope has been defined.

8.   **A.** It is important to understand the processes and their inputs and outputs! Whereas all of these choices may be important, the only one that is listed as a part of Validate Scope is to get customer acceptance of the product. The other activities may be done during the project, but they aren't part of the Validate Scope process. 'D' is close, but that is formally part of the Perform Quality Control process.

9.   **D.** This question was not easy. Organizational process assets include things like templates, financial control procedures, and standardization guidelines; however, the PMIS (project management information system) is classified as an enterprise environmental factor since it is generally part of your environment.

10.   **A.** This is the only choice that is not part of the scope baseline. It is used to help create the baseline, but it is not a part of it. 'B', 'C', and 'D' represent the three components of the scope baseline.

11. **B.** This one is tricky. If you missed it, don't feel bad, but it is important to know that questions like this are on the exam. The reason 'B' is correct is that the requirements management plan contains a plan for how changes will be handled. If too many changes are pouring in, it is likely that the requirements management plan was not well defined. 'A' is incorrect because it is not the sponsor's role to control change. He or she is paying you to handle that. 'C' is incorrect because if the change control board exists on your project, it only evaluates changes. The board is almost always reactive, not proactive. 'D' is incorrect since the change evaluation system is a made up term not found in PMI's processes.

12. **C.** It is the sponsor's job to pay for the project and to accept the product. Choice 'A' is really the project manager's job. 'B' is the project manager's job as well. It is not a clearly defined job for the sponsor. 'D' is not a function of the sponsor. If more control were needed over the functional managers, that would be the role of senior management.

13. **B.** The project manager and customer are involved in the Validate Scope process, and the tool used here is inspection. The product is inspected to see if it matches the documented scope. 'A', 'C', and 'D' are not documented as part of the processes.

14. **A.** The Nominal Group Technique typically starts by gathering a large field of candidate items (in this case they are scope items) and voting on them to sort them from highest down to lowest in order of priority. It is designed to rapidly identify the scope items that would provide the highest value to the most people. 'B' is not a good choice since brainstorming doesn't involve interviews or voting. 'C' is a means of voting, but it is not a good fit for the scenario here since this also involved interviews. 'D' is a model of team building and performance and does match the question being asked.

15. **D.** This is the best choice here. The WBS dictionary contains attributes about each work package such as an explanation of the work package (which invalidates choice 'A'), who is assigned responsibility for the work package (which invalidates choice 'B'), and a cost account code (which invalidates choice 'C'). If a work package were changed, that would most likely alter the scope baseline, and information on how to go about this would be found in the scope management plan and not the WBS dictionary.

16. **C.** Notice the use of the word 'FIRST'. 'A' is wrong because the customer should never bypass the project manager to authorize changes directly. It is the project manager's job to authorize changes on the project. 'B' is incorrect since all changes might not go to the change control board. Even if a change control board exists on the project, the project manager doesn't automatically just send everything their way. The project manager should deal with it first. 'D' is incorrect because the requirements management plan is not even the place this would be reflected. The scope baseline would need to be updated, but only after the change had been properly evaluated to see if it even belonged.

17. **A.** The customer accepts the scope of the product in Validate Scope.

18. **B.** The Nominal Group Technique is a method used to promote creativity in the Collect Requirements process, and the two outputs that match that process are the requirements documentation and the requirements traceability matrix.

19. **C.** It may make sense to benchmark against other internal projects or departments or against external organizations. Either one is acceptable, which eliminates 'A' and 'B' as good choices. 'D' is not a good choice since metrics may be used at any time to provide good working targets. Waiting until operations have stabilized would likely miss out on many of the benefits of benchmarking.

20. **B.** This can be a tough scenario and a tough question. On the PMP Exam, gravitate toward answers that have words like "understand" and "evaluate" in them. The product cannot be formally accepted without understanding its impact on the entire project. There is a strong bias on the exam against the practice of adding extra scope to the project, known as gold plating. Wherever you see this, your first instinct should be against doing it or accepting it.

21. **C.** Choices 'A' and 'B' are no-nos on the PMP Exam. You don't just make changes because they "add value." Does the customer want the change? Does the change increase the project risk or put the quality in jeopardy? Between 'C' and 'D', the best answer is 'C'. The reason is that just because the project manager thinks this is a good piece of functionality doesn't mean that he should automatically add it. The customer should have input into this decision as well. Choice 'D' might be correct in limited circumstances if you knew that you were at or near the end of the project, but changes on a project rarely require the automatic initiation of a new project.

22. **A.** The requirements documentation is typically created quite early on the project. In this case, it would be created well before the work breakdown structure and the scope baseline (which is made up of the scope statement, the WBS, and the WBS dictionary). The activity list would be created last in this list, so the order of creation of the documents listed would be A, B, D, and C.

23. **C.** Answers 'A', 'B', and 'D' are all incorrect, since they encourage adding or keeping the additional functionality. It is important not to add extras to the project for many reasons. The final product should be true to the scope. If you missed this, reread the section on scope management and gold plating.

24. **A.** The project manager needs to be proactive and influence the root causes of change. 'B' would be ridiculous in the real world. Imagine getting a change request near the end of the project that is good for the project and refusing to do it until you completed the original scope. Some change is good! 'C' is incorrect because although some change may introduce an unacceptable level of risk, all change certainly does not. Some changes could dramatically reduce the project risk and help the project. 'D' is incorrect, because value is not the primary criterion for evaluating change. A change may deliver high value, but also introduce too much risk or cost, or delay the project unacceptably.

25. **B.** These are all group decision-making techniques. Although 'A', 'C', and 'D' may sound like good choices, you need to know these five (Unanimity, Majority, Consensus, Plurality, and Dictatorship) before sitting for the exam.

6 Time Management

Difficulty	Memorization	Exam Importance
HIGH	HIGH	MEDIUM

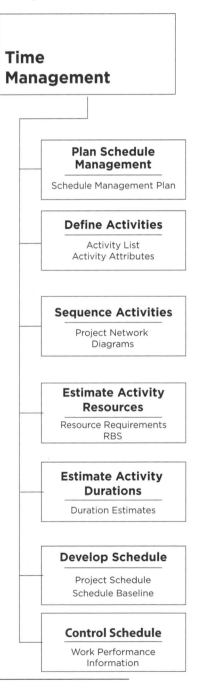

Time Management

Plan Schedule Management
Schedule Management Plan

Define Activities
Activity List
Activity Attributes

Sequence Activities
Project Network Diagrams

Estimate Activity Resources
Resource Requirements
RBS

Estimate Activity Durations
Duration Estimates

Develop Schedule
Project Schedule
Schedule Baseline

Control Schedule
Work Performance Information

From the indicators at the top of the page, you can tell that you may find this chapter to be more difficult than the previous chapter on scope management. In order to help you prepare for this topic, this book has clearly broken down the practices and outlined the techniques and formulas you will need to know in order to ace the questions on the exam. By the time you have completed this chapter, you may well have a higher level of confidence here than on any other section of the test.

Spending extra time here will yield direct dividends on the exam! Make sure that you learn both the processes and the techniques so that you may approach these questions with absolute confidence.

Philosophy

Project Time Management is concerned primarily with resources, activities, scheduling, and schedule management. The philosophy here, as elsewhere, is that the project manager should be in control of the schedule, and not vice versa. The schedule is built from the ground up, derived from the scope baseline and other information, and rigorously managed throughout the life of the project.

There are seven processes related to time management that you should understand. They are:

1. Plan Schedule Management (planning out the next six processes)
2. Define Activities (list the project activities)
3. Sequence Activities (order the activities and create the project network diagram)
4. Estimate Activity Resources (estimating the resources needed to complete each activity)
5. Estimate Activity Durations (determine time estimates for each activity)
6. Develop Schedule (create the schedule)
7. Control Schedule (monitor schedule performance)

You will see from reading this chapter that the driving philosophy behind time management is mathematical; it is primarily cold, hard analysis. The project manager does not merely accept whatever schedule goals are handed down or suggested. Instead, he builds the schedule based on the work to be done and then seeks to make it conform to other calendar requirements, constraints, and strategic goals.

Additionally, while most of the topics within this book are related, the topics of scope, time, and cost are particularly tightly linked. Changes made to one area will almost certainly have direct impacts on the other two.

As in other areas, it is best that project managers begin from the bottom up. The WBS, which was covered in the previous chapter, is a key input to time management processes. Using this comprehensive list of deliverables, you now define the work that must be done in order to produce these deliverables.

The individual schedule activities are then sequenced, and the resource and duration estimates are applied to these activities.

This approach has many similarities to the practices in scope management. Most similar is that your analysis and the resulting deliverables are comprehensive and complete.

Importance

Time management is important, both in the application of PMI's processes and on the exam.

Preparation

Modern project managers typically rely on software to perform complex schedule and time calculations. While this is not a bad thing, being a PMP requires that you understand the theories and practices for time management that underlie the software.

Some people are intimidated by the mathematical and logical aspects of this section because they do not understand the diagramming techniques and processes. A reliance on intuition will not get you very far on these questions. You either know how to calculate them or you do not. It is far better to spend time learning the techniques than to try to fumble your way through them on the exam. A heavier reliance on memorization and understanding is necessary here.

This book's approach to these exam questions falls into two categories:

1. There are several key terms that may be new to you, or they may have slightly different meanings than you are used to. Many of the questions on the exam will test your knowledge of specific terms and nuances, so it is important to be able to recognize and clearly understand them even if you do not memorize the definitions word for word.
2. There are formulas and techniques for estimating and diagramming. Memorization alone is not sufficient here. You must be able to calculate estimates, float, and critical path, among others.

Although the logic and math portions can be daunting to some people as they approach the exam, it should be pointed out that with each of the hard logic questions, the right answer is often much easier to determine than with the situational questions. Once you master the techniques presented in this chapter, you can work out the right answer on your own and simply match it to the list of choices. For many, these questions become favorites on the exam.

Time Management Processes

Time Management Processes

There are seven processes in the time management knowledge area. Following are the break-outs that show to which process group each item belongs:

Process Group	Time Management Process
Initiating	(none)
Planning	Plan Schedule Management, Define Activities, Sequence Activities, Estimate Activity Resources, Estimate Activity Durations, Develop Schedule
Executing	(none)
Monitoring & Controlling	Control Schedule
Closing	(none)

In the knowledge area of time management, it is also essential that you know the main outputs that are produced during each process. The different key outputs that are created in each process are summarized in the chart below.

Process	Key Output(s)
Plan Schedule Management	Schedule Management Plan
Define Activities	Activity list, Activity attributes
Sequence Activities	Project schedule network diagrams
Estimate Activity Resources	Activity resource requirements, Resource breakdown structure
Estimate Activity Durations	Activity duration estimates
Develop Schedule	Project schedule, Schedule baseline
Control Schedule	Work performance information, Change requests

Planning

Plan Schedule Management

What it is:

Time management has a total of seven processes, and Plan Schedule Management is the one that defines how the subsequent six will be carried out.

Why it is important:

Time management follows the same pattern you observed in scope management, with a process at the beginning (Plan Schedule Management) to define how everything will go and one at the end (Control Schedule) that reviews how the plan went. By properly defining the processes up front, it will create a plan against which results may be compared and controlled.

When it is performed:

The process of Plan Schedule Management may be performed early in the project. It should be performed before the other six processes are carried out.

How it works:

Inputs

Project Management Plan — See Ch. 2, Common Inputs

Project Charter — See Ch. 4, Integration, Develop Project Charter

Enterprise Environ. Factors — See Ch. 2, Common Inputs

Organizational Process Assets — See Ch. 2, Common Inputs

Tools

Expert Judgment — See Ch. 2, Common Tools

Analytical Techniques — See Ch. 2, Common Tools

Meetings — See Ch. 2, Common Tools

Plan Schedule Management

Outputs

Key Fact

Schedule Management Plan

As you can see, the inputs and tools are predictable and are unlikely exploits for the exam. This particular output is the point of this process. The schedule management plan becomes part of the project plan, and it defines how the schedule will be defined, how it will be measured, how and how often the team will track progress, and what will happen if the project veers from the plan. It also describes how progress will be reported and any other relevant details on how the remaining six time management processes will be carried out.

Plan Schedule Management

Planning

Define Activities

What it is:

Once the scope baseline has been created, it can be used to decompose the work into activity detail. The main result of this planning process is the activity list. This list represents all of the schedule activities that need to take place for the project to be completed. This is primarily accomplished by taking the WBS and decomposing the work packages even further until they represent schedule activities. The difference between work packages in a WBS and an activity list is that the activity list is more granular and is decomposed into individual schedule activities. Work packages will often contain bundles of related activities that may involve multiple groups of people. It is these activities that comprise the activity list. The activity list is used as the basis for the next five time management processes: Sequence Activities, Estimate Activity Resources, Estimate Activity Durations, Develop Schedule, and Control Schedule.

If the project is being performed under procurement, this planning process will most likely be performed by the subcontracting organization, with the results being provided to the organization that is responsible for the management of the overall project.

Why it is important:

In project scope management, we focused on what work needed to be performed on the project. Now, in time management, we need to focus on how and when it is accomplished. The activity list will be an essential input into building the schedule, so it is important that it be both complete and correct.

When it is performed:

The process of Define Activities is often performed as soon as the scope has been baselined. In other words, it is common to create the activity list after the requirements documentation, project scope statement, work breakdown structure, and the WBS dictionary have been created and are in a stable form (i.e., they are under control).

Define Activities

How it works:

Inputs

Key Fact

Schedule Management Plan

The output of the previous process is going to be an important input into all of the other processes in time management. It describes how the process of Define Activities will be carried out.

Key Fact

Scope Baseline

The scope baseline is made up of the approved project scope statement, the WBS, and the WBS dictionary. The scope baseline provides the primary input into this process. Each resulting schedule activity should tie back to a specific deliverable in the scope baseline.

Enterprise Environ. Factors— See Ch. 2, Common Inputs

Organizational Process Assets — See Ch. 2, Common Inputs

Tools

Key Fact

Decomposition

If you understood decomposition as it was used in the Create WBS process, you should have no problem understanding it here. Each work package at the bottom of the WBS is simply decomposed into smaller pieces, known as schedule activities. The project manager should solicit heavy involvement from the project team or the functional managers to leverage their expertise when performing this process.

Define Activities

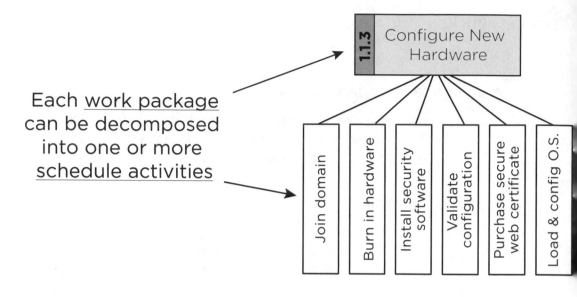

Each <u>work package</u> can be decomposed into one or more <u>schedule activities</u>

Key Fact

Rolling Wave Planning

The concept of rolling wave planning is a form of progressive elaboration that models project planning the way we see things in the real world.

Suppose, for example, that you are standing at the edge of a field. You may be able to see some things in great detail, even counting individual blades of grass at your feet. The further off you look, however, the less detail you will be able to perceive. Distant objects, such as a mountain range miles away, would appear general and hazy.

Rolling wave planning mirrors this construct by assuming that things in the near future should be relatively clear, while project activities in the distant future may not be as detailed or as easily understood. Armed with that perspective a project manager may choose to carefully decompose certain work packages, with anticipated execution in the near term, in great detail, while delaying analysis on work packages that will not be accomplished until later in the project.

This type of planning must be revisited throughout the project, much as waves continually pound the shore.

Rolling wave planning is used more frequently on projects like the creation of an information technology system, and less often on projects within the construction industry where unknowns may cost millions of dollars.

Expert Judgment

Expert judgment in decomposing activities may come from numerous sources, including team members, consultants, and functional managers. One of the best sources for expertise in decomposing a work package into an activity may be the person who will ultimately be responsible for executing the work package or the schedule activity, although that may not be known at this point.

Outputs

Key Fact

Activity List

All of the schedule activities that need to be performed in order to complete the project are compiled into the activity list. Each activity in the list should map back to one and only one work package (a work package, however, typically has more than one activity belonging to it). One major difference between a work package and a schedule activity is that the work packages are deliverables-based, focusing on the scope of the project, while the activities are focused on the work that needs to be done in order to execute the work packages. The activities should include enough information to transition them to the project team so that the work may be performed.

The activity list's usefulness is tied to its completeness and accuracy. It is important to identify and document each activity that must be performed in order to complete the project.

It is important to note that a line exists between the work breakdown structure and the activity list. Although the activity list is an extension of the work breakdown structure, it is not a part of the work breakdown structure. The WBS belongs to the scope baseline, while the activity list is more closely related to the project's schedule.

The activity list by itself is generally limited only to an identifier, such as an activity name or a unique numeric identifier, and a description.

Key Fact

Activity Attributes

As planning progresses, there will be a need to store additional information about activities. For example, the person responsible for this activity, the parts that need to be procured before this activity may be started, and the location at which the work will be performed could be highly important.

Activity attributes may be stored with the activity list or in a separate document and are typically added after the initial activity list has been created.

Note that any time you see the activity list, you will also see the activity attributes. The activity attributes may be thought of as an expansion of the activity list.

Milestone List

The key project milestones are produced as a part of this process. These milestones may be related to imposed dates (such as a contractual obligation), schedule constraints, or projected dates based on historical information.

Define Activities

Sequence Activities

What it is:

The Sequence Activities process is primarily concerned with taking the activity list defined in the Define Activities process and arranging those activities in the order they must be performed.

This process is all about understanding and diagramming the relationships that schedule activities have with each other.

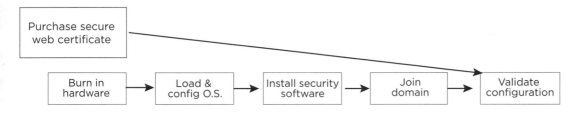

Schedule activities logically sequenced

Why it is important:

A network logic diagram is a picture in which each activity is drawn in the order it must be performed, and the amount of time each activity takes is represented with numbers. Sequence Activities is the planning process in which network diagrams are produced.

Network diagramming is the preferred method for representing activities, their dependencies, and sequences. The precedence diagramming method (also known as activity on node) is discussed later in this chapter.

Sequence Activities

When it is performed:

Because of the flow of inputs and outputs between other processes, the process of Sequence Activities must be performed after Define Activities and before Develop Schedule.

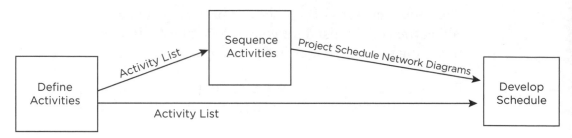

Define Activities must be performed before Sequence Activities or Develop Schedule

How it works:

Inputs

Key Fact

Schedule Management Plan

The schedule management plan will be an important input here, because it defines how this process will be carried out.

Key Fact

Activity List

The activity list is the most important input into Sequence Activities. It is in this process that the schedule activities from the activity list will be arranged, or sequenced, into a diagram that represents the order in which they must be performed.

Activity Attributes

The activity attributes, produced in Define Activities, are brought into this process since they contain additional information about each activity that may influence how it is sequenced.

Milestone List

Milestones are events that must be considered in the life of the project.

There is an interesting relationship between milestones and the process of Sequence Activities. Milestones are often imposed from outside the project (e.g., the project sponsor indicates an overall deliverable date), and activities typically come from within the project (e.g., the decomposition of work packages). Because of this, activities will often need to be arranged in a specific way in order to meet key milestones. For instance, if the customer specified a milestone of a pre-construction walkthrough at a certain point in time, then the activity of cleaning up the work site may need to be sequenced in earlier than would otherwise be necessary.

Project Scope Statement

The description of the project's scope will often give you information about the project that will influence the order in which certain activities are performed. For instance, if a computer system contained hardware and software, it might be necessary to procure and configure the hardware before constructing the software.

This may seem like common sense, but the project scope statement is used to ensure that nothing is missed.

Enterprise Environ. Factors — See Ch. 2, Common Inputs

Organizational Process Assets — See Ch. 2, Common Inputs

Tools

Key Fact

Precedence Diagramming Method (PDM)

The precedence diagramming method creates a graphical representation of the schedule activities in the order in which they must be performed on the project.

Activities are represented by the nodes (rectangles), with arrows representing the dependencies that exist between the activities.

The project network diagram illustrated uses the activity on node convention to represent the activities. In this case, the nodes are shown as rectangles, and the activities are represented inside the node, usually by letters of the alphabet. Units of duration are shown above the nodes.

The second half of this chapter has a special focus on project network diagramming including the precedence diagramming method.

Sequence Activities

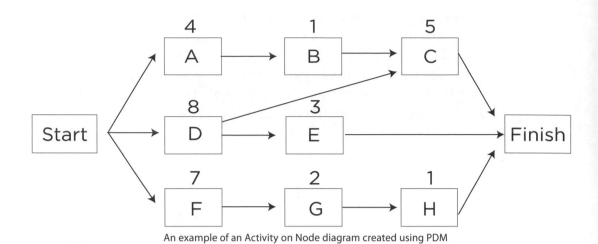

An example of an Activity on Node diagram created using PDM

Key Fact

Dependency Determination

Dependencies are those things that influence which activities must be performed first. For example, a road must be graded before it can be paved. If grading and paving the road were two activities on the project, then we would say that the start of the activity of paving the road is dependent upon the finish of the activity of grading the road, thus these two activities have a finish-to-start relationship.

Two activities with a dependency, creating a finish-to-start relationship

There are three main kinds of dependencies that may exist among activities.

Mandatory Dependencies

A mandatory dependency is one that cannot be broken. Given the example where paving the road is dependent upon grading it, the dependency is unavoidable, or mandatory. Mandatory dependencies are also known as hard logic, since a mandatory dependency is considered unmovable and always true.

Discretionary Dependencies

Discretionary dependencies, unlike the preceding example, are not always true. These would often be the result of best practices, and may vary organization to organization and even project to project. For instance, the project of managing the remodeling of a house may have a discretionary dependency between painting the walls and carpeting the floors, where painting must be completed before carpeting could be installed. There is no absolute rule that says the carpet could not be installed before the painting begins.

Discretionary dependencies are also known as soft logic or preferred logic and are typically based on historical information, expert judgment, and best practices.

External Dependencies

External dependencies are those dependencies that must be considered but are outside of the project's control and scope. For instance, if an automobile is being developed to use alternative technology, there may be an external dependency on a supplier providing a battery that meets certain specifications before the project can meet its schedule. Because these are dependencies, they must be identified and documented as part of this process.

Key Fact

Leads and Lags

A lead is simply one activity getting a jump-start on another. Consider, for instance, a software project that has a dependency between finishing the development of a section of code and beginning the quality inspection. Since the development has to finish before the testing begins, we would say that a mandatory finish-to-start dependency exists between the two activities.

An example of a lead would be if the individual or group performing the quality inspection gets an unfinished beta copy of the software in order to get a head start. Note that leads do not do away with the finish-to-start relationship that exists. Instead, it simply "cheats" that relationship.

Leads, and the rationale behind them, must be clearly explained and documented.

Sequence Activities

Think of a lag as a waiting period that exists between two activities. A lag is a situation where a waiting period must occur between one activity and another dependent activity. An example of a lag would be if one activity was to order a computer server and another activity was to configure the server, then a lag might exist between the time the server is ordered and the time it arrives and can be configured. During this lag, there is no work being performed by the organization against this activity; no resources are being expended. They are simply waiting.

Outputs

Key Fact

Project Schedule Network Diagrams

The name of this output may be slightly misleading. Although it is used later in creating the schedule, the schedule network diagram is not the schedule. In other words, no start or finish dates are assigned to the activities yet. They are simply arranged in the order they need to be performed on the project.

A project schedule network diagram may include a full representation of every activity in the project, or it may include summary nodes. In the event that a summary node is used, enough documentation should be included so that the basic flow of activities may be understood.

Project Documents Updates — See Ch. 2, Common Outputs

Sequence Activities

Estimate Activity Resources

What it is:

How long an activity takes is usually a function of determining the effort needed to perform the activity, the number of resources that will be applied to it, and the resource availability. This process is all about analyzing the project's schedule activities to determine the resource requirements.

Why it is important:

Understanding the number of resources required to complete an activity and determining how long they will be used for that activity is an important step in project planning and an essential ingredient to the schedule, which will be developed later.

When it is performed:

Because the process of Estimate Activity Resources uses the activity list and activity attributes, it must be performed after Define Activities. Additionally, since the output of this process is used to build the project schedule, this process must be performed before Develop Schedule. This process often goes hand in hand with Estimate Costs, since cost and time are closely linked, so they may be performed at the same time, or in an iterative cycle.

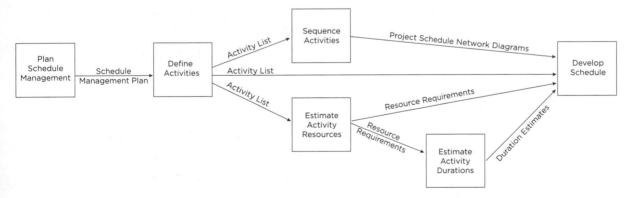

A diagram showing the order of Time Management's planning processes

Estimate Activity Resources

How it works:

Inputs

 Schedule Management Plan

The schedule management plan will be an important input here, because it defines how this process will be carried out. In this case, it may describe the methods that will be used to estimate activity resources and the accuracy that is desired.

 Activity List

The activity list is the most important input into this process. Each activity in the list will be evaluated and the resources will be estimated for it.

Activity Attributes

In your mind, the activity attributes should be virtually indistinguishable from the activity list. The two always go together. In this case, the activity attributes give expanded information on each activity in the activity list.

 Resource Calendars

Resources may include both physical resources and human resources, and their availability needs to be factored into the process of Estimate Activity Resources. For instance, a piece of heavy machinery may currently be available only during the months of April and May, which must be considered. The resource calendars provide the dates that human and physical resources will be available.

Risk Register

The risk register (discussed in chapter 11) is a list of the risks that have been identified on the project. This helps in making decisions in light of risks that might impact the choices of resources.

Activity Cost Estimates

The costs (discussed in the next chapter) influence the resource requirements, and the resource requirements influence the costs. In this process we bring the cost estimates in if they have been determined.

Enterprise Environmental Factors

Every project environment is different, and different factors will influence how long an activity will take. For instance, an activity could require access to an aircraft manufacturer's flight simulation systems, or a project that has some manufacturing as an activity might require access to the organization's facilities in order to perform this activity.

Organizational Process Assets — See Ch. 2, Common Inputs

Tools

Key Fact

Expert Judgment

There is no substitute for asking for expert opinion on how to estimate resource needs for an activity. Asking someone who has performed this type of activity previously, a functional manager, or even the resource who will be performing the work can bring insight into the resource needs for the activities.

Alternative Analysis

The old saying goes that "there is more than one way to skin a cat," implying that just because one way has been identified, alternatives may still be helpful. This could include outsourcing an activity, purchasing a software component off the shelf rather than building one, or using a totally different approach to complete the activity.

Key Fact

Published Estimating Data

Some industries have extensive data available through published, recognized sources that can help in estimating. For instance, if you take a car to a body shop for repair, they often have books provided by the insurance industry with almost every conceivable repair listed, along with how long the repair should take for an experienced person to complete.

This type of data can help give insight into the Estimate Activity Resources process.

Estimate Activity Resources

Bottom-Up Estimating

It may be that you encounter an activity that cannot be estimated, either because it has not been broken down enough, or because it is simply too complex. In this case, it is appropriate to break down the activity further into progressively smaller pieces of work until these pieces may be estimated for their resource requirements.

Once these estimations have been performed, the pieces may be summed up from the bottom back up to an activity level.

Project Management Software

Software is a means and not an end. It can help the project manager store and organize information, experiment with alternatives, and rapidly perform the routine calculations.

Outputs

Key Fact

Activity Resource Requirements

The resources required for each schedule activity are the primary output of Estimate Activity Resources. These resources include the kind of resource and the number of these resources. The activity resource requirements need to specify, for instance, if two senior programmers are required for four months or if three junior programmers are required for five months.

Each activity resource requirement should be documented with sufficient detail to explain the decision-making process used to arrive at these estimates.

Key Fact

Resource Breakdown Structure

The resource breakdown structure, or RBS, is similar in many ways to the WBS. It is graphical and hierarchical, logically arranged from top to bottom, and it arranges the resources by category and type.

Project Documents Updates

Because this is a detailed planning process, it is common for several project documents to be updated as a result. The activity list, and particularly the activity attributes, would normally get updated.

Also, the resource calendar would need to be updated since this process is estimating the resources that will be needed, and perhaps tentatively pre-assign specific resources on the resource calendar if those can be anticipated at this point.

Planning

Estimate Activity Durations

What it is:

This process is exactly what it sounds like. Each activity in the activity list is analyzed to estimate how long it will take.

There is an important difference between duration and level of effort, and this process focuses on determining duration.

The duration of an activity is a function of many factors, including who will be doing the work, when they are available, how many resources will be assigned to this activity, and the amount of work contained in the activity.

Why it is important:

These activity duration estimates will become a primary input into creating the schedule when the overall project time line has been created.

When it is performed:

Estimate Activity Durations is performed after the activity resource requirements have been gathered and before the schedule is developed.

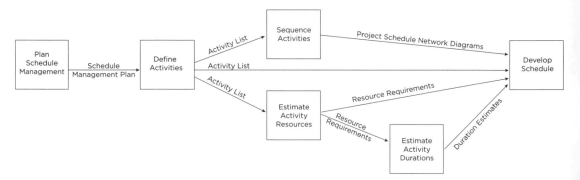

A diagram showing the order of Time Management's planning processes

How it works:

Inputs

Schedule Management Plan

The schedule management plan will be an important input here, because it defines how this process will be carried out. For Estimate Activity Durations, it would likely describe how the activity duration estimates will be derived and how accurate and precise they need to be.

Activity List

The activity list is a primary input for this process. Every activity in the list should be estimated to determine its duration.

Activity Attributes

The activity attributes always accompany the activity list. These attributes provide additional information about each activity in the list.

Activity Resource Requirements

Since the duration is a function of the amount of work associated with an activity and the resources assigned to perform that work, the activity resource requirements need to be brought into this process.

Resource Calendars

These are the resource calendars that were updated in the Estimate Activity Resources process. These calendars show physical and human resource usage across the entire project and sometimes the entire enterprise.

Project Scope Statement

The project scope statement, created earlier in Define Scope, has the constraints and assumptions for the project that can affect this process.

Estimate Activity Durations

For instance, a constraint that a particular component of a house had to be built at a different facility and transported to the construction site would influence the activity's duration. Likewise, an assumption that a particular component of a software product could be completed by a subcontracting firm faster than it could be built internally would be helpful in performing Estimate Activity Durations.

Risk Register

The risk register contains a list of all identified risks, and since risk plays a big part in the creation of estimates, it needs to be reviewed carefully as part of this process.

Resource Breakdown Structure

The resource breakdown structure provides an organized chart of resources by category or type.

Enterprise Environmental Factors

Factors such as what records an organization requires, safety standards, and regulations can all affect how long an activity takes. For instance, it may take far longer to perform an activity in a nuclear power plant than it does in a conventional power plant due to enterprise environmental factors, and these must be considered in order to accurately estimate the duration of activities.

Organizational Process Assets

Organizational process assets could take the form of a rich database of historical information that shows the estimated and actual durations for activities for a previous project, while another organization may have specific calendar requirements when shifts or resources are available. Anything that gives structure or guidance to your activity duration estimates would be considered an organizational process asset.

Tools

Expert Judgment

Anyone who has managed a project will attest that the duration of an activity can be notoriously hard to estimate in advance. The expert providing the judgment should follow some basis, such as historical information, whether documented or experiential.

Key Fact

Analogous Estimating

Analogous estimating, also known as top-down estimating, is where an activity from a project previously performed within the organization is used to help estimate another activity's duration.

Typically, the previous actual time spent on the similar activity is used as the estimate for another similar activity. The technique is combined with expert judgment to determine if the two activities are truly alike.

Parametric Estimating

If one team can install 100 feet of fence in one day, then it would take 10 teams to install 1,000 feet of fence in one day. This kind of linear extrapolation is an example of parametric estimating.

Parametric estimating can work well for activities that are either linear or easily scaled. It is not as effective for activities that have not been performed before or those for which little or no historical information has been gathered.

Key Fact

Three-Point Estimating

Three-point estimating, also called PERT estimates, use three data points for the duration instead of simply one. These are pessimistic, most likely (also known as realistic), and optimistic estimates.

There are two primary ways of calculating a three-point estimate: beta distribution and triangular distribution.

Beta Distribution

We will begin by looking at beta distribution. As an example of how this is used, suppose a developer estimates that it will most likely take 9 days to write a module of code; however, he also supplies an optimistic estimate of 7 days and a pessimistic estimate of 17 days.

The project manager then applies a formula, usually in the form of a weighted average, to these estimates to distill them down to a single estimate. The traditional formula is:

$$(Pessimistic + 4 \times Realistic + Optimistic) \div 6$$

In the example above, the numbers would be substituted as $(17 + 4 \times 9 + 7) \div 6 = 10$ days. This number is used as the activity duration estimate for this schedule activity.

When considering beta distribution, another important formula to memorize for the exam is one used to calculate the standard deviation (expressed as σ) for an estimate.

$$\sigma = (Pessimistic - Optimistic) \div 6$$

This formula is not the actual standard deviation, but a shortcut that makes quite a few assumptions about the data. It's a good idea to know for the exam, but be careful before using this in actual practice.

Given these formulas, let us consider the following estimates for activities A, B, and C.

Activity	Optimistic	Pessimistic	Realistic
A	22	35	25
B	60	77	70
C	12	40	20

Now, using the formulas above, we will calculate the three point estimate for each of these activities.

Activity	Optimistic	Pessimistic	Realistic	3 Point Estimate
A	22	35	25	26.17
B	60	77	70	69.5
C	12	40	20	22

Triangular Distribution

The technique of triangular distribution is very similar to beta distribution; however, it is a bit easier. For our purposes in estimating, triangular distribution is a simple average of the values of the pessimistic, optimist, and most likely estimates.

$$(Pessimistic + Realistic + Optimistic) \div 3$$

You also need to be prepared to recognize beta and triangular distribution graphs for the exam. Simply being able to identify which one is beta and which one is triangular should be sufficient. The triangular shape associated with triangular distribution makes that a snap.

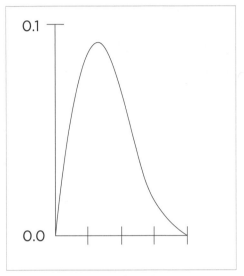

Beta Distribution

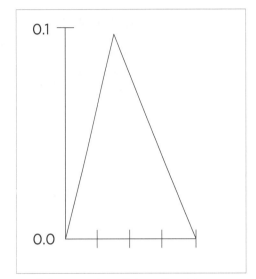

Triangular Distribution

A graphical representation of beta and triangular distributions

Group Decision-Making Tech. — See Ch. 2, Common Tools

Key Fact

Reserve Analysis

Reserve time, also called contingency, is extra time added to an activity duration estimate.

Reserve time estimates are revisited throughout the life of the project, being revised up or down as more information on schedule risk becomes available.

Outputs

Key Fact

Activity Duration Estimates

All of the preceding inputs and tools for this process are used together to produce this key output: the activity duration estimates.

The activity duration estimates contain an estimated duration for each activity in the activity list. Ideally these estimates represent a range such as the optimistic-pessimistic-realistic ones covered in the three-point estimate technique discussed earlier in this process.

Project Documents Updates

As each activity is being estimated at a low level, updates to the activity attributes are a normal by-product of this process. Additionally, any assumptions made as part of the estimates should be documented.

Develop Schedule

What it is:

The process of Develop Schedule is one of the largest of the 47 processes, containing a heart-stopping 27 combined inputs, tools, and outputs.

As anyone who has managed a complex project will attest, developing the schedule can be one of the most daunting parts of the project.

Why it is important:

The schedule is one of the most visible and important parts of the project plan. In fact, many inexperienced project managers often mistakenly refer to the depictions of the schedule as the project plan or use the two terms interchangeably.

As you could guess by the name, this process is the one where the project's schedule is created.

When it is performed:

The process of Develop Schedule is typically performed after the processes of Estimate Activity Resources, Estimate Activity Durations, and Sequence Activities have been performed and before Determine Budget is performed.

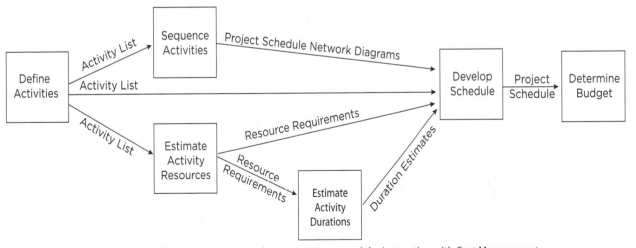

A diagram showing the order of Time Management's planning processes and the integration with Cost Management

How it works:

Inputs

Key Fact

Schedule Management Plan

The schedule management plan will specify how the schedule will be calculated, and developed, and what forms it will ultimately take.

Key Fact

Activity List

The activity list is the list of all activities that need to be scheduled and performed on the project. It is a bit redundant here as an input since the project schedule network diagrams (covered later in the list of inputs to this process) implicitly contain the activity list.

Activity Attributes

The activity attributes always accompany the activity list. They provide expanded information on each activity in the list, and these details may be important when scheduling the activity.

Key Fact

Project Schedule Network Diagrams

The project schedule network diagrams were created earlier in Sequence Activities, and they now become a primary input into Develop Schedule. The project schedule network diagrams show the order in which activities must be completed, while the schedule assigns dates to each of these activities.

Activity Resource Requirements

The activity resource requirements were developed previously in Estimate Activity Resources. They show which physical and human resources will be required for each activity.

Key Fact

Resource Calendars

The resource calendars show resource usage across the organization and will assist in developing the schedule since the resource calendar may put additional constraints on when resources are available.

Key Fact

Activity Duration Estimates

This is another important input into the process of Develop Schedule. The activity duration estimates, created earlier in Estimate Activity Durations, specify how long an activity will take, which has a direct bearing on the schedule.

Project Scope Statement

The project scope statement, created earlier in the Define Scope process, is the document that defines the scope of the project. It is particularly helpful here in Develop Schedule because it also contains constraints and assumptions for the project.

Since most constraints and assumptions ultimately relate to cost and time, they need to be factored into this process.

Risk Register

The risk register contains a list of all identified risks. Risk plays a big part in the development of the schedule and will often influence decisions that are made.

Project Staff Assignments

The staff assignments show the resources assigned to an activity. When resource availability is taken into account, this can have a significant impact on how the schedule is developed.

Resource Breakdown Structure

The resource breakdown structure provides an organized chart of resources by category or type.

Enterprise Environ. Factors — See Ch. 2, Common Inputs

Organizational Process Assets

As is true with other processes, assets come in many forms. For this process, organizational process assets include anything the performing organization owns that would help with the process of developing the schedule. Items such as an overall resource calendar or examples from previous projects would be particularly helpful in performing Develop Schedule.

Develop Schedule

Tools

Schedule Network Analysis

This technique actually refers to a group of techniques used to create the schedule. Any of the other specific tools or techniques that are part of the process of Develop Schedule may be used as part of this general tool.

Critical Path Method (CPM)

Before trying to understand the critical path method, it is important to understand what the critical path is. A project's critical path is the combination of activities that, if any are delayed, will delay the project's finish.

The critical path method is an analysis technique with three main purposes:

1. To calculate the project's finish date.

2. To identify how much individual activities in the schedule can slip (or "float") without delaying the project.

3. To identify the activities with the highest risk that cannot slip without changing the project finish date.

A more detailed explanation of the critical path method appears later in this chapter under the heading, "Special Focus: Critical Path Method." The section shows specific techniques and provides exercises that you will need to be able to perform.

Critical Chain Method

Based on the theories of Eliyahu Goldratt, critical chain provides a way to view and manage uncertainty when building the project schedule.

The traditional way of building the schedule, using the critical path method, gathers realistic activity duration estimates and assembles the schedule, identifying the longest (critical) path through the network. Buffers may be added to certain high-risk activities in order to ensure that their uncertainty is managed.

The critical chain method modifies this technique by estimating each activity as aggressively as possible, building the schedule network, and then adding one lump-sum buffer to the end of the network before the finish date. This lump-sum buffer is then used to manage any individual activity that might be in danger of slipping, whether it is on the critical path or in danger of affecting the critical path. One advantage of this approach is that the team is not made aware of the buffers and therefore they are kept on an aggressive schedule. A buffer, however, does exist, and it is under the control of the project manager.

Key Fact

Resource Optimization Techniques

These two techniques seek to use resources in the most efficient ways, and they are important to know for the exam.

Resource Leveling

When many people think about the technique of resource leveling, they may mistakenly consider only what their project management software does to level resources. Resource leveling is when your resource needs meet up with the organization's ability to supply resources.

In order to resource-level the project, you first use the critical path method to calculate and analyze all of the network paths for the project. Then you apply resources to that analysis to see what effect it has on schedule outcome.

Consider the following scenario. After performing the processes of Estimate Activity Durations and Estimate Activity Resources, you end up with the following project schedule network diagram.

Activity ID	Activity	Preceding Activity	Resources Needed	Quantity of Resource Required	Estimated Duration (in days)
A	Database Design	Start	Database Administrator	2	8
B	Data Entry	A	Data Entry Clerk	10	5
C	Write stored procedures	A	Programmer	8	5
D	Test stored procedures	B,C	Quality Control Engineer	1	2

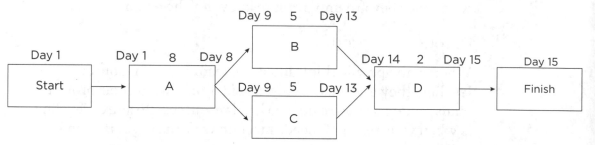

The project network diagram above was created from the preceding table using the critical path method. Now, however, consider what would happen if the organization could not provide eight programmer resources as reflected in this scenario. Instead, they can only supply two. The scenario must be resource leveled, resulting in a longer overall network diagram as follows:

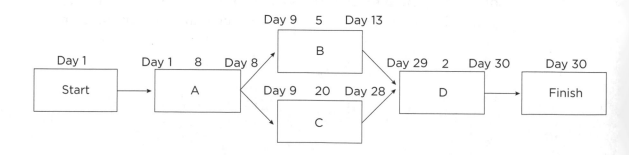

After the resource calendar has been applied and the schedule has been leveled, a schedule is created based on the resources applied, where each activity is assigned a projected start and finish date.

Resource Smoothing

Resource smoothing looks at the schedule in light of resource constraints. When resource smoothing is used, the critical path and the completion date do not change. The activities may change within their float, but that is all. Resource smoothing is usually less disruptive to the schedule than resource leveling.

Modeling Techniques

Modeling techniques are used to explore various schedule scenarios, and may include "what-if analysis" and simulation.

"What-if analysis" typically uses Monte Carlo analysis to predict likely schedule outcomes for a project and identify the areas of the schedule that are the highest risk.

This analysis is performed by computer and evaluates probability by considering a huge number of simulated scheduling possibilities or a few selected likely scenarios. A computer employing Monte Carlo analysis can perform what-if analysis and identify the highest risk activities that may not otherwise be apparent, showing the impact of these changes on the schedule.

Leads and Lags

This technique, mirroring the one in the Sequence Activities process, ensures that the leads and lags are accurately applied to the schedule and adjusted appropriately.

Schedule Compression

On many projects, there are ways to complete the project schedule earlier without cutting the project's scope. That is the purpose of schedule compression.

Two types of questions that you will probably encounter on the exam involving schedule compression are crashing and fast tracking. Crashing involves adding resources to a project activity so that it will be completed more quickly. Crashing almost always increases costs.

Original Estimate

Activity	Resources	Estimated days
200 yards of pipeline construction	1	12

Crashed Estimate

Activity	Resources	Estimated days
200 yards of pipeline construction	4	4

An example of crashing the schedule by adding more resources to an activity

Note that in the example above, as is often the case, increasing the number of resources does decrease the time but not by a linear amount. This is because activities will often encounter the law of diminishing returns when adding resources to an activity. The old saying "too many cooks spoil the broth" applies to projects as well as cooking.

Fast tracking means that you re-order the sequence of activities so that some of the activities are performed in parallel, or at the same time. Fast tracking does not necessarily increase costs, but it almost always increases risk to the project since discretionary dependencies are being ignored and additional activities are happening simultaneously. (Discretionary dependencies were discussed under the process of Sequence Activities.)

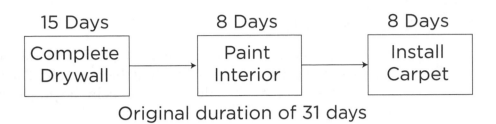

Original duration of 31 days

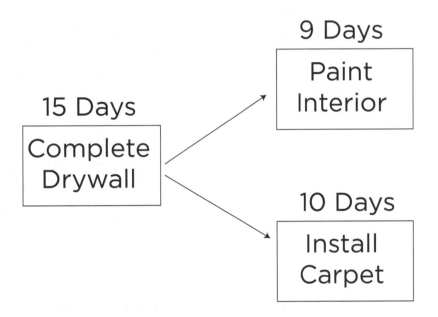

Fast tracked duration of 25 days

Note that fast tracking often results in some individual activities taking longer, and it increases the risk. In the example above, the workers may have a harder time moving around each other, thus increasing the time to paint and install carpet. Also, there is an increased risk associated with these activities. For example, the painters could damage the carpet, or the carpet installers could be hampered by the fresh paint.

Develop Schedule

Develop Schedule

Scheduling Tool

A tool to help with scheduling simply helps to facilitate the math and logic-intensive process of building the schedule. The tool can perform the routine schedule analysis to help the project manager and team produce a viable schedule.

Outputs

Key Fact

Schedule Baseline

The schedule baseline is the approved schedule that has been placed under control. Keep in mind that a baseline is the original plan plus all approved changes, so it may be changed, but only through a formal process. If the schedule slips, that does not become incorporated into the baseline.

Key Fact

Project Schedule

The project schedule shows when each activity is scheduled to begin and end; it also shows a planned start and finish date for the overall project. The schedule is typically represented graphically, and there are different forms it may take. The most common forms are covered as follows:

Milestone Chart

A milestone chart, as the name implies, only represents key events (milestones) for the project. Milestones may be significant events or deliverables that are the responsibility of the project team or external parties.

Milestone charts, because of the general level of information they provide, should be reserved for brief, high level project presentations where a lot of schedule detail would be undesirable or even distracting.

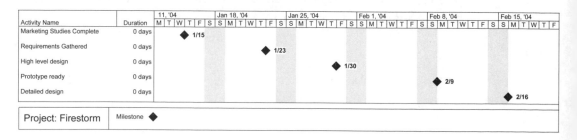

Bar Charts (also called Gantt Charts)

Bar charts, or Gantt charts, show activities represented as horizontal bars and typically have a calendar along the horizontal axis. The length of the bar corresponds to the length of time the activity should require.

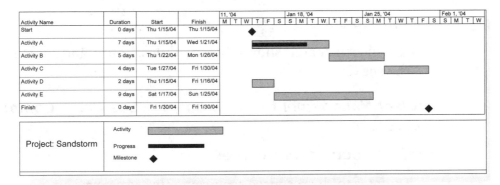

A bar chart, or Gantt chart, can be easily modified to show percentage complete (usually by shading all or part of the horizontal bar). It is considered to be a good tool to use to communicate with management, because unlike the project network diagram, it is easy to understand at a glance.

Project Network Diagram

The project network diagram is a useful detail-driven tool that provides a powerful view of the dependencies and sequences of each activity. It is the best representation for calculating the critical path and showing dependencies on the project.

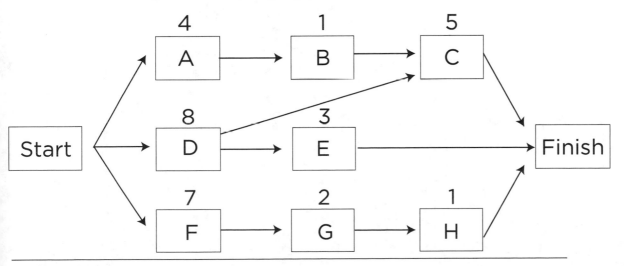

Schedule Data

Schedule data refers to the information the project team used to model and create the project schedule. It would include schedule templates that were used, the activities and their attributes, estimated durations, and any constraints and assumptions. This output is simply the data which supports how this schedule was developed.

Project Calendars

A project calendar shows the schedules, hours, and shifts for all of the activities.

Project Management Plan Updates — See Ch. 2, Common Outputs

Project Documents Updates

Updates to the resource requirements are a very common output in Develop Schedule, especially in the case of the tool of resource leveling, which adjusts the resources that are required in light of the organization's ability to supply them. Updates to activity attributes, risk logs, and calendars are also common.

Develop Schedule

Control Schedule

What it is:

As you can tell from its name, Control Schedule is a monitoring and controlling process. The concept behind monitoring and controlling processes in general is to compare the work results to the plan and ensure that they line up. In this process, the schedule is controlled to make sure that time-related performance on the project is in line with the plan.

One of the more important concepts to master with Control Schedule (and most monitoring and controlling processes in general) is that schedule changes are not only reacted to, but the schedule is controlled proactively. That is, the project manager should be out in front of the project, influencing changes before they affect the project. Of course, at times, changes to the schedule may occur and the project manager will have to react to them, but the project manager should be proactive whenever possible.

Why it is important:

Any time the schedule changes or a change request that affects the schedule occurs, the change should be evaluated and planned. The schedule should be monitored continuously against the actual work performed to ensure that things stay on target.

When it is performed:

The process of Control Schedule is performed throughout the life of the project from the moment the schedule is developed until all scheduled activities have been completed.

How it works:

Inputs

Project Management Plan

The project management plan contains the schedule management plan and the schedule baseline, both of which are essential components for this process. The schedule management plan is important since it defines how the schedule will be managed and changed, and Control Schedule is the process that processes and manages those changes, while the schedule baseline provides the latest approved version of the project schedule. As changes are made or change requests are approved, the schedule baseline is updated to reflect those changes. Both of these components have been officially melded into the project management plan at the point at which Control Schedule is performed.

Key Fact

Project Schedule

The project schedule is the primary input to this process since it is the source against which the results are controlled.

Work Performance Data

Work performance data gives information on how the work is being performed. In this case, it will tell us how particular schedule activities are being completed. This can help spot trends and provide helpful information to compare against the schedule.

Project Calendars

Projects may have multiple calendars, possibly spanning multiple organizations. For example, if components of a project were being developed in both China and France, the holidays and working periods would differ significantly. These calendars will be necessary when controlling (and likely adjusting) the schedule.

Schedule Data

Supporting information is almost always a good thing to have, and the schedule data is the supporting information that may contain explanations of why certain scheduling decisions were made and the factors that went into those decisions.

Organizational Process Assets

Anything that the organization has that can make this process run more smoothly could be considered an organizational process asset. For example, a system for formally evaluating schedule change or a software system to help detect changes or measure variances would be an organizational process asset.

Tools

Key Fact

Performance Reviews

The project schedule shows planned start and finish dates for each activity; however, it is the actual dates that determine when the project is delivered. Performance reviews are used so that the project manager can determine how the project is progressing against the schedule.

Project Management Software

Software simply automates and simplifies the analysis used in the other tools and techniques described for Control Schedule.

Resource Optimization Techniques

When the schedule changes, whether or not those changes were anticipated, it can cause a ripple effect throughout the whole project. In this case, the resources that had been carefully allocated across the project may need to be leveled or smoothed again to ensure they match the changed schedule. This technique was described in detail under the Develop Schedule process.

Modeling Techniques

This technique analyzes multiple scenarios and uses what-if analysis to find the best way to align the plan with reality and potential risks.

Leads and Lags

Leads and lags will always have some effect on the schedule, even if they do not affect the delivery date. As the project management plan is executed, the leads and lags need to be adjusted to reflect reality so as to provide the most realistic view of the schedule possible.

Schedule Compression

Compression techniques, covered under Develop Schedule, are used to search for ways to shorten the plan in order to make it match reality or meet commitments.

Control Schedule

Control Schedule

Scheduling Tool

Optimizing and managing a schedule can be a very mathematically demanding process. In this case, a software tool can help manage the large number of options and decisions to help find the preferred schedule.

Outputs

Work Performance Information

Key Fact

The updated schedule performance index (SPI), schedule variance (SV) and other earned value measurements relevant to the schedule need to be calculated and communicated out. These concepts are covered in the next chapter on Cost Management.

Schedule Forecasts

Key Fact

The schedule is only a plan, but when it is compared against actual performance data, meaningful forecasts can be made. The most common forecasts are the Estimate At Completion (EAC) and Estimate To Completion (ETC), covered in the next chapter under the topic of Earned Value Management.

Change Requests

Key Fact

Change requests are a normal byproduct of Control Schedule. For instance, if actual performance is far ahead of schedule, a change request may be introduced to consider a new piece of functionality previously considered impossible to deliver on time. Conversely, if the project is running behind schedule, a change request to outsource key components may be introduced.

Project Management Plan Updates

As the schedule changes, impact to the project's scope and budget are to be expected. As components of the project management plan change, they need to be captured as updates.

Project Documents Updates — See Ch. 2, Common Outputs

Organizational Process Assets Updates

Any time a lesson is learned in Control Schedule, it becomes a reusable asset for the performing organization.

Control Schedule

Special Focus:
CRITICAL PATH METHOD

Key Fact

Everything in this section is of key importance

One very important tool used in Develop Schedule is a mathematical analysis technique called critical path method. You should be very comfortable with this technique, so a good portion of the rest of this chapter is dedicated to the subject.

Network Paths

The term "network path" refers to a sequence of events that affect each other on the project from start to finish. These activities form a path through the project. Paths are important because they illustrate the different sets of sequences in which activities must be performed, and they are used to identify areas of high risk on the project. In a real project plan, there will usually be numerous paths through the network diagram, and software is typically used to represent and calculate them.

To understand the paths, refer to the network diagram and corresponding tables that follow.

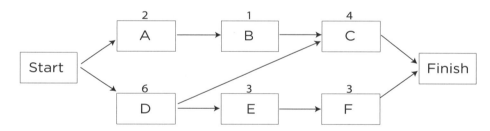

Figure 6-1: Network Logic Diagram – Activity on Node
Duration units shown in weeks

Activity	Duration (weeks)
A	2
B	1
C	4
D	6
E	3
F	3

Table 6-2: Individual activities

In the preceding diagram and tables, each node has a corresponding duration as listed in Table 6-2. Each possible path through the network is determined by following the arrows in the diagram in Figure 6-1.

Critical Paths

Determining the critical path through the network is a tool used heavily in creating the schedule. Critical path calculations show you where most of the schedule risk exists.

The critical path is made up of activities that cannot be delayed without delaying the finish of the project. By following the steps taken in creating the network diagram, the critical path is determined simply by identifying the longest path through the system. In the previous example, it is Start-D-E-F-Finish, because activities D (6) + E (3) + F (3) will take 12 weeks, and this is the longest path through the system.

Keep in mind that it is not unusual to have more than one critical path on a project. This occurs when two or more paths tie for the longest path. In this event, schedule risk is increased because there are an increased number of ways the project could be delayed.

Float

After you have mastered the concepts for activity on node, calculating float (sometimes referred to as "slack") is also easy. Before attempting any exercises, it is critical to understand the following:

1. Float is simply how much time an activity can slip before it changes the critical path. Another way of thinking about float is that it is the maximum amount of time an activity can slip without pushing out the finish date of the project.
2. If an item is on the critical path, it has zero float. Although there are technical cases where this might not be true, you should not encounter any such examples on the exam.

Keeping the preceding two items in mind, let us revisit the activity on node network diagram in figure 6-1 using this example:

Question: What is the float for Activity D?

Answer: 0 weeks. Activity D cannot slip without affecting the finish date because it is on the critical path.

Question: What is the slack for Activity C?

Answer: 2 weeks. If activity C slips by more than 2 weeks, then the path Start-D-C-Finish would delay the finish of the project.

There is a simple way to do this that will allow you to breeze through the questions on the exam. The method is a brute force approach. If the exam asks you to calculate the slack for an activity, simply look at the project network diagram and find the duration you can substitute for that activity that will put it on the critical path. You should be able to zero in on the float right away. If you have created a path chart, such as the one in Table 6-3, this method is a snap.

Path	Activities	Path Duration (weeks)
Start-A-B-C-Finish	2+1+4	7
Start-D-C-Finish	6+4	10
Start-D-E-F-Finish	6+3+3	12

Table 6-3

In this example:

- Activity A has float of 5 weeks, because this activity may be delayed up to 5 weeks without delaying the finish of the project
- Activity B also has float of 5 weeks, because paths with Activity B could slip up to 5 weeks without changing the project's finish date.
- Activity C is slightly trickier. It has a float of only 2 weeks. Even though it could slip 5 weeks in the first path listed in Table 6-3, if it slipped from 4 weeks to 6 weeks, then path Start-D-C-Finish would be on the critical path. Therefore, we take the *smallest slippage possible*, and that becomes the float for this activity.

After a little practice, this will become the easiest and quickest way to calculate float. There are detailed exercises at the end of this chapter to help cement your understanding of this.

Critical Path Method

Note that on the exam you may see the terms *forward pass* or *backward pass* related to the critical path. These methods of determining early or late start or early or late finish are presented below.

Early Start

The early start date for an activity is simply the earliest date it can start when you factor in the other dependencies. This is the date the activity will start if everything takes as long as it was estimated. Consider the figure that follows (this diagram is the same as Figure 6-1, referenced earlier).

Question: Given the following diagram, what is the early start for Activity B?

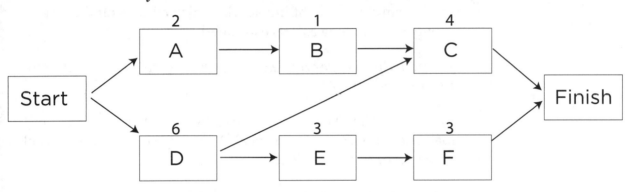

Units shown in weeks

The answer is week 3. The reason is that Activity A is scheduled to take 2 weeks. It begins on week 1, and finishes on week 2. Activity B could then begin on the first day of week 3.

This technique is called a "forward pass" because we have moved "forward" through the diagram, starting from the start date to perform our calculations.

Early Finish

The early finish date is the early start date plus the duration estimate minus 1 unit. In the example above, the early finish date for Activity 'A' would be 2 weeks after the early start date. Since the early start date is week 1, the early finish would be week 2.

This makes sense since the activity takes all of week 1 and all of week 2, finishing at the end of week 2.

Here we also performed a "forward pass," as again we based our calculations on the start date and worked forward through the network.

Late Start

The late start date for activity turns the problem around and looks at it from the other end of the network diagram. It asks, "What is the *latest* this activity could start and not delay the project's finish date?" Although there are many methods that may be used to calculate late start, the easiest way is to simply add the float to the early start. This will give us the absolute latest date that the activity can start and not impact the finish date, assuming that the activity takes as long as was estimated.

Question: Given the example in the previous table, what is the late start for Activity 'B'?

Answer: Week 8. The reason is that this activity has 5 weeks of float, and if the early start is week 3, the late start would be week 3 + 5 weeks of float = week 8.

Remember that for activities with zero float or slack, the late start and the early start will be the same.

This technique is called a "backward pass." The reason is that you must begin at the end of the network diagram and work your way backward, evaluating how close activities may slide toward the finish without moving the finish.

Late Finish

An activity's late finish will be the late start plus the activity's duration estimate minus 1 unit.

In the example above, the late start for Activity B is week 8, and the duration is 1 week, so the late finish date would also be week 8. If the fact that both the start and finish are shown as week 8 confuses you, keep in mind that the start represents the first day of week 8, and the finish represents the last day of week 8.

Remember that for activities with zero float or slack, the late finish and the early finish will be the same.

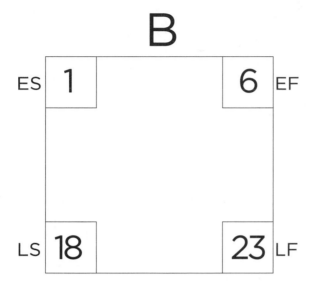

Calculating the late finish date by adding the activity's duration to the late start date is another example of a "backward pass."

ES, EF, LS, and LF

Often a node on the project network diagram may be represented as in the preceding diagram, with the early start in the upper left corner (represented by ES), the early finish in the upper right (EF), the late start in the bottom left (LS) and the late finish in the bottom right (LF). By dividing each node on a project network diagram into quadrants, all four of these may be represented for every node in the diagram.

Free Float

Also known as "free slack," free float is the amount of time an activity can be delayed without affecting the early start date of subsequent dependent activities. If this leaves you scratching your head, consider the diagram below:

The free float of activity E would be determined by calculating how long it could slip before it impacted the early start of activity

C. In this example, activity E has 4 units of free float. Note that this is different from its float, which is 19 units.

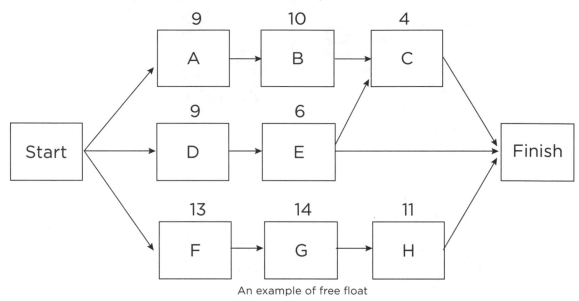

An example of free float

Negative Float

Negative float is a situation that occurs when an activity's start date occurs before a preceding activity's finish date. For instance, suppose that there is a constraint for an activity (Activity D) that involves a 1 day final inspection of a building that is to begin and be completed on July 15th; however, a preceding activity (Activity C) that encompasses testing the electrical components of the project does not finish until July 25th. If work is scheduled 7 days per week, then it could be stated that Activity D has a negative float of 10 days.

Technically, negative float exists when an activity's finish date happens before its scheduled start date. In the example above, Activity D is supposed to finish at the end of the 15th; however, it cannot even begin until 10 days later. There Activity D has 10 days of negative float.

Negative float for an activity tells you that your schedule has problems. It most often occurs when immovable constraints or milestones are imposed by forces outside the project, causing an impossible situation. Negative float may be resolved by several methods, such as reworking the logic of the schedule, crashing, or fast-tracking.

Kev Fact

Summary of Key Terms

You need to understand each of the following key terms. You do not have to memorize every term word for word, but you should be able to recall the general definition and apply them on the exam.

Activity Decomposition – Similar to scope decomposition (remember the asteroids metaphor), except that the final result here is an activity list instead of the WBS.

Activity Duration Estimates – Probable number of periods (weeks, hours, days, months, etc.) this activity should take with the probable range of results. Example:

Activity Duration Estimate	Explanation
1 week +/- 3 days	The activity should take between 2 and 8 days, assuming a 5 day work week
1 month + 20% probability it will be accomplished later	There is an 80% likelihood that the activity will be completed within a month and a 20% chance that it will exceed a month.

Activity List – A list of every activity that will be performed on the project.

Activity on Arrow Diagram - A rarely used type of network diagram where activities are represented by the arrows connecting the nodes. Nodes are typically represented by circles in this type of project network diagram.

Activity on Node Diagram - A type of network diagram where activities are represented on rectangular nodes with arrows representing the dependencies.

Analogous Estimating – A form of expert judgment often used early on when there is little information available. Example: "This project is similar to one we did last year, and that one took three months, so we will estimate three months for this project." It is performed from the top down, focusing on the big picture.

Backward Pass – The method for calculating late start and late finish dates for an activity (see explanation of float, early and late starts and finishes earlier in this chapter for a detailed explanation).

Summary of Terms

Beta Distribution – a method of estimating activity duration using the formula $(\text{Pessimistic} + 4 \times \text{Realistic} + \text{Optimistic}) \div 6$

Critical Path – The paths through the network diagram that show which activities, if delayed, will affect the project finish date. For schedule, the critical path represents the highest risk path in the project.

Dependencies – Activities that must be completed before other activities are either started or completed.

Dependencies	Description	Example
Mandatory	Also called "hard logic," these activities must be followed in sequence.	Clearing the lot on a construction site before pouring the foundation.
Discretionary	Also called "soft logic." Expert judgment and best practices often dictate that particular activities are performed in a particular order. The dependencies are discretionary because they are based on expert opinion rather than mandatory or hard logic.	Painting the interior before putting down carpet.
External	Dependencies relying on factors outside of the project.	Zoning approval for a new building. Weather for a rocket launch.

Dummy Activity – An activity in a network diagram that does not have any time associated with it. It is only included to show a relationship, and is usually represented as a dotted or dashed line. Dummy activities only exist in activity on arrow diagrams.

Duration compression - A technique primarily made up of two means of compressing the schedule: crashing and fast-tracking, described in the following table:

Technique	Description	Example
Crashing	Applying more resources to reduce duration. Crashing the schedule usually increases cost.	If setting up a computer network takes one person 6 weeks, three resources may be able to do it in two weeks. Note – Crashing usually does not reduce the schedule by a linear amount.
Fast tracking	Performing activities in parallel that would normally be done in sequence. Fast tracking activities usually increases project risk, and these activities have a higher probability of rework.	Example: In XYX Corp, no coding on software modules is allowed until after the database design is complete, but when fast tracking, the activities could be done in parallel if it is not a mandatory dependency.

Delphi Technique - A means of gathering expert judgment where the participants do not know who the others are and therefore are not able to influence each other's opinion. The Delphi technique is designed to prevent groupthink and to find out a participant's real opinion.

Expert Judgment – A method of estimating in which experts are asked to provide input into the schedule. Combining expert judgment with other tools and methods can significantly improve the accuracy of time estimates and reduce risk.

Float – How much time an activity can be delayed without affecting the project's finish date. Also known as "slack."

Forward Pass – The method for calculating early start and early finish dates for an activity (see explanation of float and early and late starts and finishes earlier in this chapter).

Free float – Also known as "free slack." How much time an activity can be delayed without affecting the early start date of subsequent dependent activities.

Heuristics – Rules for which no formula exists. Usually derived through trial and error.

Lag – The delay between an activity and the subsequent one dependent upon it. For example, if you are pouring concrete, you may have a 3 day lag after you have poured the concrete before your subsequent activities of building upon it can begin. Since no work is taking place during that 3 day period, it is considered to be a lag and not part of the actual activity.

Lead – Activities with finish-to-start relationships cannot start until their predecessors have been finished; however, if you have 5 days of lead time on an activity, it may begin 5 days before its predecessor activity has finished. Think of it as getting a head start, like runners in a relay race. Lead time lets the subsequent task begin before its predecessor has finished.

Mathematical Analysis – A technique to show scheduling possibilities where early and late start and finish dates are calculated for every activity without looking at resource estimates.

Milestones – High level points in the schedule used to track and report progress. Milestones usually have no time associated with them.

Monte Carlo Analysis – Computer simulation that throws a high number of "what if" scenarios at the project schedule to determine probable results.

Network Diagram – (Also called network logic diagram or project network diagram.) A method of diagramming project activities to show sequence and dependencies.

Negative Float – A situation that occurs when an activity's start date comes before a preceding activity's finish date. Technically, negative float exists when an activity's finish date happens before its scheduled start date. Negative float for an activity indicates a schedule with problems. Reworking the logic of the schedule, crashing, or fast-tracking are potential solutions.

Precedence Diagramming Method – (Also called Activity on Node.) A type of network diagram where the boxes are activities, and the arrows are used to show dependencies between the activities.

Reserve Time (Contingency) – A schedule buffer used to reduce schedule risk. The chart below represents the most common types of reserve for a project.

Contingency	Example
Project %	Add 15% to the entire project schedule
Project lump sum	Add 2 months calendar schedule to the project
Activity %	Add 10% to each activity (or to key, high-risk activities)
Activity lump sum	Add 1 week to each activity (or to key, high risk activities)

Schedule Baseline – The approved schedule that is used as a basis for measuring and reporting. It includes the original project schedule plus all approved updates.

Slack – See "Float."

Triangular Distribution – a method of estimating activity duration using the formula   (Pessimistic + Realistic + Optimistic) ÷ 3

Variance Analysis – Comparing planned versus actual schedule dates.

Summary of Terms

Exercises

In order to test yourself on time management, complete the following questions based on Figure 6-7 below.

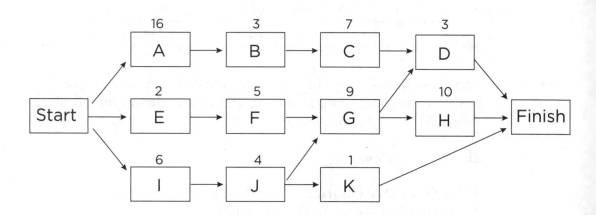

Figure 6-7: Project Network Diagram.
Durations shown in days

1. List all the paths through the network logic diagram as illustrated in Figure 6-7.

2. What is the critical path through the network diagram shown in Figure 6-7?

3. List the slack for each activity in the network diagram shown in Figure 6-7.

4. Provided the following table, how many weeks long is the critical path?

Activity	Preceding Activity	Duration (in weeks)
Start		0
A	Start	6
B	A, E	2
C	B	2
D	C	3
E	Start	1
F	A,E	1
G	F, B	7
Finish	D, G	0

5. Given the table in question 4 above, describe the effect of Activity D taking twice as long as planned.

6. An activity has 3 estimates, provided below:

   Optimistic   =   10 days
   Pessimistic   =   25 days
   Realistic   =   15 days

   What is the three-point estimate for this activity?

7. What is the standard deviation for the activity in question 6?

8. Given the project network node depicted below, fill in the value in the missing quadrant, and calculate the duration and the float for the activity.

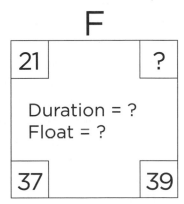

Answers to Exercises

1. There are six possible paths through the system, listed in the table below:

Path
Start-A-B-C-D-Finish
Start-E-F-G-D-Finish
Start-E-F-G-H-Finish
Start-I-J-G-D-Finish
Start-I-J-G-H-Finish
Start-I-J-K-Finish

2. Because two paths tie for the longest duration, there are two critical paths:

- Start-A-B-C-D-Finish – duration 29 days
- Start-I-J-G-H-Finish – duration 29 days

Path	Durations	Total
Start-A-B-C-D-Finish	16+3+7+3	29 days
Start-E-F-G-D-Finish	2+5+9+3	19 days
Start-E-F-G-H-Finish	2+5+9+10	26 days
Start-I-J-G-D-Finish	6+4+9+3	22 days
Start-I-J-G-H-Finish	6+4+9+10	29 days
Start-I-J-K-Finish	6+4+1	11 days

3. This task is easier than it first appears since over 70% of the activities were on the critical path. Those activities automatically have zero slack; thus, no calculations are necessary for most of the activities.

The way to solve for these is to take each path listed above and go through them one at a time. If the path is a critical path, or if the activity is found on the critical path, simply skip it. If the path is not the critical path, then take the sum of the items on that path and subtract it from the total critical path. For activity E, it is found on 2 paths above. One of them totals 19, and the other 26. We always use the larger one and subtract it from the critical path total of 29. That leaves a slack of 29-26, or 3 for activity E.

Time Management
Exercises

Activity	On Critical Path?	Slack (Float) in days
A	Y	0
B	Y	0
C	Y	0
D	Y	0
E	N	3
F	N	3
G	Y	0
H	Y	0
I	Y	0
J	Y	0
K	N	18

4. Your first step in solving this problem is to draw out a network logic diagram. Your diagram should look similar to the one shown below:

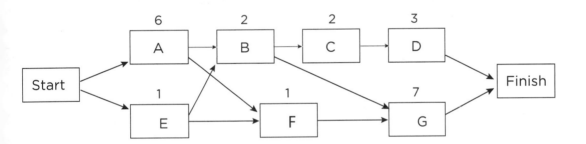

The next step is to list out all paths through the network:

Path	Durations	Total
Start-A-B-C-D-Finish	6+2+2+3	13
Start-A-B-G-Finish	6+2+7	15
Start-A-F-G-Finish	6+1+7	14
Start-E-B-C-D-Finish	1+2+2+3	8
Start-E-B-G-Finish	1+2+7	10
Start-E-F-G-Finish	1+1+7	9

The answer is 15 weeks, based on the fact that Start-A-B-G-Finish has a duration of 15 weeks, and that is the longest duration of any path.

5. If Activity D were to take twice as long as planned, that would change its duration from 3 to 6 weeks. This would have two effects:

•   The critical path would change. The new critical path would be Start-A-B-C-D-Finish.

•   The project finish date would be extended by 1 additional week, meaning the overall project would take 16 weeks.

    To arrive at this solution, reconstruct the table as follows:

Path	Durations	Total
Start-A-B-C-D-Finish	6+2+2+6	16
Start-A-B-G-Finish	6+2+7	15
Start-A-F-G-Finish	6+1+7	14
Start-E-B-C-D-Finish	1+2+2+6	11
Start-E-B-G-Finish	1+2+7	10
Start-E-F-G-Finish	1+1+7	9

Note how the longest path has changed to the first one in the table above.

6. The formula for three-point estimates is:

    (Pessimistic + 4 × Realistic + Optimistic) ÷ 6

    Which is equivalent to...

    (25 + 4 × 15 +10) ÷ 6

    This yields a three-point duration estimate of 15.83.

7. The formula for standard deviation is:

    (Pessimistic - Optimistic) ÷ 6

    or...

    (25-10) ÷ 6

    This yields a standard deviation of 2.5.

8. For this exercise, the early finish (top right quadrant), the duration, and the float were in question.

   Given the example, it is easiest to begin with the duration. This may be calculated easily by subtracting the late start (bottom left) from the late finish (bottom right) and adding one. 39-37+1 yields an activity duration of 3 (if this confuses you, consider that days 37, 38, and 39 are all working days). Now, simply count 3 days from the early start (top left), using day 21 as a working day, and it gets you to an early finish of day 23 (day 21, 22, and 23). The float is the late start - the early start, represented as 37 - 21 = 16. Even though this is the only node we have, we could further deduce that the early start or early finish date could slip 16 days without affecting the critical path and endangering the finish date.

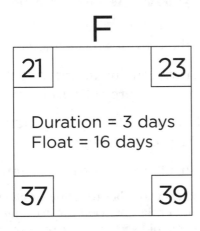

F

| 21 | 23 |

Duration = 3 days
Float = 16 days

| 37 | 39 |

IMPORTANT

In addition to this quiz, use your Key to InSite, found on the inside back cover of this book, to access additional content, including new exam questions, expanded content, and simulated PMP exams. If your book did not come with a Key to InSite on the inside back cover, it may not be authentic. If you do not have a Key to InSite, you may purchase one at *insite.velociteach.com*.

Time Management Questions

1. **You are the project manager for the construction of a commercial office building that has very similar characteristics to a construction project performed by your company two years ago. As you perform Define Activities, what is the BEST approach?**

   A. Use the activity list from the previous project as your activity list.

   B. Generate your activity list without looking at the previous project's list and compare when your project's list is complete.

   C. Use the gap analysis technique to identify any differences between your project and the previous project.

   D. Use the previous activity list to help construct your list.

2. **The customer has called a project team member to request a change in the project's schedule. The team member asks you what the procedure is for handling schedule changes. Where should you refer the team member to help him understand the procedure?**

   A. The project office.

   B. The change control board.

   C. The schedule management plan.

   D. Inform the team member that the customer is always right.

3. **If you were creating duration estimates for a schedule activity, which of the following tools or techniques would NOT be appropriate to use?**

   A. Expert judgment.

   B. Reserve analysis.

   C. Three-point estimating.

   D. Least-squares estimating.

4. Senior management has called you in for a meeting to review the progress of your project. You have been allocated 15 minutes to report progress and discuss critical issues. Which of the following would be BEST to carry with you in this case?

   A. Milestone chart.

   B. The project network diagram.

   C. An expert from each functional area of the project so that all questions may be answered.

   D. Project status reports from your team members.

5. Which of the following is FALSE concerning an activity's early finish and/or late finish?

   A. Early finish represents the earliest possible date an activity could finish.

   B. Late finish represents the latest possible date an activity could finish without lengthening the critical path.

   C. The difference between an activity's early finish and late finish is the same as the difference between the early start and late start.

   D. Early finish is typically depicted in the node's lower left quadrant, and late finish is depicted in the lower right quadrant.

6. The amount of time that an activity may be delayed without extending the critical path is:

   A. Lag.

   B. Grace period.

   C. Free factor.

   D. Slack.

7. Crashing differs from fast tracking because crashing:

   A. Usually increases value.

   B. Usually increases the cost.

   C. Usually saves more time.

   D. Usually saves more money.

8. **If senior management tells you "The last project we did like this cost us almost five million dollars," what estimating method is being used?**

    A. Delphi technique.

    B. Principle of equivalency of activities.

    C. Analogous estimating.

    D. Bottom-up estimating.

9. **You are advising a project manager who is behind schedule on his project. The sponsor on his project is very unhappy with the way things have progressed and is threatening to cancel the project. The sponsor has accepted a revised due date from the project manager but did not allow any increased spending. Which of the following would represent the BEST advice for the project manager in this case?**

    A. Fast track the schedule.

    B. Ask senior management for a new sponsor within the organization.

    C. Crash the schedule.

    D. Talk with the customer to see if budget may be increased without the sponsor's involvement.

10. **Based on the diagram below question 14, which is the correct match?**

    A. ES = 16, Float = 19.

    B. EF = 40, LS = 21.

    C. Float = 5, Duration = 19.

    D. Float = 5, LF = 40.

11. **Which Develop Schedule tool inserts non-working buffer time to be managed by the project manager?**

    A. Critical chain method.

    B. Critical path method.

    C. Resource leveling.

    D. Schedule modeling.

12. **What is the BEST tool to use to calculate the critical path on a project?**

A. Work breakdown structure.

B. GERT diagram.

C. Gantt chart.

D. Project network diagram.

13. **Consider the table at right: What is the critical path?**

Activity	Duration	Dependent on
Start	0	
A	3	Start
B	4	Start
C	2	Start
D	2	B
E	5	A,C
F	1	B
G	6	D, F
H	11	E
I	8	D, F
Finish	0	G, H, I

A. Start-A-E-H-Finish.

B. Start-C-E-H-Finish.

C. Start-B-D-I-Finish.

D. Start-B-D-G-Finish.

14. **Based on the diagram below, which of the following statements is true?**

A. This activity is on the critical path.

B. This activity is not on the critical path.

C. The activity shown should be decomposed further.

D. In order for the project to stay on schedule, the activity needs to finish on day 35 or earlier.

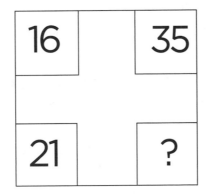

15. **Referring to the table in question 13, what is the float for Activity D?**

A. 0 days.

B. 3 days.

C. 5 days.

D. 7 days.

16. An activity has a duration estimate that is best case = 30 days, most likely = 44 days, and worst case = 62 days. What is the three-point estimate for this activity?

   A.   44.67 days

   B.   34.67 days

   C.   5.33 days

   D.   59.33 days

17. A government contracting firm that builds large infrastructure projects is analyzing the time it will take to plan phase one of a bridge renovation. The program manager's opinion is that approximately 24% of the time should be added to the beginning of the schedule for planning; however, the project manager states that his experience is that when the existing infrastructure is already in place, the general rule is that planning should take about half this much time. The project manager's beliefs are an example of:

   A.   An heuristic.

   B.   An organizational process asset.

   C.   An attribute.

   D.   Value engineering.

18. Which of the following choices best fits the description of a project manager applying the technique of what-if scenario analysis?

   A.   Using project management software to build three versions of the project schedule.

   B.   Using Monte Carlo analysis to identify what would happen if schedule delays occurred.

   C.   Using critical path method to analyze what would happen if the critical path actually occurred.

   D.   Discussing with the functional managers what they would do if certain project team members quit the project early.

19. **How do the activity list and activity attributes relate to each other?**

    A. The activity list focuses on schedule activities, while the activity attributes apply to WBS activities.

    B. The activity attributes are created prior to the activity list.

    C. The activity list may be substituted for the activity attributes in most processes.

    D. Activity attributes provide additional information for each activity on the activity list.

20. **You are discussing the schedule with members of your team when one of them describes a group of activities that can start at any time but must finish in a specific order. You decide to investigate this further. What would be the best way to recognize these activities?**

    A. Look for a Gantt chart with a group of activities that have staggered or stair-stepped finish dates.

    B. Look for a group of activities with a start-to-finish relationship.

    C. Look for a group of activities with a finish-to-finish relationship.

    D. Look for this information on the activity attributes.

21. **Which of the following is the BEST description of the critical path?**

    A. The activities that represent critical functionality.

    B. The activities that represent the largest portions of the work packages.

    C. The activities that represent the highest schedule risk on the project.

    D. The activities that represent the optimal path through the network.

22. **Which of the following is TRUE about Estimate Activity Durations?**

    A. It must be performed after Sequence Activities.

    B. It must be performed after Develop Schedule.

    C. Parametric estimates may be used to derive the durations.

    D. The activity duration estimates must be validated during Develop Schedule.

23. If schedule activities are not properly decomposed, which of the following would NOT be an expected outcome?

    A. The team encounters difficulty estimating cost and time.

    B. The team encounters difficulty in building the schedule.

    C. The team encounters difficulty in calculating earned value.

    D. The team encounters difficulty in creating the responsibility assignment matrix.

24. Your project schedule has just been developed, approved, and distributed to the stakeholders and presented to senior management when one of the resources assigned to an activity approaches you and tells you that her activity cannot be performed within the allotted time due to several necessary pieces that were left out of planning. Her revised estimate would change the schedule but would not affect the critical path. What would be the BEST way for the project manager to handle this situation?

    A. Stick with the published schedule and allow for any deviation by using schedule reserve.

    B. Go back to Estimate Activity Durations and update the schedule and other plans to reflect the new estimate.

    C. Hire an independent consultant to validate her claim.

    D. Replace the resource with someone who says they can meet the published schedule.

25. Jan is working with the project team to produce an estimate for a particular activity. They have gathered expert opinions and have determined that the optimistic estimate is 4.5 days, and the pessimistic estimate is 13 days. The most likely estimate is 7 working days. Given the team's preference for triangular distribution, what estimate should they use?

    A. 7 days.

    B. 7.6 days.

    C. 8.2 days.

    D. 11 days.

Answers to Time Management Questions

1.   D. The previous activity list would make an excellent tool to help you ensure that you are considering all activities. Any historical information such as this is thought of as an organizational process asset. 'A' is incorrect because you cannot simply substitute something as intricate as a complete activity list. 'B' is incorrect because the other activity list would provide a good starting point and should be considered before you create your activity list. 'C' (gap analysis) is a tool that is used in the real world that is not defined by PMI, nor is it used in activity list definition.

2.   C. The schedule management plan, discussed in chapter 4, is part of the project plan. This is the best source of information on how changes to the schedule are to be handled. 'A' is incorrect because the project office's job is to define standards – not to make decisions on tactical items such as this. 'B' is incorrect because the change control board may or may not even exist, and if it does exist, it usually approves or rejects scope changes. Answer 'D' would be the worst choice. The customer is not always right when it comes to requesting changes. Procedures should be defined and followed in order to improve the project's chances of success.

3   D. Since we are creating activity duration estimates, we are performing the process of Estimate Activity Durations. Answers 'A', 'B', and 'C' are all tools used in Estimate Activity Durations, but 'D' is a made up term.

4.   A. Milestone charts show the high level status, which would be appropriate given the audience and time allocated for this update.

5.   D. The early finish is typically depicted in a node's upper right quadrant, while the late finish is in the lower right. 'A' was not a good choice because that accurately defines the early finish, given the activity's estimated duration. 'B' is not correct because that is the definition of the late finish. 'C' is not a good choice, because the float (or slack) determines the gap between early finish and late finish and between the early start and late start. Since the float is the same, the difference between those dates should also be the same.

6.   D. The slack (or float) is the amount of time an activity may be delayed without affecting the critical path.

7. B. Crashing adds more resources to an activity. This usually increases the cost due to the law of diminishing returns which predicts that 10 people usually cannot complete an activity in half the time that 5 people can. The savings from crashing are rarely linear. 'A' is incorrect because crashing does not directly affect the project's value. 'C' is incorrect because crashing may or may not save more time than fast tracking – depending on the situation. 'D' is incorrect because crashing usually costs more money than fast tracking.

8. C. In this example management is providing you with analogous estimates. These estimates use actual costs from previous projects (historical information or organizational process assets) to produce estimates for a similar project.

9. A. In this case, you must compress the schedule without increasing the costs. Fast tracking does not directly add cost to the project and is the best choice in this case. 'B' is incorrect. The sponsor is paying for the project. Do this, and your sponsor will probably be asking for a new project manager instead! 'C' is incorrect because crashing usually adds cost to the project, and that is not allowed in this scenario. 'D' is incorrect because the sponsor authorizes budget. Doing an end-run around the sponsor and going to the customer would be very inappropriate.

10. D. In order to answer this question, you'll need to calculate the duration, the float, and the late finish. The early finish is given to us as 35 (eliminating 'B' as a potential correct answer). To calculate the duration, subtract the early start (top left) from the early finish (top right) and add one. This works out to $35 - 16 + 1 = 20$, eliminating 'C' as a possible answer. To calculate the float, subtract the early start from the late start. This is $21 - 16 = 5$. Now we can also eliminate 'A' as a possibility, so we actually have enough information to guess 'D' as the correct answer. To confirm it, we need to calculate the late finish (LF). Late Finish = Late Start + duration – 1, or $LF = 21 + 20 - 1 = 40$.

11. A. The critical chain method provides a buffer to be used by the project manager to protect the critical path. Typically, the team is not aware of this buffer.

12. D. The project network diagram shows duration and dependencies which would help you calculate the critical path. 'A' is incorrect because the WBS does not show durations or activity dependencies. 'B' is incorrect because GERT is most helpful for

showing conditions and branches. 'C' is incorrect because a Gantt chart is very useful for showing percentage complete on activities but is not the best tool for showing activity dependencies or calculating the critical path.

13.   A. The critical path is determined in 3 steps. The first step is to draw out the project network diagram. Yours should look similar to the one depicted as follows (note that activities B and C were moved to make the diagram neater – don't worry if your diagram does not look this neat):

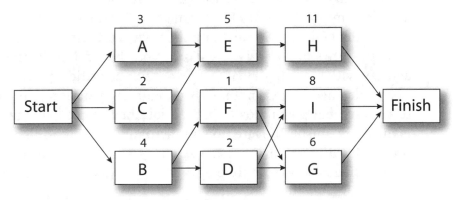

The next step is to list out all of the paths through the network. The six paths are:

Start-A-E-H-Finish

Start-C-E-H-Finish

Start-B-F-I-Finish

Start-B-F-G-Finish

Start-B-D-I-Finish

Start-B-D-G-Finish

The last step is to add up all of the values associated with each path as is done below:

Start-A-E-H-Finish = 0+3+5+11+0 = **19**

Start-C-E-H-Finish = 0+2+5+11+0 = 18

Start-B-F-I-Finish = 0+4+1+8+0 = 13

Start-B-F-G-Finish = 0+4+1+6+0 = 11

Start-B-D-I-Finish = 0+4+2+8+0 = 14

Start-B-D-G-Finish = 0+4+2+6+0 = 12

The critical path emerges as Start-A-E-H-Finish because the path adds up to 19, which is longer than any of the other paths. If any of the activities in this path are delayed, the finish of the project will be delayed.

14.   B. This diagram was used elsewhere in this quiz in a different way. That is common to see on the exam as well. This activity has 5 days of float (slack). To calculate the float, subtract the early start from the late start. This is 21 – 16 = 5. You should assume that any activity with a positive float (>0) is not on the critical path. 'C' does not work since there is not nearly enough information to point you toward further decomposition. 'D' might have fooled you, but 35 is the early finish. The late finish is actually 40 (Late Finish = Late Start + duration – 1, or LF = 21 + 20 - 1 = 40). This means that this activity needs to be complete by day 40 in order for the project to stay on schedule.

15.   C. The float (or slack) of an activity is the amount of time it can slip without moving the critical path. In this case, we must calculate the float of Activity D. If Activity D was on the critical path, we would immediately know that the float was 0, but in this case it is not.

To solve this problem, we must first list out all of the paths. We will use the list from the previous question.

Start-A-E-H-Finish = 0+3+5+11+0 = 19

Start-C-E-H-Finish = 0+2+5+11+0 = 18

Start-B-F-I-Finish = 0+4+1+8+0 = 13

Start-B-F-G-Finish = 0+4+1+6+0 = 11

Start-B-D-I-Finish = 0+4+2+8+0 = 14

Start-B-D-G-Finish = 0+4+2+6+0 = 12

The next step is to identify the ones that have Activity D in them. They are:

Start-B-D-I-Finish = 0+4+2+8+0 = 14

Start-B-D-G-Finish = 0+4+2+6+0 = 12

Now the task is simple. We simply subtract the path sums from the length of the critical path for each (19-14 = 5, and 19-12 = 7), and finally we take the smaller of those two values which is 5. Therefore, the float for Activity D is 5.

16.   A. The formula for a three-point estimate, also called a PERT estimate, is (Pessimistic + 4 × Realistic + Optimistic) ÷ 6. In this example, the terms were switched around slightly, but it equates to (62 + 4 × 44 + 30) ÷ 6 = 268 ÷ 6 = 44.67.

17.   A. An heuristic is a process or method that exists when the rules are loosely defined or when there are no rules at all. The question asked what do the project manager's beliefs exemplify. Since the project manager has a "general rule" that the planning should take less time but it is only based on experience and not a firm rule, it fits the definition well. 'B' is not a good answer since there are opinions and general rules at work here but no real assets. 'C' is not a good answer since you would have to ask "an attribute of what?" It simply doesn't fit well here. 'D' does not work because value engineering (discussed more in the next chapter) is all about trying to squeeze the most value out of a deliverable without affecting the cost. Cutting planning time in half would not accomplish this in any direct way.

18.   B. What-if analysis can take on many forms, but the form you are most likely to see on the exam is Monte Carlo analysis, which throws a large number of scenarios at the schedule to see what would happen if one or more bad scenarios occurred.

19.   D. The activity attributes simply expand on the information for each activity. 'A' is incorrect since the activity attributes tie back to the activity list and not the WBS. 'B' is incorrect since the activity attributes may be created at the same time or after the activity list, but not before. 'C' is incorrect since the activity attributes may never be substituted for the activity list. Instead the activity attributes accompany the activity list, providing additional information on each activity.

20.   C. This scenario describes tasks that have finish dates linked in finish-to-finish order.

21.   C. This one may have been difficult for you, because it is a non-traditional definition of the critical path. The critical path is the

series of activities, which if delayed, will delay the project. This makes these activities the highest schedule risk on the project. 'A' is incorrect because the critical path has no relationship with functionality. 'B' is incorrect because the size of the work packages does not directly correlate to the critical path. 'D' is incorrect because the critical path does not represent the optimal path through the network.

22.   C. One of the important tools used in Estimate Activity Durations is parametric estimates. 'A' was incorrect because none of the outputs of Sequence Activities is an input into Estimate Activity Durations, meaning that there is no reason one has to be performed before the other. 'B' is incorrect because Develop Schedule should always be performed after Estimate Activity Durations (how will you be able to create the schedule if you don't know how long the component activities will take?). 'D' is incorrect because validation of the activity durations sounds like a great thing to do, but it is not a part of the Develop Schedule process.

23.   D. This is a problem many project managers have faced. As you answer this question, keep in mind that WBS nodes are decomposed into work packages first. Then schedule activities are decomposed from the work packages. 'A', 'B', and 'C' all relate to problems you would have if the schedule activities are not properly decomposed, but 'D' is related to the work packages, and you are not given anything in the question that suggests there is a problem with the way they were decomposed.

24.   B. Changes happen. Some of them are submitted as change requests, and some of them come out of nowhere. In this case, you would want to return to planning and update the plans. The project will not be delayed, and the resource has given a good reason why the dates need to be revisited (a common occurrence in the real world). 'A' is incorrect, because the plan should reflect reality – not an unrealistic estimate. 'C' is incorrect, because you cannot possibly get an outside opinion every time a resource needs to change a date. 'D' is incorrect, because the resource gave a good reason for the adjustment. It was not that she was lacking in training or ability, but that pieces were left out of planning. Therefore, 'B' represents the all-around best answer.

25.	C. Triangular distribution for these purposes is really nothing more than a simple average, which is $(4.5 + 13 + 7) \div 3 = 8.16$ (rounded to 8.2). 'A' was a trap for someone who simply saw the most likely estimate of 7 days and wanted to avoid doing any math. 'B' worked out for beta distribution $(P + 4R + O) \div 6$, but that was not what was asked here. 'D' was a random number.

CHAPTER SIX

7 Cost Management

Difficulty	Memorization	Exam Importance
HIGH	HIGH	HIGH

The topic of cost management, like time management, has critical formulas that must be learned and understood. This chapter will explain these formulas clearly and provide methods and exercises for quick retention.

Most of the principles and techniques explained here, such as earned value, did not originate with PMI but were derived from long-standing practices in the fields of cost accounting, managerial accounting, and finance.

From the indicators at the top of the page, you can tell that most people find this chapter to be one of the more difficult ones. In order to help you prepare for this topic, this book has clearly broken down the practices and outlined the techniques and formulas needed to ace the questions on the exam.

It is also essential that you know the main outputs that are produced during each of the four processes. The different tasks that are performed in each process are summarized in the chart on the right.

The processes of Project Cost Management with their *primary* outputs

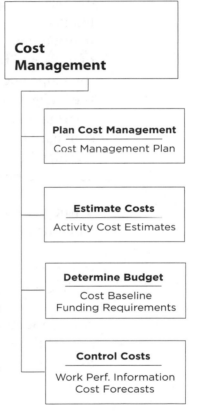

Cost Management

Plan Cost Management
Cost Management Plan

Estimate Costs
Activity Cost Estimates

Determine Budget
Cost Baseline
Funding Requirements

Control Costs
Work Perf. Information
Cost Forecasts

Philosophy

While the actual tools and techniques behind cost management may be different from time management, the driving philosophy has several similarities. Costs should be planned, quantified, and measured. The project manager should tie costs to activities and resources and build the estimates from the bottom up.

It is common practice for high-level budgets to be determined prior to knowing costs. The reason for this is that many companies use fiscal year planning cycles that must be done far in advance of their project planning. Budgetary constraints are a fact of life, but instead of blindly accepting whatever budget is specified by management, the project manager carefully reviews the scope of work and the duration estimates and then reconciles them to the scope and projected costs. Adjustments to the project scope, the budget, or the schedule are much easier to justify by working up from a detailed level instead of from the top down. Although summary budgets are often the first thing created in the real world, when it comes to detailed planning, the overall approach advocated here is scope first, schedule second, and budget third.

Throughout this book, you will see that estimates should be built from the bottom up. At the point in the process where budgets are created, you should have a well-defined work breakdown structure, an activity list with resource and duration estimates for each activity, and a schedule.

Now budgeting becomes a task of applying rates and schedule against those resources and activities to create activity cost estimates and a cost baseline, following the cost management plan.

It is the project manager's job to constantly monitor and control cost against time, scope, quality, and risk to ensure that all projections remain realistic and clearly defined.

Importance

The topic of cost management is of high importance for the exam, both in the understanding of PMI's processes and in the application of key formulas, which play a part here as well.

Preparation

Learning the 13 key formulas for Cost Management is a must. Learning to apply them is equally as important. The good news is that the formulas are not overly difficult, and there are plenty of explanations and examples in this book to help cement the concepts.

As mentioned briefly above, memorization is important; however, understanding the formulas is even more important. Once you grasp the formulas and concepts, the memorization will be a snap. In fact, some people studying for the exam only memorize the concepts and reconstruct the formulas as needed. This is possible because each formula does make sense, so read and reread this chapter until they are clear to you.

Important Concepts

Before you begin to explore the four processes that make up this knowledge area, take a moment to familiarize yourself with the following two important terms. While these do not fit within any particular process, they are important concepts for you to understand.

Key Fact

Life-Cycle Costing

Instead of simply asking "how much will this product cost to develop?" Life-cycle costing looks at the total cost of ownership from purchase or creation, through operations, and finally to disposal. It is a practice that encourages making decisions based on the bigger picture of ownership costs.

For instance, it may be less expensive for the project to use generic computer servers to develop a software product; however, if the organization will have to maintain those servers, and if that organization has expertise and existing service contracts with IBM, then the project may be making a short-sighted decision that will have adverse effects downstream.

Key Fact

Value Engineering

Value engineering is the practice of trying to get more out of the project in every possible way. It tries to increase the bottom line, decrease costs, improve quality, shorten the schedule, and generally squeeze more benefit and value out of each aspect of the project. The key to value engineering is that the scope of work is not reduced by these other efforts.

ning

Plan Cost Management

What it is:

This process follows the same pattern as the Plan Scope Management and Plan Schedule Management processes. It is the process that creates the plan that will guide and direct the activities in the other three cost management processes.

Why it is important:

This process gives guidance to the other cost management processes, and cost is an important area, both in actual projects and on the exam.

When it is performed:

The general rule (and one that will help you on the exam) is that scope activities are performed first, time and schedule activities second, and cost and budget activities third, but as is true with most rules, there are exceptions to this one. The exception is that overall budgets or budgetary constraints are very often determined before the project is initiated, so while the cost details will not be determined until after the scope has been planned and resources assigned and activity duration determined, the high-level constraints and perhaps even the funding schedules will often be specified in the project charter.

How it works:

Plan Cost Management is a relatively streamlined process with a few common inputs and tools and a single, important output.

Inputs

Project Management Plan — See Ch. 2, Common Inputs

Project Charter — See Ch. 4, Develop Project Charter

Enterprise Environ. Factors — See Ch. 2, Common Inputs

Organizational Process Assets — See Ch. 2, Common Inputs

Tools

Expert Judgment — See Ch. 2, Common Tools

Analytical Techniques — See Ch. 2, Common Tools

Meetings — See Ch. 2, Common Tools

Outputs

Key Fact

Cost Management Plan

The cost management plan is the only significant component of this process. It is the plan that describes how the processes of Estimate Costs, Determine Budget, and Control Costs will be carried out. It will describe the units, precision, accuracy, and thresholds, and will specify how performance is measured. The cost management plan will ultimately become an important part of the project management plan.

Estimate Costs

Planning **Estimate Costs**

What it is:

Most of the processes in this book are intuitively named, making it that much easier to understand them. Estimate Costs is a good example of that. Its name indicates exactly what it does.

In Estimate Costs, each schedule activity is analyzed to evaluate the activity time estimates and the resource estimates associated with them, and a cost estimate is produced.

Why it is important:

If you've heard the old saying that the devil is in the details, then you know why Estimate Costs is important. In this process, you gain a detailed understanding of the costs involved in performing a project.

When it is performed:

It may be misleading to suggest that Estimate Costs is only performed once. This process, like many others, may be performed over and again throughout the project; however, there are a few essential predecessor processes that must be completed before it can be performed adequately. Costs are estimated against schedule activities, so the project's schedule has to be created first.

The order of certain processes from Define Scope to Estimate Costs

How it works:

Cost estimates, prepared for each activity, are categorized in terms of their accuracy. In other words, how much leeway are you giving yourself with your estimating?

When it comes to estimates that result from this process, there are many options.

Estimate Costs

Consider the table that follows:

Estimate Type	Range
Order of Magnitude Estimate	-50% to +100%
Conceptual Estimate	-30% to +50%
Preliminary Estimate	-20% to +30%
Definitive Estimate	-15% to +20%
Control Estimate	-10% to +15%

These five different types of estimating are used, depending on the need. For instance, in the initiation of a project, an order of magnitude estimate may suffice, while later in the project, a definitive estimate may be in order. For activities with relatively few unknowns, a control estimate may be appropriate. Typically, the closer in time you get to actually spending money for an activity, the more precise you want that activity's estimate to be.

Inputs

Cost Management Plan

By this time, it should be a familiar pattern that a management plan is created at the beginning of a knowledge area, and that management plan guides the other processes in that knowledge area. In this case, the cost management plan guides the process of Estimate Costs. Specifically, it tells how costs estimates will be derived and how accurate and precise they are expected to be.

Human Resource Management Plan

Information on what types of resources the project will need and how the project will be procuring them can affect the cost estimates. For example, if the organization is required to staff project resources from a particular vendor, that will have a direct impact on the associated activity costs.

Scope Baseline

The project scope statement, one of the three components of the scope baseline created earlier in Define Scope, ties each element of the scope back to the underlying need it was designed to address. Also, the project scope statement provides information on constraints and assumptions related to the scope, and these can dramatically affect the cost estimates.

Project Schedule

Cost estimates are largely a function of the activity's duration and the resources required. The schedule contains all of the activities, and costs are estimated at a schedule activity level, but there may be additional ways in which the schedule can affect the cost estimates. For example, certain types of seasonal materials or labor may be more expensive at some times than others, and the schedule can help the project team anticipate that impact.

Risk Register

The risk register may have specific information on identified risks related to costs. Any such information should be factored in to this estimating process.

Enterprise Environ. Factors — See Ch. 2, Common Inputs

Organizational Process Assets — See Ch. 2, Common Inputs

Tools

Expert Judgment — See Ch. 2, Common Tool

Kev Fact

Analogous Estimating

The tool of analogous estimating uses the actual results of projects that have been performed by your organization as the estimates for your activities. Analogous estimates are typically easier to use, and their accuracy depends on how similar the two projects actually are.

Kev Fact

Parametric Estimating

Parametric estimating is a tool often used on projects with a high degree of historical information, and it works best for linear, scalable projects. For instance, if you knew that it cost $4,000,000 to build a mile of roadway, then you could estimate that it would cost $32,000,000 to build 8 miles of road.

Estimate Costs

Bottom-Up Estimating

Key Fact

The technique of bottom-up estimating produces a separate estimate for each schedule activity. These individual estimates are then aggregated up to summary nodes on the WBS.

Bottom-up estimating is considered to be highly accurate; however, it can also be time consuming and labor-intensive.

Three-Point Estimating — See Ch. 6, Estimate Activity Durations, Tools

Key Fact

Reserve Analysis

Key Fact

It is normal for the cost estimates that will be produced as a result of this process to include reserve amounts, also called contingency. This is simply a buffer against slippage on the project.

The reserve amounts should be analyzed as part of the Estimate Costs process simply to ensure that the amount of reserve being planned properly reflects the risk associated with the project.

Cost of Quality

The technique of evaluating the cost of quality, often abbreviated as COQ, looks at all of the costs that will be realized in order to achieve quality. This tool is also used in the Plan Quality process. The costs of items that are not conformant to quality standards are known as "cost of poor quality," often abbreviated as CoPQ.

Project Management Software

The tool of project management software is most useful in facilitating the other tools and techniques, performing the routine calculations, and organizing and storing the large amounts of information used to build the cost estimates.

Vendor Bid Analysis

Bids should be analyzed, and most specifically the winning bid, if for no other reason than to improve the project team's understanding of costs.

Estimate Costs

Group Decision-Making Techniques

Cost estimates should have team consensus, and in order to get that, you may use any of several techniques to help the team form agreement on the results.

Outputs

Key Fact

Activity Cost Estimates

The activity cost estimates are the primary output of this process. These estimates address how much it would cost to complete each schedule activity on the project.

Basis of Estimates

When it comes to the PMBOK Guide, you can never have too much supporting detail. Here, especially, it is important to include enough information on how you derived the activity cost estimates.

Project Documents Updates

The cost management plan details how the project costs will be managed and how change or requested changes to the project costs will be managed. As the activity cost estimates are created, it is normal that this plan would be updated, sometimes significantly.

Estimate Costs

Planning

Determine Budget

Determine Budget

What it is:

In order to understand this process, it is necessary to understand what a budget is. A budget, also known as the cost performance baseline, takes the estimated project expenditures and maps them back to dates on the calendar. In other words, the Determine Budget process time-phases the costs so that the performing organization will know how to plan for cash flow and likely expenditures.

Why it is important:

A good cost baseline will help the organization plan its expenditures appropriately and will prevent the organization from tying up too much money throughout the life of the project. For instance, a construction project may have relatively low costs early on, but these costs may rise dramatically in the construction phase. The cost performance baseline will reflect this, helping the organization to plan accordingly.

Although a high-level budget, similar to a cost constraint, may be determined early in the project, this cost baseline describes a detailed budget that shows costs and time lines for each work package or activity.

When it is performed:

Because the budget typically maps back to schedule activities, it should be performed after Define Activities, Estimate Activity Durations, and Estimate Activity Resources have been performed. Additionally, because the cost performance baseline is time-phased, it should be performed after Develop Schedule since that is where the project's time line is determined, also since it is based on the activity costs estimates, it should be performed after the process of Estimate Costs.

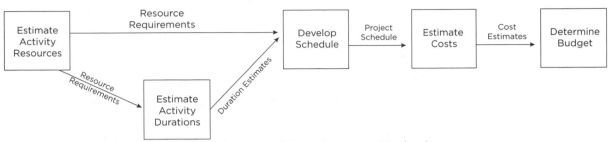

A diagram showing the order of Time Management's planning processes and the integration with Cost Management

How it works:

Inputs

Cost Management Plan

The cost management plan specifies how the budget will be created, as well as the role the budget will play in the management of the project.

Scope Baseline

The scope baseline contains the project scope statement, the WBS, and the WBS dictionary. All of these comprise the information on why the scope was set where it was, what its limits are, and what other scope-related constraints exist. For instance, certain elements of scope may be non-negotiable since they are required by contract, while other requirements may be easily changed. As the project's budget is being created, the scope should be carefully considered.

Also, the budget is not only mapped back to the schedule (that is, time-phased), but costs are also tied back to a node on the work breakdown structure, and the WBS dictionary will provide expanded attributes, information, and details on each of the work packages.

Key Fact

Activity Cost Estimates

The activity cost estimates are a primary input into this process. They provide details on what each schedule activity is estimated to cost.

Because every schedule activity maps back to a single work package, these activity cost estimates are added together to get the cost for their parent work package.

Determine Budget

Determine Budget

Basis of Estimates

As in other areas, you can never have too much supporting detail. The basis for estimates for the activity cost estimates describes how you derived the cost estimates you are using here.

Project Schedule

The cost performance baseline is time-phased, meaning that it shows what costs will be incurred and when they will be incurred. The schedule helps tie these costs back to periods of time for planning purposes.

Resource Calendars

Resource calendars show when resources are going to be used and when they will be available. This, along with the project schedule, will help plan for when costs will be incurred.

Risk Register

The risk register contains all of the identified risks on the project. These risks need to be carefully considered as the budget and funding requirements are developed.

Agreements

Agreements and contracts may provide information on what costs the project is contractually obliged to incur. For instance, the contract may specify that only one specific brand of computer server may be used in a data center or that the project is obligated to use at least five of these servers. Any contractual information that affects the cost or expenditures should be factored into the Determine Budget process.

Organizational Process Assets — See Ch. 2, Common Inputs

Tools

Cost Aggregation

Even though costs are estimated at an activity level, these cost estimates should be aggregated to the work package level where they will be measured, managed, and controlled during the project.

Reserve Analysis

The tool of reserve analysis is related to risk. Almost all projects maintain a financial reserve to protect them against cost overrun. How much they keep and how they track it vary from project to project. These buffers go by various names such as management reserve and contingency reserve. For instance, one project may decide to pad each activity cost estimate by 10% across the board, while another project may only pad the activities that are considered to be at highest risk for cost overrun. Still another project may add a total cost buffer of 20% as a lump sum to the entire project cost baseline.

There is no one prescribed way to perform reserve analysis; however, the reserve amount should be in keeping with the risk levels and tolerances on the project.

Expert Judgment

This is, perhaps, the most important tool used in the Determine Budget process. Good estimates (whether they are for cost, time, or another resource) should almost always have some expert judgment applied. In most scenarios, the person doing the work or responsible for the activity should be consulted for input.

Historical Relationships

The term "historical relationships" means a parametric estimating model based on historical data. An example of parametric estimating would be basing the cost of the development of a software application on the estimated number of lines of code or screens involved, or based the cost of an airport runway on its planned length.

Parametric estimates work best when the project being undertaken is highly similar to previous projects and there is significant historical information available within your organization or industry.

Funding Limit Reconciliation

Kev Fact

Because companies typically operate on fiscal years, they are required to budget for projects long before the actual scope is known, and a single project may span several fiscal years. Because of that, it is normal for a project to receive a funding limit or constraint as the project is begun.

It is important for the project to reconcile planned spending with these funding limits. For instance, the organization may specify that they will only be able to provide $200,000 in the first month of a project, but $450,000 in the second month. The project's cost baseline ultimately needs to be compatible with these limitations.

Outputs

Cost Baseline

Kev Fact

The cost baseline is another term for the project's budget, and you should expect to see questions related to it on the exam. It not only specifies what costs will be incurred, but when they will be incurred. Larger projects may be divided into multiple cost baselines. For instance, one cost baseline may track domestic labor costs, while a second cost baseline is used to track international labor costs. In traditional projects, the funding forms an S curve, meaning that the costs start off slowly, accelerate throughout construction phase of the project, and begin to slow down during testing and closure. When analyzed cumulatively, this pattern forms a characteristic S pattern as is shown in the following illustration.

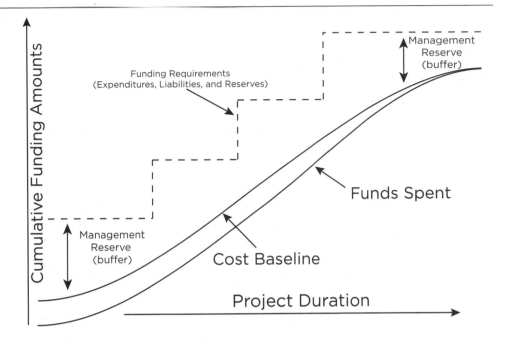

S-Curve diagram showing the relationship of cost and time

Project Funding Requirements

Kev Fact

It would be impractical for most projects to petition management for authorization on each individual cost, so instead, the project determines funding requirements using the cost baseline. The funding requirements are almost always related to the planned expenditures, but they are not identical to them. For instance, a project may request $20,000 per month throughout the life of the project, or they may require a larger portion early on in order to purchase equipment or incur other fixed costs.

Project Documents Updates

Oftentimes performing the process of Determine Budget results in changes to the project's scope, schedule, or costs. If any of these changes affect the way in which costs are managed (or the way change requests to the costs are managed) then the corresponding plan or document should be updated to reflect this.

Monitoring & Controlling

Control Costs

What it is:

Control Costs, in many ways, is the quintessential monitoring and controlling process. There are two important things to keep in mind about controlling processes:

1. They are proactive. They do not merely wait for changes to occur. Instead, they try to influence the factors that lead to change.

2. Controlling processes measure what was executed against what was planned. If the results of what was executed do not match the cost baseline, then appropriate steps are taken to bring the two back in line. This could either mean changing future plans or changing the way the work is being performed.

Control Costs is primarily concerned with cost variance. In project management, cost variances are described as either being positive (good) or negative (bad). Even a positive cost variance needs to be understood and the plan must be adjusted. Accurate planning is paramount.

Why it is important:

Control Costs is an essential process for ensuring that costs are carefully monitored and controlled. It ensures that the costs stay on track and that change is detected whenever it occurs.

When it is performed:

Control Costs is not a process that is performed only once. Instead, it is performed regularly throughout the project, typically beginning as soon as project costs are incurred. The activities associated with Control Costs are usually performed with more frequency as project costs increase. For instance, many projects will perform Control Costs monthly during planning phases and weekly (or even more frequently) during construction phases, where costs typically peak.

How it works:

Inputs

Kev Fact

Project Management Plan

The cost performance baseline is the most important component of the project management plan used in Control Costs. A baseline is the original plan plus all approved changes. The cost performance baseline (also known as the budget) shows what costs are projected and when they are projected to be incurred. The cost performance baseline is the plan against which the actual costs are measured.

Another important component of the project management plan for this process is the cost management plan. This plan lays out how costs will be managed throughout the life of the project.

Kev Fact

Project Funding Requirements

Like the preceding input, which contained the cost baseline, the project funding requirements are also part of the plan against which the actual funding is measured. In this case, positive or negative variances from the planned funding requirements will be evaluated so that corrective action may be taken if necessary.

Work Performance Data — See Ch. 2, Common Inputs

Organizational Process Assets — See Ch. 2, Common Inputs

Tools

Kev Fact

Earned Value Management

Earned Value, covered in the next section of this chapter, is a method of measuring actual performance against the original plan. Earned value measurement can help identify areas where the project is performing differently than the plan. Earned value measurement would identify variances (such as CV) as well as trends (such as CPI) that directly influence the Control Costs process.

Control Costs

Estimate Costs

Forecasting

The technique of forecasting uses current and previous cost information to predict future costs. This focuses on the concepts of Estimate At Completion (EAC) and Estimate To Completion (ETC), covered later in this chapter under the heading of Earned Value.

TCPI

The concept of TCPI is an earned value technique that focuses on the performance needed in order to achieve your earned value targets. TCPI is covered in more detail in the special focus section on earned value later in this chapter.

Performance Reviews

Performance reviews can be helpful to uncover areas where costs may be under or over performing. This is most typically used as part of earned value management to compare the plan with the actual results and forecast indexes and project trends.

Project Management Software

Because the calculations involved in Control Costs (especially the earned value calculations) can be tedious and complex, project management software is typically used to calculate actual values and assist with "what if" analysis.

Reserve Analysis

Reserves are pools of money set aside to keep the project running smoothly in case a risk event occurs. Periodic analysis is needed in order to ensure that the project still has the right amount set aside. It does not serve the performing organization well if there is too much reserve set aside, and it puts the project at risk if there is too little. Reserve Analysis is the technique used to evaluate and adjust this as needed.

Outputs

Key Fact

Work Performance Information

Work performance information shows how the project is performing against the plan. For the process of Control Costs, the performance measurements of CV, SV, CPI, SPI, TCPI, and VAC are especially applicable, since they help show variances and trends on how the project is performing against the plan.

Key Fact

Cost Forecasts

Budget forecasts are your projections for how much funding will be needed and when it will be needed from this point forward in the project.

The two values that relate most closely to completion are Estimate At Completion (EAC) and Estimate To Completion (ETC). These numbers are used to help forecast a likely completion for the project. Both EAC and ETC are covered in more detail later in this chapter.

Change Requests

As Control Costs is performed, requested changes are a normal output. For instance, if the process of Control Costs showed that the project was going to cost significantly less or more than the cost baseline, then certain changes would likely result to bring the project back in line. These changes could take the form of reducing the scope, increasing the budget, or changing factors related to execution.

Project Management Plan Updates

Anything that changes the project plan, such as changes to the cost baseline, changes to the cost management plan, or changes to any other parts of the project management plan, should be updated back into the project management plan.

Estimate Costs

Estimate Costs

Project Documents Updates

This output, like the preceding one, is seen frequently. The thing to keep in mind is that anytime you update one plan that causes other documents or plans to change, it needs to be captured as an output.

Organizational Process Assets Updates

Even mistakes are potentially assets if they are documented in the form of lessons learned, but lessons learned can document more than errors. Organizational process assets could also include things done well that resulted in costs falling into line.

Special Focus: Earned Value

Kev Fact

The following section is of key importance

If you are wrestling with your understanding of earned value, think about the concept of debits and credits. In a double entry accounting system, for every debit to one account, there is a corresponding credit to another account. Earned value is similar in that if you spend a dollar on labor for your project, that dollar doesn't just evaporate into thin air. You are "earning" a dollar's value back into your project. If you buy bricks or computers, write code or documentation, or perform any work on the project, those activities earn value back into your project.

There are 13 key formulas associated with earned value management that often appear on the test, and they require both memorization and understanding. Following is a chart that presents a summary of the key terms used in earned value calculations.

Note that for Planned Value, Earned Value, and Actual Cost, there are older, equivalent terms that still show up on the exam. These older terms and their associated abbreviations are shown along with the current terms on the chart on the following page, and you must be able to recognize and apply either one on the exam.

Earned Value

Earned Value

Term	Abbrev.	Description	Formula
Budgeted At Completion	BAC	How much was originally planned for this project to cost.	No one formula exists. BAC is derived by looking at the total budgeted cost for the project.
Planned Value (also known as Budgeted Cost of Work Scheduled)	PV (or BCWS)	How much work should have been completed at a point in time based on the plan. Derived by measuring planned work completed at a point in time.	$PV = $ Planned % Complete X BAC
Earned Value (also known as Budgeted Cost of Work Performed)	EV (or BCWP)	How much work was actually completed during a given period of time. Derived by measuring actual work completed at a point in the schedule.	$EV = $ Actual % Complete X BAC
Actual Cost (also known as Actual Cost of Work Performed)	AC (or ACWP)	The money spent during a given period of time.	Sum of the costs for the given period of time.
Cost Variance	CV	The difference between what we expected to spend and what was actually spent.	$CV = EV - AC$
Schedule Variance	SV	The difference between where we planned to be in the schedule and where we are in the schedule.	$SV = EV - PV$
Cost Performance Index	CPI	The rate at which the project performance is meeting cost expectations during a given period of time.	$CPI = EV \div AC$
Cumulative CPI	CPI^C	The rate at which the project performance is meeting cost expectations from the beginning up to a point in time. CPI^C is also used to forecast the project's costs at completion.	$CPI^C = EV^C \div AC^C$
Schedule Performance Index	SPI	The rate at which the project performance is meeting schedule expectations up to a point in time.	$SPI = EV \div PV$
Estimate At Completion	EAC	Projecting the total cost at completion based on project performance up to a point in time.	$EAC = BAC \div CPI^C$
Estimate To Completion	ETC	Projecting how much more will be spent on the project, based on past performance.	$ETC = EAC - AC$
Variance At Completion	VAC	The difference between what was budgeted and what will actually be spent.	$VAC = BAC - EAC$
To-Complete Performance Index	$TCPI_C$	Performance that must be achieved in order to meet financial or schedule goals.	$TCPI_C = (BAC - EV) \div$ Remaining Funds

EVM Example

Consider the following example:
You are the project manager for the construction of 20 miles of sidewalk. According to your plan, the cost of construction will be $15,000 per mile and will take 8 weeks to complete.

2 weeks into the project, you have spent $55,000 and completed 4 miles of sidewalk, and you want to report performance and determine how much time and cost remain.

Below, we will walk through each calculation to show how we arrive at the correct answers.

Budgeted at Completion

In the approach outlined by this book, we will always begin by calculating BAC. Budgeted at completion simply means, "how much we originally expected this project to cost." It is typically very easy to calculate. In our example, we take 20 miles of sidewalk X $15,000 per mile. That equates to a BAC of $300,000.

BAC = $300,000

Planned Value

The planned value is how much work was planned for this point in time. The value is expressed in dollars.

Planned Value = Planned % complete X BAC

We do this by taking the BAC ($300,000) and multiplying it by our % complete. In this case, we are 2 weeks complete on an 8 week schedule, which equates to 25%. $300,000 X .25 = $75,000. Therefore, we had planned to spend $75,000 after two weeks.

PV = $75,000

Earned Value

If you have been intimidated by the concept of earned value, relax. Earned value is based on the assumption that as you complete work on the project, you are adding value to the project. Therefore, it is simply a matter of calculating how much value you have "earned" on the project.

Earned Value

Planned value is what was planned, but earned value is what actually happened.

EV = Actual % Complete X BAC

In this case, we have completed 4 miles of the 20 mile project, which equates to 20%. We multiply that percentage by the BAC to get EV. It is $300,000 × 20% = $60,000. This tells us that we have completed $60,000 worth of work, or more accurately, we have earned $60,000 of value for the project.

EV = $60,000

Actual Cost

Building on the above illustration, we will calculate our actual costs. Actual cost is the amount of cost you have incurred at this point, and we are told in the example that we have spent $55,000 to date. In this example, no calculation is needed.

AC = Actual Cost

AC = $55,000

Cost Variance

Cost variance (CV) is how much actual costs differ from planned costs. We derive this by calculating the difference between EV and AC. In this example, it is EV of $60,000 – AC of $55,000. A positive variance (as in this case) reflects that the project is doing better on cost than expected.

For those who are curious, the reason we use EV in this formula instead of PV is that we are calculating how much the actual costs have varied. If we used PV, it would give us the variance from our plan, but the cost variance measures actual cost variance, EV is based on actual performance, whereas PV is based on planned performance.

A positive CV is a good thing. It indicates that we are doing better on costs than we had planned. Conversely, a negative CV indicates that costs are running higher than planned.

CV = EV–AC

CV = $5,000

Schedule Variance

Schedule variance (SV) is how much our schedule differs from our plan. Where people often get confused here is that *this concept is expressed in dollars*. SV is derived by calculating the difference between EV and PV. In this example, the schedule variance is EV of $60,000 – PV of $75,000. A negative variance (as in this case) reflects that we are not performing as well as we had hoped in terms of schedule. A positive SV would indicate that the project is ahead of schedule.

$$SV = EV - PV$$

SV = –$15,000

Cost Performance Index

The cost performance index gives us an indicator as to how much we are getting for every dollar. It is derived by dividing Earned Value by the Actual Cost. In this example, Earned Value = $60,000, and our Actual Cost = $55,000. $60,000 ÷ $55,000 = 1.09.

This figure tells us that we are getting $1.09 worth of performance for every $1.00 we expended. A CPI of 1 indicates that the project is exactly on track. A closer look at the formula reveals that values of 1 or greater are good, and values less than 1 are undesirable.

$$CPI = EV \div AC$$

CPI = 1.09

Schedule Performance Index

A corollary to the cost performance index is the schedule performance index, or SPI. The schedule performance index tells us how fast the project is progressing compared to the project plan. It is derived by dividing earned value by the planned value. In this example, earned value = $60,000, and our planned value = $75,000. $60,000 ÷ $75,000 = 0.8. This tells us that the project is progressing at 80% of the pace that we expected it to, and when we look at the example, this conclusion makes sense. We had expected to lay 20 miles of sidewalk in 8 weeks. At that rate, after 2 weeks, we should have constructed 5 miles, but instead the example tells us that we had only constructed 4 miles. That equates

Earned Value

to 4÷5 performance, which is 80%. Like the cost performance index, values of 1 or greater are good, and values that are less than 1 are undesirable.

SPI = EV ÷ PV

SPI = 0.8

A common way for the cost performance and schedule performance index to be used is to track them over time. This is often displayed in the form of a graph, as illustrated below. This graph may be easily interpreted if you consider that a value of 1 indicates that the index is exactly on plan.

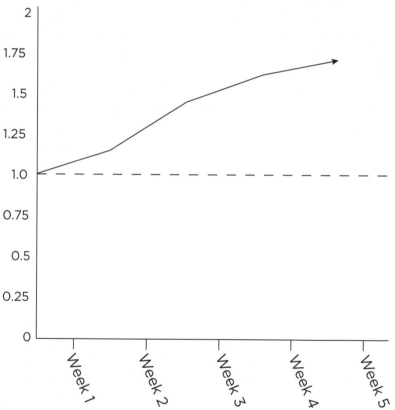

Schedule Performance Index Over Time
(same view with Cost Performance Index)

Earned Value

Estimate At Completion

Estimate at completion is the amount we expect the project to cost, based on where we are relative to cost and schedule. If that sounds confusing, think of it this way. If you know you are half way through the project, and you are currently 20% over budget, then the estimate at completion factors that variance out to the end of the project. There are many ways to calculate EAC; for the exam, the most straightforward way to calculate it is to take the BAC and divide it by our cost performance index. In this example, we expected to spend (BAC) $300,000 and our CPI is 1.09. $300,000 ÷ 1.09 = $275,229.36. This should make sense. We are doing better on costs than we had originally planned, and this value reflects that.

$$EAC = BAC \div CPI^c$$

EAC = $275,229.36

Estimate To Completion

Estimate to completion is simply how much more we expect to spend from this point forward based on what we've done so far. It can be easily backed into by taking our estimate at complete (what we expect to spend) and subtracting what we have spent so far (Actual Cost). Given the numbers above, it would be EAC of $275,229.36 - AC of $55,000 = $220,229.36. This tells us that we expect to spend $220,229.36 more, given our performance thus far.

$$ETC = EAC - AC$$

ETC = $220,229.36

Variance at Completion

Variance at completion is the difference between what we originally budgeted and what we expect to spend. A positive variance indicates that we are doing better than projected, and a negative variance indicates that we expect the project to run over on costs.

In this example, our BAC was $300,000; however, our EAC is now $275,229.36. $300,000 − $275,229.36 = $24,770.64.

Earned Value

$$VAC = BAC - EAC$$

VAC = $24,770.64

Cumulative CPI (CPIc)

Once you understand the concept of earned value, the cumulative cost performance index (expressed as CPI^c) is not as intimidating as it may first look. Recall that the regular CPI is simply $EV \div AC$, the efficiency indicator of performance during a given period of time. The CPI^c is simply all of the periodic earned value calculations added together (EV^c) and divided by all of the periodic actual cost calculations added together (AC^c).

Consider a company that took earned value measurements at monthly intervals for the past three months, as summarized in the table below.

	EV	AC
Month 1	$22,000	$13,700
Month 2	$151,000	$137,900
Month 3	$107,000	$98,400

The following table, using the same example, conveys the usefulness of CPI and CPI^c.

	EV	EV^c	AC	AC^c	CPI	CPI^c
Month 1	$22,000	$22,000	$13,700	$13,700	1.61	1.61
Month 2	$151,000	$173,000	$137,900	$151,600	1.09	1.14
Month 3	$107,000	$280,000	$98,400	$250,000	1.09	1.12

Given this information, the CPI^c would be calculated by adding up all of the earned value figures ($280,000) and dividing by the sum of the actual costs ($250,000). This yields a cumulative CPI of 1.12.

Earned Value

Cost Performance Index (CPI) was calculated by applying the formula CPI = EV÷AC, which gave us a calculation of the monthly performance. For the Cumulative Cost Performance Index (CPI^C), we applied the formula $CPI^C = EV^C \div AC^C$, which calculates the project's performance up to a point in time.

These values are useful, because the monthly CPI only provided a snapshot of your earned value performance during a certain period of time, but the cumulative CPI can show a number that factors in performance efficiency in all months up to a point in time. The cumulative CPI has been shown to be a good predictor of performance at completion, even when used very early in the project.

TCPI (also expressed as $TCPI_C$)

The To-Complete Performance Index is the performance which must be achieved on all remaining work in order to meet either financial or schedule goals. TCPI can come in two varieties: $TCPI_C$ for cost, and $TCPI_S$ for schedule. Since the PMBOK Guide only mentions the cost version, this book will focus on that index. It is calculated as follows:

$TCPI_C$ = (BAC - EV) ÷ Remaining funds. Remaining funds = BAC - AC if targeting original budget, or EAC - AC if targeting the current forecast.

As an important note, this breaks the general rule that an index of 1 or greater is good, and less than one is undesirable. Since this is looking at the performance the project would need to achieve to end on target, a lower index is good, since it means that you could underperform and still meet your target, while an index of greater than one is bad since you are essentially saying that you would need to overperform against the plan in order to meet your estimates.

Earned Value

Types of Cost

Several types of questions regarding cost may appear on the exam. It is important to understand the difference between the different types of cost presented as follows:

Cost Type	Explanation
Fixed	Costs that stay the same throughout the life of a project. An example is a piece of heavy equipment, such as a bulldozer.
Variable	Costs that vary on a project. Examples are hourly labor, and fuel for the bulldozer.
Direct	Expenses that are billed directly to the project. An example is the materials used to construct a building.
Indirect	Costs that are shared and allocated among several or all projects. An example could be a manager's salary. His people might be direct costs on a project, but his salary is overhead and would be considered an indirect cost.
Sunk	Costs that have been invested into or expended upon the project. Sunk costs are like spilt milk. If they are unrecoverable, they are to be treated as if they are irrelevant! This is difficult for many people to understand, but the statement "we've spent over 10 million dollars on this project, and we're not turning back now" is not good decision-making if the costs are unrecoverable, or "sunk."

Exercises

Example 1

You are constructing 6 additional rooms on an office building. Each of the six rooms is identical, the projected cost for the project is $100,000, and construction is expected to take 5 weeks.

At the end of the 2nd week, you have spent $17,500 per room and have finished 2 rooms; you are ready to begin on the 3rd.

1. **Based on the information provided in the example above, fill in the values for the following table:**

	Value
Budgeted At Completion	
Planned Value	
Earned Value	
Actual Cost	
Cost Variance	
Schedule Variance	
Cost Performance Index	
Schedule Performance Index	
Estimated At Completion	
Estimated To Completion	
Variance At Completion	
To-Complete Performance Index (cost)	

2. **Is the project ahead of or behind schedule?**

3. **Is the project going to be completed over or under budget?**

Example 2

Here is another example to test your understanding of these concepts.

You have planned for a project to write a software application to take 1 year. The costs on this project are budgeted at $12,500 per month.

Six months into the project, you find that the software application is 50% completed, and you have spent $70,000.

4. **Based on the information provided, fill in the values for the following table:**

	Value
Budgeted At Completion	
Planned Value	
Earned Value	
Actual Cost	
Cost Variance	
Schedule Variance	
Cost Performance Index	
Schedule Performance Index	
Estimated At Completion	
Estimated To Completion	
Variance At Completion	
To-Complete Performance Index (cost)	

5. **Is the project ahead of or behind schedule?**

6. **Is the project going to be completed over or under budget?**

7. **For each column, circle the one cell that shows the most desirable value in that column.** (Note that some of these attributes are covered in Chapter 5 – Project Scope Management.)

IRR	SPI	CPI	NPV	Payback Period	BCR	ROI	TCPI$_C$
22%	1	.5	$25,000	16 mos	2	9%	.5
0%	0	1	$95,000	2 yrs	1.5	12%	.9
12%	.8	1.2	$50,000	16 wks	1	-2%	1
-3%	1.2	1.15	$71,000	25 mos	.2	3%	2

8. **Project X was expected to take four months and cost $70,000 per month. At the end of month one, the project was 20% complete, and had spent $89,000. At the end of month two, it was 40% complete and had spent $151,000. What is the cumulative CPI for Project X at the end of month two?**

Answers to Exercises

1. **Your answers should look like these:**

	Value
Budgeted At Completion	$100,000
Planned Value	$40,000.00
Earned Value	$33,333.33
Actual Cost	$35,000.00
Cost Variance	-$1,666.67
Schedule Variance	-$6,666.67
Cost Performance Index	0.95
Schedule Performance Index	0.83
Estimated At Completion	$105,263.15
Estimated To Completion	$70,263.15
Variance At Completion	-$5,263.15
To Complete Performance Index (cost)	1.03

- **BAC = $100,000.00**
- **PV = 2 weeks ÷ 5 weeks = 40% complete × 100,000 = $40,000**
- **EV = 2 rooms ÷ 6 rooms = 33.3% complete × 100,000 = $33,333.33**
- **AC = $17,500 per room × 2 rooms = $35,000**
- **CV = (EV) $33,333.33 – (AC) $35,000.00 = -$1,666.67**
- **SV = (EV) $33,333.33 – (PV) $40,000.00 = -$6,666.67**
- **CPI = (EV) $33,333.33 ÷ (AC) $35,000.00 = 0.95**
- **SPI = (EV) $33,333.33 ÷ (PV) $40,000.00 = 0.83**
- **EAC = (BAC) $100,000.00 ÷ (CPI) 0.95 = $105,263.15**
- **ETC = (EAC) $105,263.15 – (AC) $35,000.00 = $70,263.15**
- **VAC = (BAC) $100,000.00 – (EAC) $105,263.15 = –$5,263.15**
- **$TCPI_c$ = ((BAC) $100,000.00 – (EV) $33,333.33) ((BAC) $100,000.00 – (AC) $35,000) = 1.03**

2. **Is the project ahead of or behind schedule?**

   The project is behind schedule. The easiest way to determine this is by looking at the SPI. Since it is less than 1, we can determine that the project is not doing well in terms of the schedule.

3. **Is the project going to be completed over or under budget?**

   There are two ways to see that the project is going to run over budget. First, the CPI is less than 1. Second, the VAC is negative.

   Check your answers against the values in the following table:

	Value
Budgeted At Completion	$150,000.00
Planned Value	$75,000.00
Earned Value	$75,000.00
Actual Cost	$70,000.00
Cost Variance	$5,000.00
Schedule Variance	$0
Cost Performance Index	1.07
Schedule Performance Index	1.0
Estimated At Completion	$140,186.91
Estimated To Completion	$70,186.91
Variance At Completion	$9,813.09
To Complete Performance Index (cost)	0.94

Earned Value Exercises

- BAC = $150,000.00
- PV = 6 months ÷ 12 months = 50% complete X 150,000 = $75,000
- EV = Project is 50% complete X 150,000.00 = $75,000.00
- AC = $70,000 .00
- CV = (EV) $75,000.00 – (AC) $70,000.00 = $5,000.00
- SV = (EV) $75,000.00 – (PV) $75,000.00 = $0
- CPI = (EV) $75,000.00 ÷ (AC) $70,000.00 = 1.07
- SPI = (EV) $75,000.00 ÷ (PV) $75,000.00 = 1
- EAC = (BAC) $150,000.00 ÷ (CPI) 1.07 = $140,186.91
- ETC = (EAC) $140,186.91 – (AC) $70,000.00 = $70,186.91
- VAC = (BAC) $150,000.00 – (EAC) $140,186.91 = $9,813.09
- TCPIc = ((BAC) $150,000.00 – (EV) $75,000) (BAC) $150,000 – (AC) $70,000) = 0.94

4. **Is the project ahead of or behind schedule?**
This would be classified as a "trick" question, as neither answer is correct. Since the SPI is 1, we can see that the project is exactly on schedule.

5. **Is the project going to be completed over or under budget?**
The project is projected to finish ahead of (under) budget, due to the cost performance index being greater than 1.

6. The most desirable project attributes for each column are shaded in the chart below. Note that some of these formulas came from Chapter 4, Scope Management. If you found the $TCPI_c$ answer confusing, remember that TCPI breaks the index rule where the larger number is usually more desirable. TCPI looks forward, so with a $TCPI_c$ of .5, we are saying that the project could spend at twice the projected rate from this point until the end and still end on budget.

IRR	SPI	CPI	NPV	Payback Period	BCR	ROI	$TCPI_c$
22%	1	.5	$25,000	16 mos	2	9%	.5
0%	0	1	$95,000	2 yrs	1.5	12%	.9
12%	.8	1.2	$50,000	16 wks	1	Ð2%	1
Ð3%	1.2	1.15	$71,000	25 mos	.2	3%	2

7. Did you notice that for most of these measurements, the bigger value is the best one? That is true for all except for the payback period, where you want the shortest time to recoup project costs, and for $TCPI_c$ where smaller numbers are better.

8. If you got this one, give yourself a big pat on the back! In order to answer it, you first had to calculate the earned value for months one and two.
Month 1 EV = 0.2 × $280,000 = $56,000
Month 2 EV = 0.2 × $280,000 = $56,000
Month 2 AC = $151,000

After getting these values, the CPI^C is a snap. It is simply the sum of the earned value numbers divided by the sum of the actual costs. Since you already know the sum of the actual costs is $151,000, all you have to do is add the earned values together and divide. This yields $112,000 ÷ $151,000 = a cumulative CPI (CPI^C) of 0.74.

IMPORTANT

In addition to this quiz, use your Key to InSite, found on the inside back cover of this book, to access additional content, including new exam questions, expanded content, and simulated PMP exams. If your book did not come with a Key to InSite on the inside back cover, it may not be authentic. If you do not have a Key to InSite, you may purchase one at *insite.velociteach.com*.

Cost Management Questions

Note: Some of these questions are based on material covered in previous chapters as well as this chapter.

1. 1. **Your schedule projected that you would reach 50% completion today on a road construction project that is paving 32 miles of new highway. Every 4 miles is scheduled to cost $5,000,000. Today, in your status meeting, you announced that you had completed 20 miles of the highway at a cost of $18,000,000. What is your Planned Value?**

    A. $12,800,000.

    B. $18,000,000.

    C. $20,000,000.

    D. $40,000,000.

2. **If the CPI is 0.1, this indicates:**

    A. The project is performing extremely poorly on cost.

    B. The project is costing 10% over what was expected.

    C. The project is only costing 90% of what was expected.

    D. The project is performing extremely well on cost.

3. **Activity cost estimates are used as an input into which process?**

    A. Estimate Costs.

    B. Determine Budget.

    C. Analyze Costs.

    D. Control Costs.

4. **Based on the following Benefit Cost Ratios, which project would be the best one to select?**

   A. BCR = −1.

   B. BCR = 0.

   C. BCR = 1.

   D. BCR = 2.

5. **The difference between present value and net present value is:**

   A. Present value is expressed as an interest rate, while net present value is expressed as a dollar figure.

   B. Present value is a measure of the actual present value, while net present value measures expected present value.

   C. Present value does not factor in costs.

   D. Present value is more accurate.

6. **Kayla is reviewing the budget and spending to ensure that she has enough money to pay vendors for the next projected phase. The CFO of the company has provided extra funds to allow for contingencies, but Kayla is not yet certain that it is enough. Which process is Kayla most likely performing?**

   A. Plan Cost Management.

   B. Estimate Costs.

   C. Analyze Budget.

   D. Control Costs.

7. **Your best cost estimate for an activity is $200,000, but the estimate you document has a range of $100,000 to $400,000. This ranged estimate represents a(n):**

   A. Cost estimate.

   B. Budgeted estimate.

   C. Order of magnitude estimate.

   D. Variable estimate.

8. **Which of the following process sequences is correct?**

    A.   Create WBS, then Determine Budget, then Estimate Costs.

    B.   Create WBS, then Estimate Costs, then Determine Budget.

    C.   Determine Budget, then Estimate Costs, then Create WBS.

    D.   Estimate Costs, then Budget Costs, then Create WBS.

9. **One of your team members makes a change to the budget with your approval. In what process is he engaged?**

    A.   Plan Costs.

    B.   Estimate Costs.

    C.   Cost Management.

    D.   Control Costs.

10. **After measuring expected project benefits, management has four projects from which to choose. Project 1 has a net present value of $100,000 and will cost $50,000. Project 2 has a net present value of $200,000 and will cost $75,000. Project 3 has a net present value of $500,000 and will cost $400,000. Project 4 has a net present value of $125,000 and will cost $25,000. Which project would be BEST?**

    A.   Project 1.

    B.   Project 2.

    C.   Project 3.

    D.   Project 4.

11. **Your project office has purchased a site license for a computerized tool that assists in the task of cost estimating on a very large construction project for a downtown skyscraper. This tool asks you for specific characteristics about the project and then provides estimating guidance based on materials, construction techniques, historical information, and industry practices. This tool is an example of:**

    A.   Bottom-up estimating.

    B.   Parametric modeling.

    C.   Analogous estimating.

    D.   Activity duration estimating.

12. **If the Earned Value of a project on January 16 was $127,253, the Budgeted at Completion was $275,000, and the Schedule Performance Index was 0.77, how much work was expected to have been completed at that point?**

   A. $97,985

   B. $127,253

   C. $165,264

   D. $211,750

13. **You are managing a project that is part of a large construction program. During the execution of your project you are alerted that the construction of a foundation is expected to experience a serious cost overrun. What would be your FIRST course of action?**

   A. Evaluate the cause and size of the overrun.

   B. Halt execution until the problem is solved.

   C. Contact the program manager to see if additional funds may be released.

   D. Determine if you have sufficient budget reserves to cover the cost overrun.

14. **If earned value = $10,000, planned value = $8,000, and actual cost = $3,000, what is the schedule variance?**

   A. −$2,000

   B. $2,000

   C. $5,000

   D. $-5,000

15. **Estimate to completion indicates:**

   A. The total projected amount that will be spent, based on past performance.

   B. The projected remaining amount that will be spent, based on past performance.

   C. The difference between what was budgeted and what is expected to be spent.

   D. The original planned completion cost minus the costs incurred to date.

16. The project team has been working significant overtime on a project for the past three months. The sponsor wants to know what the CPI will need to be from this point forward in order to meet original cost expectations. You know that at this point the Earned Value is $1,124,767, the total budget is $3,111,845, the Planned Value is $950,000, and the project has spent $1,000,975. What should you tell the sponsor?

A.   0.84

B.   0.94

C.   1.0

D.   1.21

17. If a project has a CPI of .95 and an SPI of 1.01, this indicates:

A.   The project is progressing slower and costing more than planned.

B.   The project is progressing slower and costing less than planned.

C.   The project is progressing faster and costing more than planned.

D.   The project is progressing faster and costing less than planned.

18. The best definition of Earned Value is:

A.   The measure of work performed expressed in terms of the budget authorized to perform that work.

B.   Actual % Complete X the BAC.

C.   The value of the project at a point in time expressed in terms of the work performed.

D.   Managing project performance in order to achieve expected results.

19. Project A would yield $100,000 in benefit. Project B would yield $250,000 in benefit. Because of limited resources, your company can perform only one of these. They elect to perform Project B because of the higher benefit. What is the opportunity cost of performing Project B?

A.   −$150,000.

B. $150,000.

C.   −$100,000.

D. $100,000.

20. **As a project manager, your BEST use of the project cost baseline would be to:**

    A.   Measure and monitor cost performance on the project.

    B.   Track approved changes.

    C.   Calculate team performance bonuses.

    D.   Measure and report on variable project costs.

21. **The value of all work that has been completed so far is:**

    A.   Earned value.

    B.   Estimate at complete.

    C.   Actual cost.

    D.   Planned value.

22. **If the EAC for a project is $201,500, the ETC is $25,010, the SPI is 1.0, and the CPIc is 1.06, what is the BAC?**

    A.   23,594.

    B.   190,094.

    C.   201,500.

    D.   213,590.

23. **If you have a schedule variance of $500, this would indicate:**

    A.   Planned value is less than earned value.

    B.   Earned value is less than the estimate at completion.

    C.   Actual cost is less than earned value.

    D.   The ratio of earned value to planned value is 5:1.

24. **If budgeted at complete = $500, estimate to complete = $400, earned value = $100, and actual cost = $100, what is the estimate at complete?**

    A. $0.

    B. $150.

    C. $350.

    D. $500.

25. **You have spent $322,168 on your project to date. The program manager wants to know why costs have been running so high. You explain that the resource cost has been greater than expected and should level out over the next six months. What does the $322,168 represent to the program manager?**

A. Earned value.

B. Actual cost.

C. Planned value.

D. Cost performance index.

Answers to Cost Management Questions

1. **C.** Planned Value is calculated by multiplying the Budgeted At Completion by planned % complete. Our cost per mile is planned at $1,250,000 ($5,000,000 ÷ 4 miles), and our Budgeted At Completion is 32 miles x 1,250,000/mile = $40,000,000. We planned to be 50% complete. Therefore, $40,000,000 x .50 = $20,000,000.

2. **A.** Understanding the concepts behind the earned value calculations is important for the exam and will help you with questions like this one. In this question, the terrible cost performance index indicates that we are getting ten cents of value for every dollar we spent; thus the project is doing very poorly on cost performance.

3. **B.** Determine Budget takes the activity cost estimates and uses them (along with other inputs) to create a budget. 'A' is incorrect because Estimate Costs is the process that creates the activity cost estimates, so it stands to reason that they would be an output and not an input. 'C' sounds like a decent guess, but it is not a real process. 'D' is incorrect because the process of Control Costs is not concerned with just the individual activity cost estimates. Instead, it uses inputs of the cost baseline.

4. **D.** With Benefit Cost Ratios, the bigger the better! BCR is calculated as benefit ÷ cost, so the more benefit, and the less cost, the higher the number.

5. **C.** There is a difference between present value and net present value. Present value tells the expected value of the project in today's dollars. Net present value is the same thing, but it subtracts the costs after calculating the present value.

6. **D.** Kayla is performing reserve analysis. Knowing that would have narrowed the choice down to two potential answers 'B' and 'D'. To decide which one, look at what she is doing and why she is doing it. She is making sure that she has enough money, which is not an estimating activity, which eliminates 'B'. It is more of a monitoring and controlling activity. Choice 'C' is not a real process, and 'A' would have been performed much earlier and is not descriptive of what Kayla is doing. 'D' emerges

as the best choice since she is comparing the plan (budget) with actual performance (spending). This is classic for a monitoring and controlling process, and Control Costs is the only monitoring and controlling process in the list of choices.

7. **C.** Order of magnitude estimates are −50% to +100%. In this example, $100,000 and $400,000 are −50% to +100% of $200,000.

8. **B.** This question may not look like it is about inputs and outputs, but it actually is. Create WBS is performed first out of the three processes, and the output is the Work Breakdown Structure (WBS). The WBS is used as an input for the next process of the three, Estimate Costs, where the costs of the activities are estimated and aggregated back to the WBS. Finally, the output of that process, the Activity Cost Estimates, is used as an input into Cost Budgeting, which occurs last out of the three processes listed. By understanding how the outputs of one process **become the inputs into** another, it becomes simpler to understand the logical order of many of these processes.

9. **D.** The main clue here is "change." If they are making approved changes, they are in a control process. 'A' is not a real process. 'B' is incorrect since Estimate Costs is the process where the original estimates are developed and not where they are updated. 'C' is the knowledge area (careful not to get these confused with processes).

10. **C.** This one was very tricky! Net present value already has costs factored in, so they can be ignored here. The net present value is the only value you need to consider, and bigger is better!

11. **B.** This is an example of parametric modeling. Parametric modeling is common in some industries, where you can describe the project in detail, and the modeling tool will help provide estimates based on historical information, industry standards, etc.

12. **C.** The first step in answering any question is to determine what is being asked. In this case, the question asked "how much work was expected to have been completed" at a point in time. That is the definition of Planned Value (PV). In most scenarios, PV is given to you in order to calculate something else, but in this case you have to calculate it.

One way to do this using the information we have is to use the formula for SPI.

SPI = EV ÷ PV. Using simple algebra, we can change it around to also say that PV= EV ÷ SPI, or PV = $127,253 ÷ 0.77 = $165,264.

We can see that the project is behind schedule at this point and has not earned as much value as was expected.

The Budgeted at Completion (BAC) is not of any use here since we don't know when the project was supposed to be completed or other helpful variables.

13.   **A.** This question illustrates one of the biggest exam biases. Your job as a project manager is almost always to evaluate and understand first. Know what you are dealing with before you take action, and don't just accept anyone's word for it. Verify the information yourself!

14.   **B.** Schedule Variance is calculated as EV–PV. In this example, $10,000 – $8,000 = $2,000.

15.   **B.** The Estimate To Completion is what we expect to spend from this point forward, based on our performance thus far.

16.   **B.** 0.94. The sponsor is asking for the To-Complete Performance Index for cost (TCPIc). This scenario was a little bit tricky. Just because the team has been working overtime does not necessarily mean that they are behind schedule or over budget. In this situation they have recently been working overtime and are still under budget.

To calculate the TCPIc, we'll use the standard formula:

TCPIc = (BAC – EV) ÷ Remaining funds.

The BAC is given as the total budget in this question and is $3,111,845. The EV is also given at $1,124,767. Now we have to calculate remaining funds, which is the original budget minus actual costs. We know that the original budget was $3,111,845 and the project has incurred actual costs so far of $1,000,975, which leaves $2,110,870 remaining funds. Now it becomes a matter of plugging numbers into the formula.

TCPIc = (BAC – EV) ÷ Remaining Funds

TCPIc = ($3,111,845 - $1,124,767) ÷ $2,110,870

TCPIc = $1,987,078 ÷ $2,110,870

TCPIc = 0.94

Cost Management Answers

This value of 0.94 means that the project could run somewhat over budget for the remainder of the time and still finish on target.

17.   **C.** Did the wording trip you up on this one? Make sure you read the questions and answers carefully since things were switched around on this one. A schedule performance index greater than 1 means that the project is progressing faster than planned. A cost performance index that is less than 1 means that the project is costing more than planned. Therefore choice 'C' is the only one that fits.

18.   **A.** This is the definition of Earned Value. 'B' is a formula for Earned Value, but it is not the definition. 'C' does not work since Earned Value is about the value earned and not just the costs expended. For example, it is possible to expend a lot of cost, materials, and manpower and earn very little value. 'D' is close to a definition of earned value management (EVM), but it is too generic and does not match the definition of Earned Value.

19.   **D.** Opportunity cost is simply how much benefit you are passing up. In this case, by choosing project B. You are foregoing $100,000 in expected benefit from project A, and that $100,000 represents the opportunity cost.

20.   **A.** The cost baseline is used to track cost performance based on the original plan plus approved changes.

21.   **A.** Earned value is defined as the value of all work completed to this point.

22.   **D.** The formula for EAC is EAC = BAC ÷ CPIc. There is quite a bit of information here, but the only numbers that are relevant are the EAC and the CPIc. In this case we can use simple algebra to restate the formula as BAC = EAC × CPI, or BAC = $21,3590, which is answer 'D'.

23.   **A.** This is another tricky question because of the way it is worded. Schedule variance is calculated as earned value – planned value. In this case, schedule variance could only be positive if earned value is greater than planned value (or stated otherwise, if planned value is less than earned value). 'A' is the only choice that has to be true.

24.   **D.** The estimate at complete is what we expect to have spent at the end of the project. It is calculated by taking our budgeted at complete and dividing it by our cost performance index. Step 1

is to calculate our cost performance index. It is earned value ÷ actual cost, and in this case, it equals 1. Budgeted at complete is $500, and $500 ÷ 1 = $500. Therefore, 'D' is the correct answer, indicating that we are progressing exactly as planned. Note that there are many ways to calculate the EAC, and not all of them agree perfectly. One other common way is EAC = AC + ETC, which yields the same answer of $500 for this example.

25.   **B.** Look at the first sentence "You have spent $322,168..." Actual Cost is what you have spent to date on the project.

8 Quality Management

Difficulty	Memorization	Exam Importance
MEDIUM	MEDIUM	HIGH

Philosophy

The philosophy of quality, covered in this chapter, is derived from several leading quality theories, including TQM, ISO-9000, Six Sigma, and others. We will look at each of these theories in terms of the tools and techniques they provide.

The philosophy of quality, contained in the three processes of quality management, is also a very proactive approach. Whereas early theories on quality relied heavily on inspection, current thinking is focused on prevention over inspection. This evolution of thought is based on the fact that it costs more to fix an error than it does to prevent one.

The responsibility of quality lies heavily with the project manager. Everyone on the team has an important contribution to make to project quality; however, it is management's responsibility to provide the resources to make quality happen, and the project manager is ultimately responsible and accountable for the quality of the project.

The process, as it relates to quality, is perhaps more important here than most other places. Plan Quality Management, Perform Quality Assurance, and Control Quality map closely to the Plan-Do-Check-Act cycle as described by

The processes of Project Quality Management with their primary outputs

Quality Management

Plan Quality Management
Quality Management Plan
Quality Metrics
Quality Checklists

Perform Quality Assurance
Change Requests

Control Quality
Quality Control Measurements
Validated Changes
Verified Deliverables

Deming, and you should expect that several questions on the exam will rely heavily on your understanding of how quality activities flow and connect.

It is also important to understand that some of the investment in quality is usually borne by the organization since it would be far too expensive for each project to have its own quality program. An example would be a company investing in a site license for a software testing product that can be used across numerous projects.

Importance

Project quality management is one of the slimmer chapters, but it is of high importance on the exam. You should expect to see several exam questions that will relate directly to this chapter, so it will be necessary to become acquainted with the terms and theories as described below. Then reread this chapter to ensure that you have mastered the topic.

In real world practice, quality formulas abound; however, you do not need to memorize or apply them here. This chapter focuses on the processes, concepts and terms.

Some parts of this topic will be revisited in later chapters in order to show how quality fits into the overall project management context.

Preparation

The quality processes, tools and techniques, and outputs found in this chapter must be learned and understood. You should expect to see questions on the exam that relate directly to these concepts. Special attention will be paid to the key quality theories that show up on the exam, as well as terminology that you need to know.

Pay careful attention to the differences between Plan Quality Management, Perform Quality Assurance, and Control Quality. These distinctions are a tricky area for many people on the exam.

Definition of Quality

The definition of quality you should know for the exam is "the degree to which a set of inherent characteristics fulfills requirements." It is also important to realize that the requirements or needs of the project may be stated or implied. This means that a product may be low-grade and high-quality at the same time if the requirements call for a low-grade product. If you find this concept confusing, this chapter should help clear things up and get you ready for the exam.

Quality Management Processes

There are only three processes within project quality management, as listed in the table below. In the framework, these processes touch three process groups: planning (Plan Quality Management), executing (Perform Quality Assurance), and monitoring & controlling (Control Quality).

Process Group	Quality Management Process
Initiating	(none)
Planning	Plan Quality Management
Executing	Perform Quality Assurance
Monitoring & Controlling	Control Quality
Closing	(none)

The primary outputs associated with the three quality management processes are shown in the table below.

Process	Primary Outputs
Plan Quality Management	Quality management plan Quality metrics Quality checklists
Perform Quality Assurance	Change requests
Control Quality	Quality control measurements Validated changes Verified deliverables

Quality Terms and Philosophies

 All of these quality management terms are important for the exam.

Kev Fact

Total Quality Management (TQM)

A quality theory popularized after World War II that states that everyone in the company is responsible for quality and is able to make a difference in the ultimate quality of the product. TQM applies to improvements in processes and in results. TQM also includes statistical process control.

TQM shifts the primary quality focus away from the product that is produced and looks instead at the underlying process of how it was produced.

In other words, how something is produced becomes more important than what is actually produced.

Continuous Improvement

Also known as "Kaizen," from the Japanese management term. A philosophy that stresses constant process improvement, in the form of small changes in products or services.

Kaizen

(See Continuous Improvement)

Just-In-Time (JIT)

A manufacturing method that brings inventory down to zero (or near zero) levels. It forces a focus on quality, since there is no excess inventory on hand to waste.

ISO 9000

Part of the Organization for International Standards to ensure that companies document what they do and do what they document.

ISO 9000 is not directly attributable to higher quality, but may be an important component of Perform Quality Assurance, since it ensures that an organization follows their processes.

Statistical Independence

When the outcomes of two processes are not linked together or dependent upon each other, they are statistically independent. Rolling a six on a die the first time neither increases nor decreases the chance that you will roll a six the second time. Therefore, the two rolls would be statistically independent.

Mutually Exclusive

A statistical term that states that one choice excludes the others. For example, painting a house yellow and painting it blue or white are mutually exclusive events.

Standard Deviation

The concept of standard deviation is an important one to understand for the exam. Standard deviation is a statistical calculation used to measure and describe how a set of data is organized. The following graphic of a standard bell curve illustrates standard deviation.

The standard deviation, represented by the Greek symbol σ, is calculated first by averaging all data points to get the mean, then calculating the difference between each data point and the mean, squaring each of the differences, and dividing the sum of the squared differences by the number of data points minus one. Finally, take the square root of that number, and you have the standard deviation of the data set. If the data set is "normally distributed," as it is in the following chart, the following statistics will be true:

- 68.25% of the data points (or values) will fall within 1 σ from the mean.

- 95.46% of the values will fall within 2 σ from the mean.

- 99.73% of the values will fall within 3 σ from the mean.

- 99.99966% of the values will fall within 6 σ from the mean.

The standard deviation may be used in a few different ways in quality. For instance, the higher your standard deviation, the more diverse your data points are. It is also used to set quality levels (see the Six Sigma topic later in this chapter), and to set control limits to determine if a process is in control (see the Control Charts topic later in this chapter).

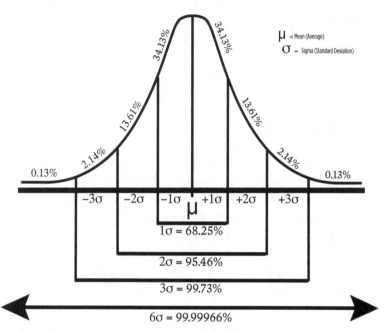

Even though you should not expect to have to perform standard deviation calculations for the exam, you will likely see questions related to the application of the standard deviation. The more you understand about this concept, the more prepared you will be for the exam.

Six Sigma

Six Sigma is a popular philosophy of quality management that focuses on achieving very high levels of quality by controlling the process and reducing defects (a defect is defined as anything that does not meet the customer's quality standards).

As you will remember from the section on standard deviation, a σ (sigma) is defined as 1 standard deviation from the mean. At the level of one sigma quality, 68.25% of all outputs will meet quality standards.

Quality Terms

At the three sigma quality level, that number jumps to 99.73% of all outputs that meet quality standards. At the six sigma level, the number is 99.99966% of all outputs that meet quality standards. This means that when quality reaches six sigma standards, the results will be such that only 3.4 out of every 1,000,000 outputs do not meet quality standards.

Six sigma quality strives to make the overwhelming majority of the bell curve fall consistently within customer quality limits.

Six sigma puts a primary focus on quantifying, measuring, and controlling the quality of products, services, and results. It is based on the underlying theory that anything will vary if measured to a fine enough level. The goal is to refine the process so that human error and outside influence no longer exist, and any remaining variations are completely random.

If done properly, the statistical outcome should follow the bell curve illustrated previously under the topic of standard deviation. The goal is to make six standard deviations (sigmas) of the outputs fall within the customer's quality limits.

If this seems like a lot of information, the most important things to know for the exam are that six sigma is a quality management philosophy that sets very high standards for quality, one sigma quality is the lowest quality level, allowing 317,500 defects per 1,000,000 outputs, three sigma quality is higher, allowing 2,700 defects per 1,000,000, and six sigma quality is the highest of these, allowing only 3.4 defects per 1,000,000.

Also know that six sigma quality levels may not be high enough for all projects or all industries. For instance, the pharmaceutical industry, the airline industry, and power utilities typically strive for higher levels of quality than six sigma would specify in some areas of their operations.

Prevention vs. Inspection

Prevention is simply keeping defects from occurring, while inspection is about catching the errors that have occurred before they impact others outside the project.

Modern project management strongly favors prevention over inspection.

Quality Terms

Attribute Sampling vs. Variable Sampling

Attribute sampling is binary; either a work result conforms to quality or it does not. Variable sampling, on the other hand, measures how well something conforms to quality. Consider, for example, a production facility making prescription drugs. Using attribute sampling, they would define tolerances, a batch of product would be tested, and it would either pass or fail that inspection. Using variable sampling, however, the batch of product would be rated on a continuous scale (perhaps on parts per million) that showed how well the batch conformed to ideal quality.

Special Causes vs. Common Causes

Within the topic of statistical process control (see Control Charts later in this chapter), there is a concept of special causes and common causes.

Special causes are typically considered unusual and preventable, whereas common causes are normal. For instance, if your manufacturing process produced 250 defects per 1,000,000 due to assembly errors, that might be considered a special cause, whereas if your manufacturing process produced one defect in a million due to bad raw materials, that might be considered a common cause. In general, special causes are considered preventable by process improvement, while common causes are generally accepted.

Tolerances vs. Control Limits

Tolerances deal with the limits your project has set for product acceptance. For instance, you may specify that any product will be accepted if it weighs between 12 and 15 grams. Those weights would represent your tolerances for weight. Control limits, on the other hand, are a more complex concept. Typically, control limits are set at three standard deviations above and below the mean. As long as your results fall within the control limits, your process is considered to be in control.

Control limits are discussed further under the topic of Control Charts, covered later in this chapter.

Quality Terms

If that explanation still leaves you scratching your head, consider that tolerances focus on whether the product is acceptable, while control limits focus on whether the process itself is acceptable.

Planning

Plan Quality Management

What it is:

Plan Quality Management is named appropriately. It is the process where the project team identifies what the quality specifications are for this project and how these specifications will be met.

Why it is important:

As stated earlier in this chapter, quality is "planned in" from the start, and not "inspected in" after the product has been constructed. Plan Quality Management is the process where this planning is performed to make sure that the resulting product is of acceptable quality.

When it is performed:

Plan Quality Management begins early in the planning phase of the project. In fact, it typically is performed concurrently with other planning processes and the development of the project management plan.

The reason Plan Quality Management is performed early in project planning is that decisions made about quality can have a significant impact on other decisions such as scope, time, cost, and risk.

How it works:

Inputs

Project Management Plan

The project management plan is brought into Plan Quality Management, with particular attention paid to the three baselines, covered here.

Scope Baseline

Most project management practitioners view scope and quality as inseparable, which is why the scope baseline is so important to Plan Quality Management. The scope baseline defines the full project requirements, and it also specifies the acceptance criteria for these requirements.

Cost Baseline

Since quality and scope are tightly linked, the cost baseline is also important. Changes to the scope will need to be evaluated against the budget and the schedule.

Schedule Baseline

The schedule baseline is important for the same reasons as the cost performance baseline (see previous point).

Stakeholder Register

The purpose of the stakeholder register is to identify stakeholders who may have specific needs, interests, or expertise related to the project. In this case there may be stakeholders with expertise in quality, or who work in a quality-related department, who should be involved in the Plan Quality Management process.

Risk Register

Quality can be a very significant area of project risk. For example, it may be identified that there may be issues related to customer acceptance or satisfaction if quality is not satisfied. The risk register will list all of the identified areas of risk related to quality and which may affect this process.

Requirements Documentation

The requirements are very closely tied to quality. Since quality is "planned in" from the beginning of the project, the requirements must be thoroughly understood and carefully considered.

Enterprise Environ. Factors — See Ch. 2, Common Inputs

Organizational Process Assets

Assets such as quality management plans from previous projects should be considered and used as part of the project plan. Also, the performing organization's quality policy should be brought into this process. The quality policy is usually brief and defines the performing organization's attitudes about quality across all projects. It must be considered if it exists. If it does not exist, the project team should write one for this project.

Tools

Kev Fact

Cost-Benefit Analysis

Quality can be expensive to achieve; however, there is a golden rule in quality that all benefits of quality activities must outweigh the costs.

No activities should be performed that cost more (or even the same) as the expected benefits. These benefits potentially include acceptance, less rework, and overall lower costs.

Kev Fact

Cost of Quality

The technique of evaluating the cost of quality (often abbreviated as COQ) looks at all of the costs that will be realized in order to achieve quality. The costs of items that do not conform to quality are known as "cost of poor quality," often abbreviated as CoPQ.

Kev Fact

Seven Basic Quality Tools

There are seven quality tools that are commonly used to measure and implement quality. They are:

1. Cause-and-Effect Diagrams

Also called Ishikawa or fishbone diagrams, these charts are used to help identify root causes. Quality problems are traced back to their root causes so that prevention may be used instead of inspection.

2. Flowcharting

Flowcharts show how various components relate in a system. Flowcharting can be used to predict where quality problems may happen. In addition to traditional flow charts, cause-and-effect diagrams, described above, are a type of flowcharting.

3. Checksheets

Checksheets are used to keep running totals of quality-related incidents and facts. They are useful to help gather totals for how often situations occur so that they may be analyzed later.

Plan Quality Management

4. Pareto Diagrams

The Pareto chart is a histogram showing defects ranked from greatest to least. It is used to focus energy on the problems most likely to change results.

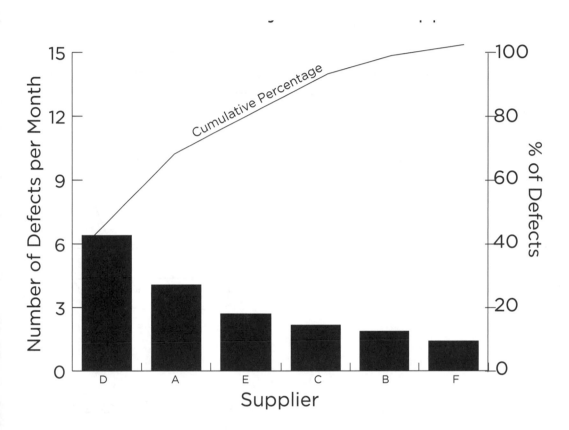

A Pareto chart, showing problems ranked from greatest to least

Pareto diagrams are based on Pareto's Law, which is also known as the 80/20 rule. This rule states that 80% of the problems come from 20% of the causes, but there are variations on this theme. For the exam, know that Pareto's Law is also known as the 80/20 rule and that a Pareto chart is used to help determine the few root causes behind the majority of the problems on a project

Plan Quality Management

5. Histograms

Histograms are column charts that allow stakeholders to visualize the distribution of data. Each column in a histogram represents a frequency of occurrences.

6. Control Charts

Control charts are part of a set of quality practices known as Statistical Process Control. If a process is statistically "in control,"

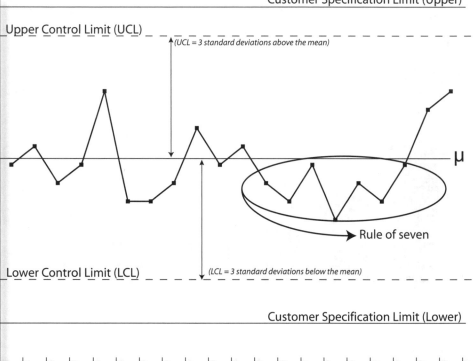

Customer Specification Limit (Upper)

Upper Control Limit (UCL)

(UCL = 3 standard deviations above the mean)

μ

Rule of seven

Lower Control Limit (LCL)

(LCL = 3 standard deviations below the mean)

Customer Specification Limit (Lower)

it does not need to be corrected. If it is "out of control," then there are sufficient variations in results to the point where production is generally stopped until it can be brought back statistically in line. A control chart is one way of depicting variations and determining whether or not the process is in control.

A sample control chart

Control charts graph the results of a process to show whether or not they are in control. The *mean* of all of the data points is represented by a line drawn through the average of all data points on the chart. The upper and lower control limits are set at three standard deviations above and below mean.

If measurements fall outside of the control limits, then the process is said to be out of control. The assignable cause should then be investigated and determined.

An interesting rule that is used with control charts is known as the rule of seven. It states that if seven or more consecutive data points fall on one side of the mean, they should be investigated. This is true even if the seven data points are within the control limits.

Some control charts, especially those used in a manufacturing environment, represent the upper and lower limits of a customer's specification for quality as lines on the control chart. Everything between those lines would be considered within the customer's

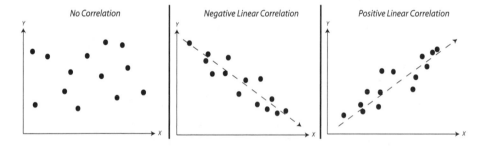

quality specification.

7. Scatter Diagrams

Scatter diagrams are a particularly powerful tool for spotting trends in data. Consider the following three scatter diagrams:

Three scatter diagrams indicating varying correlations

Scatter diagrams are made using two variables (a dependent variable and an independent variable). What you are looking for is correlation between the two variables. Considering the previous examples, suppose that the horizontal, or X axis, represented hours of study, which is your independent variable. The vertical, or Y axis, represented your score on the exam, which is the dependent variable. In that case, the third graph would make sense, since the more people studied, the higher their scores tended to be. When you see a graph that looks like the second graph, where the more the person studied, the lower their score, you might deduce that the book they are reading is actually having a negative effect. The first example graph might lead you to deduce that the study material being used has no effect at all and therefore there is no correlation.

Benchmarking

The technique of benchmarking is where a project's quality standards are compared to those of other projects that will serve as a basis for comparison. These other projects may be from the industry, such as an automaker setting quality standards based on those of other automobiles in their class, or it may be based on projects previously executed by the performing organization.

Design of Experiments

The technique of design of experiments, often abbreviated as DOE, is an important technique in Plan Quality Management. It uses data analysis to determine optimal conditions. For instance, rather than conducting a series of individual trials, an information technology project may use design of experiments analysis and optimize hardware and bandwidth needed to run an Internet-based application, finding the optimal match of system response time and overall cost.

Statistical Sampling

Statistical sampling is a powerful tool where a random sample is selected instead of measuring the entire population. By sampling properly, you can dramatically cut down on the number of measurements you need to take. Do not be concerned with how to actually statistically sample. Instead, focus on the reason it would be used.

Additional Quality Planning Tools

There are nearly countless additional Plan Quality Management tools that are designed by specific industries or for use with specific types of projects. While this is mentioned in the PMBOK Guide, focus energy on the tools presented here for the exam.

Meetings — See Ch. 2, Common Tools

Outputs

Kev Fact

Quality Management Plan

The quality management plan is a key output of the Plan Quality Management process. It describes how the quality policy will be met. It becomes a part of the overall project management plan.

Kev Fact

Process Improvement Plan

The concept of process improvement is tightly linked to quality, and the process improvement plan, part of the project management plan, deals with how quality activities will be streamlined and improved.

Kev Fact

Quality Metrics

Quality metrics specifically define how quality will be measured. For instance, it is not adequate for the team to say that the system needs to have a rapid response time. Instead, a quality metric might specify that a system must respond within two seconds to 99% of all requests up to 1,000 simultaneous users. Quality metrics may relate to any quality measure.

Kev Fact

Quality Checklists

A checklist is a Plan Quality Management output created to ensure that all steps were performed, and that they were performed in the proper sequence. They are created here and used in the process of Control Quality.

Project Documents Updates

As Plan Quality Management is performed, it is normal to update the project management plan and other project documents (specifically the process improvement plan and the quality management plan).

Plan Quality Management

Executing

Perform Quality Assurance

What it is:

For many people, Perform Quality Assurance can be one of the trickiest of the 47 processes to understand. One of the most common mistakes exam takers make is to confuse Perform Quality Assurance with Control Quality (covered next), and the difference between the two can appear subtle.

Perform Quality Assurance is an executing process, and the most important thing for you to remember about this process is that it is primarily concerned with overall process improvement. It is not about inspecting the product for quality or measuring defects. Instead, Perform Quality Assurance is focused on steadily improving the activities and processes undertaken to achieve quality. Numerous questions on the exam are missed because of a misunderstanding of this key distinction!

Why it is important:

Too often, people think of quality as simply measuring, testing, and inspecting the final product; however, quality management should be about improving the process as well as the product.

Perform Quality Assurance is important because if the quality of the process and activities is improved, then quality of the product should also improve, along with an overall reduction of cost.

When it is performed:

The process of Perform Quality Assurance is performed as an ongoing activity in the project life cycle. It typically begins early and continues throughout the life of the project. Because Perform Quality Assurance uses many of the outputs of Plan Quality Management, it is not undertaken until after Plan Quality Management has been performed.

How it works:

Inputs

Quality Management Plan

The quality management plan gives guidance as to how the process of Perform Quality Assurance will be executed. As changes are made to the way quality is managed, they should be documented back into the quality management plan.

Process Improvement Plan

The process improvement plan takes a look at how the work is being performed, and what steps might be taken to improve the way it is being performed as well as the results. This defines much of what the process of Perform Quality Assurance is about.

Quality Metrics

The quality metrics created earlier in Plan Quality Management are used here. Since Perform Quality Assurance is primarily concerned with process improvement, the metrics provide an objective means of measurement.

Key Fact

Quality Control Measurements

The quality control measurements can be thought of as a feedback loop. As changes are evaluated here in the process of Perform Quality Assurance, they are measured in Control Quality and fed back into this process for evaluation.

Project Documents — See Ch. 2, Common Inputs

Tools

Quality Management and Control Tools

Affinity Diagrams

Affinity diagrams help visually relate bits of information to other bits of information. They are used to help discover or create meaningful systems of organization. Most mind mapping techniques make use of affinity diagrams to help represent information the way the human brain processes and stores information.

Perform Quality Assurance

Another hypothetical use of an affinity diagram would be to initially write production problems onto individual sticky note cards and place them randomly on the wall, then use the affinity system to create four categories and move each note card under one of the categories.

Process Decision Program Charts (PDPC)

PDPC charts identify risks and steps to take in the event of these risks. PDPC charts are most useful because they may help identify the paths that show the early stages of a risk event.

Interrelationship Digraphs

Used for complex problems, interrelationship digraphs show all of the causes and effects related to a problem.

Tree Diagrams

This diagram breaks things down into categories so that the problem may be more easily understood. In a tree diagram, each node or branch may have zero to multiple sub-nodes or branches. The WBS is one type of tree diagram. An organizational breakdown structure or risk breakdown structure would be another example.

Prioritization Matrices

Solutions to problems are placed in the matrix and are assigned a priority based on pre-determined criteria.

Activity Network Diagrams

This type of network diagram (Activity On Node or Activity On Arrow) shows the order in which things need to take place and the dependency relationships between tasks.

Matrix Diagrams

A matrix diagram shows the relationship between the different elements by describing the type of relationship for each cell where a row and column intersect. This description could be the characteristic of the relationship or the quality or strength of it. Different shapes and dimensions are useful, depending on how many items there are to evaluate.

Quality Audits

Quality audits are the key tool in Perform Quality Assurance. The reason for this is that audits review the project to evaluate which activities taking place on the project should be improved and which meet quality standards. The goal of the audits is to improve both the acceptance of the product and the overall cost of quality.

Process Analysis

The process analysis carefully reviews the quality process to ensure that it is working efficiently and effectively.

Outputs

Change Requests

When this much analysis and evaluation is taking place, requested changes are a normal and expected outcome of this process. It is rare that change requests would be represented as a key fact, but in this case, they are the primary output of the process. It is important to point out that most of the change requests resulting from this process would be procedural changes.

Project Management Plan Updates

As the process of Perform Quality Assurance changes the way in which the project is managed, the project management plan (and specifically the quality management plan and the process improvement plan) should be updated.

Project Documents Updates

Quality activities can potentially affect every aspect of the project, such as scope, schedule, budget, risk, and human resources (to name only a few). Any of the knowledge areas and corresponding plans can, and often do, change because of quality-related issues. As these areas of the project are changed as a result of Perform Quality Assurance, the appropriate documents should be updated.

Perform Quality Assurance

Organizational Process Assets Updates

These assets are anything that can be borrowed, built-upon, and reused for future projects within an organization. Any such assets should be updated as new practices are implemented or new information is learned.

Control Quality

What it is:

Control Quality looks at specific results to determine if they conform to the quality standards. It involves both product and project deliverables, and it is done throughout the project, not just at the end.

Control Quality typically uses statistical sampling rather than looking at each and every output. Many volumes have been written about sampling techniques, and the practice is often very complex and is highly tailored to industry.

This process uses the tool of inspection to make sure the results of the work are what they are supposed to be. Any time you find a part being inspected for quality, you can be sure that you are in the control process.

Why it is important:

Control Quality is the process where each deliverable is inspected, measured, and tested. This process makes sure that everything produced meets quality standards.

When it is performed:

This process typically takes place throughout much of the project. It is performed beginning with the production of the first product deliverable and continues until all of the deliverables have been accepted.

How it works:

Inputs

Project Management Plan

The quality management plan is the main component of the project management plan that is of interest here. It provides the plan for how Control Quality will be carried out.

Control Quality

Quality Metrics

The quality metrics will be used to measure whether or not the work results meet quality specifications.

Quality Checklists

The quality checklists show the steps that were taken to achieve quality on the product. Now that the product is in Control Quality, the checklists will assist in assessing its conformance to quality.

Work Performance Data

The work performance data can shed light on the current state of the deliverable and where it should be. For example, if a software project is scheduled to have the database completed by this date and the work performance measurements show that it is still in design, that will affect the Control Quality process. In this example, you would likely use the work performance measurements to alter your testing scenarios to reflect the database's unfinished state.

Approved Change Requests

Change requests can not only change the product, but also the way the product is constructed, and either of these types of changes will affect quality management.

Deliverables

The project's deliverables are a primary input into this process. The deliverables are inspected and measured to ensure that they conform to quality standards.

Project Documents — See Ch. 2, Common Inputs

Organizational Process Assets

Any informational assets (or other types of assets) should be brought into this process. For instance, if a company invested in a license for a tool that assisted in software testing, that would be appropriate to bring into this process.

Tools

Seven Basic Quality Tools — See Plan Quality Management, Tools

Key Fact

Statistical Sampling

Key Fact

Statistical sampling is a powerful tool where a random sample is selected instead of measuring the entire population. By sampling properly, you can dramatically cut down on the number of measurements you need to take.

Inspection

Key Fact

The tool of inspection is exactly what it sounds like. Inspection may be testing a module of a software application or performing a walkthrough on a building.

Approved Change Requests Review

When change requests are made to any part of the project, the results must be evaluated for their compliance with quality standards.

Outputs

Quality Control Measurements

As the process of Control Quality is performed, important measurements of quality levels and compliance are a normal output and should be documented.

Control Quality

Validated Changes

Defects need to be corrected, and as they are corrected, deliverables need to be inspected again to validate that they now meet quality standards. This also covers other changes that might impact quality.

Kev Fact

Verified Deliverables

The verified deliverables are the key output of Control Quality. They are validated because they pass inspection and meet quality standards.

Work Performance Information — See Ch. 2, Common Outputs

Change Requests — See Ch. 2, Common Outputs

Project Management Plan Updates — See Ch. 2, Common Outputs

Project Documents Updates — See Ch. 2, Common Outputs

Organizational Process Assets Updates — See Ch. 2, Common Outputs

Quality Management Questions

1. **You are a project manager, and your manager wants to meet with you to evaluate your project's performance in order to see how it is meeting the quality standards supplied by the company. In what process is your boss engaged?**

   A. Total Quality Management.

   B. Control Quality.

   C. Plan Quality Management.

   D. Perform Quality Assurance.

2. **If you were using a fishbone diagram to determine root causes of problems, you would be involved in:**

   A. Perform Quality Inspection.

   B. Perform Quality Prevention.

   C. Control Quality.

   D. Perform Quality Audits.

3. **Plan Quality Management includes all of the following outputs EXCEPT:**

   A. Quality management plan.

   B. Accepted deliverables.

   C. Metrics.

   D. Checklists.

4. **In a control chart, the mean is represented as a horizontal line. This represents:**

    A. The average of the control limits.

    B. The average of all data points.

    C. The average of all data points that are within control limits.

    D. A means of identifying assignable cause.

5. **The quality team is meeting to discuss quality as it pertains to a new building product. The group is having some difference of opinion as to the Cost of Quality (COQ). Which of the four statements made by the team is true regarding the cost of quality?**

    A. COQ does not include testing, destructive tests, and inspections in the calculations.

    B. COQ should categorize all product failures as preventable or non-preventable.

    C. COQ should include all costs to prevent nonconformance over the life of the product.

    D. All other things being equal, a lower overall COQ is indicative of a higher-quality product.

6. **Quality audits are an important part of quality management because:**

    A. They allow for quantification of the risk.

    B. They randomly audit product results to see if they are meeting quality standards.

    C. They check to see if the quality process is being followed.

    D. They are conducted without prior notice and do not allow team members time to cover up defects.

7. **If the results of Activity A have no bearing on the results of Activity B, the two activities would be considered:**

    A. Statistically unique.

    B. Statistically independent.

    C. Correlated, but not causal.

    D. Mutually exclusive.

8. **The BEST tool to use to look for results that are out of control is:**

   A. Pareto chart.

   B. Control chart.

   C. Ishikawa diagram.

   D. Statistical sampling.

9. **You are a project manager with limited resources on the project. Several quality defects have been discovered, causing the stakeholders concern. You wish to begin by attacking the causes that have the highest number of defects associated with them. Which tool shows defects by volume from greatest to least?**

   A. Pareto chart.

   B. Control chart.

   C. Ishikawa diagram.

   D. Cause-and-effect diagram.

10. **The process improvement plan looks at which of the following?**

    A. The quality of the product.

    B. The quality of the team.

    C. The project management and product development.

    D. The phases of the project.

11. **In the process of managing a construction project, you discover a very serious defect in the way one particular section has been built. Your engineers analyze the section of the building and decide that the problem is actually relatively minor. In which process are you involved?**

    A. Plan Quality Management.

    B. Perform Quality Assurance.

    C. Control Quality.

    D. Project Quality Management.

12. **You are performing a project that has a lot in common with a project completed by your company two years ago. You want to use the previous project to help you determine quality standards for your project. Which of the following tools would be the BEST one to help you with this?**

    A. Benchmarking.

    B. Control chart.

    C. ISO 9000.

    D. Total Quality Management.

13. **Which of the following is most representative of the Total Quality Management philosophy?**

    A. Decreasing inventory to zero or near zero levels.

    B. Everyone can contribute to quality.

    C. Zero defects.

    D. Continuous improvement is preferred over disruptive change.

14. **Which of these quality standards is the highest?**

    A. It is impossible to determine without further information.

    B. 99% quality.

    C. Three sigma quality.

    D. Six sigma quality.

15. **Which quality process is performed first?**

    A. Plan Quality Management.

    B. Perform Quality Assurance.

    C. Control Quality.

    D. Quality Definition.

16. **If a project team is drawing a tree diagram on the board, which of the following would mostly likely be used?**

    A. An organizational breakdown structure.

    B. A cause-and-effect diagram.

    C. A finite branch diagram.

    D. A network diagram.

17. **A project team is having their first quality meeting and plans to review the organization's quality policy when it is discovered that the company has never developed an organizational quality policy. The project manager is very concerned about this discovery. What would be the BEST course of action?**

   A. Document the absence of a quality policy in the quality management plan and take corrective action.

   B. Write a quality policy just for this project.

   C. Substitute benchmark data for the quality policy.

   D. Suspend execution until the organization provides a quality policy.

18. **On a control chart, the customer's acceptable quality limits are represented as:**

   A. Control limits.

   B. Mean.

   C. Specification.

   D. Normal distribution.

19. **A customer is concerned that the quality process is not being followed as laid out in the quality management plan. The best way to see if this claim is accurate is:**

   A. Random sampling.

   B. Kaizen.

   C. Personally participate in the quality inspections.

   D. Audits.

20. **Mind mapping techniques are most closely related to:**

   A. Lateral Diagrams.

   B. Affinity Diagrams.

   C. Seven Basic Quality Tools.

   D. Plan Quality Management.

21. **Your organization practices just-in-time management. Which of the following would be the highest concern for a project manager operating in this company?**

    A. Absenteeism.

    B. Lower quality of parts.

    C. Conflicting quality processes.

    D. Inventory arriving late.

22. **Reduced quality on a project would MOST likely lead to which of the following?**

    A. Rework and increased cost risk.

    B. Absenteeism and decreased cost.

    C. Increased inspections and decreased cost.

    D. Reduced quality limits.

23. **An organization had a defective unit of product returned. They have asked the team that designed the product to investigate the cause of the failure. After a careful review, the team determines that the product failure is unusual and is related to poor raw materials. They have sampled products from the same batch and have determined that it was not affected by the same problem. The project manager has to report to the Vice President of Quality. How should she describe this problem?**

    A. A process problem.

    B. A quality assurance issue.

    C. A Special Cause.

    D. A Common Cause.

24. **Which of the following is NOT a part of the Plan Quality Management process?**

    A. Benchmarking.

    B. Audits.

    C. Cost-benefit analysis.

    D. Design of experiments.

25. **A project manager wants to perform a code review, but over two million lines of code have already been written for this project, and more are being produced every day. Rather than reviewing each line of code, the manager should consider:**

A. Automated testing tools.

B. Trend analysis.

C. Statistical sampling.

D. Regression analysis.

Answers to
Quality Management Questions

1. **D.** In this example your boss is auditing you to see if you are following the process. Remember that audits are a tool of Perform Quality Assurance.

2. **C.** Control Quality is the correct answer here.

3. **B.** This one should have been one of the easier questions. Accepted deliverables is not an output of Plan Quality Management. It is an output of Verify Scope.

4. **B.** The mean represents the average of all of the data points shown on the chart, calculated simply by adding the values together and dividing by the number of values. 'C' is not correct because the mean includes everything. If only the values that were within the control limits were used, it could make the mean look better than it should.

5. **C.** The Cost of Quality (COQ) looks at all costs incurred to prevent nonconformance throughout the life of the product. 'A' is incorrect because it includes all costs related to producing a product that conforms to quality. The ones listed are prime examples of costs that should be included. 'B' is incorrect because product failures are categorized as "Internal" (found through inspection or testing, and "External" (found by the customer) and not as preventable or non-preventable. 'D' is incorrect because spending less overall on quality is not indicative of a higher-quality product. If anything, the opposite would likely be true.

6. **C.** Audits are a tool of Perform Quality Assurance that checks to see if the process is being followed. Choices 'A' and 'D' are incorrect, and choice 'B' is referring to inspection, which is a tool of Control Quality.

7. **B.** If two events have no bearing on each other, they are statistically independent. Choice 'D' is when two events cannot both happen at the same time.

8. **B.** That is how a control chart is used. It visually depicts whether a process is in or out of control. Choice 'A' is used in Control Quality to rank problems by frequency. 'C' is used in Control Quality to anticipate problems in advance. Choice 'D' is used in Control Quality to pick random samples to inspect.

9.   **A.** Pareto charts rank defects from greatest to least, showing you what should get the most attention.

10.   **C.** The process improvement plan is all about the quality of the project and the quality of the product development processes.

11.   **C.** Control Quality is the best choice here. Your clue here was the fact that your engineers had inspected something specific. This wasn't related to planning or process – it was a physical inspection of a work result, and that is what happens during the Control Quality process.

12.   **A.** Benchmarking takes results from previous projects and uses them to help measure quality on your project. Benchmarks give you something against which you can measure.

13.   **B.** Total Quality Management stresses, among other things, that everyone contributes to the quality of the product and process.

14.   **D.** Six sigma represents that 99.99966% of all work results will be of acceptable quality in the manufacturing process. This is higher than 99% or 3 sigma, which represents a 99.73% quality rate.

15.   **A.** Plan Quality Management should always happen first. Perform Quality Assurance and Control Quality would come after the quality management plan is in place. 'D' is not a PMI process. Keep in mind that the quality processes do run in a cycle, but planning should always happen first.

16.   **A.** The WBS, RBS, and OBS are examples of tree diagrams. 'B' was a close guess, but it is not a type of tree where one parent node may have multiple child nodes. 'C' was a made up term. 'D' does not work well. Network diagram is its own category and does not fit the concept of a tree diagram.

17.   **B.** If no organizational quality policy exists, you should develop one for this project. 'A' and 'C' are incorrect since you should not proceed without a quality policy. 'D' would be a good way to lose your job! You should try to fix this problem yourself rather than force your organization to write a quality policy.

18.   **C.** The quality specification is the customer's quality requirements. 'A' represents the limits for what is in and out of statistical control, typically set at three standard deviations from the mean. 'B' is the average of all of the data points. 'D' is a statistical term relating to the way the data points are scattered.

19.   **D.** Audits, part of the Perform Quality Assurance process, review the process and make sure that the process is being followed.

20.   **B.** Affinity diagrams are closely related to mind mapping. 'A' is a made up term. 'C' has nothing to do with mind mapping. 'D' might have seemed like a good choice since it is an actual process name, but mind mapping has no relationship with Plan Quality Management as it is presented in this book.

21.   **D.** The PMP Exam has several questions structured like this one. You could have any of the problems listed here, but the one you would be most concerned with is parts arriving late. An organization that practices just-in-time (JIT) does not keep spare inventory on hand. Instead, the inventory is ordered so that the parts arrive only slightly before they are needed.

22.   **A.** Rework and increased cost and risk are likely outcomes of low quality. 'B' and 'C' are incorrect since decreased cost is not related to low quality. 'D' is incorrect, because you would not lower the quality limits or specifications just because the quality is bad.

23.   **D.** This was a tougher question. A common cause is one that is generally considered not to be preventable, and this falls into that category. 'A' and 'B' are not good answers since we are given no information that points to the fact that there is a process failure that contributed in any way. This problem is related to product failure, and that should have narrowed it down to 'C' or 'D'. 'C' would have been correct if the product had been assembled incorrectly or if there were something that was purely preventable by the project team, but that is not the case. 'D' emerges as the best answer.

24.   **B.** Audits are part of Perform Quality Assurance. Choices 'A', 'C', and 'D' are all part of Plan Quality Management.

25.   **C.** Statistical sampling (may appear as random sampling) is the best choice. If the overall population is too large, accurate sampling can give you the same statistical results as measuring the entire population. 'A' might be a good choice in the real world, but you should focus on the inputs, tools, and outputs contained in the PMBOK Guide for the exam, and automated testing tools are not a part of quality management.

9 Human Resource Management

Difficulty	Memorization	Exam Importance
HIGH	MEDIUM	HIGH

Although the PMBOK Guide treats the subject of human resource management lightly, you should expect several questions on the exam that cover a variety of theories, including leadership, motivation, conflict resolution, and roles within a project.

The content for this area of the test is drawn from basic management theory, organizational behavior, psychology, and of course, the field of human resources. If you have ever formally studied these subjects, you have probably been exposed to most of the theories in this chapter.

In managing a project, the project manager must also lead people. Some project managers may excel at organizing tasks and planning activities and be dismal at motivating other people; however, in order to be successful, a manager should be able to do both.

This chapter covers the four processes, along with the inputs, tools, and outputs you will need to know in order to pass the exam.

The processes of Project HR Management with their primary outputs

Philosophy

The approach to the area of human resource management is to define a role for everyone on the project and to define the responsibilities for each of these roles. Many people make the mistake of only understanding the role of the project manager and never understanding the proper role of senior management, the sponsor, or the team. Project managers must help define the roles and influence everyone on the project.

The philosophies of leadership and power are based on the realization that the project manager is rarely given complete and unquestioned authority on a project. Instead, he must be able to motivate and persuade people to act in the best interest of the project and must be able to build a team and lead members to give their best efforts to the project.

Finally, it is important to understand that although the project manager is ultimately responsible for the project, he should delegate assignments to the team. This delegation takes the form of responsibility and authority. The project manager gives responsibility and authority to the team and expects reliability and accountability in return.

Importance

Human resource management questions are considered by many people to be the easiest questions on the exam. This is because this is one of the few sections where many of the questions can often be answered by using common sense. Unless you find these questions particularly difficult, it is a good idea to get comfortable with the information in this chapter and focus your attention on more challenging subject matter. A careful review of the theories and content prior to taking the exam should be adequate to help you through this section.

Preparation

The focus of this chapter will be on roles and responsibilities, motivational theories, forms of power, and leadership styles. While this knowledge area is considered to be one of the easiest ones, take the time to learn it. Questions from this section will appear on the exam.

HUMAN RESOURCE MANAGEMENT

You should expect to see questions relating to Tuckman's Ladder, Maslow's Heirarchy, Herzberg's Hygiene Factors, and other theories covered in this chapter on your exam.

This chapter, in particular, contains a significant amount of content that is not found in the PMBOK Guide.

Human Resource Management Processes

There are four processes within project human resource management. In the PMI framework, these processes touch two process groups: planning (Plan Human Resource Management), and executing (Acquire Project Team, Develop Project Team, and Manage Project Team).

Process Group	Human Resource Management Process
Initiating	(none)
Planning	Plan Human Resource Management
Executing	Acquire Project Team, Develop Project Team, Manage Project Team
Monitoring & Controlling	(none)
Closing	(none)

The primary outputs associated with the four human resource management processes are shown in the table below.

Process	Primary Outputs
Plan Human Resource Management	• Human resource management plan
Acquire Project Team	• Staff assignments • Resource calendars
Develop Project Team	• Team performance assessment
Manage Project Team	• Change requests

Planning

Plan Human Resource Management

What it is:

It is a common pattern throughout the PMI processes to have a knowledge area that starts off with a planning process to set the tone for the remaining processes in that area. This is the case with human resource management, which begins with Plan Human Resource Management. This process gives guidance to the rest of the human resource processes, defining the roles and responsibilities and creating the human resource management plan.

Why it is important:

This process lays out how you will staff, manage, team-build, assess, and improve the project team.

When it is performed:

Plan Human Resource Management typically takes place very early on the project, and it may be performed iteratively. In other words, you may do some work on the scope, some work on the schedule, and then plan human resources, and then do more work on the scope, returning again to human resources, and so on. It should not be thought of as a process that is tackled only one time.

How it works:

Inputs

Project Management Plan — See Ch. 2, Common Inputs

Activity Resource Requirements

The activity resource requirements provide information on what resources will be needed to complete the work on the project. General estimates for human resource needs were developed during the time management planning processes, and now they will be more thoroughly evaluated and estimated in Plan Human Resource Management.

Enterprise Environmental Factors — See Ch. 2, Common Inputs

Organizational Process Assets — See Ch. 2, Common Inputs

Tools

Kev Fact

Organization Charts and Position Descriptions

There are many ways to represent who will be working on the project and what they will be responsible for doing. For the exam, you need to know about three primary formats:

Hierarchical

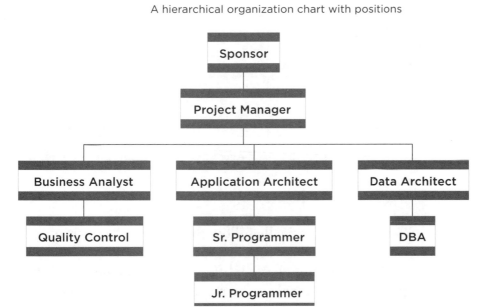

A hierarchical organization chart with positions

Matrix

Matrix charts are another way to depict which roles on the project will be working with specific work packages and what their responsibilities will be. One of the most popular categories is the Responsibility Assignment Matrix (RAM), which displays work packages in the rows and roles in the columns. Each cell shows how a specific role will work on a particular work package.

One popular type of the RAM is known as the RACI chart (pronounced "ray-cee"). RACI charts, such as the one that follows, list each work package in the rows and list the roles in the columns. RACI charts derive their name from the way each cell is assigned either an 'R' for Responsible, 'A' for Accountable, 'C' for

Consult, or 'I' for Inform. Generally, only one person is assigned accountability for a work package, but more than one person may be responsible for performing the work on a work package.

An example of a RAM chart in RACI format

Work Package \ Role	Project Manager	Business Analyst	Data Architect	Application Architect	Jr. Programmer	Sr. Programmer	Quality Control
Document scope	C	A					R
Review scope	A	I	C	C	C	C	C
Approve scope	A	R	R	R	R	R	R
Create database	C	C	A	I			
Design application	I	I	I	A	I	R	C
Code application	I	I	I	I	R	A	C
Application testing	I	I	I	I	I	I	A

R = Responsible, A = Accountable, C = Consult, I = Inform

Text-Oriented Formats

Text formats basically follow the format of a position description, detailing out what responsibilities each position on the project will involve and what qualifications will be needed to fill these positions. This tool can be particularly useful in recruiting.

Networking

Networking is the process of communicating with others within your "network" of contacts. By networking within the organization, the project manager can understand the political and organizational forces that will influence the project.

Organizational Theory

Groups behave differently than individuals, and it is important to understand how organizations and teams behave. Familiarizing yourself with the vast amount of work that has been done to understand organizational theory can pay dividends throughout the project.

Plan Human Resource Mgt.

Expert Judgment — See Ch. 2, Common Tools

Meetings — See Ch. 2, Common Tools

Outputs

Key Fact

Human Resource Management Plan

As you might expect, the human resource management plan is the sole output of the Plan Human Resource Management process. It is mainly comprised of three components: roles and responsibilities, organization charts, and the staffing management plan.

The roles and responsibilities component should define each role on the project and specify a title, a level of responsibility and authority, and the skill level or competency needed to be able to perform this role.

The staffing management plan, which is part of the human resource management plan, details how and when the project will be staffed, how and when the staff will be released, and other key human resources components such as how they will be trained.

One common component of the human resource management plan is a resource histogram. A resource histogram (see example following) simply shows the resource usage for a given period of time. On most projects, resource usage increases from the conceptual phase through planning, hits its peak in construction and testing, and falls off through implementation and closure.

The timeline for the staffing needs is also a component of the human resource management plan. It helps the project and the organization anticipate and plan for the staffing needs.

Another element of the human resource management plan is a release plan. How the project team will be released from the project is important: especially to individual members and their

Plan Human Resource Mgt.

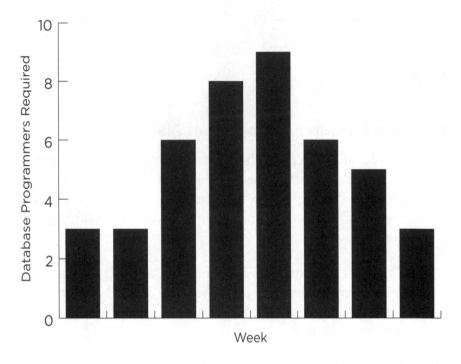

functional managers.

An example of a resource histogram, showing usage by weeks

Other elements of this plan are the staff training needs, rewards systems, safety procedures, compliance needs, and a plan for how the staff will be released at the appropriate time. The human resource management plan tells how those specific needs will be addressed on the project.

Acquire Project Team

What it is:

Acquire Project Team is another process that sounds exactly like what it is. This process focuses on staffing the project. Because it is an executing process, you can think of it as a key process that carries out the human resource management plan.

Why it is important:

This process gets the right people working on the project. Careful attention to this process should pay off in the form of the quality of staff you bring on.

When it is performed:

Make sure that you understand that the process of Acquire Project Team is typically performed throughout the project, as you may need different skill sets throughout the life of the project. For instance, you may need business analysts early on in the life of the project, while you may need more quality engineers later in the project. Acquire Project Team would be performed as long as the project was adding team members or replacing existing staff.

How it works:

Inputs

Human Resource Management Plan

The human resource management plan details when resources will be needed and how long they will be needed, and includes roles and responsibilities, organizational charts, and other information that would be helpful in formally bringing team members into open project positions.

Enterprise Environ. Factors — See Ch. 2, Common Inputs

Organizational Process Assets — See Ch. 2, Common Inputs

Acquire Project Team

Tools

Kev Fact

Pre-Assignment

It is normal on a project for the roles to be defined first. Later, resources are assigned to perform those roles and fulfill the responsibilities; however, occasionally specific resources will be pre-assigned to fill a role. This may occur before the human resource management plan has been created and even before the project formally begins.

Negotiation

Negotiating is an important skill for project managers to cultivate. Project managers often have to negotiate for resources, both inside and outside the organization.

Acquisition

The tool of acquisition, as used here, can be a bit misleading since the overall process is "Acquire Project Team." The tool of acquisition refers to looking outside the organization for resources when they cannot be provided by your organization or when the organization elects not to provide those resources internally.

Virtual Teams

As the Internet has transformed the way most of us do our jobs, virtual teams have become much more popular. A virtual team is a group of individuals who may or may not see each other in person. Instead, they typically use electronic tools to communicate, meet online, share information, and collaborate on documents and deliverables.

Multi-Criteria Decision Analysis

This is a weighted matrix that can be used to objectively score potential candidates on the various factors that matter the most to the project. The criteria and weightings are determined in advance, and candidates are scored against them, with the highest-scoring candidate being selected for the position.

Outputs

Kev Fact

Project Staff Assignments

The assigned staff is the primary output of this process. Each role that was defined should have a resource assigned to it. Understand that these assignments may happen several times throughout the process as resources are needed. For instance, it would typically be difficult to assign a particular person to a role that will not be needed for a year.

Kev Fact

Resource Calendars

As resources are assigned to the project, the time they are assigned to work on activities should be documented on the resource calendar. Each resource's forecasted time on the project should be noted so that the functional manager or performing organization will know how to account for their resources.

Project Management Plan Updates

It is normal for the human resource management plan to undergo revisions and updates as staff members are assigned. Specifically, as things work or do not work when staffing a project, elements of the human resource management plan may be updated to reflect re-planning and corrective action.

Acquire Project Team

Executing

Develop Project Team

What it is:

Where the exam is concerned, Develop Project Team is the most important process in Project Human Resource Management. It is an executing process that focuses on building a sense of team and improving its performance.

Why it is important:

A team performs better than a group of disconnected individuals. This is true not only for sports teams, but also for project teams.

When it is performed:

The process of Develop Project Team is performed throughout the project. In other words, as long as there is a team on the project, you should perform this process. It is considered to be most effective when it is begun early in the project's lifecycle.

How it works:

Inputs

Human Resource Management Plan

The human resource management plan, which is a component of the project management plan, provides the guidance for this entire process. It outlines how project team members will be trained and how Develop Project Team will be conducted. This may include such things as offering flex time, bonus pay, or the option of telecommuting.

Project Staff Assignments

The staff assignments, which were made as part of the Acquire Project Team process, are brought into this process. The rationale behind this is that the staff assignments contain a list of all team members for the project.

Resource Calendars

Resource calendars specify when project team members would be available to take part in team-building activities.

Develop Project Team

Tools

Kev Fact

Interpersonal Skills

The tool of interpersonal skills is often called soft skills. This tool represents the ability to get along with others, to ensure their cooperation, and to motivate people to give extra effort and do their best for the project.

The Alpha Study of project managers found that many of the project managers who ranked themselves highly in the areas of soft skills were often ranked among the lowest in soft skill competency by their stakeholders.

Strong interpersonal skills are very important where the team is concerned. Soft skills can be a thorny area for project managers. Many project managers are not fully aware of how they are relating to their teams.

Kev Fact

Training

Training can include a wide range of activities, but it may be thought of as any instruction or acquisition of skills that increases the ability of the team or individuals to perform their jobs.

If a team member does not have the skills needed to carry out his responsibilities, then training may be a good option. In general, training is highly favored for the exam. In most cases you encounter on the exam, it should be paid for by the performing organization or the functional manager and not by the customer or the project.

Kev Fact

Team-Building Activities

A team-building activity is any activity that enhances or develops the cohesiveness of the team. This usually occurs by focusing on building bonds and relationships among team members. It is important to keep in mind that although team-building may be treated as a special event, it can occur while performing regular project responsibilities, and it actually becomes more important as the project progresses.

Develop Project Team

Team-building cannot be forced. It should be modeled by the project manager, who should work to include all members of the team and create a shared goal.

One important theory that speaks to the development of the team is Tuckman's Ladder of Team Developent. It defines five levels of performance: Forming, Storming, Norming, Performing, and Adjourning.

- Forming is the first stage where the team understands the project and their roles.
- Storming is the stage where the team begins to do the work, but there is typically a good bit of conflict and difficulty. This stage may be chaotic.
- Norming is the stage where the behavior normalizes and members begin to work as a team. In this stage, the project manager shares more leadership with the team.
- Performing is the stage where the team is working at an efficient level that exceeds what individuals could accomplish alone. The project manager's role changes to be one of overseeing and delegating.
- Adjourning is the stage where the project is closed and the team is released. Since individuals tend to fear change, this stage can be difficult on everyone.

Ground Rules

Kev Fact

A project's ground rules are the formal or informal rules that define the boundaries of behavior on the project. For instance, a project may lay down ground rules that say that everyone on the project shares responsibility for protecting the security of project data. In this case, everyone on the project would be expected to treat information with the same general caution. It is important that ground rules be defined and communicated to the team members.

Colocation

Kev Fact

Colocation is the act of physically locating team members in the same general space. The most common example of this is to create a war room where all the team members work or to colocate the project team at the customer's site.

Kev Fact

Recognition and Rewards (Theories of Motivation)

Recognition and reward systems are typically defined as part of the human resource management plan. In general, desirable behaviors should be rewarded and recognized. For the exam, you should focus on win-win rewards as the best choices for team building. Win-lose rewards, such as a contest where one team member wins and the others do not, can be detrimental to the sense of team.

There is a substantial body of knowledge on recognition and reward theories. These theories, also known as Theories of Motivation, are traditional exam favorites. A thorough understanding of several theories is needed to be fully prepared to pass the exam, including Maslow's Hierarchy of Needs, McGregor's Theory X and Y, Contingency Theory, Herzberg's Motivation-Hygiene Theory, and McClelland's Theory of Needs.

Maslow's Hierarchy of Needs

Maslow's Hierarchy of Needs is a basic theory of human motivation that project managers should understand. Abraham Maslow grouped human needs into five basic categories as illustrated in the following diagram.

Maslow's theory states that these needs form a hierarchy since the needs at the bottom must be satisfied before the upper needs will surface. As an example, people cannot reach their full potential if they do not have sufficient food or safety.

Every project manager should understand the

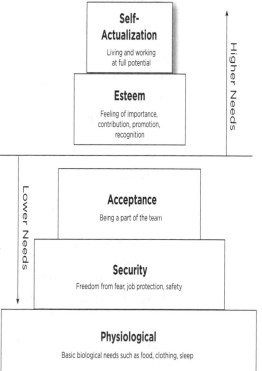

Develop Project Team

needs of the team members and how they interrelate so that he can help them to perform at their full potential.

Expectancy Theory

Expectancy Theory is a motivational theory developed by Victor Vroom. It says that team members make choices based on the expected outcomes. For project work, it most directly applies by saying that team members will only work hard toward a goal if they believe that goal is achievable.

McGregor's Theory X and Theory Y

McGregor's organizational theory states that there are two ways to categorize and understand people in the workplace.

Managers who ascribe to Theory X presume that team members are only interested in their own selfish goals. They are unmotivated, they dislike work, and they must be forced to do productive work. Theory X managers believe that constant supervision is necessary to achieve desired results on a project.

Those who practice Theory Y assume that people are naturally motivated to do good work. "Y managers" believe that their team members need very little external motivation and can be trusted to work toward the organization's or project's goals.

An assembly-line organization may treat everyone as an "X Person," monitoring and measuring every move, whereas an organization that encourages telecommuting might be more prone to treat employees as "Y People." However, it should be understood that it is the manager, not the organization, that ascribes to Theory X or Theory Y, and the style of management is not necessarily determined by the type of work being performed.

Contingency Theory

The Contingency Theory, developed by Fred E. Fiedler in the 1960s and 1970s, states that a leader's effectiveness is contingent upon two sets of factors. The first set of factors measures whether the leader is task-oriented or relationship-oriented. The second set evaluates situational factors in the workplace, such as how stressful the environment is.

Develop Project Team

The practical application of this theory suggests that in stressful times, a task-oriented leader will be more effective, while in relatively calm times, a relationship-oriented leader will function more effectively. The inverse is also true. What makes a leader effective in one setting may actually work against him in another.

Herzberg's Motivation-Hygiene Theory

This theory has nothing to do with personal hygiene as the name might incorrectly cause you to conclude. Instead, Herzberg conducted studies to quantify what factors influence satisfaction at work.

Similar to Maslow's theory, Herzberg's Motivational-Hygiene theory states that the presence of certain factors does not make someone satisfied, but their absence will make someone unsatisfied. In this case, hygiene factors must be present, but they do not motivate by themselves. Motivation factors will motivate, but they will not work without the hygiene factors in place.

Hygiene Factors	Motivation Factors
Company policy	Achievement
Supervision	Recognition
Good relationship with boss	Work
Working conditions	Responsibility
Paycheck	Advancement
Personal life	Growth
Status	
Security	
Relationship with co-workers	

McClelland's Three Need Theory

Also called Achievement Theory, or McClelland's Theory of Needs, this theory states that employees are motivated out of three primary needs:

Achievement

Team members with a high need for achievement (nAch) have a need to stand out. They gravitate toward other team members with a high nAch. They may also prefer to work alone. High risk projects are often not appealing to nAch team members since their individual effort may be thwarted by the risk of the project. Also, very low risk projects may not appeal since individual effort may not be recognized.

Power

Team members with the need for power (nPow) generally desire either institutional (social) power or personal power. Individuals with a desire for social power are usually more effective team members than those with a desire for personal power.

Affiliation

Individuals with the need for affiliation (nAff) want to belong to a team. They seek to maintain good relationships and do well in customer-facing team positions.

By understanding the needs of individual team members (nAch, nPow, or nAff), the project manager can work to manage roles and motivate the overall project team to reach peak performance.

Forms of Power

Another topic that needs to be covered as part of this tool is the various forms of power.

Project managers, especially those in matrix and functional organizations, are often tasked with responsibility for the project without much formal authority in the organization. Understanding the forms of power can help the project manager maximize his ability to influence and manage the team.

Reward Power

Reward power is the ability to give rewards and recognition. Examples include a pay raise, time off, or any other type of reward that would motivate a team member.

Expert Power

Expert power exists when the manager is an expert on the subject. For instance, the person who architected a part of a software system would probably have significant expert power on a project that used that system. People would listen to the architect because he had credibility. A subject matter expert usually has significant power to influence and control behavior.

Legitimate

Also known as formal power, legitimate power is the power that the manager has because of his position. This type of power comes from being formally in charge of the project and the people and has the backing of the organization.

Strong, broad-based, formal authority for a project manager is unusual and would typically indicate a projectized organizational structure.

Referent

Referent power is a form of power that is based on respect or the charismatic personality of the manager. It is ultimately rooted in a persuasive ability with people. Another usage of referent power is when a less powerful person allies with a more powerful person and leverages some of the superior's power. For instance, if the project manager is very close to the CEO of the company, his power will probably be higher because of that alliance.

Punishment

Also known as coercive power, this type of influence is the ability to punish an employee if a goal is not met. "If this module does not pass quality control by the end of next week, you are all fired," would be an example of a manager using punishment power.

Develop Project Team

Best Forms of Power

In addition to being able to identify the different types of power a project manager can use, you should also know that the exam favors reward and expert as the most effective forms of power and punishment as the least effective.

Personnel Assessment Tools

Personnel assessments are powerful ways for team members and managers to gain insights into relational styles, strengths, and weaknesses. In addition, 360 degree feedback assessments can help individuals understand how they are perceived by others both inside and outside of the organization. Assessments are not the end goal. They are a means to create awareness so that an improvement plan may be undertaken.

Outputs

Key Fact

Team Performance Assessments

Team evaluations are performed by the project manager to focus on areas that should be improved. It is the project manager's job to increase team performance. It is also important for the project manager to identify the right resources needed to help develop the team.

Enterprise Environmental Factors Updates

As the project team develops new skills or acquires new training, these need to be updated at an organizational (enterprise) level for the benefit of future projects and for functional managers.

Manage Project Team

What it is:

This process has most of the attributes of a monitoring and controlling process. In fact, it used to be a monitoring and controlling process in a previous edition of the PMBOK Guide, but it is an executing process now. This is important to know. In this process, you are actively managing the project team to ensure that they perform according to the plan.

Why it is important:

Out of all the areas on the project, the human resource side often has the most trouble with project execution. People can be unpredictable. Some leave the project, teams experience unexpected conflict, individuals suffer from low morale, and all of these events directly affect objective measures such as the budget, the schedule, and quality.

This uncertainty becomes even more challenging when you consider that team members often report to different functional managers and have "dotted line" responsibilities to the project manager.

In the Manage Project Team process, the project manager considers all of these factors and works to keep the team at optimal performance.

When it is performed:

Manage Project Team is performed as long as there is a team on the project.

How it works:

Inputs

Human Resource Management Plan

The human resource management plan, which is a component of the project management plan, provides the plan for managing the team through each phase of the project.

Develop Project Team

Manage Project Team

Project Staff Assignments

The project staff assignments, an output of the process Acquire Project Team, provide a main input here. This is essentially a list of human resources that should be considered as part of this process.

Team Performance Assessments

The team performance assessments are an important and ongoing input into the Manage Project Team process. The project manager should regularly assess the performance of the team so that issues can be identified and managed. The format and frequency of the assessments may vary.

Issue Log

An issue may be thought of as anything that threatens project progress. It could be specific, such as a technical concern, or general, such as a personality conflict among team members. A documented log of issues is important since it gives the project team a place to record issues that require resolution. Along with each issue, the person or people responsible for resolving the issue should be documented.

Work Performance Reports

The performance reports are an objective measure of progress against the plan. Such items as scope, time, and cost are measured carefully, and any difference between these and the plan is documented.

Organizational Process Assets — See Ch. 2, Common Inputs

Tools

Observation and Conversation

These informal tools are used to monitor team morale and identify problems, whether potential or real. The point of this tool is that project managers should remain close to their team throughout the project.

Project Performance Appraisals

A project performance appraisal is where the project manager and other personnel managers on the project meet with the people who report to them on the project and provide feedback on their performance and how they are conducting their job.

In recent years, the tool of 360 degree feedback has gained in popularity. Using this tool, feedback is provided from all directions and often from individuals both internal and external to the project, occasionally even including vendors and external contractors.

Conflict Management

Managing conflict in a constructive way helps improve team morale and performance. As discussed earlier in this chapter, conflict may occur between any individuals or groups on the project, but it most often occurs between project managers and functional managers. It is important to manage and resolve conflict; however, if conflict cannot be resolved among the parties involved, it should be escalated.

Conflict that hurts the project should be dealt with in progressively more official channels, such as escalation to the project manager, escalation to the functional managers, and ultimately escalation to the human resources department.

Methods of Conflict Management

Consider for a moment the problem of a door that is stuck shut. There are several ways to approach this problem:

• You may want to throw your weight against the door, pounding it with your shoulder.

• You might elect to try to go in the room from another point of entry.

• You could try to take the hinges off the door to make it come apart.

• You might choose to ignore the problem of the stuck door, avoiding it altogether, or hope that someone else will take care of it.

• You could attempt to find out why the door was stuck in the first place and deal with that problem.

Manage Project Team

In the same way there are several ways to approach conflict resolution. Because conflict is inevitable, you should be aware of the common ways of handling it:

Problem-Solving

Problem-solving involves confrontation, but it is confrontation of the problem and not the person! It means dealing with the problem head on. Using this technique, the project manager gets to the bottom of the problem and resolves the root causes of the conflict.

One common term in problem-solving is "confrontation." Although the word confrontation may have negative connotations, this type of conflict resolution is highly favored as it is proactive, direct, and deals with the root of the problem. Consequently, it is most often the correct answer on the exam when questions of conflict resolution arise.

Collaboration

Collaboration is a favored technique for resolving conflict. When collaborating, individuals (or teams) work together with other individuals (or teams) to come to a solution. This is a favored technique for the exam, second only to problem-solving.

Compromise

Compromise takes place when both parties sacrifice something for the sake of reaching an agreement. On the test, compromise may be presented as "lose – lose" since both parties give up something.

Forcing

Forcing is exactly what the name implies. It is bringing to bear whatever force or power is necessary to get the door open. Although forcing may work well in the case of a stuck door, this is considered to be the worst way to resolve project conflict. Forcing doesn't help resolve the underlying problems, it reduces team morale, and it is almost never a good long-term solution.

Smoothing

Using smoothing, the project manager plays down the problem and turns attention to what is going well. The statement "We shouldn't be arguing with each other. Look at how well we've done so far, and we're ahead of schedule," would be an example of smoothing.

Smoothing downplays conflict instead of dealing with it head on and does not produce a solution to the conflict. Instead, smoothing merely tries to diminish the problem.

Withdrawal

Withdrawal is technically not a conflict resolution technique but a means of avoidance. A project manager practicing withdrawal is merely hoping the problem will go away by itself. Needless to say, this is not a favored method of conflict resolution because the conflict is never resolved. It will never be a correct answer on the exam unless the question describes a bad behavior or asks you about something not to do.

Constructive and Destructive Team Roles

Related to the area of conflict management is the project manager's ability to recognize and deal with constructive and destructive roles on his or her team.

Constructive Team Roles	
Initiators	Clarifiers
Information Seekers	Harmonizers
Information Givers	Summarizers
Encouragers	Gate Keepers

Destructive Team Roles	
Aggressors	Topic Jumpers
Blockers	Dominators
Withdrawers	Devil's Advocates
Recognition Seekers	

Manage Project Team

Constructive Team Roles

Initiators

An initiator is someone who actively initiates ideas and activities on a project. This role is considered positive because it is proactive and can be highly productive.

Information Seekers

Information seekers are people on the team who actively seek to gain more knowledge and understanding related to the project. This is a positive role because fostering an understanding among the team is important, and open communication should be valued.

Information Givers

An information giver, as its name implies, is someone who openly shares information with the team. Although not all information may be shared (for instance classified or secret information must be kept confidential), the overarching principal is to foster good communication and a good flow of information on the project.

Encouragers

Encouragers maintain a positive and realistic attitude. On the project, they focus on what can be accomplished, not on what is impossible. This is a positive role because it contributes to team morale.

Clarifiers

A clarifier, as the name suggests, is someone who works to make certain that everyone's understanding of the project is the same. This is a positive role because it ensures that everyone has a common understanding of the project goals and details.

Harmonizers

In music, harmony is not the same as the melody, but it complements and enhances the melody. Similarly, a harmonizer on the project will enhance information in such a way that understanding is increased. This is a positive role because the overall understanding of the project and the project context, or the details surrounding it, are enhanced.

Summarizers

Summarizers take the details and restate them succinctly or relate them back to the big picture. This is a positive role because details on the project may become overwhelming, but the summarizer can keep things simple enough for everyone to understand the higher purpose of the tasks.

Gate Keepers

The term gate keeper has two possible uses in project management literature. The first definition is used differently in project management than it is in other business disciplines. A gate keeper is someone who draws others in. Someone who says, "We haven't heard from the other end of the table today," would be an example of a gate keeper. This is a very positive role because it encourages the entire team to participate on the project.

The other usage comes from someone who judges whether or not the project should continue at different stages (known as the stage-gate approach). This gate keeper makes decisions about whether the project is still achieving the business need and if it is justified in continuing to a subsequent phase.

Both of these usages of gate keeper are considered to be constructive roles on the project.

Destructive Team Roles

The effective project manager will be able to identify destructive roles within the team and diminish or eliminate them.

Aggressors

An aggressor is someone who is openly hostile and opposed to the project. This is a negative role because it serves no productive purpose on the project.

Blockers

A blocker is someone who blocks access to information and tries to interrupt the flow of communication. This is a negative role because of the disruptive effect poor communication can have on a project.

Withdrawers

A withdrawer does not participate in discussion, resolution, or even the fleshing out of ideas. Instead, he is more likely to sit quietly or not participate at all. This is a negative role because it usually produces a team member that does not buy into the project and can have a negative effect on the overall team morale.

Recognition Seekers

A recognition seeker looks at the project to see what is in it for him. He is more interested in his own benefit rather than the project's success. This is a negative role because of the damaging effect on team morale and because a recognition seeker may ultimately jeopardize the project if doing so somehow personally benefits him.

Topic Jumpers

A topic jumper disrupts effective communication by constantly changing the subject and bringing up irrelevant facts. This is a negative role because it prevents issues from being fully discussed and brought to closure.

Dominators

The dominator is someone who disrupts team participation and communication by presenting opinions forcefully and without considering the merit of others' contributions. He will likely talk more than the rest of the group and will bully his way through the project. This is a negative role because valid opinions are often quashed, and the project may take on a one-dimensional quality.

Devil's Advocates

A devil's advocate is someone who will automatically take a contrary view to most statements or suggestions that are made. This may be a positive or negative role on the project, but it is most often associated with a negative role since it often disrupts and frustrates communication, discourages people from participating, and stalls progress.

Sources of Conflict

One last area of conflict management you should understand is based on research that suggests that the greatest project conflict occurs between project managers and functional managers. Most conflict on a project is the result of disagreements over schedules, priorities, and resources. This finding runs contrary to a commonly held belief that most conflicts are the result of personality differences.

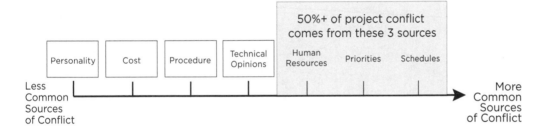

A diagram showing the primary sources of conflict on a project

Key Fact

Interpersonal Skills

As discussed in the process Develop Project Team, the project manager's interpersonal skills play a significant part in regular management responsibilities.

General management skills cover a whole host of topics, but are particularly focused on producing key results by driving and managing tasks and motivating team members. Among the most important of these are:

Manage Project Team

Manage Project Team

Leadership

There is a difference between leading and managing on a project. Managing has been defined as being about producing key results, while leading involves establishing direction, aligning people to that direction, and motivating and inspiring.

There are several different styles of leading that are recognized throughout the field of project management. The following graphic may prove very helpful for the exam. In the early phases of the project, the project manager should take a very active role in the leadership of the project, usually directing the activities and providing significant leadership. As the project progresses, however, other styles of leading may be more appropriate. These styles of leading are less heavy-handed. Of course, the particular style of leading needed will vary from one project to the next.

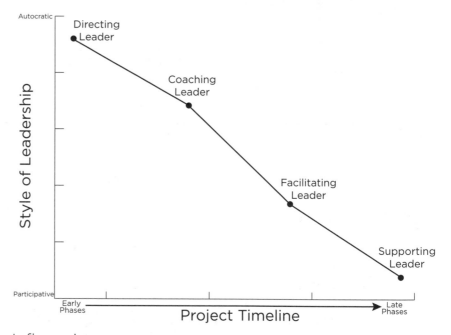

Influencing

Most project managers have limited authority on a project, and this is particularly true when it comes to the team. In this case, the skill of influencing becomes particularly important. Project managers have to be able to influence stakeholders through persuasion, listening, and building trusting relationships.

Effective Decision Making

Good decision making involves several components, including following a process, keeping focused on the goals, and taking all information into consideration.

Outputs

Change Requests

Requested changes to the staff could occur for a number of reasons. The team could be dysfunctional, the workers could be under-qualified or over-qualified, or you may need to augment the staff with more resources than previously planned. Any of these or other scenarios that change the human resource management plan should be documented and processed through the change control system. Enterprise Environmental Factors Updates — See Ch. 2, Common Outputs

PM Plan Updates— See Ch. 2, Common Outputs

Project Documents Updates— See Ch. 2, Common Outputs

Ent. Environ. Factors Upd. — See Ch. 2, Common Outputs

Org. Process Assets Updates — See Ch. 2, Common Outputs

Manage Project Team

IMPORTANT

In addition to this quiz, use your Key to InSite, found on the inside back cover of this book, to access additional content, including new exam questions, expanded content, and simulated PMP exams. If your book did not come with a Key to InSite on the inside back cover, it may not be authentic. If you do not have a Key to InSite, you may purchase one at *insite.velociteach.com*.

Human Resource Management Questions

1. **If you hear a project manager saying to a customer "We all agree that this project is important. Let's not fight over a few thousand dollars," what conflict resolution technique is the project manager trying to use?**

   A. Smoothing.

   B. Problem Solving.

   C. Forcing.

   D. Compromising.

2. **Who manages the resources in a matrix organization?**

   A. Senior management.

   B. Functional managers.

   C. Project manager.

   D. Human resources.

3. **Trey, a functional manager of his organization's information technology domain, has supplied a database developer to a project managed by Vickie; however, it has become apparent that the developer lacks the knowledge to work on the operating environment the team is using. Trey and Vickie meet and determine that the resource can attend a training class and close the gap in skills, but there is a question as to who should pay for it. How should they resolve this?**

    A. They should escalate the conflict to senior management.

    B. Trey's department should pay for the training.

    C. Vickie's project should pay for the training.

    D. They should seek a compromise.

4. **What is considered the LEAST desirable form of power for a project manager to exercise?**

    A. Formal.

    B. Referent.

    C. Punishment.

    D. Forcing.

5. **Which statement below BEST matches a Theory X manager's beliefs?**

    A. People want to be rewarded for their work.

    B. People have higher needs that will not emerge until the lower needs have been satisfied.

    C. People will contribute to work if left alone.

    D. People cannot be trusted.

6. **The human resource management plan:**

    A. Should be created by the human resources department.

    B. Is a part of the resource management plan.

    C. Is a tool of Develop Project Team.

    D. Is an output of the Plan Human Resource Management process.

7. **A project manager is tracking his team through a process of development that includes Storming and Adjourning. Which expert developed the theory this is based upon?**

   A. Maslow.

   B. Herzberg.

   C. McClelland.

   D. Tuckman.

8. **Which technique produces the most lasting results?**

   A. Problem-solving.

   B. Smoothing.

   C. Compromising.

   D. Withdrawing.

9. **The most important role of the project sponsor is to:**

   A. Manage and resolve conflicts between the team and upper management.

   B. Provide and protect the project's financial resources.

   C. Provide and protect the project's human resources.

   D. Balance the project's constraints regarding time, scope, and cost.

10. **Human resource management encompasses:**

    A. Organizational Planning, Acquire Project Team, Report Performance, and Manage Project Team.

    B. Plan Human Resource Management, Acquire Project Team, Report Performance, and Develop Project Team.

    C. Plan Human Resource Management, Staff Acquisition, Develop Project Team, and Release Project Team.

    D. Plan Human Resource Management, Acquire Project Team, Develop Project Team, Manage Project Team.

11. **Which of the following is NOT an input into Plan Human Resource Management?**

   A. Enterprise environmental factors.

   B. Role and responsibility assignments.

   C. Organizational process assets.

   D. Activity resource requirements.

12. **Which of the following is a constructive team role?**

   A. Information seeker.

   B. Recognition seeker.

   C. Blocker.

   D. Devil's advocate.

13. **A project manager is trying to rank and quantify three variables for his team which he has labeled on a dry-erase board as follows: nAch, nPow, and nAff. Which expert developed the theory this is this based upon?**

   A. Maslow.

   B. Herzberg.

   C. McClelland.

   D. Tuckman.

14. **Maslow's Hierarchy of Needs theory states that:**

   A. The strongest motivation for work is to provide for physiological needs.

   B. Hygiene factors are those that provide physical safety and emotional security.

   C. Psychological needs for growth and fulfillment can be met only when lower-level physical or security needs have been fulfilled.

   D. The greater the financial reward, the more motivated the workers will be.

15. **Which of the following is NOT true of team building?**

    A. Team agreement should be obtained on all major actions.

    B. Team building requires role modeling on the part of the project manager.

    C. Team building becomes less important as the project progresses.

    D. Teamwork cannot be forced.

16. **Team building is primarily the responsibility of:**

    A. The project team.

    B. The project manager.

    C. Senior management.

    D. The project sponsor.

17. **A war room is an example of:**

    A. Contract negotiation tactics.

    B. Resource planning tools.

    C. A functional organization.

    D. Colocation.

18. **Which processes make use of the project manager's interpersonal skills?**

    A. Acquire Project Team and Manage Project Team.

    B. Develop Project Team and Manage Project Team.

    C. Acquire Project Team and Develop Project Team.

    D. Develop Project Team and Transition Project Team.

19. **Which of the following is NOT a human resource process?**

    A. Plan Human Resource Management.

    B. Acquire Project Team.

    C. Report Team Performance.

    D. Develop Project Team.

20. **A project coordinator is distinguished from a project manager in that:**

    A. A project coordinator has no decision-making power.

    B. A project coordinator has less decision-making power.

    C. A project coordinator has no authority to assign work.

    D. A project coordinator has more decision-making power.

21. **Which of the following is NOT a tool used in Develop Project Team?**

    A. Interpersonal Skills.

    B. Training.

    C. Ground Rules.

    D. Encouragement.

22. **An organization is undertaking a strategic project to develop a new technology that would provide them with a market advantage. The project manager has been brought in early to help with pre-planning, when a senior manager informs him that there is a specific resource that he wants to be on the project as a quality engineer. Is this situation acceptable?**

    A. No. The project manager is ultimately responsible for the project and should have the opportunity to approve or reject the acquisition of all resources.

    B. No. If a resource is pre-assigned, the functional manager should be the one to make that assignment to ensure that the individual has the proper skills.

    C. Yes. Pre-assignment may occur as a part of Acquire Project Team.

    D. Yes, as long as it does not adversely affect the project.

23. **One potential disadvantage of a matrix organization is:**

    A. Highly visible project objectives.

    B. Rapid responses to contingencies.

    C. Team members must report to more than one boss.

    D. The matrix organization creates morale problems.

24. **A project manager in Detroit is having difficulty getting the engineers in his company's Cleveland office to complete design documents for his project. He has sent numerous requests to the VP of Engineering (also in Cleveland) for assistance in getting the design documents, but so far his efforts have been unsuccessful. What kind of organization does this project manager work in?**

    A. Functional.

    B. Hierarchical.

    C. Strong matrix.

    D. Projectized.

25. **Which of the following is not true about a project's ground rules?**

    A. Ground rules should be communicated to all team members.

    B. Ground rules should be consistent across projects in an organization.

    C. Ground rules should be clearly defined.

    D. Ground rules define behavioral boundaries on a project.

Answers to Human Resource Management Questions

1. A. Smoothing occurs when the person trying to resolve the conflict asks everyone to focus on what they agree upon and diminishes the items on which there is disagreement.

2. B. The functional manager has resource responsibilities in a matrix organization. In this type of organizational structure, the project manager must work with the functional managers to secure resources for a project. If you were tempted to choose 'C', keep in mind that the project manager primarily manages the project. The benefit of a matrix organization is that the project manager does not need to divert as much attention to managing the resources as he or she would in a projectized organization.

3. B. Remember this: unless it is a very unusual circumstance, the project does not pay for training. Trey supplied the developer to work on the project, and it is the functional organization's responsibility to provide competent and trained resources. If you were in a hurry, you might have chosen 'A'. After all, senior management does resolve conflict between project managers and functional managers; however, not every disagreement or conflict should be escalated in such a hair-trigger manner. 'D' is incorrect since compromise is not overly favored for the exam to begin with, and compromise would not be in the project's best interest here.

4. C. Punishment. 'D' is a problem solving technique – not a form of power.

5. D. Theory X managers believe that people cannot be trusted and must be watched and managed constantly.

6. D. The human resource management plan is created during the Plan Human Resource Management process.

7. D. Tuckman's theory of team development, also known as Tuckman's Ladder, includes the phases of Forming, Storming, Norming, Performing, and Adjourning.

8. A. Problem-solving (sometimes referred to as confrontation) is getting to the root of the problem and is the best way to produce a lasting result and a real solution.

Human Resource Answers

9. B. This question comes from Chapter 2 – Foundational Terms and Concepts. The project sponsor provides the funds for the project. He may or may not take on other roles, but this is his defining role on the project.

10. D. The four processes are Plan Human Resource Management, Acquire Project Team, Develop Project Team, Manage Project Team, and yes, you do need to know all of them before taking the PMP Exam.

11. B. The easiest way to answer questions like this one is to start by narrowing the choices down. Three of the answers will be valid inputs, and enterprise environmental factors and organizational process assets are inputs into almost every planning process. That will eliminate answers 'A' and 'C'. In order to narrow it down between 'B' and 'D', think about the process and consider what it does. The process creates a human resource management plan, and choice 'D' sounds like something that would be produced as part of that plan and not an input. The activity resource requirements would be useful to produce the human resource management plan. 'B' emerges as the best choice.

12. A. Information seeker. Recognition seekers are more concerned with getting in the spotlight than with facilitating communication. Blockers reject others' viewpoints and shut down discussion. Devil's advocate – bringing up alternative viewpoints - can be either positive or negative, but it is listed in most project management literature as a destructive team role because when it is negative it is very negative! Information seekers are constructive because they ask questions to gain information.

13. C. McClelland developed the Three Need Theory that states that people have the basic needs for Achievement (generally abbreviated as nAch), Power (nPow), and Affiliation (nAff). This is what the project manager is analyzing on the dry-erase board.

14. C. This question might have been difficult for you. 'A' is not necessarily true, because Maslow stated that any level of his "pyramid" provides the greatest level of motivation when the needs of the levels below have already been met. Thus physiological needs such as food and shelter will be the greatest motivator for workers to do a good job when those needs are

unmet. But once the lower level needs are met, the needs of the next level become the greatest motivators.

15. C. Successful team building begins early in project development, but it is a continuous process throughout the life of the project.

16. B. Team building must be carried out under the direction of a strong leader. The project manager has the only project role that allows for regular, direct interaction with the team.

17. D. Colocation is the practice of locating all team members in a central location. Another variation of a war room is a conference room devoted exclusively for a particular project team. It is a tool of Develop Project Team used in human resource management.

18. B. Develop Project Team and Manage Project Team both have interpersonal skills as a tool. Even if you did not have that memorized, the answer might have been intuitive since team development and management are enhanced by strong interpersonal skills. 'D' had the name of a made-up process in it and should have been eliminated immediately.

19. C. Report Team Performance is not a real process. It does sound similar to the Communications process of Report Performance, but this question asked which of the processes did not belong to the knowledge area of human resource management.

20. B. A project coordinator has some authority and some decision-making power, but less than a project manager.

21. D. Encouragement may be a great idea, but it is not specified as a tool of Develop Project Team. 'A', 'B', and 'C' all are. If you missed this question keep in mind that you should favor the terms, vocabulary, and phrases you see here on the exam. Few people can commit all of the inputs, tools and techniques, and outputs to memory, but you should learn to recognize them and pick out the ones that do not belong.

22. C. Pre-assignment of individuals to a defined role is a tool of Acquire Project Team. There are many reasons this might be necessary, including contractual agreements. Many times the project manager is not the first person recruited onto the project, making pre-assignment a reality for many projects and project

managers. 'A', 'B' and 'D' all have some merit to them, but they are not the best answer in this case since pre-assignment is a formally-defined tool.

23. C. In a matrix organization, team members report to both the project manager and the functional manager. This can sometimes cause confusion and can lead to conflict on a project and within the organization.

24. A. The clue in the question that indicates a functional organization is the project manager's low authority; he must appeal to the head of the engineering department rather than making his request directly to the team members.

25. B. Ground rules may be unique to the project, and they certainly don't have to be the same across all projects in an organization. For instance, a project that has high security might have more stringent ground rules than a less secure one. 'A' and 'C' are incorrect because clearly defining ground rules and communicating them to everyone helps to make sure they are understood and will be followed. 'D' is incorrect because that is exactly what ground rules do – they define the boundaries of behavior that team members should respect.

10 Communications Management

Difficulty	Memorization	Exam Importance
MEDIUM	MEDIUM	MEDIUM

People who study this chapter are often surprised that it is not related to the skill of communication through verbal and written media, in areas such as project writing styles, persuasion, and presentation methods. Rather, communications management covers all tasks related to producing, compiling, sending, storing, distributing, and managing project records. This knowledge area is now made up of only three processes to determine what to communicate, to whom, how often, and when to reevaluate the plan. It involves understanding who your stakeholders are and what they need to know.

Communications management also requires that you accurately report on the project status, performance, change, and earned value, and that you pay close attention to controlling the information to ensure that the communication management plan is working as intended.

The processes of Project Communications Management with their *primary* outputs

Communications Management

Plan Communications
Communications Management Plan

Manage Communications
Project Communications

Control Communications
Work Performance Info.

Philosophy

There is an old joke in project management circles about

"mushroom project management" in which you manage projects the same way you grow mushrooms – by keeping everyone buried in manure, leaving them in the dark, and checking back periodically to see what has popped up.

The philosophy presented here is, as you may have guessed, quite different. It focuses on keeping the stakeholders properly informed throughout the project. Communication under this philosophy may be a mixture of formal and informal, written and verbal, but it is always proactive and thorough. It is essential that the project manager distribute accurate project information in a timely manner and to theright audience.

Importance

Communications management is of medium importance on the exam, bordering on high. You may see several questions that relate directly to this chapter, so it will be necessary to become acquainted with the processes, terms, and theories presented here.

Preparation

Although the volume of material in communications management is smaller than most of the other areas, there are key concepts that must be learned. Be prepared for several questions on the test specifically related to the inputs, tools and techniques, and outputs for each process. The reason the focus is on these areas is that they are critical to the smooth operation of the processes, and most test-takers do not find them intuitive.

Two other areas of key importance are the communications model and understanding channels of communication. You can expect to see questions about these on the exam.

There are not as many exam questions related to this section as there are to some of the others, and by carefully reviewing this chapter and the exercises, you should be in good shape for the exam

Communications Management Processes

There are three processes within project communications management, following the familiar pattern of plan, execute, and control. These processes touch three process groups: planning (Plan Communications Management), executing (Manage

Communications), and monitoring and controlling (Control Communications).

Process Group	Communications Management Process
Initiating	(none)
Planning	Plan Communications Management
Executing	Manage Communications
Monitoring & Controlling	Control Communications
Closing	(none)

The primary outputs associated with the three communications management processes are shown in the table below.

Process	Primary Outputs
Plan Communications Management	Communications Management Plan
Manage Communications	Project Communications
Control Communications	Work Performance Information

Project Manager's Role in Communications

The project manager's most important skill set is that of communication. It is integral to everything the project manager does. You may see questions on your exam asking you what the project manager's most important job or most important skills are, or how most of the project manager's time is spent. The answer is almost always related to communications. It is estimated that an effective project manager spends about 90% of his time communicating, and fully 50% of that time is spent communicating with the project team.

Also note that while communications take up a majority of the project manager's working day, one individual cannot control everything that is communicated on a project, nor should he try. Project managers who ask that every single e-mail or conversation be filtered through them first are generally demonstrating that they are not in control on the project. Instead, the project manager should be in control of the communications process. This is done by creating a strong communications management plan, adhering to it, and regularly monitoring and controlling the results.

Communications Processes

Planning

Plan Communications Management

What it is:

For the exam you should consider that Plan Communications Management is all about the communications management plan, its only significant output. The communications management plan is, as you might guess, the plan that drives communication on the project. It defines:

- How often communications will be distributed and updated
- In what format the communications will be distributed (e.g., e-mail, printed copy, web site, etc.)
- What information will be included in the project communications
- Which project stakeholders will receive these communications

Why it is important:

This plan sets stakeholders' expectations on the project, letting them know what information they will receive and when and how they will receive it. If the project manager invests time in defining these lines of communication up front, conflict should be less than if it were undefined. Keep in mind that projects will vary greatly in how formally they define the communications management plan. On a small project, it may not make sense for the project manager to go to great lengths to define an overly formal communications management plan.

When it is performed:

Like many planning processes, Plan Communications Management is typically performed early on the project, before regular project communications commence; however, it may be revisited as often as needed. It does depend on the process of Identify Stakeholders, so it would be performed after that process.

How it works:

Inputs

Project Management Plan — See Ch. 2, Common Inputs

Stakeholder Register

This input provides a list of all identified project stakeholders that will be used to construct the communications management plan.

Enterprise Environ. Factors — See Ch. 2, Common Inputs

Organizational Process Assets — See Ch. 2, Common Inputs

Tools

Kev Fact

Communication Requirements Analysis

This one tool can cover quite a bit of ground. It is relatively simple to define, but sometimes quite tricky to perform on an actual project. The goal of this technique is to identify which stakeholders should receive project communications, what communications they should receive, how they should receive these communications, and how often they should receive them.

Kev Fact

Communication Channels

A significant part of analyzing the project's communication requirements is determining the communication channels, or paths of communication, that exist within it. Expect at least a couple of questions on the exam to relate directly to this topic. Because the project manager needs to manage and be in control of project communications, it is important to understand that adding a single person on a project can have a significant impact on the number of paths or channels of communication that exist between people.

Channels = n × (n-1) ÷ 2

(Where n = the number of people on the project)

The formula above for calculating communication channels looks complicated, but is actually a simple geometric expansion. Before memorizing the formula, refer to the two illustrations below. You can see from the drawing that four people produce six communication channels, as is confirmed by the formula:

4 × (4-1) ÷ 2 = 6.

If there were five people, the formula would be applied as:

$5 \times (5\text{-}1) \div 2 = 10$

By understanding the illustrations that follow and the way people interrelate to form communication channels, the concept should be easy to comprehend.

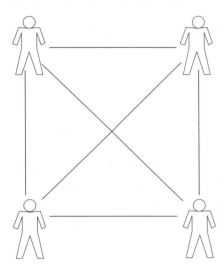

Four people create six communication channels, as illustrated above.

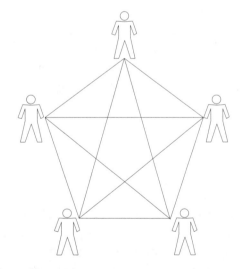

Five people create ten communication channels, or paths, as depicted in the illustration above.

Official Channels of Communication

The number of communication channels is of specific concern when analyzing the project's communication requirements. If there are a large number of channels of communication on the project, the project manager should work to define which communication channels are official. For example, it may be necessary to determine who can officially communicate with the customer or with key subcontractors.

Communication Technology

Technology is a tool, and the right tool should be selected for a given communications need. Whereas face-to-face meetings may be needed for some projects, a project web site, portal, or e-mail may be more appropriate for others. The technology should be tailored to the need. Sensitivity and security of information should also come into consideration when choosing the right technology.

Key Fact

Communication Models

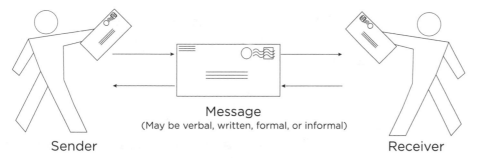

Message
(May be verbal, written, formal, or informal)

Sender   Receiver

Communication Model

The communication model is a formal way of understanding how messages are sent and received. This model defines the responsibilities between the sender and the receiver.

The sender's responsibilities are to:

- Encode the message clearly
- Select a communication method
- Send the message
- Confirm that the message was understood by the receiver

Plan Communications Mgt.

The receiver's responsibilities are to:

- Decode the message
- Acknowledge (Confirm that the message was received)
- Respond and give feedback

Often, it is not so easy to simply transmit a message and assume it will be received, decoded, and understood properly. "Noise" can interfere with a message's transmission. Noise can be anything that interferes with the receiver's ability to understand a message. For instance, language and cultural issues, method of transmission, distance, and bias can all inject noise into the message. Both the sender and receiver must be consciously aware of noise and work to prevent it from compromising the message.

Messages can be conveyed in verbal and nonverbal ways. Below are some terms related to different ways of communicating:

Active listening

Active listening requires that the receiver takes active steps to ensure that the sender was understood. It is similar to effective listening (below).

Effective listening

Effective listening requires the listener's full thought and attention. To be effective as a listener means to monitor nonverbal and physical communication and to provide feedback indicating whether the message has been clearly understood.

Feedback

Feedback refers to the verbal and nonverbal cues a speaker must monitor to see whether the listener fully comprehends the message. Nodding and smiling might be considered positive feedback and indicate that the message is understood and received, whereas nodding and a blank stare might indicate that the message needs to be re-coded for better communication. Asking questions or repeating the speaker's words are also ways to give feedback.

Nonverbal

Nonverbal communication takes place through body language such as facial expressions, posture, hand motions, etc. In fact, most communication between the sender and receiver is nonverbal. Therefore, in order to understand the message, a good listener must carefully attend to nonverbal communication.

Paralingual

Paralingual communication is vocal but not verbal – for example, tone of voice, volume, or pitch. A high-pitched squeal does not employ words, but it certainly communicates!

Communication Blockers

A communication blocker is anything that interferes with the sender encoding the message or the receiver decoding it. It can include anything that disrupts the communication channels.

Key Fact

Communication Methods

There are four basic methods of communication you will need to know, and it is very important to understand what they are and how and when they are used. Many people find the difference between formal and informal to be non-intuitive the first time they encounter it. The methods of communication are covered in the following table.

Method	Examples	When used
Informal written	E-mail messages, memorandums	Used frequently on the project to convey information and communicate.
Formal written	Contracts, legal notices, project documents (e.g., the Charter), important project communications	Used infrequently, but essential for prominent documents that go into the project record. The project plan is a formal written document.
Informal verbal	Meetings, discussions, phone calls, conversations	Used to communicate information quickly and efficiently.
Formal verbal	Speeches, mass communications, presentations	Used for public relations, special events, company-wide announcements, sales.

Plan Communications Mgt.

Be aware that not just the message but also the medium determines whether a form of communication is formal or informal.

Another way of framing communications is to think of them in one of the following three categories:

Category	Examples
Interactive	A meeting where people can ask questions
Push	A bulk e-mail blast
Pull	A website where a video presentation or white paper can be downloaded

Meetings — See Ch. 2, Common Tools

Outputs

Kev Fact

Communications Management Plan

The communications management plan is part of the project management plan, and it defines the following:

• Who should receive project communications

• What communications they should receive

• Who should send the communication

• How the communication will be sent

• How often it will be updated

• Definitions so that everyone has a common understanding of terms

Project Doc. Updates — See Ch. 2, Common Outputs

Manage Communications

What it is:

It is easiest to consider the process of Manage Communications as the execution of the communications management plan. In other words, the communications management plan lays out how communications will be handled, and the process of Manage Communications carries that out.

Keep in mind that while Manage Communications is performed according to the communications management plan, it must also be flexible so that unplanned information requests may be handled.

Why it is important:

Manage Communications is the process where the bulk of project communications takes place.

When it is performed:

Manage Communications generally updates stakeholders on the progress of the project according to the communications management plan. It may start quite early on the project, but it typically elevates in importance and activity during the construction phase of the project.

How it works:

Inputs

Communications Management Plan

The communications management plan, a component of the project management plan, is an ingredient here. It is indispensable to this process since it defines how this process will be carried out.

Work Performance Reports

Much of project communication will be related to the project's performance, and the performance reports provide that information to this process.

Enterprise Environ. Factors — See Ch. 2, Common Inputs

Org. Process Assets — See Ch. 2, Common Inputs

Tools

Communication Technology

See description under the tools of previous process, Plan Communications Management.

Communication Models

See description under the tools of previous process, Plan Communications Management.

Communication Methods

See description under the tools of previous process, Plan Communications Management.

Information Management Systems

This represents tools that facilitate communication and the distribution and management of information. For example, an intranet portal site would be a good example of an information management system, as would an e-mail system, text messaging, electronic document archival system, or even the postal service. Anything that helps manage information and get information into the hands of stakeholders qualifies.

Kev Fact

Performance Reporting

Performance reporting used to be organized in its own process. Now it is a tool under Manage Communications. It involves creating reports for the stakeholders that show how the project is progressing against the plan. The tool is used early on the project and takes on increasing importance as the project enters the construction phase where more resources and costs are expended.

The essential point is to create performance reports and use them as a communication tool. The performance reports show how the project is progressing against the various baselines (scope, time, cost, and quality). They may have numerous formats and content, including graphics for schedules and earned value information. The performance reports are tailored to the audience. For instance, the project manager may produce only a one-page executive summary for the sponsor, while a more detailed report may be prepared and distributed for the team.

Outputs

Kev Fact

Project Communications

Any time information is being exchanged with stakeholders, this output comes into play. Recall from earlier in this chapter that communications may be formal or informal, oral or written.

PM Plan Updates — See Ch. 2, Common Outputs

Project Documents Updates — See Ch. 2, Common Outputs

Organizational Process Assets Updates

This includes the normal components outlined in Chapter 2, Common Inputs, but would also contain the obvious output of the information you distributed in whatever format.

Manage Communications

Monitoring & Controlling

Control Communications

What it is:

Monitoring and controlling processes look at what was planned and compare that with the work that was executed. Control Communications does exactly that. It compares the results of the previous process (Manage Communications) and compares it with the communications management plan. If there are differences, adjustments are made to the plan or to the way the work is being carried out.

Why it is important:

Communication issues are responsible for more than their share of project problems and failures. Getting the plan right and then executing it well is extremely important.

When it is performed:

Control Communications is started early in the project and is performed periodically throughout. As long as there are project communications taking place, it would be an appropriate time to perform this process.

How it works:

Inputs

Project Management Plan - See Ch. 2, Common Inputs

Key Fact

Project Communications

All of the project communications that were produced in the previous process (Manage Communications) are brought into Control Communications. This way you have the plan and the results to compare.

Key Fact

Issue Log

The issue log may contain communications-related issues that need to be carefully considered in this process.

Work Performance Data — See Ch. 2, Common Outputs

Organizational Process Assets — See Ch. 2, Common Inputs

Tools

Information Management Systems

Information management systems facilitate storing and sharing information in the right format.

Expert Judgment — See Ch. 2, Common Tools

Meetings — See Ch. 2, Common Tools

Outputs

Work Performance Information

WPI explains the performance data that was gathered.

Change Requests

Most times that you see the output of change requests in this book, it is marked as a common output with no further commentary. The only exception here is that change requests are a very predictable output when communication is reviewed. They may be changes to the project scope, changes to the work being performed, changes to how the work is carried out, or (most likely) changes to how progress is being communicated.

PM Plan Updates — See Ch. 2, Common Outputs

Project Documents Updates — See Ch. 2, Common Outputs

Org. Process Assets Upd. — See Ch. 2, Common Outputs

Control Communications

Exercises

1. **Calculate the number of communication channels that would exist between eight people.**

2. **Draw a line connecting the specific form of communication on the left to the corresponding type of communication on the right.**

E-mail

Testimony before congress

Speech at a trade show

Contract addendum

Hallway conversation with a coworker

Informal Written

Formal Written

Informal Verbal

Formal Verbal

Answers to Exercises

1. Calculate the number of communication channels for 8 people.

With 8 individuals, there are 28 communication channels as proven by the formula $8 \times (8\text{-}1) \div 2 = 28$

A graphical depiction of the 28 communication channels between the 8 people

2. The forms of communication are illustrated below:

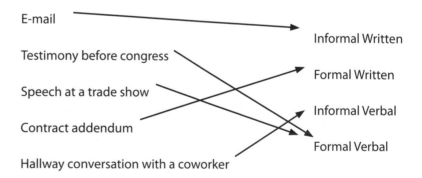

E-mail — Informal Written

Testimony before congress — Formal Written

Speech at a trade show — Informal Verbal

Contract addendum — Formal Verbal

Hallway conversation with a coworker

IMPORTANT

In addition to this quiz, use your Key to InSite, found on the inside back cover of this book, to access additional content, including new exam questions, expanded content, and simulated PMP exams. If your book did not come with a Key to InSite on the inside back cover, it may not be authentic. If you do not have a Key to InSite, you may purchase one at *insite.velociteach.com*.

Communications Management Questions

1. **If there were 4 people on the project team and 9 more are added, how many additional channels of communication does this create?**

    A.   6.

    B.   30.

    C.   36.

    D.   72.

2. **The process to create a plan showing how all project communication will be conducted is known as:**

    A.   Communications Modeling.

    B.   Plan Communications Management.

    C.   Information Method.

    D.   Communication Distribution Planning.

3. **The responsibility of decoding the message rests with:**

    A.   The sender.

    B.   The receiver.

    C.   The communications management plan.

    D.   The communications model.

4. **Which of the following is FALSE regarding Manage Communications?**

    A.   Manage Communications is an executing process.

    B.   Manage Communications ends when the product has been accepted.

    C.   Manage Communications may involve unexpected requests from stakeholders.

    D.   Manage Communications carries out the communications management plan.

5. **Acknowledgement in the context of the communication model indicates:**

    A.   Confirmation of receipt.

    B.   Comprehension of the sender's message.

    C.   Agreement with the sender's message.

    D.   Agreement upon a protocol and frequency of communication.

6. **Your latest review of the project status shows it to be more than three weeks behind schedule. You are required to communicate this to the customer. This message should be:**

    A.   Formal and written.

    B.   Informal and written.

    C.   Formal and verbal.

    D.   Informal and verbal.

7. **Which of the following statements is TRUE regarding issues?**

    A.   All issues must be resolved in order for the project to be closed.

    B.   The issue log is a tool for stakeholders to manage project issues.

    C.   Each issue should be assigned to a single owner.

    D.   Issue management may be treated as a sub-project on larger, more complex projects.

8. **The majority of a person's communication is:**

   A. Verbal.

   B. Nonverbal.

   C. Documented.

   D. Unnecessary.

9. **Which of the following communication techniques is the most effective for resolving conflict?**

   A. Instant messaging.

   B. Conference calls.

   C. Formal written communication.

   D. Face-to-face communication.

10. **Communication skills would be used most during which of the following processes?**

    A. Manage Communications.

    B. Status Meetings.

    C. Report Performance.

    D. Communications Change Control.

11. **The communications management plan typically contains all of the following EXCEPT:**

    A. The expected stakeholder response to the communication.

    B. The stakeholder communication requirements.

    C. What technology will be used to communicate information.

    D. A glossary of terms.

12. **You are about to attend a biweekly status meeting with your program manager when she calls and asks you to be certain to include earned value analysis in this and future meetings. Why is earned value analysis important to the communications process?**

    A. It communicates the project's long term success.

    B. It communicates how the project is doing against the plan.

    C. It communicates the date the project deviated from the plan.

    D. It communicates the value-to-cost ratio.

13. **You receive a last-minute status report from a senior member of the project team that you believe is incorrect. It shows tasks as complete that you are almost certain are no more than 60% complete, and it documents deliverables as having been turned over to the customer that you do not believe are even finished yet. You are walking into a communication meeting with key stakeholders. What is the BEST way to handle this problem?**

A. Ask the team member who wrote the report to sign the bottom of it.

B. Ask the stakeholders to wait a few minutes while you try to verify the information.

C. Summon the project team to the meeting and get to the bottom of the discrepancy.

D. Do nothing with this status and provide an amended report at the next meeting with the stakeholders.

14. **The MOST important skill for a project manager to have is:**

A. Good administrative skills.

B. Good planning skills.

C. Good client-facing skills.

D. Good communication skills.

15. **Performance reporting is a tool that is most closely associated with which process?**

A. Plan Communications Management.

B. Manage Communications.

C. Report Performance.

D. Control Communications.

16. **The best definition of noise is:**

   A.   Any unsupportable information that finds its way onto written or verbal project communications.

   B.   Anything that interferes with transmission and understanding of a message.

   C.   Any communication that takes place through unofficial project channels.

   D.   A communications acronym for Normal Operational Informing of Select project Entities.

17. **A project manager is holding a meeting with stakeholders related to the status of a large project for constructing a new runway at a major airport. The runway project has a CPI of 1.2 and an SPI of 1.25, and the manager is going to have to deliver the message to the stakeholders that a crucial quality test has failed. What kind of communication does this meeting represent?**

   A.   Formal verbal.

   B.   Informal verbal.

   C.   Paralingual.

   D.   Nonverbal.

18. **You have just taken over as the project manager for the construction of a new runway for a major airport. The project is already in progress, and there are over 200 identified stakeholders on the project. You want to know how to communicate with these stakeholders. Where should you be able to find this information?**

   A.   It depends on the type of project.

   B.   The stakeholder management plan.

   C.   The communications management plan.

   D.   Communication requirements.

Communications Questions

19. **Mary is using forecasting to determine her project's estimate at complete. What would be the most likely place to include this information?**

   A. The communications management plan.

   B. The project activity report.

   C. The performance reports.

   D. The stakeholder management report.

20. **Marie is a project manager who is involved in a meeting with the customer. After the customer makes a statement, Marie carefully reformulates and restates the message back to them. What is Marie practicing in this case?**

   A. Listening skills.

   B. Project communications management.

   C. Professional courtesy.

   D. Passive listening.

21. **Lessons learned should contain:**

   A. The collective wisdom of the team.

   B. Feedback from the customer as to what you could have done better.

   C. Information to be used as an input into administrative closure.

   D. Analysis of the variances that occurred from the project's baseline.

22. **In which process would earned value analysis be used?**

   A. Plan Communications Management.

   B. Manage Communications.

   C. Report Performance.

   D. Report Project Value.

23. **Information sent to specific recipients who need to receive it but that is not confirmed to be received or understood by the receiver is known as:**

    A.   The communication model.

    B.   Push communication.

    C.   Pull communication.

    D.   Noise.

24. **Information sensitivity and security would be of greatest concern when:**

    A.   Working on government projects.

    B.   Evaluating the communications model.

    C.   Choosing the appropriate communications technology.

    D.   Rumors or inaccurate information are being circulated.

25. **The issue log is used in which communications management process?**

    A.   Plan Communications Management.

    B.   Push Communication.

    C.   Manage Communications.

    D.   Control Communications.

Answers to Communications Questions

1. D. If you tried to take a shortcut here, chances are you missed this one and guessed 'C'. If there were 4 people, there would have been 6 communication channels. 9 more would create 13, which equals 78 communications channels. The question is asking how many additional channels were created, so the answer is 78-6 = 72.

2. B. Plan Communications Management is the process for determining how the overall communication process will be carried out. It is the general plan for communications. None of the other three answers were terms used in this book, but the real giveaway was that only one answer 'B' was even the name of a process.

3. B. In the communication model, it is the sender that encodes, and the receiver decodes the message.

4. B. Did you get tricked by this one? Manage Communications doesn't always end when acceptance has occurred, so this is the answer that doesn't fit. Some stakeholders will need information distributed on the closure of the contracts and projects. 'A' is true, because Manage Communications is an executing process. 'C' is true because Manage Communications carries out predetermined communication, but also will be used to respond to unplanned requests from stakeholders. 'D' is true because Manage Communications is the process that executes the communications management plan.

5. A. Within the communication model, acknowledgement only indicates confirmation of receipt. It does not mean that the receiver understood the message or agreed with the message.

6. A. Communication on schedule slippage, cost overruns, and other major project statuses should be formal and in writing. That doesn't mean you can't pick up the phone to soften the blow, but the formal and written aspects of the communication are what count here.

7. C. Each issue should be assigned to an owner and be assigned a target completion date. 'A' is incorrect since a project could be closed (successfully) and still have outstanding issues. Sometimes the issues are out of the project manager's control. 'B' is incorrect since the issue log is not for the stakeholders – it is for the project manager to use to manage issues. 'D' is incorrect because issues are managed within the context of a project. If you were even considering creating a separate project to manage issues, your project is probably beyond hope.

Communications Answers

8. B. Most of a person's communication takes place non verbally. It is body language that carries much of the message. 'A' is the opposite of the correct answer. 'C' is incorrect since most of the communication is nonverbal, but not written (documented). 'D' may well be true for some people, but it is not the right answer here.

9. D. Face-to-face communication is the most effective means of resolving conflict. This fits an overall theme that direct, clear, and personal communication is favored for project managers. If you guessed 'A', go find a place to hide in shame, or at least go sit in time out for a few minutes. 'B' and 'C' might seem like appropriate choices in some situations, but face-to-face is still more effective.

10. A. Your communications skills are used as a tool in Manage Communications. 'B', 'C', and 'D' should have been easy to eliminate since they are not real processes.

11. A. The expected response you will receive is not part of the communications management plan. The communications management plan focuses on how you will communicate to stakeholders and not how they will communicate to you. 'B', 'C', and 'D' are all typically part of the communications management plan.

12. B. Earned value analysis is a communication tool, and it's all about how the project is doing against the plan.

13. B. This is a hard question, but be prepared for questions like this on the PMP! The reasoning behind it is this: a project manager should always communicate good information and should always report the truth. 'A' is wrong because it isn't about getting your team member to sign off. Accurate information is more important than accountability. 'C' is incorrect because it is not the team's job to go to these meetings. They should be doing the work on the project. 'D' is incorrect because waiting only postpones the situation and delays getting accurate information to the stakeholders. Choice 'B' is best in this case because it is the only one that gets accurate information to the stakeholders as quickly as possible.

14. D. Good communication skills are the most important skills a project manager can have! Project managers spend more time communicating than anything else.

15. B. Performance reporting is a tool of the Manage Communications process. 'C' would have been a good choice years ago when such a process existed, but it is not a process for this edition of the exam.

16. B. Noise is anything that interferes with the transmission and understanding of a message. If you guessed 'D', then you were indeed guessing.

17. B. Many people incorrectly guess 'A' for this question, but meetings are classified as informal verbal - even when the subject matter is important!

18. C. The stakeholder's communication needs are all contained in the communications management plan.

19. C. Performance reporting is a tool in the Manage Communications process, and it uses forecasting to show how the project is progressing. Performance reports often contain the estimate at complete and the estimate to complete, as well as the cost and schedule performance indexes. 'A' was the only other answer that contained a term that is used in this book, and it is not an appropriate match for this question.

20. A. Marie is practicing good listening skills to make sure she communicates well with her customer.

21. D. This is important! Lessons learned focus on variances from the plan and what would be done differently in the future in order to avoid those variances.

22. B. Earned value analysis factors in the difference between what was planned and the work that was actually accomplished. This information can then be distributed out to the appropriate stakeholders, which is done in the Manage Communications process.

23. B. Push communication is communication that is pushed out (think bulk email), but the drawback is that there is no confirmation by the receiver that it was received or understood.

24. C. One of the key, deciding factors when selecting the right communication technology is how sensitive or confidential the information is. 'A' might look like a good answer at first, but not all government projects are particularly confidential or sensitive.

25. D. Even if you didn't know the inputs, tools, and outputs, it may have been intuitive to you that the issue log was tied to the monitoring and controlling process here. It is used as an input into Control Communications.

11 Risk Management

Difficulty	Memorization	Exam Importance
HIGH	MEDIUM	HIGH

If the previous chapter seemed light and somewhat easy, you are about to make up for that. Risk management is a very rich field, full of information and tools for statistical analysis. In the real world, actuaries anticipate risk and calculate the probability of risk events and their associated costs, and entire volumes are written on risk analysis and mitigation. In this section, you do not need to know every tool and technique associated with risk. Instead, focus your study on the high level interactions within the different risk processes.

Philosophy

By this time, you should have picked up on the fact that very few of these processes are reactive. The overriding philosophy is that the project manager is in control and proactively managing events, avoiding as many problems as possible. The project manager must understand how to anticipate and identify areas of risk, how to quantify and qualify them, and how to plan for them.

The processes of Project Risk Management with their *primary* outputs

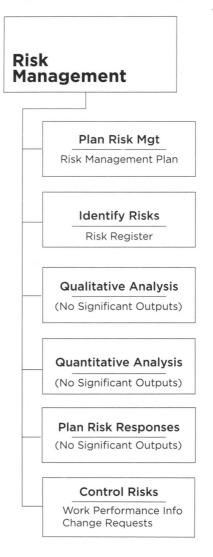

Risk Management

Plan Risk Mgt
Risk Management Plan

Identify Risks
Risk Register

Qualitative Analysis
(No Significant Outputs)

Quantitative Analysis
(No Significant Outputs)

Plan Risk Responses
(No Significant Outputs)

Control Risks
Work Performance Info
Change Requests

Importance

Risk is one of the areas many people find difficult on the exam. The material may be new or unfamiliar, and the techniques may take some work in order to master.

Preparation

In order to pass this section of the exam, you need to understand the risk management plan and the terms related to risk. The 6 risk management processes contain 75 inputs, tools, and outputs! All of these components to the processes are important, but the secret is that most of them are either common sense or they rarely are exploited on the exam. This chapter puts more emphasis on the essential elements that you need to know. Material is organized around these six processes, building upon the different components that go with each one.

There are six processes within project risk management, and these processes touch only two process groups: planning (Plan Risk Management, Identify Risks, Perform Qualitative Risk Analysis, Perform Quantitative Risk Analysis, Plan Risk Responses), and monitoring and controlling (Control Risks).

Process Group	Risk Management Process
Initiating	(none)
Planning	Plan Risk Management, Identify Risks, Perform Qualitative Risk Analysis, Perform Quantitative Risk Analysis, Plan Risk Responses
Executing	(none)
Monitoring & Controlling	Control Risks
Closing	(none)

The primary outputs associated with the six risk management processes are shown in the table below.

Process	Primary Outputs
Plan Risk Management	Risk management plan
Identify Risks	Risk register
Perform Qualitative Risk Analysis	Project Documents Updates
Perform Quantitative Risk Analysis	Project Documents Updates
Plan Risk Responses	Project Documents Updates
Control Risks	Work performance information Change requests

Risk

The usage of the word "risk" here has a different meaning than many project managers and organizations may have encountered before. Risk has two characteristics that must be understood for the exam:

1. Risk is related to an uncertain event.

2. A risk may affect the project for good or for bad. Although risk usually has negative connotations, it may well have an upside. This is a favorite exploit on the exam.

Planning   ## Plan Risk Management

What it is:

Plan Risk Management is the process that is concerned with one thing: creating the risk management plan. Your understanding of that plan is the key to unlocking this process and will form the foundation for the other risk management processes.

In Plan Risk Management, the remaining five risk management processes are planned. How they will be conducted is documented in the risk management plan, which is typically general and high-level in nature. This means that when performing Plan Risk Management, you usually are not concerned with specific project risks. Instead, you will focus on how risk will be approached on the project.

Why it is important:

Think of this process as creating your roadmap for the five processes of Identify Risks, Perform Qualitative Risk Analysis, Perform Quantitative Risk Analysis, Plan Risk Responses, and Control Risks. By creating a plan (the risk management plan) for these five processes, you are being deliberate and proactive with risk on the project.

The more risk that is inherent on the project, and the more important the project is to the organization, the more resources you would typically apply to performing this process.

When it is performed:

This process is general and high-level in nature and therefore takes place early on the project, usually before many of the

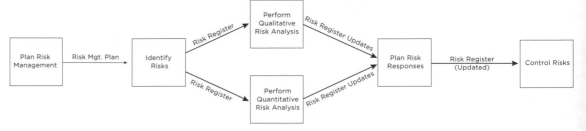

A diagram showing the order of the Risk Management processes

other planning processes are performed. The reason it usually takes place very early is that the results of this (and other risk processes) can significantly influence decisions made about scope, time, cost, quality, and procurement.

How it works:

Inputs

Project Management Plan

This process brings in as much information as is known about the project in order to create a risk management plan with an approach compatible with the project plan's.

Project Charter

The charter may contain information about risk tolerance or constraints and assumptions that need to be factored into the risk management plan.

Stakeholder Register

The stakeholder register is important to this process because it lists stakeholders who may be able to give input about risk approaches and who may be affected by risk management decisions.

Enterprise Environ. Factors — See Ch. 2, Common Inputs

Organizational Process Assets — See Ch. 2, Common Inputs

Tools

Key Fact

Analytical Techniques

As is stressed in this process, the risk management plan outlines the project's overall approach to risk, and this is determined through careful analysis to determine the appropriate level of risks for the various areas and the approach warranted on the project.

Expert Judgment — See Ch. 2, Common Tools

Meetings — See Ch. 2, Common Tools

Outputs

Kev Fact

Risk Management Plan

As stated in the introduction to this process, creating the risk management plan is the real purpose of this process. In fact, it is the process's sole output.

The risk management plan is a roadmap to the other five risk management processes. It defines what level of risk will be considered tolerable for the project, how risk will be managed, who will be responsible for risk activities, the amounts of time and cost that will be allotted to risk activities, and how risk findings will be communicated.

Another important part of the risk management plan is a description of how risks will be categorized. This will be a significant help in the subsequent risk processes. One tool for creating consistent risk categories is the risk breakdown structure (RBS).

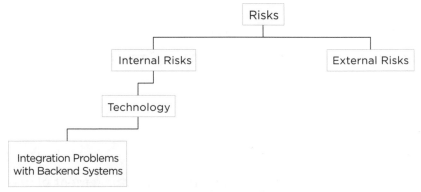

An example RBS showing risk categories

The RBS, like its cousin the WBS, is a graphical, hierarchical decomposition used to facilitate understanding and organization.

In this case, however, we are breaking down the categories of risks and not the work. One important thing to note with the RBS is that we are not breaking down the actual risks (they won't be known until we perform the Identify Risks process). Instead, we are breaking down the categories of risks that we will evaluate.

The risk management plan may contain more information such as standard vocabulary about probability and impact that apply to the project.

Identify Risks

Planning

Identify Risks

What it is:

Identify Risks is a planning process that evaluates the project to identify which risks could impact the project and to understand the nature of these risks.

There is a single output from this process, and that should help you understand it better. The output is the risk register, which is a list of all risks, their causes, and any possible responses to those risks that can be identified at this point in the project.

Be aware that Identify Risks, like many processes discussed in this book, is often performed multiple times on the project. This may be especially true in this case since your understanding of risk, and the nature of the risks themselves, will change and evolve as the project progresses.

Why it is important:

Identify Risks builds the risk register, which is needed before the remaining four risk processes (Perform Qualitative Risk Analysis, Perform Quantitative Risk Analysis, Plan Risk Responses, and Control Risks) may be performed. This list of risks will drive the other risk processes.

When it is performed:

Although Identify Risks is typically performed early on in the project, risks change over time, and new risks arise. It may be necessary to perform this process multiple times throughout the project.

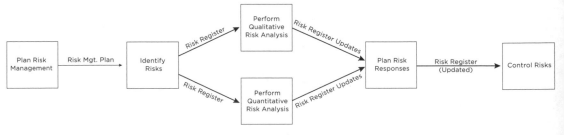

A diagram showing the order of the Risk Management processes

Identify Risks

How it works:

Inputs

There are 13 inputs into this process, but don't let the sheer number concern you. Do not focus your time on memorizing the list. Most of them are closely related and are easily understood.

Risk Management Plan — See Plan Risk Mgt, Outputs

Cost Management Plan

The cost management plan, schedule management plan, quality management plan, and human resource plan all explain how these components will be managed and implemented on the project. The information in any of these three plans may increase or reduce project risk.

Schedule Management Plan

See description under the Cost Management Plan input above.

Quality Management Plan

See description under the Cost Management Plan input above.

Human Resource Plan

See description under the Cost Management Plan input above.

Kev Fact

Scope Baseline

This input, combined with the next two inputs (Activity Cost Estimates and Activity Duration Estimates), documents the understanding of the scope, schedule, and budget. These inputs represent the typical areas of greatest project risk and should be reviewed carefully to see if they present risks to this particular project.

Kev Fact

Activity Cost Estimates

See description under the Scope Baseline input above.

Activity Duration Estimates

See description under the Scope Baseline input above.

Stakeholder Register — See Identify Stakeholders, Outputs

Project Documents

The project documentation contains information that may help identify the risks present on the project. These documents are necessary because of the tool of documentation review used in this process.

Procurement Documents

Procurement activities introduce their own unique risks due to the fact that they are using external entities to perform project work.

Enterprise Environ. Factors — See Ch. 2, Common Inputs

Organizational Process Assets — See Ch. 2, Common Inputs

Tools

Documentation Reviews

A documentation review is a review of all project documentation that exists to date. The documentation is reviewed for completeness, correctness, and consistency. For instance, if the plan appears sketchy or quickly thrown together, that could identify a significant risk, especially if the project were of high importance.

Information Gathering Techniques

There are numerous techniques for gathering information to create the risk register. The techniques most commonly discussed in the context of risk are: brainstorming, Delphi technique, expert interviews, and root cause identification.

Kev Fact

Checklist Analysis

Checklist analysis uses a Risk Breakdown Structure (RBS), either from this project or from a previous project, to check off items and ensure that all significant risks or categories are being evaluated.

Although it may not be exhaustive, this tool provides structure to the Identify Risks process.

Assumptions Analysis

Assumptions should not only be documented, they should also be analyzed and challenged if necessary.

Key Fact

Diagramming Techniques

Ishikawa diagrams, also called cause-and-effect diagrams and fishbone diagrams, are one way to show how potential causes can lead to risks.

Another diagramming method used to identify risks is influence diagrams. This category shows how one set of factors may influence another. For instance, late arrival of materials may not be a significant risk by itself, but it may influence other factors, such as triggering overtime work or causing quality problems later on in the project due to inadequate time to properly perform the work.

Finally, flow charts are useful in identifying risks. Flow charts are graphical representations of complex process flows. They are especially useful because they can break down something very complex into an understandable diagram.

Strengths, Weaknesses, Opportunities, and Threats (SWOT) Analysis

SWOT analysis is particularly useful since it is a tool used to measure each risk's strengths (S), weaknesses (W), opportunities (O), and threats (T). Each risk is plotted, and the quadrant where the weaknesses (usually internal) and threats (usually external) are highest, and the quadrant where strengths (again, usually internal), and opportunities (usually external) are highest will represent the highest risks on the project.

SWOT analysis can give you another perspective on risk that will often help you identify your most significant project risk factors.

	Helpful	Harmful
Internal	**Strength** J F	**Weakness** N L D O E
External	**Opportunity** G A C M H	**Threat** P K I B

Illustration of one type of SWOT analysis where each letter corresponds to a specified risk from the risk register

Expert Judgment — See Ch. 2, Common Tools

Outputs

Kev Fact

→ *Risk Register*

As stated earlier, the risk register provides a list of all identified risks on the project, what the possible reactions to this risk are, what the root causes are, and what categories the risks fall into. It is also common to update the RBS with the more specific information as the following example illustrates.

The risk register is an essential input into the remaining risk management processes and may be updated throughout the life of the project.

Identify Risks

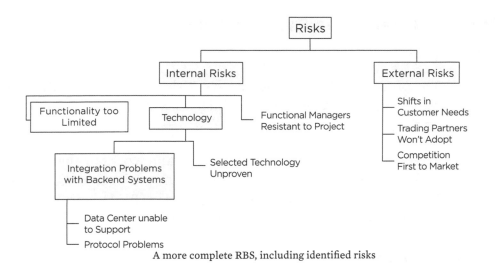

A more complete RBS, including identified risks

Risk ID	Risk	Responses	Root Cause	Categories
R001	Threat of being hacked	Firewall; intrusion detection software	Poorly designed security; Outdated technology	Security

Fragment of a Risk Register

Identify Risks

Planning

Perform Qualitative Risk Analysis

What it is:

The process of Perform Qualitative Risk Analysis is usually done rapidly in order to determine which risks are the highest priority on the project.

It takes each risk from the risk register and works to analyze its probability of occurring and impact to the project if it did occur. By using the probability and impact matrix (PIM), a prioritization and ranking can be created, which is updated on the risk register.

Why it is important:

This process helps you rank and prioritize the risks so that you can put the right emphasis on the right risks. It helps to ensure that time and resources are spent in the right risk areas.

When it is performed:

Perform Qualitative Risk Analysis, like many other risk processes, is usually performed more than once on a project. The reason for this is twofold:

1. Perform Qualitative Risk Analysis can usually be performed fairly quickly relative to other planning processes.

2. It is normal for risks and their underlying characteristics to change over the life of the project, making this process important to revisit often.

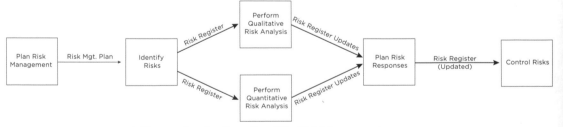

A diagram showing the order of the Risk Management processes

Identify Risks

How it works:

Inputs

Risk Management Plan

The risk management plan should define the overall approach to risk on the project, including how much risk is acceptable and who will be responsible for carrying out the analysis of the risks.

Scope Baseline

The scope has a large influence on risk. Items in the scope that are well-known and understood will have less uncertainty, while items that are not understood as well will have higher uncertainty.

Risk Register

The risk register specifies each risk to be analyzed as part of this process.

Enterprise Environ. Factors — See Ch. 2, Common Inputs

Organizational Process Assets — See Ch. 2, Common Inputs

Tools

The next two tools, because of their similarities, will be discussed together. Although they are different, it is highly unlikely you would be called upon to differentiate between them for the exam.

Kev Fact *Risk Probability and Impact Assessment / Probability and Impact Matrix*

When evaluating risks to determine what the highest priorities should be, the two tools and techniques mentioned above can assist you. The way they are used is that each risk in the risk register is evaluated for its likelihood of occurring and its potential impact on the project. Each of these two values is given a ranking (such as low, medium, high, or 1 through 10) and are multiplied together to get a risk score. This resulting score is used to set the priorities.

Qualitative Risk Analysis

Risk Data Quality Assessment

The data used should be objectively evaluated to determine whether or not it is accurate and of acceptable quality. For instance, if you were evaluating weather risk for a construction project, you would need to evaluate the quality of the weather data you were using.

Risk Categorization

Categorizing the detailed risks can help you build a better big-picture of the risks. This may help you understand which parts of the project have the highest degree of uncertainty. The RBS is a common way to help organize the identified risks into categories.

Risk Urgency Assessment

Urgent risks are those that cannot wait. As you are evaluating the risks, it is important to determine which risks are the most urgent, requiring immediate attention. For instance, if you determined that a building's structural support may be inadequate, that would require immediate attention, while other risks, such as future weather threats, although equally important, might be less urgent.

Expert Judgment— See Ch. 2, Common Tools

Outputs

Project Documents Updates

Project documents (especially the risk register) are going to be updated as a part of this analysis. Now that more detail is known, it should be added to the register, including the priority of the risks, the urgency of the risks, the categorization of the risks, and any trends that were noticed while performing this process.

nning

Perform Quantitative Risk Analysis

What it is:

This process is very easy to confuse with the previously covered Perform Qualitative Risk Analysis, and in reality the processes have quite a lot in common; however, Perform Quantitative Risk Analysis seeks to assign a projected value to *quantify* the risks that have been ranked by Perform Qualitative Risk Analysis. This likely value is most often specified in terms of cost or time. Make sure to be able to differentiate between this process and the previous one before taking the exam.

Why it is important:

Perform Quantitative Risk Analysis updates the risk register, and this information will be used by the subsequent two processes (Plan Risk Responses and Control Risks). Without performing this process, the information about the identified risk is less complete and less useful.

When it is performed:

Perform Quantitative Risk Analysis relies on the prioritized list of risks from the Perform Qualitative Risk Analysis process. Therefore, it is usually performed right after Perform Qualitative Risk Analysis; however, in some cases they may be performed at the same time.

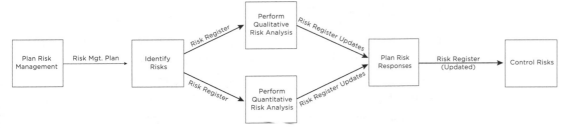

A diagram showing the order of the Risk Management processes

How it works:

Inputs

Risk Management Plan — See Plan Risk Mgt., Outputs

Qualitative Risk Analysis

Cost Management Plan

In case you are wondering why the cost and schedule management plans are included and the scope management plan is not, consider that the cost and schedule are easily quantified, and this process is concerned with quantifying the risks. Although scope may present important risks to the project, it generally fits better into the qualitative risk analysis.

Schedule Management Plan

See explanation for Cost Management Plan input above.

Risk Register — See Identify Risks, Outputs

Enterprise Environ. Factors — See Ch. 2, Common Inputs

Organizational Process Assets — See Ch. 2, Common Inputs

Tools

Data Gathering and Representation Techniques

Interviewing

Interviewing uses a structured interview to ask experts about the likelihood and impact of identified risks. After interviewing several experts, for instance, the project manager might create pessimistic, optimistic, and realistic values associated with each risk.

Probability Distributions

Probability distributions are mathematical representations that show the probability of an event occurring. The probability is usually expressed as a table or graph. Consider flipping a coin as an example. You would have two possible outcomes from this event: heads or tails. Now imagine flipping this coin six times. Doing this, we can analyze the probability of the coin landing on heads a given number of times.

Number of "heads" seen over six coin tosses	Probability
0	1.56%
1	9.38%
2	23.44%
3	31.24%
4	23.44%
5	9.38%
6	1.56%
Total:	100%

Pay particular attention to the way the probability first rises and then falls as the number of occurrences increases. This is typical with probability distributions. The most likely outcome here is 3 heads. Also notice that in this case, the probabilities add up to 100%. This is because heads has to show up from 0 to 6 times when the coin is tossed 6 times. There are no other outcomes, therefore this accounts for 100% of the possibilities.

Probability distributions are very useful for analyzing risks. They allow the project manager to take a good look at the real probability of an event occurring and to make a rational decision about how to approach the risk.

Kev Fact

Quantitative Risk Analysis and Modeling Techniques

Sensitivity Analysis

Sensitivity analysis is used to analyze your project and determine how sensitive it is to risk. In other words, you are analyzing whether the occurrence of a particular negative risk event would ruin the project or merely be an inconvenience.

Expected Monetary Value Analysis

Expected monetary value analysis takes uncertain events and assigns them a most likely monetary value (i.e., dollar amount). It is typically calculated by using decision trees, covered next.

Decision Tree Analysis

Decision trees are used to show probability and arrive at a dollar amount associated with each risk.

Quantitative Risk Analysis

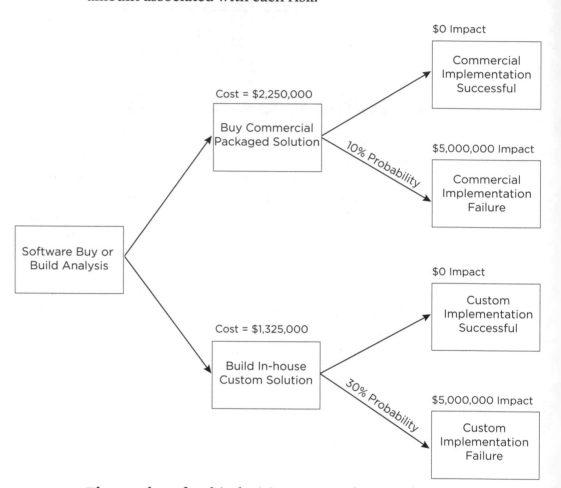

The numbers for this decision tree work out as follows:

	Initial Cost	Risk Cost	Probability	Total
Commercial Package	$2,250,000	$5,000,000	10%	$2,750,000
Custom Software	$1,325,000	$5,000,000	30%	$2,825,000

The totals above were calculated by multiplying the risk cost by the probability and adding that value to the initial cost.

Tornado Diagrams

Tornado diagrams, named for the funnel shape of their bars, are one way to analyze project sensitivity to cost or other factors.

Change in project cost due to a 10% change in labor costs with all other project costs held constant.

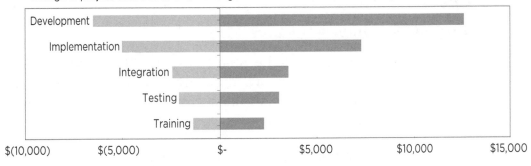

Change in Project Costs

A tornado diagram, used to depict risks

The tornado diagram above depicts the effects of a 10% change in labor costs on the project. If labor costs increase by 10% and all other costs hold steady, development will be affected the most. Specifically, if the costs rise by 10%, then the development costs will rise by approximately $13,000. If the labor costs fall by 10%, development costs will fall by approximately $7,000. This shows how sensitive each analyzed area of the project is to risk (in this case, the risk of a cost increase).

A tornado diagram ranks the bars from greatest to least on the project so that the chart takes on a tornado-like shape.

Modeling and Simulation

There are almost as many types of simulation as there are projects; however, one technique for simulating the schedule is Monte Carlo analysis.

This is a favorite topic on the exam. Monte Carlo analysis, also discussed in Chapter 6 – Time Management, is a tool that takes details and assembles a big picture. Performed by computer, Monte Carlo analysis throws large numbers of scenarios at the schedule to see the impact of certain risk events. This technique will show you what is not always evident by simply looking at the schedule. It will often identify tasks that may not appear inherently high risk, but in the event they are delayed, the whole project may be adversely affected.

Expert Judgment

People with expertise in the areas of risk that you are evaluating are one of the richest sources of data gathering. Asking experts to review your data and your methodology can be very useful.

Outputs

Project Documents Updates

Several documents could be updated as a result of this process. For example, the scope or schedule might be changed in order to account for risk; however, the most common document update is the risk register.

The risk register is updated with the probabilities associated with each identified risk and the probability of meeting the project's cost and time projections. Additionally, the priorities of the risks should be updated, and any trends that have been observed should be noted.

Do not forget that a risk may be beneficial! As an example, when you purchase a lottery ticket you are running the risk that you will win money, and that risk can be quantified. If you are constructing a building, you would plan for a certain amount of bad weather to impact the construction schedule; however, you run the risk that the weather will be worse than anticipated as well as the risk that the weather will be better than anticipated. This usage of the word risk is counter-intuitive to many people, but it is correct within the domain of project management because the risk is in the uncertainty, not just in the outcome.

anning

Plan Risk Responses

What it is:

Earlier, in the process of Plan Risk Management, we created a general approach to risk (the risk management plan). Then, in Identify Risks, we created a list of risks and started our risk register. Then we qualitatively and quantitatively analyzed the risks, and now we are ready to create a detailed plan for managing the risk. That is precisely what Plan Risk Responses does; it creates a plan for how each risk will be handled.

Remember that risk can be a positive or negative event (e.g., there is a risk that the project will finish late, but there is also a risk that it will finish early). Therefore, careful consideration must be given to each risk, whether the impact of that risk is positive or negative.

Why it is important:

Up to this point all we have done is identify and analyze the risks, but now that the analysis is complete we need to create a specific plan. The resulting plan is actionable, meaning that it assigns specific tasks and responsibilities to specific team members.

When it is performed:

Plan Risk Responses is performed after all of the other risk planning processes have been completed. The updated risk register flows in as an input, and emerges as its primary output.

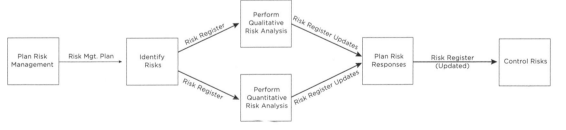

A diagram showing the order of the Risk Management processes

How it works:

Inputs

Risk Mgt. Plan — See Plan Risk Management, Outputs

Risk Register — See Identify Risks, Outputs

Tools

You will almost certainly see exam questions related to the risk responses. Be sure you can identify different responses based on behaviors described in the test questions.

Strategies for Negative Risks or Threats

Key Fact

Avoid

Avoidance is a very appropriate tool for working with undesirable risk in many circumstances. For instance, a software project may choose to avoid the risk associated with using a particular piece of cutting-edge technology in favor of using a slower but more reliable technology.

Transfer

To transfer a risk to another party is to make it their responsibility. Contractual agreements and insurance are common ways to transfer risks.

Mitigate

Mitigating a risk simply means to make it less. For instance, if you were concerned about the risk of weather damage to a construction project, you might choose to construct the building outside of the rainy season.

Accept

Acceptance is often a perfectly reasonable strategy for dealing with risk, whether positive or negative. When accepting a risk you are simply acknowledging that the best strategy may not be to avoid, transfer, mitigate, share, or enhance it. Instead, the best strategy may be simply to accept it and continue with the project. Many people miss questions on the exam related to this because they don't have the mindset that acceptance may be the best strategy if the cost or impact of the other strategies is too great. If you are struggling with this concept, consider that even the act of getting out of bed each day carries risks, but these are risks that most people readily accept.

Kev Fact

Strategies for Positive Risks or Opportunities

As is stressed throughout this chapter, risks can be positive or negative, and where positive risks are concerned, the project manager wants to take steps to make them more likely. The following are specific strategies taken to capitalize on the positive risks.

Exploit

The definition for risk is uncertainty. Where the strategy of exploitation is concerned, you are trying to remove any uncertainty. For instance, if a positive risk of finishing the project early is identified, then adding additional people to ensure that the project is completed early would be an example of exploiting the risk.

Share

In order to share a positive risk, the project seeks to improve the chances of the risk occurring by working with another party. For instance, if a defense contractor identifies a positive risk of getting a large order, they may determine that sharing that risk by partnering with another defense firm, or even a competitor, would be an acceptable strategy.

Enhance

Enhancing a positive risk first requires that you understand the underlying cause(s) of the risk. By working to influence the underlying risk triggers, you can increase the likelihood of the risk occurring. For example, an airline might add flights to a popular route during holidays in order to enhance traffic and profitability during heavy travel times.

Accept

See explanation under Strategies for Negative Risks or Threats.

Plan Risk Responses

Contingent Response Strategies

A contingent response strategy is one where the project team may make one decision related to risk, but make that decision contingent upon certain conditions. For example, a project team may decide to mitigate a technology risk by hiring an outside firm with expertise in that technology, but that decision might be contingent upon the outside firm meeting intermediate milestones related to that risk.

Expert Judgment — See Ch. 2, Common Tools

Outputs

PM Plan Updates — See Ch. 2, Common Outputs

Project Documents Updates

Now that a specific plan has been created for each risk in the risk register, the register should be updated to reflect this new information. Other documents may be affected as well.

Another area frequently updated is documents and agreements that reflect risk-related contract decisions. One of the tools for this process is to transfer the risk to another party. This tool can often result in contractual agreements. For instance, a company that has little experience in mission-critical software development may contract out that part of the project, but risk-related contract decisions would typically accompany this decision. In this example, it might be appropriate to specify cost, time, and performance targets for the subcontracting software company to meet in order to receive full payment.

Control Risks

What it is:

At this point, you should have detected a pattern with the knowledge areas. Knowledge areas have a monitoring and controlling process that looks back over the plans and any execution that has taken place and compares them. In these monitoring and controlling processes, you are asking questions such as: "Did we plan properly?" "Did the results come out the way we anticipated?" "If the results did not match the plan, should we take corrective action by modifying the plan or changing the way we are executing?" "Are there lessons learned that we need to feed into future projects?"

Why it is important:

Plans have to be reassessed and reevaluated. Where risk is concerned, we've done quite a bit of planning, identifying, analyzing, and predicting, but the process of Control Risks takes a look back to evaluate how all of that planning is lining up with reality.

When it is performed:

Control Risks is a process that is performed almost continually throughout the project. That is not to say that you do these activities without stopping or that someone is assigned full time, but rather that monitoring and controlling the risk is an ongoing concern.

How it works:

Inputs

Project Management Plan — See Ch. 2, Common Inputs

Risk Register

The risk register contains all of the identified risks on the project, and this is an important component to bring into the process. This list of risks should be reviewed to ensure that the risks were identified properly and that weights and responses that were anticipated actually match what is really occurring on the project.

Work Performance Data

Work performance data is used as an input here since monitoring and controlling processes compare the plan to the results. The plan is brought in as an input above, and the work performance data provides information on the results. For instance, the status of a deliverable provides helpful information related to schedule risk, cost risk, or other areas of concern.

Work Performance Reports

The work performance reports do not focus so much on *what* has been done as they do on *how* it was done. For instance, whereas the work performance information provides information on the status of deliverables, the work performance reports focus on cost, time, and quality performance. Where the performance reports are concerned, the actual results are compared against the baselines to show how the project is performing against the plan.

Tools

Key Fact

Risk Reassessment

As you perform a project, your information about risks, and even the very nature of the risks, changes. You should reassess this information as often as necessary in order to make sure that the risk needs of the project are current and accurate. Note that a constant reassessment may not be required by all projects. Some projects may not need to reassess their risk information at all, while others may need more frequent updates.

Key Fact

Risk Audits

The important thing to know about risk audits is that they are focused on overall risk management. In other words, they are more about the top-down process than they are about individual risks. Periodic risk audits evaluate how the risk management plan and the risk response plan are working as the project progresses and also whether or not the risks that were identified and prioritized are actually occurring.

Variance and Trend Analysis

Variance analysis focuses on the difference between what was planned and what was executed. Trend analysis shows how performance is trending. The reason trend analysis is important is that a one-time snapshot of cost may not cause concern, but a trend showing worsening cost performance may indicate that things are steadily worsening and may indicate that a problem is imminent.

Technical Performance Measurement

Performance can take on many flavors. In this case, technical performance measurement focuses on functionality, looking at how the project has met its goals for delivering the scope over time.

Reserve Analysis

The project's reserve (also called contingency) can apply to schedule or cost. Periodically, the project's reserve, whether cost or time, should be evaluated to ensure that it is sufficient to address the amount of risk the project expects to encounter.

Meetings

This particular technique is not necessarily suggesting that you have specially-called status meetings related to risk. Instead, it is suggesting that you create a project culture where bringing up items related to risk is always acceptable and risk is discussed regularly.

Outputs

Work Performance Information — See Ch. 2, Common Outputs

Change Requests

When risk events occur, change requests to the project are a normal outcome. In addition, even when the events do not occur, the project may be changed as a result of new risk-related information gathered during this process.

Control Risks

PM Plan Updates — See Ch. 2, Common Outputs

Project Documents Updates

New risk information, whether it is changes to your risk estimates or actual numbers (such as costs related to weather damage), should be regularly updated in the risk register.

Org. Process Assets Updates — See Ch. 2, Common Outputs

Control Risks

Control Risks

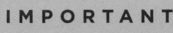

IMPORTANT

In addition to this quiz, use your Key to InSite, found on the inside back cover of this book, to access additional content, including new exam questions, expanded content, and simulated PMP exams. If your book did not come with a Key to InSite on the inside back cover, it may not be authentic. If you do not have a Key to InSite, you may purchase one at *insite.velociteach.com*.

Risk Management Questions

1. **You are managing the construction of a data center, but the location is in an area highly prone to earthquakes. In order to deal with this risk, you have chosen a type of building and foundation that is particularly earthquake-resistant. This is an example of:**

    A. Risk transfer.

    B. Risk avoidance.

    C. Risk mitigation.

    D. Risk acceptance.

2. **You are evaluating the risk by trying to produce a risk score for each risk. This is an example of which tool?**

    A. Monte Carlo analysis.

    B. Probability impact matrix.

    C. RACI Chart.

    D. Cause-and-effect diagrams.

3. **As part of your project, you have identified a significant risk of cost overrun on a software component that is integral to the product. Which represents the BEST strategy in dealing with this risk?**

    A. Outsource the software development.

    B. Insure the cost.

    C. Double the estimate.

    D. Eliminate the need for this component.

4. **Planning meetings and analysis are used in which process?**

    A.   Manage Stakeholder Expectations.

    B.   Perform Quantitative Risk Analysis.

    C.   Plan Risk Responses.

    D.   Plan Risk Management.

5. **Refer to the diagram below. What is the expected value of Result A?**

    A. $200,000.

    B. $100,000.

    C. $50,000.

    D. $25,000.

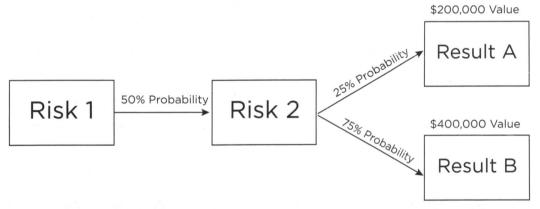

6. **Refer to the diagram from the previous question. What risk management tool is employed in this diagram?**

    A.   Earned value management.

    B.   Sensitivity analysis.

    C.   Decision tree analysis.

    D.   Flowcharting.

Risk Questions

7. Marie is meeting with her project team to evaluate each identified risk and try to assign an estimated dollar amount or time impact estimate to it. Which process is her team performing?

    A. Perform Quantitative Risk Analysis.

    B. Perform Qualitative Risk Analysis.

    C. Plan Risk Responses.

    D. Control Risks.

8. The project team has missed an important milestone, and their SPI is 0.77. The sponsor has notified the project manager that she intends on getting more involved in project decisions until they are back on track. She has asked the team to activate their contingency response strategy for this scenario. Which choice below best describes what the team would likely do?

    A. Implement the contingency plan to deal with the missed milestone and poor performance.

    B. Spend reserve money to get the SPI back to 1.0 or greater.

    C. Perform a root cause analysis on the late milestone and performance.

    D. Identify the risks associated with the missed milestone.

9. If a project manager is recommending that immediate corrective action be taken, which process is he involved in?

    A. Perform Qualitative Risk Analysis.

    B. Plan Risk Management.

    C. Identify Risks.

    D. Control Risks.

10. What is the BEST source of information about potential risk on your project?

    A. Computer risk analysis.

    B. Interviews with team members from other projects.

    C. Historical records from similar projects.

    D. Your own experience in this industry.

11. **You have just finished a thorough Monte Carlo analysis for your project. Which of the following would the analysis MOST likely identify?**

    A. Divergent paths causing risk.

    B. Points of schedule risk.

    C. Points of schedule conflict that lead to risk.

    D. Gaps in the project path that could create risk.

12. **Senior management in an organization is concerned about risk on a project. The concern has escalated to the sponsor who has asked the project manager to evaluate a particular risk. The project manager responded by saying this risk had numerous interdependencies and was related to many other potential risks, but the sponsor asked that its potential impact be evaluated while holding all of the other risks at their current state. What would be the best tool for the project manager to use in this case?**

    A. Root cause analysis.

    B. Tornado diagram.

    C. Decision tree analysis.

    D. Assumptions analysis.

13. **Your company is beginning a new building project and has assigned you the role of project manager. During the first few meetings with stakeholders you become aware of several risks that are of concern to the project sponsor. The topic of risk management, however, has yet to be addressed. What is the first thing you should do to address the project risks?**

    A. Develop a risk management plan.

    B. Identify project risks.

    C. Plan responses to project risks.

    D. Determine how risks will be controlled.

14. **Plan Risk Management is:**

    A. A process of identifying potential risks for a project.

    B. Deciding how risk management activities will be structured and performed.

    C. Assessing the impact and likelihood of project risks.

    D. Numerical analysis of the probability of project risks.

15. **Which of the following is an output of Identify Risks?**

    A. Risk register.

    B. Probabilistic analysis.

    C. Risk-related contractual agreements.

    D. Recommended cash reserves.

16. **Which of the following would NOT be a strategy for dealing with negative risk?**

    A. Avoid.

    B. Transfer.

    C. Share.

    D. Mitigate.

17. **A risk probability and impact assessment is used in:**

    A. Identify Risks.

    B. Perform Qualitative Risk Analysis.

    C. Perform Quantitative Risk Analysis.

    D. Plan Risk Responses.

18. **A project team is meeting to look at the things they considered to be true for the purposes of planning as they relate to risks. Other stakeholders are present and are challenging the team about the decisions they initially made. What technique is being employed in this scenario?**

    A. Root cause analysis.

    B. Tornado diagram.

    C. Sensitivity analysis.

    D. Assumptions analysis.

19. **The BEST definition of risk management is:**

    A. The process of identifying, analyzing, and responding to risk.

    B. The process of reducing risk to the minimum level possible for the project.

    C. The process of proactively ensuring that all project risk is documented and controlled.

    D. Creation of the risk response plan.

20. **The analysis where future outcomes are estimated and opportunities are expressed as positive numbers while threats are expressed as negative values is known as:**

    A. Sensitivity analysis.

    B. SWOT analysis.

    C. Expected monetary value analysis.

    D. Probability distributions.

21. **Which of the following is NOT a tool or technique for gaining expert opinion as it relates to risk?**

    A. Brainstorming.

    B. Delphi technique.

    C. Monte Carlo analysis.

    D. Expert interviews.

22. **Which of the following would NOT be contained in the risk management plan?**

    A. A risk breakdown structure.

    B. A description of the overall approach to risk on the project.

    C. Risk roles and responsibilities.

    D. A list of identified risks.

23. **Which of the following statements is TRUE regarding risk?**

    A. All risk events must have a planned workaround.

    B. All risk events are uncertain.

    C. All risk events are negative.

    D. All risk events should be covered by a contingency budget amount.

24. **Which of the following is NOT a valid way to reduce risk?**

    A. Select a contract type that reduces risk.

    B. Insure against the risk.

    C. Create a workaround for the risk.

    D. Plan to mitigate the risk.

25. **You are the project manager for a global change management project. The Vice President of Operations is a key project stakeholder, and she has expressed concern about the way risk is being managed on the project. She is particularly concerned that the project may fail if even one of several risk events occur. She has called a meeting to discuss this with you. What would be the best document to bring to this meeting.**

    A. The results of your project's sensitivity analysis.

    B. The results of your project's risk modeling.

    C. The results of your project's EMV analysis.

    D. The results of your probability distributions.

Risk Management Answers

1.   C. The best answer here is risk mitigation since you are taking steps to lessen the risk. 'A' is incorrect because you are not transferring the risk to anyone else. 'B' is incorrect because you would need to relocate in order to completely avoid the risk of earthquake. 'D' is incorrect because you are not merely accepting the risk – you are taking steps to make it less severe.

2.   B. The probability impact matrix (PIM) derives a risk score by multiplying the probability of the risk by its impact (both of these numbers are estimated). This resulting risk score may be used to help prioritize the risk register.

3.   A. Outsourcing the software development could allow you to cap the cost. 'B' is not a good choice because costs for development such as this cannot be insured in a cost-effective manner. 'C' is not correct because doubling the estimate does not deal with the root of the problem. It only arbitrarily changes the estimate. 'D' is incorrect because you cannot simply eliminate every high risk component in the real world.

4.   D. Planning meetings and analysis are a tool of the process of Plan Risk Management.

5.   D. The way this problem is solved is by multiplying out the probabilities times the value. In this case, it is the 50% probability of Risk 1 × the 25% probability of Risk 2 × the $200,000 value of Result A. $.5 \times .25 \times 200{,}000 = \$25{,}000$.

6.   C. This is an example of decision tree analysis.

7.   A. You should have seen the fact that Marie's team was quantifying the risks by seeking to assign a dollar or time estimate to them, and Perform Quantitative Risk Analysis is the process that does this.

8.   A. Contingency response strategies are generally only activated once a milestone is missed or some key measurement is triggered. At that point a contingency plan kicks in. 'B' is not a bad answer, but it assumes too much. For instance, we don't even know if there

Risk Answers

are reserve monies. 'C' and 'D' might be very reasonable steps, but it wasn't what the sponsor specifically requested.

9.   D. Recommended corrective action is the result of monitoring and controlling processes, and the only monitoring and controlling process in the choices was Control Risks.

10.   C. Historical records from similar projects would provide you with the best source of information on potential risks. 'A', 'B', and 'D' are all good sources, but they would not be as pertinent or helpful as the records from other similar projects. Historical information gets brought into your planning processes as an organizational process asset.

11.   B. One of the things Monte Carlo analysis would show you is where schedule risk exists on the project. 'A' is incorrect, because it is typically convergent and not divergent tasks that create schedule risk. 'C' is incorrect because it is not looking for schedule conflicts – those would be corrected in Develop Schedule. 'D' is incorrect because gaps in the project path do not, by themselves, cause risk.

12.   B. The sponsor is asking to evaluate the impact of one risk while holding the others at a baseline, and a tornado diagram is the tool to accomplish that. 'A', 'C', and 'D' are all tools used in risk assessment, but the tornado diagramming technique is custom-made for this assignment.

13.   A. You should develop the risk management plan. A risk management plan will outline how all risk planning activities and decisions will be approached. Methods of identification, qualification, quantification, response planning, and control will all follow the development of the risk management plan.

14.   B. Plan Risk Management is not planning for actual risks (which include choices 'A', 'C', and 'D'); it is the PROCESS of deciding how all risk planning activities and decisions will be approached. It is the plan for how to plan.

15.   A. The risk register is the only output of Identify Risks, and it is updated in Perform Qualitative Risk Analysis, Perform Quantitative Risk Analysis, Plan Risk Responses, and Control Risks.

16.   C. There are four identified strategies for dealing with negative risks. They are: mitigate, transfer, avoid, and accept. The reason that 'C' was incorrect is that share is a strategy for managing a positive risk or opportunity.

17.   B. The hardest part about risk is keeping the various processes straight. Since the outputs are similar (for the most part), focus more of your study on the processes themselves and their tools. In this question, the tool of risk probability and impact assessment is a tool of Perform Qualitative Risk Analysis.

18.   D. The big clue to this question was the phrase "considered to be true for the purposes of planning." The definition of an assumption is "anything considered to be true or certain for the purposes of planning." Assumptions analysis is a tool used in risk (specifically in Identify Risks) to challenge and test the underlying assumptions the team has made and to identify the risks of those assumptions not bearing out.

19.   A. The process of identifying, analyzing, and responding to risk is the definition of risk management.

20.   C. EMV analysis statistically calculates the average outcome, and expresses opportunities as a positive amount and the risks or threats as negative amounts.

21.   C. Monte Carlo analysis, which is a computer-based analysis, might be useful for revealing schedule risk, but it would not be useful for gaining expert opinion. Choices 'A', 'B', and 'D' are all tools used as part of project risk management.

22.   D. The risk management plan does not contain the identified risks. It is more general and high-level than that. The identified risks will be listed in the risk register, produced after the risk management plan.

Risk Answers

23.   B. Risk events are, by definition, uncertainties. These could either be positive or negative. 'A' is incorrect because some risks are simply accepted and have no workaround. 'C' is incorrect because a risk may be positive or negative. 'D' is incorrect because not all risks are budgeted. Some are transferred to other parties or are too small or unlikely to consider.

24.   C. Read these questions carefully! The workaround is what you do if the risk occurs, but it does not reduce the risk as the question specified. 'A', 'B', and 'D' all focus on reducing risk by transferring or mitigating it.

25.   A. Your VP of Operations is concerned about your project's sensitivity to risk. All of these answers might be applicable to one degree or another, but 'A' stands out as the best match to the problem you are trying to address. The results of sensitivity analysis directly addresses your stakeholder's concern.

12 Procurement Management

Difficulty	Memorization	Exam Importance
HIGH	MEDIUM	MEDIUM

Procurement management is the set of processes related to obtaining goods, services, or scope from outside the organization.

Procurement management can be a very challenging knowledge area on the exam. One reason it can be so difficult is that relatively few project managers have formal procurement training in their backgrounds, and even if they do, it may differ in key ways from what is presented here.

Philosophy

This procurement management approach is steeped in formal government procurement practices. In fact, many of the processes, tools, techniques, and outputs found here are near duplicates of those used by many government and military institutions in the United States.

The overarching philosophy of procurement management is that it should be formal. Many people's practical experience may differ from this rigid approach, but it is necessary to understand it and to be able to apply this philosophy on the exam.

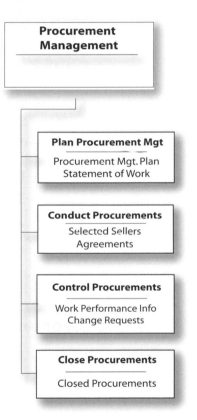

The processes of Project Risk Management with their *primary* outputs

Procurement Management

Plan Procurement Mgt
Procurement Mgt. Plan
Statement of Work

Conduct Procurements
Selected Sellers
Agreements

Control Procurements
Work Performance Info
Change Requests

Close Procurements
Closed Procurements

Importance

Several questions on the exam will be drawn from procurement management. If formal procurement is new to you, this material is especially important.

There is a significant volume of material presented in this chapter; however, Point of Total Assumption (PTA) is the only complex technique you will need to learn how to apply.

Preparation

As mentioned earlier, it would be wise to take special care in this section if you do not have a background in formal procurement activities.

Keep in mind as you approach this material that it was not written to be memorized. It was written to be practiced and applied. For this chapter in particular, understanding is more important than memorizing.

This also applies to key terms, concepts, the processes, and their components.

These procurement management processes are quite involved. Test-takers would do well to read this chapter carefully and then read Chapter 12, Project Procurement Management, in the 5th Edition PMBOK Guide.

Procurement Processes

There are four processes in procurement management. These processes are displayed in the figure at the beginning of the chapter and summarized in the following tables.

Process Group	Procurement Management Process
Initiating	(none)
Planning	Plan Procurement Management
Executing	Conduct Procurements
Monitoring & Controlling	Control Procurements
Closing	Close Procurements

Process	Key Outputs
Plan Procurement Management	Procure. Mgt. Plan, Procure. S.O.W.
Conduct Procurements	Selected Sellers, Agreements
Control Procurements	Work Performance Info, Change Req.
Close Procurements	Closed Procurements

Procurement Roles

In procurement management, there are two primary roles defined, and the project manager could play either of these roles. In fact, it is not uncommon for project managers to play both roles on the same project. The roles are:

Buyer

The organization or party purchasing (procuring) the goods or services from the seller.

Seller

The organization or party providing or delivering the goods or services to the buyer.

Contract Types

When procuring goods or services, the type of contract that governs the deal can make a significant difference in who bears the risk. There are three categories of contracts you must know for the test. They are listed below with information on each one:

Fixed Price Contracts (AKA Lump Sum Contracts)

Fixed price contracts are the easiest ones to understand. There is generally a single fee, although payment terms may be specified so that the cost is not necessarily a lump sum payable at the end.

This type of contract is very popular when the scope of work is thoroughly defined and completely known. Three types of fixed price contracts are:

Firm Fixed Price (FFP)

The price is fixed, with no provision for cost or performance overruns. The risk is entirely shifted to the seller.

Fixed Price Incentive Fee (FPIF)

The price is fixed, with an incentive fee for meeting a target specified in the contract (such as finishing the work ahead of schedule).

Fixed Price Economic Price Adjustment (FP-EPA)

This type of contract is popular in cases where fluctuations in the exchange rate or interest rate may impact the project. In this case, an economic stipulation may be included to protect the seller or the buyer. The economic stipulation may be based on the interest rate, the consumer price index, cost of living adjustments, currency exchange rates, or other indices.

Cost Reimbursable Contracts

There are two common types of cost reimbursable contracts:

Cost Plus Fixed Fee (CPFF)

The seller passes the cost back to the buyer and receives an additional fixed fee upon completion of the project.

Cost Plus Incentive Fee (CPIF)

The seller passes the cost back to the buyer and gets an incentive fee for meeting a target (usually tied back to keeping costs low) specified in the contract.

Time and Materials Contracts

In a time and materials contract, the seller charges for time plus the cost of any materials needed to complete the work.

Type of Contract	Who Bears the Risk	Explanation
Fixed Price	Seller	Since the price is fixed, cost overruns may not be passed on to the buyer and must be borne by the seller.
Cost Plus Fixed Fee	Buyer	Since all costs must be reimbursed to the seller, the buyer bears the risk of cost overruns.
Cost Plus Incentive Fee	Buyer and Seller	The buyer bears most of the risk here, but the incentive fee for the seller motivates that seller to keep costs down.
Time and Materials	Buyer	The buyer pays the seller for all time and materials the seller applies to the project. The buyer bears the most risk of cost overruns.

Point of Total Assumption

Because there are numerous types of contracts where the risk is shared to one degree or another, it is important to be able to calculate how risk is allocated between the buyer and seller. One consideration, particularly when using Fixed Price Incentive Fee contracts, is the Point of Total Assumption.

The Point of Total Assumption (PTA) is the cost point in the contract where a subcontractor assumes responsibility for all additional costs. This concept can be challenging to understand at first, so to help with this, consider the following situation. Company ABC is subcontracting out the installation of industrial shelving to company XYZ for an estimated $75,000. The selected contract is Fixed Price Incentive Fee, so ABC pushes for a cap (called a price ceiling) to protect them from serious cost overruns. The terms of the contract are that XYZ's target cost is $71,000, the target price to ABC is $75,000 and XYZ's ceiling price to ABC is $84,000; however, for every dollar over the target cost, the share ratio is 3:1. This means that ABC (the buyer) will pay $0.75, while XYZ (the seller) will have to pay $0.25 of every dollar overrun. Knowing this information, it is fairly simple to calculate the PTA.

The formula is:

Target cost + (ceiling price – target price) ÷ ABC's % share of cost overrun.

In this case, it would be $71,000 + ($84,000 - $75,000) ÷ .75, which simplifies to $71,000 + $12,000 = $83,000.

In other words, at the point the cost reaches $83,000, the subcontractor (XYZ) would assume the total burden of cost overrun. The ceiling price is still $84,000, but XYZ is bearing 100% of the cost overrun burden above $83,000 in cost (the PTA). The PTA is important, because it helps identify the cost point in the contract where the seller has the most motivation to bring things to completion.

Plan Procurement Management

What it is:

This process involves looking at the project and determining which components or services of the project will be made or performed internally and which will be "procured" from an external source. After that decision is made, the project manager must determine the appropriate type of contracts to be used on the project.

Why it is important:

Currently best practices in the field of project management favor buying externally vs. building internally, all other things being equal; however, there are numerous factors that should go into your decision on whether to "make or buy."

Carefully planning what to procure and how to go about the processes of procurement will ensure that the right things are procured in the right way.

When it is performed:

Because a project may have multiple subcontractors, potentially in every phase of the project, any of the procurement processes could be performed repeatedly and at any time throughout the project.

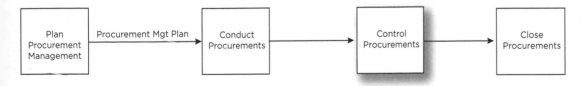

A diagram showing the order of the four Procurement Management processes

How it works:

Inputs

Project Management Plan

The project management plan describes what will be done and how it will be accomplished. This information will be useful to review when considering what components of the scope should be procured (i.e., performed by groups outside the organization).

Requirements Documentation

Key Fact Requirements may carry legal or contractual obligations that need to be considered in procurement.

Risk Register

The risk register provides a complete list of anticipated risks that may include risks to the procurement processes.

Activity Resource Requirements

The resources needed to complete each activity will influence make vs. buy and other procurement-related decisions.

Project Schedule

Like the previous input, the schedule for the work to be performed and completed can also influence make vs. buy and other procurement-related decisions.

Activity Cost Estimates

The cost estimates can help the buyer and seller form a basis for bidding.

Stakeholder Register

The stakeholder register provides a list of all parties interested in the project. When it comes to procurement activities, these stakeholders may well be outside of the organization.

Enterprise Environmental Factors

There may be factors at work in an organization that have a strong influence on procurement. For instance, an organization may have a strong culture of building internally rather than buying, or they could have a strong culture of buying from a few trusted sellers. All of this should be factored in when making procurement decisions.

Org. Process Assets — See Ch. 2, Common Inputs

Tools

Kev Fact

→ Make-or-Buy Analysis

Make-or-buy analysis is difficult to sum up succinctly. The analysis looks at all of the factors that could sway the decision toward making internally or buying externally, including risk factors, cost, releasing proprietary information, and a host of other decision points.

When using this tool, the decision-makers must often look outside of the project itself. For instance, writing a software component may not make as much sense as procuring it externally where only the project is concerned; however, if the performing organization has an interest in developing the capability to build that kind of software, it may make sense for the project to make vs. buy.

Expert Judgment

Where procurement planning is concerned, expert judgment can be of tremendous value. There will often be scope, technical, legal, cost, and schedule considerations, and bringing in people with expertise in this area can help the project team make the best decisions.

Market Research

This tool is used to analyze the market and understand what different vendors could potentially do for the project. This tool might also include analyzing new technologies that are available.

Meetings — See Ch. 2, Common Tools

Outputs

Kev Fact

→ Procurement Management Plan

The procurement management plan is an important output of the Plan Procurement Management process. It defines how all of the other procurement management processes will be carried out. This includes defining what will be procured on the project, how a seller will be selected, what types of contracts will be used, how risk will be managed, and how sellers will be managed, including how their performance will be measured.

Procurement Statement of Work

Key Fact   Many people find this document confusing on first approach, but it is highly important for the exam! If you recall the project scope statement, produced as part of the Define Scope process, then you will know that the project's scope has been defined at this point. A procurement statement of work is not merely a replication of what was done in Define Scope. Instead, a procurement statement of work helps explain a section of the scope to potential sellers in enough detail so that they can decide whether or not they want to (or are qualified to) pursue the work in question. Expect statements pertaining to the previous sentence to be on the exam!

Procurement Documents

Key Fact   There are quite a few types of procurement documents that vary from organization to organization. Don't worry about the differences between an Invitation For Bid (IFB) and a Request For Proposal (RFP). For the exam, know that the procurement statements of work are written by the buyer and provided to the prospective seller(s). They provide a narrative description of the work to be performed.

Source Selection Criteria

Key Fact   The key to remember for this output is that the source selection criteria are determined before the seller is selected. This helps keep the procurement process objective and unbiased. For instance, it may be that you will choose the lowest-priced qualified bidder (in which case the qualifications need to be spelled out), or you may want the bidder that represents the highest technical competency or the lowest risk. Whatever the criteria, ensure that they are specified before the other procurement activities are conducted. Also keep in mind that these source selection criteria may or may not be shared with the prospective sellers.

Make-or-Buy Decisions

Key Fact   During this process, the project team performed make-or-buy analysis as a tool, and now it is time to act upon the data gathered. The decisions should be made and documented, and enough information to justify why these decisions were made should be included.

Change Requests

Sometimes changes need to be made to the project in order to facilitate procurement. For instance, a software application may be redesigned in order to allow a subcontractor to use their own database and keep their work and data separate from that of the core team. These requested changes should be channeled back through Perform Integrated Change Control to evaluate their impacts on the rest of the project.

Project Documents Updates — See Ch. 2, Common Outputs

Plan Procurement Management

Executing

Conduct Procurements

What it is:

Most of the processes in this book do exactly what they sound like. In this case, the process of Conduct Procurements does just that. It carries out the procurement management plan, selects one or more sellers, and awards the procurement, usually in the form of a contract.

Why it is important:

This one gets the ball rolling with procurement. So far you have decided what you want to procure and written the procurement management plan. Now it's time to issue the bid package to potential sellers, hold bidder conferences, evaluate proposals you receive from potential sellers, and select one of them. You know, however, that real life isn't that simple, and this can be a very tricky area on the exam as well.

When it is performed:

To state the obvious, this process is performed when you are ready to conduct your procurement activities. This means that it will occur after Plan Procurement Management.

Like the other procurement processes, Conduct Procurements is performed as needed. It may be performed multiple times if there are multiple contracts, or it is not performed at all if the project is not procuring anything.

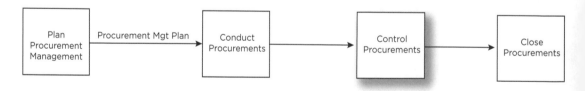

A diagram showing the order of the four Procurement Management processes

How it works:

Be forewarned that this process has quite a few inputs, tools, and outputs (21 to be exact). Do not try to memorize all of these. Instead, know that almost all of the outputs from the previous process, Plan Procurements, flow into Conduct Procurements as inputs. The most important tools and outputs are indicated.

Conduct Procurements

Inputs

Procurement Management Plan

This is the plan that describes how the process of Conduct Procurements will be carried out.

Procurement Documents — See Plan Procurement Management, Outputs

Source Selection Criteria — See Plan Procurement Management, Outputs

Seller Proposals

These are the proposals that sellers provide to the buying organization, showing how they would approach the work and how much they would charge.

Project Documents

The Conduct Procurements process could be initiated quite early in the project, so there may be a lack of available documentation at this point; however, whatever documents have been developed should be brought into the process. This is especially true for risk-related documentation as it may influence your source selection.

Make or Buy Decisions — See Plan Procurement Management, Outputs

Procurement Statement of Work

The procurement statement of work, created in the Plan Procurement Management process, defines the scope of work to be performed as part of this procurement effort. It is primarily used to help potential sellers determine whether or not they are qualified to perform the work.

Organizational Process Assets — See Ch. 2, Common Outputs

Conduct Procurements

Tools

Bidder Conference

Kev Fact

Bidder conferences are conducted to provide information to potential sellers, while keeping all of them on a level playing field. It is important that the project manager conduct everything out in the open, with no secret meetings or communications with some vendors.

Proposal Evaluation Techniques

Kev Fact

There is no one way to evaluate proposals. In reality, there are as many techniques as there are buyers. This tool is essentially a combination of the other tools in the Conduct Procurements process, used to evaluate the seller's bid or proposal.

Independent Estimates

Kev Fact

The buyer may go and commission independent estimates to validate the proposals and bids received from the potential sellers. For example, the buyer may go out and ask an independent group to prepare an estimate so that they have an objective source of information. These independent estimates are often referred to as "should-cost" estimates.

Expert Judgment

Expert judgment is the most favored tool you will see on the exam. In the area of selecting a seller, the buyer can use expert judgment to evaluate the bids and proposals.

Advertising

If you need to expand the seller responses you are getting, advertising the bid may be the best way. Trade publications, online sources, and even newspapers can help get your bid request in front of a large and more carefully targeted audience to improve the volume and quality of responses.

Analytical Techniques

This tool is another way of describing the thought process and the effort of sorting through the various proposals in order to select a seller.

Procurement Negotiations

Negotiations between the buyer and the potential seller are performed with the goal of reaching mutual agreement on the contractual terms and conditions.

Where the exam is concerned, the goal of negotiations is to reach a win-win scenario between the buyer and seller. When the buyer exerts too much pressure on the seller or negotiates an untenable deal, this can backfire on both of them in the long run.

Keep in mind that the project manager may or may not be the person who conducts these negotiations as this can be a highly specialized area. On large and complex contracts, professional negotiators are the norm.

Outputs

Kev Fact

Selected Sellers

The RFP has been generated, the sellers have submitted their proposals, the negotiations have taken place, and now a seller is selected to provide goods or services on the project.

Kev Fact

Agreements

The agreements that come out of this process, often in the form of a contract, are formal documents governing the relationship between the buyer and seller. In general, when you see the word "agreement" on the exam, you should think "contract."

Contracts are legal documents with highly specialized and technical language and should be written and changed only by people specializing in that field (e.g., the contracting officer, procurement office, legal counsel). The project manager should not attempt to write, negotiate, or change the contract on his own.

The contract describes the work to be performed and perhaps the way in which that work will be performed (e.g., location, work conditions). It may specify who will do the work, when and how the seller will be paid, and delivery terms.

In reality, there is very little that the contract cannot specify in one way or another, so long as the terms and conditions are legal and they are mutually agreed upon by buyer and seller. Several other legal factors may come into play, depending on the country that governs the contract, legal consideration, and other technical legal matters that are outside the scope of this discussion.

An important component to include with the contract is how disputes (also called claims) will be resolved. This includes the process of dispute resolution, the parties who will be involved, and where the dispute resolution will take place.

Key Fact

Resource Calendars

You have seen this output before in Acquire Project Team. This one is different, however, in that it applies specifically to the external resources you will be procuring. Also, as resources and their availability are modified as a result of the contract, they should be updated. For instance, if a contract specifies that a team will work on site or that a piece of equipment will be available for a range of dates, these terms need to be documented, and appropriate resource calendars should be updated.

Change Requests — See Plan Procurement Management, Outputs

PM Plan Updates — See Ch 2. Common Outputs

Project Documents Updates — See Plan Procurement Management, Outputs

Control Procurements

What it is:

In a nutshell, Control Procurements is the process where the buyer and seller review the contract and the work results to ensure that the results match the contract. This typically includes a review of:

• Are the goods or services being delivered?

• Are the goods or services being delivered on time?

• Are the right amounts being invoiced or paid?

• Are additional conditions of the contract being met?

• Is the buyer/seller relationship being properly managed and maintained?

The process of Control Procurements is a process performed by both the buyer and the seller, and because of the ramifications of any issues here, the project managers from both the buyer and seller should use whatever resources are necessary to explore the potential effects of any decisions.

Why it is important:

When looking at this from a project management perspective, the contract may be viewed as a plan (albeit a very specialized and binding type of plan). The process of Control Procurements ensures that the results of the project match this plan and that all conditions of the contract are met.

When it is performed:

Control Procurements, like the other procurement management processes, may be performed throughout the project whenever goods or services are being procured. It typically occurs for a given contract at predefined intervals, but may also be performed as requested or needed.

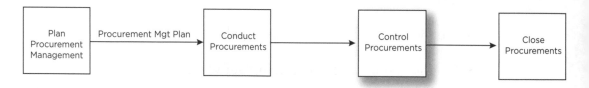

A diagram showing the order of the four Procurement Management processes

How it works:

Inputs

Project Management Plan — See Ch. 2, Common Inputs

Remember that you are in a monitoring and controlling process here, so naturally you will bring in the plan and compare it with the results.

Procurement Documents — See Plan Procurement Management, Outputs

Agreements — See Conduct Procurements, Output

Approved Change Requests

Change requests are inputs to many processes; however, in this process they are particularly important. The reason for this is that requests for changes to a contract should receive special consideration by both buyer and seller before they are formally incorporated into the contract.

Work Performance Reports

Work performance reports provide information on how deliverables are progressing against the schedule and budget, as well as technical information on the work that is being performed.

Work Performance Data

In this case, work performance data provides information on quality and costs for the work being performed.

Tools

Contract Change Control System

Key Fact The contract change control system is a component of the integrated change control system, and you may well have a separate one for each contract. This system describes the procedures for how the contract may be changed, and it would typically include the people required and the steps that need to be taken for a change request to be made, considered, approved, and implemented into the contract.

Procurement Performance Reviews

This is a periodic review, initiated by the buyer but including the seller, where the seller's progress is measured against the contract and any other applicable plans. The seller is shown the areas where they are compliant as well as any areas where performance is a problem.

Inspections and Audits

Key Fact This tool focuses on the product itself and its conformance to specifications. One important difference between this and the previous tool is that although inspections and audits do not seek to measure the seller's performance (i.e., how quickly or cost-effectively they are delivering the results), the buyer may use them to help the seller find problems in the way they are delivering the work results.

Performance Reporting

Key Fact Performance reporting is an excellent tool to help measure the seller's performance against the plan. This may include such items as earned value, the cost performance and schedule performance indices, and trend analysis. Oftentimes there are contract conditions tied to performance (e.g., seller must deliver at least 50% of the quantity of motors within 30 days of executing this contract).

Control Procurements

Payment Systems

A payment system helps ensure that invoices and payments match up and that the right amount is being invoiced for the right deliverables at the right time. Additionally, payment systems will help avoid duplicate payments (or invoices if you are the seller). This tool can be of particular importance when payments are specified in the contract.

Kev Fact

Claims Administration

Claims are basically disagreements. They may be about scope, the impact of a change, or the interpretation of some piece of the contract. The essential (legally binding) elements of the process for claims administration are defined in the contract itself, but there may be additional components in the procurement management plan.

The most important thing about claims administration is to understand that disputes must be managed and ultimately resolved and that the process for doing so should be defined in advance of the claim.

Records Management System

The project manager uses the records management system to keep track of all communications that would be relevant to the contract.

Outputs

Work Performance Info. — See Ch. 2, Common Outputs

Change Requests — See Ch. 2, Common Outputs

PM Plan Updates — See Ch. 2, Common Outputs

Project Doc. Updates — See Ch. 2, Common Outputs

Organizational Process Assets Updates

There are many items that come out of Control Procurements that may be assets, but one of the most common ones to be updated as part of this process is the information on the seller's performance during the project. This could assist future projects in deciding whether or not to use this seller in the future.

Close Procurements

What it is:

Close Procurements is the process where the contract is completed by the buyer and seller. Ideally, the contract is terminated amicably with the seller delivering all of the contracted items and the buyer making all payments on time, but it isn't always done that way. For instance, the buyer may consider a seller to be in default and cancel the contract, or a buyer and seller may mutually agree to terminate the contract for any reason.

Why it is important:

Every contract must be closed. Contracts inadvertently left open potentially put both the buyer and seller at risk. This process is tightly linked to the Close Project or Phase process in integration management as it contributes to the closure of the entire project.

When it is performed:

This process is performed at the end of each contract, whether or not that end is successful. When the contract is completed or terminated for any reason, this process is performed.

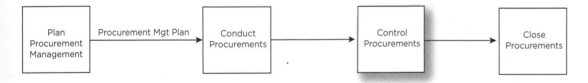

A diagram showing the order of the four Procurement Management processes

How it works:

Inputs

Project Management Plan — See Ch. 2, Common Inputs

Procurement Documents — See Plan Procurement Management, Outputs

(sidebar) **Close Procurements**

Tools

Procurement Audits

Kev Fact   The point of a procurement audit is to capture lessons learned from a contracting perspective.

Procurement Negotiations

Kev Fact   Contracts are completed when all terms, conditions, and claims against the contract are satisfied. Ideally, this is objective, and everyone agrees; however, negotiations on this point are often necessary. When negotiations break down, some other means, such as mediation or arbitration may be necessary. All of these are forms of Alternative Dispute Resolution (ADR) toward closing a contract.

Be aware that litigation is the least desirable course of action and should only be used when other ADR options have been exhausted.

Records Management System

Procurement documentation should always be archived for future reference. Many organizations have records management systems to facilitate the storing, archiving, and retrieval of records related to contracts or procurement activities.

Outputs

Closed Procurements

Kev Fact   The closed contracts are the essential outputs from Close Procurements. The buyer's contract administrator sends formal, written notice to the seller that the contract is complete.

Organizational Process Assets Updates

In addition to any other assets that may need updating, the lessons learned captured in this process (during the procurement audit) are formally documented here.

IMPORTANT

In addition to this quiz, use your Key to InSite, found on the inside back cover of this book, to access additional content, including new exam questions, expanded content, and simulated PMP exams. If your book did not come with a Key to InSite on the inside back cover, it may not be authentic. If you do not have a Key to InSite, you may purchase one at *insite.velociteach.com*.

Procurement Management Questions

1. **The contract type that represents the highest risk to the seller is:**

   A. Fixed price plus incentive.

   B. Cost reimbursable.

   C. Fixed price.

   D. Cost reimbursable plus incentive.

2. **You have been tasked with managing the seller responses to a request for proposal issued by your company. The seller responses were numerous, and now you have been asked to rank the proposals from highest to lowest in terms of their response. What are you going to use as a means to rank the sellers?**

   A. Expert judgment.

   B. Request for quotation.

   C. Seller response guidelines.

   D. Seller selection matrix.

3. **Make-or-buy analysis is a tool used in which process?**

   A. Plan Procurement Management.

   B. Conduct Procurements.

   C. Control Procurements.

   D. Analyze Procurements.

4. **Which of the following represents the right sequence of processes?**

   A. Analyze Procurements, Plan Procurement Management, Conduct Procurements, Close Procurements.

   B. Determine Make or Buy, Control Procurements, Conduct Procurements, Close Procurements.

   C. Plan Purchases and Acquisitions, Control Procurements, Conduct Procurements, Close Procurements.

   D. Plan Procurement Management, Conduct Procurements, Control Procurements, Close Procurements.

5. **An organization is trying to close out a procurement sub-project, but the vendor has not delivered on a key piece of contracted technology. The project manager has been negotiating with the vendor for several weeks to no avail. Recently the vendor representative stated that he believed the performing organization had no real legal recourse; however, the project manager disagrees. How should the project manager approach the next steps?**

   A. With the attitude that litigation is a perfectly acceptable option if negotiations fail.

   B. With the attitude that alternative dispute resolution would be preferable to litigation.

   C. With the attitude that a final, equitable settlement is to be prioritized below stakeholder satisfaction.

   D. With the attitude that alternative dispute resolution is binding, while mediation is not.

6. You are managing a large software project when the need for a new series of database tables is discovered. The need was previously unplanned, and your organization's staff is 100% utilized, so you decide to go outside the company to procure this piece of work. When you meet with prospective sellers, you realize that the scope of work is not completely defined, but everyone agrees that the project is relatively small, and your need is urgent. Which type of contract makes the MOST sense?

   A. Fixed price.

   B. Time and materials.

   C. Open ended.

   D. Cost plus incentive fee.

7. Your project plan calls for you to go through procurement in order to buy a specialty motor for an industrial robot. Because of patent issues, this motor is only available from one supplier that is across the country. After investigation, you believe that you could procure the motor from this company for a price that is within your budget. What is your BEST course of action?

   A. Revisit the design and alter the specification to allow for a comparable motor.

   B. Procure the motor from this source even though they are the sole source.

   C. See if the component may be produced in another country, avoiding your country's patent issues.

   D. Take the product out of the procurement management process.

8. **You have a supplier that is supplying parts to you under contract. The terms and conditions give you the right to change some aspects of the contract at any time, and you need to significantly lower the quantities due to a change in project scope. How should you notify the supplier?**

    A. Take them to lunch and explain the situation gently to preserve the relationship.

    B. Have your attorney call their attorney.

    C. Communicate with the supplier via e-mail.

    D. Send them a formal, written notice that the contract has been changed.

9. **Proposal Evaluation Techniques are used in which procurement process?**

    A. Plan Procurement Management.

    B. Select Sellers.

    C. Conduct Procurements.

    D. Evaluate Proposals.

10. **Your project has been terminated immediately due to a cancellation by the customer. What action should you take FIRST?**

    A. Call a meeting with the customer.

    B. Enter Close Procurements.

    C. Ask your team leads for a final status report.

    D. Verify this change against the procurement management plan.

11. **You are evaluating proposals from prospective sellers. What process are you involved in?**

    A. Analyze Procurements.

    B. Plan Procurement Management.

    C. Conduct Procurements.

    D. Control Procurements.

12. Your project scope calls for a piece of software that will control a valve in a pressurized pipeline. Your company has some experience with this type of software, but resources are tight, and it is not part of your company's core competency. You are considering involving other sellers but want to decide whether it is a better decision to produce this within your company or source it externally. What activity are you performing?

    A. Source selection.

    B. Make-or-buy analysis.

    C. Rational project procurement.

    D. Source evaluation.

13. Martina is managing a global project that will attempt to get significant portions through sourcing. When the first bids are received, they seem surprisingly high and there is very little variance among them. Which procurement management tool or technique would be the most appropriate in this case?

    A. Negotiation.

    B. Proposal Evaluation Techniques.

    C. Bidder Conferences.

    D. Independent Estimates.

14. Your organization is holding a bidder conference to discuss the project with prospective sellers, and a trusted seller you have worked with many times in the past has asked if they can meet with the project manager the day before the conference to cover some sensitive questions they do not wish to ask in front of other sellers. Should your organization meet with the seller?

    A. Yes, the more that prospective sellers know about the project, the better.

    B. Yes, they are your primary seller, and past history should be factored in.

    C. No, prospective suppliers should be kept on equal footing.

    D. No, that would represent an illegal activity.

15. **The most important thing to focus on in contract negotiations is:**

    A.   To negotiate the best price possible for your project.

    B.   To maintain the integrity of the scope.

    C.   To negotiate a deal that both parties are comfortable with.

    D.   To make sure legal counsel or the contract administrator has approved your negotiating points.

16. **If a project manager was performing Control Procurements, which of the following duties might he be performing?**

    A.   Approving seller invoices.

    B.   Negotiating the contract.

    C.   Closing the contract.

    D.   Weighing seller responses.

17. **Which document may form the basis for early termination of a seller by the buyer?**

    A.   Procurement management plan.

    B.   Seller performance evaluation.

    C.   Procurement negotiations.

    D.   Work performance information.

18. **Who generally bears the risk in a time and materials contract?**

    A.   The buyer.

    B.   The seller.

    C.   The buyer early in the project and the seller later on.

    D.   It depends on the materials used.

19. **Your company is outsourcing a project in an area where it has little experience. The procurement documents should be:**

    A. Completely rigid to ensure no deviation from sellers.

    B. Flexible enough to encourage creativity in seller responses.

    C. Informal.

    D. Reviewed by senior management.

20. **The procurement statement of work should provide:**

    A. Enough detail for the prospective seller to complete the project.

    B. Enough detail to describe the product, but not so much as to divulge trade secrets or sensitive information.

    C. Enough detail to perform make-or-buy analysis.

    D. Enough detail for the prospective seller to know if they are qualified to perform the work.

21. **You are ready to close out a procurement. Where is the best place to look for guidance in how to perform this activity?**

    A. Contract.

    B. Correspondence.

    C. Records management system.

    D. Seller performance evaluations.

22. **You are the project manager for a seller who has been selected to construct an industrial kitchen for a large food services company. Before the contract negotiations, the buyer confides in you that design is not finalized, and they want you to begin work with incomplete specifications. What type of contract should you ask for in negotiations?**

    A. Fixed price.

    B. Cost plus incentive fee.

    C. Time and materials.

    D. Cost plus fixed fee.

23. **The product or result of the project is created during which process group?**

    A.   Project life cycle.

    B.   Control Procurements.

    C.   Project executing.

    D.   Work package processing.

24. **Your customer has asked to meet with you and inspect the work you have completed to date on the project to ensure that it meets the contractual agreements. What is your customer manager engaged in?**

    A.   Close Procurements.

    B.   Seller efficiency audit.

    C.   Seller administration.

    D.   Procurement performance reviews.

25. **You have completed a project and delivered the full scope of the contract. The buyer agrees that you have technically satisfied the terms of the contract but is not satisfied with the end results. In this case, the contract is:**

    A.   Contested.

    B.   Complete.

    C.   Poorly written.

    D.   Lacking terms and conditions.

Answers to Procurement Management Questions

1. C. This question was easier than it may have first appeared to be. Fixed price is the highest risk to the seller since the seller must bear the risk of any cost overruns. Choice 'B' would provide the highest risk to the buyer.

2. A. By this time you should be thinking that if you see "expert judgment," it is likely the right answer. Expert judgment is a favored technique in project management, and it is correct in this case because you are conducting the Conduct Procurements process. It is the only tool/technique among the potential answers that is a part of that process.

3. A. Make-or-buy analysis is a tool used during the Plan Procurement Management process where you are deciding which deliverables should be procured and which should be created internally. 'D' is not a real process, and 'B' and 'C' are incorrect because by the time you conduct or Control Procurements, you need to already know what you are going to make and what you are going to buy.

4. D. Plan Procurement Management, Conduct Procurements, Control Procurements, Close Procurements. The easiest explanation for this one is that 'A', 'B', and 'C' all contain at least one made-up process.

5. B. Alternative dispute resolution (ADR), which includes mediation and arbitration, is preferable to litigation. 'A' is not a good choice because litigation should only be entered into as a last resort. 'C' is incorrect because a final, equitable resolution is very important and would not be prioritized below satisfaction. 'D' is not correct. ADR includes mediation, so the statement does not even make sense. It may be binding or non-binding.

6. B. Time and Materials. Choice 'A' is incorrect because the scope is not defined enough to establish a fair fixed price. Choice 'C' is a made-up type of contract. Choice 'D' would not make sense in this case since the seller's costs are not abundantly clear, and this type of contract would create too much risk.

7.   B. This one may trick some who think that it is wrong to use a sole source. In many cases it is the only choice. 'A' would not be good since the design has nothing to do with this. 'C' is not necessary in this case, since the issue is not a legal issue. Choice 'D' would be completely invalid since the item is still being procured outside of your organization.

8.   D. Choices 'A' and 'B' are verbal. Contract changes should always be made in writing! 'C' is written, but e-mail is not the proper forum for making important contractual changes.

9.   C. Conduct Procurements uses the tool of proposal evaluation techniques, which use a weighted decision matrix to score and select vendors.

10.   B. There are plenty of questions on the PMP Exam that defy common sense. This one asks for your FIRST action, and the most appropriate action is to enter the Close Procurements process. Choices 'A' and 'C' may be appropriate at some point, but if a project is terminated, Close Procurements needs to be performed.

11.   C. If you are evaluating seller responses, you are performing the process of Conduct Procurements. The seller proposals are brought into this process, and they are screened, weighted, rated, and evaluated against the criteria.

12.   B. Make-or-buy analysis is the process where an organization decides whether it should produce the product internally or outsource it. This is done as part of the Plan Procurement Management process.

13.   D. Independent estimates would be most appropriate. Martina needs to check and see if the bids are valid or if there may be some sort of collusion going on. 'A' might be a good step after getting some independent estimates. 'B' is a way of scoring and ranking vendors, but that might be premature at this point. 'C' is a way to inform bidders, but that should have taken place before the bids were received and would not be the best choice at this point.

14.   C. If you are involved in formal procurement, you should make every effort to keep sellers on equal footing. If one seller is provided with an advantage, it negates much of the value of the procurement process.

15. C. The most important point is to create a deal that everyone feels good about. 'A' sounds like a good choice, but it is incorrect; the best possible price might not be fair to your seller, and that could create a bad scenario for the project in the future. 'B' is important, but that is not the primary focus of negotiations. 'D' may or may not be necessary, depending on the situation.

16. A. One of the activities in Control Procurements is to pay seller invoices or generate invoices if you are the seller. Make sure to learn the primary inputs, tools, techniques, and outputs for the processes.

17. B. The seller performance evaluations, performed by the buyer, could form the basis for early termination if the contract provides for this. Note that "Contract" would have been an equally solid choice if it had been in the list. 'A' is the second best choice, since it gives information on how the subsequent procurement processes will be carried out, but it typically does not give information on how sellers might be terminated early. 'C' typically happens early in the procurement process before a seller is chosen, so this doesn't make sense as an answer. 'D' could feed helpful information into 'B', but it isn't a basis by itself.

18. A. In a time and materials contract, the buyer has to pay the seller for all time and materials, and often it involves an incomplete scope definition. Therefore, the buyer is the one most at risk.

19. B. In this scenario, you want sellers to respond with their own ideas. Procurement documents should be rigid enough to get responses to the same scope of work, and flexible enough to allow sellers to interject their own good ideas and creativity. Many people incorrectly choose 'A' because they assume that a rigid approach is almost always correct, but in this example, you do not have sufficient experience to rigidly manage the process, and you want your sellers to give you some guidance in their proposals. 'C' was clearly incorrect as procurement is something that should be done formally. 'D' is incorrect because senior management has many functions in an organization, but they would not be expected to review procurement documents.

20. D. Procurement statements of work should be as complete and concise as possible. At a minimum, they should contain enough information for the seller to determine if they are qualified to do the work.

21.   A.   The contract specifies how the procurement will be closed. Any of the other choices might provide supporting information, but the best place to look for guidance would be the contract.

22.   C. The major clue here is that the scope of work is not completely defined and they want you to begin work anyway. In that case, the project is at a higher risk, and a time and materials contract shifts much of that risk back to the buyer.

23.   C. This question ties back to Chapter 3– Process Framework. The actual work packages are completed (or executed) during the Executing process group.

24.   D. Procurement performance reviews are a tool of Control Procurements, where the buyer arranges a meeting with the seller to review the seller's performance against the plan. This question presents a near-textbook case of this.

25.   B. If the scope of the contract is complete, no other terms were breached, and no claims against the contract have been filed, then the contract is complete. 'A' is not a good choice since no claim was filed. 'C' is not a good guess here since you don't have enough information to state that the problem was that the contract was poorly written.

13 Stakeholder Management

Difficulty	Memorization	Exam Importance
LOW	LOW	LOW

Project stakeholder management is a new knowledge area represented on the exam, but the subject matter is not new. Much of the material was previously found in other knowledge areas, so that this primarily represents a reorganization of material.

Philosophy

Stakeholder management follows an approach that should be familiar, creating a plan, executing that plan, and monitoring and controlling. The idea that drives this is to work to manage the expectations that drive stakeholder satisfaction.

Stakeholder management is defined as "the creation and maintenance of relationships with the aim to satisfy needs." This is an expansive definition that covers activities throughout the project life cycle

The approach is driven by the fact that stakeholders need to be identified and have their needs understood before they are managed. They should be communicated with and involved at the proper level through the life of the project.

The processes of
Project Procurement Management
with their primary outputs.

Importance

As this is a new knowledge area, it is expected that some questions on the exam will relate back to this information; however, the content in this chapter is lighter and easier than most of the others.

Preparation

This knowledge area presents no real surprises other than the fact that there is an initiating process. Since a significant number of questions come from the initiating process group, and there are only two initiating processes, it is a safe guess that this particular process is important.

Stakeholder Management Processes

There are four processes in stakeholder management. These processes are displayed in the figure at the beginning of the chapter and summarized in the tables below.

Process Group	Stakeholder Management Process
Initiating	Identify Stakeholders
Planning	Plan Stakeholder Management
Executing	Manage Stakeholder Engagement
Monitoring & Controlling	Control Stakeholder Engagement
Closing	(none)

Process	Key Outputs
Identify Stakeholders	Stakeholder Register
Plan Stakeholder Management	Stakeholder Management Plan
Manage Stakeholder Engagement	Issue Log, Change Requests
Control Stakeholder Engagement	Work Performance Info, Change Requests

Identify Stakeholders

What it is:

Identify Stakeholders is the process that focuses on creating the stakeholder register to list all of the stakeholders and describe their involvement on the project.

Identify Stakeholders is one of only two initiating processes.

Keep in mind that a stakeholder may be anyone with an interest in the project, and that interest may be positive or negative.

Why it is important:

If the stakeholders are not properly identified on the project and their needs are not understood, then there is little chance of meeting expectations. Many projects are derailed because they did not understand the needs of the stakeholders and address them on the project.

On the exam, quite a few questions will come from the initiating process group, so you should expect several questions to be directly related to this process.

When it is performed:

Identify Stakeholders will typically be one of the first processes you perform on a project or project phase; however, it may be performed multiple times throughout the project's life cycle. For instance, if your project had six phases, you may well perform it six times (or even more). You'll need to perform it after the process of Develop Project Charter.

How it works:

Inputs

Project Charter

The charter describes the project in broad brush strokes, and it may also describe some of the stakeholders and their interests in the project or its product.

Procurement Documents

If there is a contract involved, then the procurement documents will provide information as to some of the stakeholders and their needs. Stakeholders could be the legal parties, the people who executed the contract, the team members responsible, etc.

Enterprise Environ. Factors — See Ch. 2, Common Inputs

Organizational Process Assets — See Ch. 2, Common Inputs

Tools

Kev Fact

Stakeholder Analysis

This one tool can cover quite a bit of ground. It is relatively simple to define, but it is often quite tricky to perform on an actual project. The goal of this technique is to identify which stakeholders should receive project communications, what communications they should receive, how they should receive these communications, and how often they should receive them.

Not all stakeholders should be treated equally on the project. Some are more important than others, and it is the job of the project manager (with help from the sponsor) to understand stakeholders and their abilities to influence the organization and their interests in the project.

There are many ways to accomplish this, but one technique is to plot stakeholders on a grid to visualize their impact and influence.

For the purposes of stakeholder analysis, a stakeholder would be anyone who creates or causes a need, is affected by the need, or would be affected by the solution.

When performing stakeholder analysis, the underlying needs that the stakeholders have related to this project should be ranked from greatest to least.

Expert Judgment — See Ch. 2, Common Tools

Meetings — See Ch. 2, Common Tools

Outputs

 Stakeholder Register

Key Fact
The stakeholder register is a document that lists all of the project stakeholders, describes them, and classifies them. The classification will become particularly important when you are planning the communication and want to group stakeholders together.

This document may be published with other project documentation or kept in reserve for the project manager's use only.

Identify Stakeholders

Planning

Plan Stakeholder Management

What it is:

The process of Plan Stakeholder Management is a new process for this version of the exam. It looks at how the team will relate to the stakeholders and what stakeholder involvement will be in all aspects of the project.

Why it is important:

Because this process is new, it is ripe for exploitation on the exam.

On a real project it is important because it is necessary to be proactive and deliberate when considering how to involve stakeholders on the project.

When it is performed:

This process would generally be performed very early on the project and may be revisited often as project work progresses. If it is not performed early in the project's life cycle, the project runs the risk of marginalizing and alienating stakeholders.

How it works:

Inputs

Project Management Plan — See Ch. 2, Common Inputs

Key Fact

Stakeholder Register

It is impossible to try and plan how stakeholders will be involved in the project without knowing who the stakeholders are. The register provides the stakeholders and their communication requirements.

Enterprise Environ. — See Ch. 2, Common Inputs

Organizational Process Assets — See Ch. 2, Common Inputs

Tools

Expert Judgment — See Ch. 2, Common Tools

Meetings — See Ch. 2, Common Tools

Kev Fact

Analytical Techniques

Stakeholders, and particularly their level of engagement must be understood and analyzed, with particular attention paid to the current and desired levels of engagement.

Stakeholder engagement is often plotted on a matrix such as the one that follows.

Stakeholder	Unaware	Resistant	Neutral	Supportive	Leading
Carla T.		Current			Desired
Siva S.			Current	Desired	
Ken P.	Current			Desired	

An Example of a Stakeholder Engagement Matrix

The purpose of this is to chart the current and desired states of project stakeholders, which will inform the stakeholder management plan.

Outputs

Kev Fact

Stakeholder Management Plan

The stakeholder management plan is a component of the project management plan. It describes how the team will engage the stakeholders and how it will manage expectations and deal with issues. It also describes how communication will be conducted.

The stakeholder management plan is generally not shared with most stakeholders.

Project Documents Updates — See Ch. 2, Common Outputs

Plan Stakeholder Management

Manage Stakeholder Engagement

What it is:

Manage Stakeholder Engagement is another new process, introduced in the 5th edition PMBOK Guide. It is an executing process that revolves around using communication and the issue log to help ensure that stakeholders are involved at the right level and in the right way.

For this process, know that stakeholders should be managed according to their needs and how the project scope addresses those needs.

Why it is important:

Stakeholder satisfaction may be the single most significant ingredient in project success. While much of that may have to do with product quality, quite a bit of it has to do with whether or not the stakeholders were happy with the project that was conducted, whether or not they were properly involved, and whether or not they had a voice on the project. This process helps to ensure that they are properly engaged throughout the life of the project.

When it is performed:

Stakeholders typically influence the project from very early (typically before it is even a project) until it is closed. This process happens as long as there are stakeholders with whom you need to work.

How it works:

Inputs

Stakeholder Management Plan

The purpose of this plan is fairly obvious. It describes how stakeholders will be engaged and managed throughout the project.

Communications Management Plan

The communications management plan describes how the project will communicate with the various stakeholders and groups of stakeholders. This plan complements the stakeholder management plan.

Change Log

The change log provides the raw fuel for this process since changes will trigger the need for communication. This could include changes to almost any attribute of the project including scope, time, cost, quality, vendors, or the project management plan itself.

Organizational Process Assets — See Ch. 2, Common Inputs

Tools

Communication Methods

See the next tool (interpersonal skills) for a discussion of the combined two tools.

Interpersonal Skills

Interpersonal skills and the preceding tool of communication methods combine keeping stakeholders up to date with the art of persuasion. How you communicate with stakeholders is at least as important as what you actually communicate.

Management Skills — See Ch. 2, Essential Terms

Outputs

Issue log

The issue log (and updates to it) flow out of this process. This is a very important component of this process since it captures and condenses stakeholder concerns in one single document.

Change Requests

As stakeholders are informed about the project's progress, it is normal for requested changes to result.

Manage Stakeholder Engagement

Project Management Plan Updates — See Ch. 2, Common Outputs

Project Documents Updates — See Ch. 2, Common Outputs

Organizational Process Assets — See Ch. 2, Common Outputs

Manage Stakeholder Engagement

Monitoring & Controlling

Control Stakeholder Engagement

What it is:

This process evaluates how the plan of engaging and involving stakeholders lines up with the results. While there are no real surprises with this process, it is one of the new ones for this version of the exam, so you should review it carefully for the exam.

Why it is important:

As any professional project manager can attest, stakeholder management does not always go according to plan, and when things go awry with stakeholder management, the project can quickly become derailed.

This process does the important work of monitoring and controlling the overall activities related to engaging the stakeholders and makes sure they stay on track or that the plan is updated if necessary.

When it is performed:

Like all monitoring and controlling processes, Control Stakeholder Engagement will be performed after there is a plan in place (the stakeholder management plan created in Plan Stakeholder Engagement) and after the plan has been executed (Manage Stakeholder Engagement).

This process will typically be performed from time to time throughout the project's life cycle.

How it works:

Inputs

Project Management Plan — See Ch. 2, Common Inputs

Kev Fact

Issue Log

The issue log is an important input to this process, as it will give an indication as to the volume, size, and scope of existing and new issues on the project.

Work Performance Data — See Ch. 2, Common Inputs

Project Documents — See Ch. 2, Common Inputs

Tools

Information Management Systems

An information management system facilitates the storage and reporting of information. This will represent one of the primary tools used to keep stakeholders up to date with project statuses and information.

Expert Judgment — See Ch. 2, Common Tools

Meetings — See Ch. 2, Common Tools

Outputs

None of the outputs for this process present significant fodder for the exam. The purpose of the process itself is more important.

Work Performance Info. — See Ch. 2, Common Outputs

Change Requests — See Ch. 2, Common Outputs

PM Plan Updates — See Ch. 2, Common Outputs

Project Documents Updates — See Ch. 2, Common Outputs

Org. Process Assets Updates — See Ch. 2, Common Outputs

IMPORTANT

In addition to this quiz, use your Key to InSite, found on the inside back cover of this book, to access additional content, including new exam questions, expanded content, and simulated PMP exams. If your book did not come with a Key to InSite on the inside back cover, it may not be authentic. If you do not have a Key to InSite, you may purchase one at insite.velociteach.com.

Stakeholder Management Questions

Note that this stakeholder management quiz is intentionally shorter than other chapter quizzes due to the nature of the material and its reduced importance for the exam.

1. **What are the dimensions measured on a stakeholder grid?**

   A. Access and Availability.

   B. Expertise and Influence.

   C. Interest and Power.

   D. Motive and Opportunity.

2. **Which of the following is not a tool used to manage the stakeholder engagement?**

   A. Communication methods.

   B. Interpersonal Skills.

   C. Management Skills.

   D. Issue Log.

3. **The primary purpose of the stakeholder register is:**

   A. To keep a list of all project stakeholders.

   B. To record stakeholder issues on the project.

   C. To map functional requirements back to the originating stakeholder.

   D. To serve as a project directory.

4. **The most important element in project success is:**

   A. Stakeholder satisfaction.

   B. How the product meets the requirements.

   C. Overall product quality.

   D. Overall project quality.

5. **Which of the following does not identify someone as a stakeholder during stakeholder analysis?**

   A. Someone who proposes a solution.

   B. Someone who is aware of a need.

   C. Someone who is affected by the need.

   D. Someone who would be affected by the solution.

6. **Identified stakeholder needs should all be:**

   A. Addressed by the project's product.

   B. Qualified.

   C. Ranked from greatest to least.

   D. Documented in the stakeholder management plan.

7. **Which of the following is not a classification of stakeholder engagement?**

   A. Unaware.

   B. Resistant.

   C. Leading.

   D. Participating.

8. **Ana is working on a matrix where she is measuring the stakeholder engagement on the project. What dimension would she likely be assessing and plotting?**

   A. Power and interest to influence the project.

   B. Ability and urgency to influence the project.

   C. Current and desired levels of interest.

   D. Expertise and availability to engage with the project.

9. **Which of the following statements is false regarding stakeholders?**

    A. Stakeholders may have a positive or negative interest in the success of the project.

    B. All stakeholders should be identified before the project execution begins.

    C. Stakeholders may not be affected by the outcome but may perceive that they could be affected by the outcome.

    D. Stakeholders may be people, or organizations.

10. **Which of the following is true concerning work performance data and work performance information?**

    A. Work performance data is used at the organizational level, while work performance information is used at the project level.

    B. Work performance information is more useful than work performance data.

    C. Work performance data is collected from monitoring and controlling processes.

    D. Work performance information represents raw observations and measurements.

Answers to Stakeholder Management Questions

1. **C.** When plotting stakeholder interest on a matrix, interest and influence (and sometime involvement) are measured.

2. **D.** This may have looked hard, but it was not so difficult to reason out. The issue log is the primary output of Manage Stakeholder Engagement, so it could not also be a tool. 'A', 'B', and 'C' are all tools used in that process.

3. **A.** The stakeholder register is a list of the stakeholders with their assessment and classification as it relates to the project.

4. **A.** This one should have been easy given the topic of the quiz, but you may well see questions like this on the PMP Exam. While all of the elements are important, stakeholder satisfaction is the most important.

5. **B.** The term "Stakeholder" is very broad and generally includes quite a few groups; however, someone who is aware of a need is ambiguous enough to not fit well within this list.

6. **C.** Stakeholder needs are to be ranked from greatest to least. This is key for determining project priorities. 'A' would be wonderful, but it is not realistic to think that every need a stakeholder raises will be addressed by the project. 'B' is not a bad answer, but by the time they are identified, they are essentially qualified as stakeholders. 'D' may sound like a good answer, but the stakeholder management plan is created before the stakeholders have been identified.

7. **D.** The five states of stakeholder engagement are Unaware, Resistant, Neutral, Supportive, and Leading. "Participating" might seem to make sense, but it is not a classification since the project manager does not typically need to measure the engagement of team members participating on the project.

8. **C.** The stakeholder engagement matrix plots the current and desired levels of engagement by stakeholders.

9. **B.** If you missed this one, don't feel bad. It is best to identify stakeholders early, but the key to getting it right is the word "all." Many of them may not emerge until late in the project.

10. **B**. WPI and WPD show up in Control Stakeholder Engagement. Remember that work performance data is raw, while work performance information has been analyzed and made more useful. 'A' has no grounding in reality at all, and 'C' and 'D' are opposite of the truth.

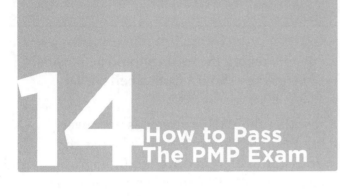

14 How to Pass The PMP Exam

Difficulty	Memorization	Exam Importance
LOW	LOW	HIGH

Passing the PMP on your first try has nothing to do with good luck. It is all about preparation and strategy. While the other chapters in this book are all about the preparation, this chapter focuses on test strategy. It includes techniques on how you can be sure to avoid careless mistakes during your exam.

The PMP Exam

This chapter covers strategies and material related to standardized tests in general and to the PMP exam specifically.

Before we get into the specifics of the PMP exam, it would be a good idea to cover standardized exams. Even if you have taken quite a few standardized exams before, now would be a good time to review some important points.

A standardized exam is a test designed to achieve some statistical consistency. Since the PMP exam is a standardized exam, this essentially means two things:

1. An individual test-taker should perform at approximately the same level on two different versions of the PMP exam.

2. The results of all people taking the exam should be normally distributed. That means they should form a bell curve.

It is important to know that the PMP exam does not cover material only from the PMBOK Guide. People who use the PMBOK Guide as a sole study reference are often surprised to find this out. This is because the PMBOK Guide is not meant to be a sole reference for practitioners or test-takers. It neither instructs you how to manage a project, nor how to study for an exam. It is, as its name suggests, a guide to the greater body of knowledge.

As we begin to talk about strategies, it would be helpful to look at how the PMP exam is actually created. The exam is made up of 200 questions, but as was pointed out in Chapter 1, only 175 of those questions count toward your pass/fail score on the exam. The trouble is that you will not be aware of which questions count and which do not. Volunteers are recruited to write questions, and these questions are then vetted, refined, and tested out before they are added to the exam.

If a question is selected, it may be introduced as one of the 25 experimental questions on the exam. Experimental questions should look like every other question on the exam. The key is that when the results for these experimental questions are evaluated, they should perform like every other question on the exam. Questions that are too difficult or too easy may be discarded.

The topic for each question may cover anything as long as it can be cited in a "contemporary project management resource." The problem for the test-taker is that PMI no longer publicly discloses what those contemporary project management resources are (although the author speculates that they are likely books currently for sale in PMI's bookstore).

There is a common way in which standardized exams are created. Questions will generally fall into three categories:

- Easier questions
- Medium questions
- Harder questions

It is important to note, however, that these questions will be scattered randomly throughout the exam.

Easier Questions

Easier questions should be answerable by most test-takers. They generally focus on topics such as ethical questions, questions that require you to support PMI, questions where you are encouraged to follow the process, and questions about obvious inputs, tools, or outputs. Most people find these to be among the easiest questions on the exam. Expect to see as many as 60 of the easier questions on the exam, although they may not seem easy at first glance.

The best way to recognize one of these questions is that after reading it through carefully a couple of times, you should find that one answer clearly stands out as the most likely candidate.

Medium Questions

Medium questions are the most common questions on the exam. You should expect to see approximately 80 questions that will fall into this category. These questions will cover topics such as the order in which processes must be performed, earned value calculations, and the application of specific risk and quality tools. They will also delve into more detail to test your understanding of the processes. In order to answer these questions, you will need to fall back to your study. If you are well prepared, you will find that you can generally trust your instincts.

Medium questions may be recognized by the fact that they should generally be more fact-based. You should be able to narrow these questions down to one or two candidate answers with a bit of careful reading.

Harder Questions

The harder questions will generally make the difference between those who pass and those who do not. One of the telltale signs of these questions is that you may be left scratching your head as to what is even being asked. This is an important clue! When you reach a question where you are not sure what is being asked, and remember that there may be as many as 60 of them, pause for a moment and shift mental gears. The harder questions on the exam are designed so that only the most prepared exam-takers will get them right.

When dealing with the harder questions, it is important to note that most test-takers will not naturally gravitate toward the right answer.

Consider the following example:

Q: **Mike is midway through execution and has a CPI of .98 and an SPI of .96 on his project. His project sponsor has requested a meeting with him to discuss the project's CPI and SPI as well as certain decisions he has made and how they might have led to recent issues that have arisen. Mike does not agree with the sponsor. What is the best way for Mike to handle this?**

A. Generate current performance reports before the meeting.

B. Meet with the sponsor to show how the project is within tolerance.

C. Explain to the sponsor why he made the decisions he did.

D. Evaluate why the sponsor wants to meet.

There are many confusing things about this question. First of all, the question is asking "what is the best way to handle this," but the reader is no more certain what 'this' even is. Beyond that, none of the answers really seems to fit.

'A' is a fine thing to do, but it doesn't really address any of the issues in the question. 'B' seems problematic since even though the project is very close to being on track, we do not know what tolerances are. 'C' sounds like a defensive response, and while 'D' looks great at first glance (trigger word: "evaluate"), it doesn't really seem to solve anything.

Now, let's look more closely. What is the question actually asking? While we cannot be certain from the way it is worded, the question basically states that the sponsor has asked for a meeting about a couple of points and that there is a disagreement on those points. Reformulating the question now adds a bit of clarity. Whenever you have to restate the question in order to understand it, you can feel confident that it is one of the harder questions on the exam.

Next, look for the trap. Remember that most exam-takers will initially pick the wrong answer on the harder questions. In this case, the most likely answer would be 'D'. It is comfortable, it does no harm, and it uses one of the trigger words we like to see. Remember, however, that a trigger word does not guarantee that it is the right answer. Instead, it should be given extra consideration. Looking at it this way, 'D' now looks like a trap. It is the answer that most test-takers would pick, and it is incorrect.

This brings us to an important strategy for strong test-takers. When you recognize a harder question, you should look for the trap and eliminate it first; however, be sure that you are, indeed, on one of the harder questions. Also keep in mind that this strategy may backfire on the easy and medium questions.

In this case, we are reasonably confident that this is one of the harder questions, so we will eliminate 'D'. Reviewing the remaining answers, 'A' does not appear to be very helpful either. Updated performance reports do not really pertain to the question in any way. That leaves answers 'B' and 'C'. Take a closer look at choice 'C'. Although the wording is such that it sounds defensive, project managers have an aspirational goal of transparency in the decision-making process. Transparency is a good thing, and 'C' fits that model.

This strategy works best with a lot of practice, so be sure to use the key in the inside back cover of your book and practice using InSite before you try it on the PMP Exam!

Reading the Questions

A critical step to passing the PMP is to read and understand each question. Questions on the exam may be long and have many twists and turns. They are often full of irrelevant information thrown in intentionally to distract you from the relevant facts. Those who pass the PMP know to read the questions carefully.

Many times the only relevant information is contained at the very the end. Consider the following example:

Q: **Mark has a project where task A is dependent on the start and has a duration of 3. Task B is dependent on start and has a duration of 5. Task C is dependent on A and has a duration of 4. Task D is dependent on B and has a duration of 6, and the finish is dependent on tasks C and D. Mark is using his project network diagram to help create a schedule. The schedule for the project is usually created during which process?**

A.   Estimate Costs.

B.   Determine Budget.

C.   Control Schedule.

D.   Develop Schedule.

Questions like the one above are not uncommon on the PMP Exam. If you take the time to draw out a complex project network diagram, you will have wasted valuable time, when the question was only asking you to pick the process (the answer is 'D').

On lengthy questions, the best practice is to quickly skip down to the last sentence for a clue as to what the question is asking. Then read the entire question thoroughly. Most of them have a very short final sentence that will summarize the actual question. Make sure, however, to read the entire question at least once! Don't simply rely on the last sentence.

Just as important as carefully reading the questions is reading each of the four answers. You should never stop reading the answers as soon as you find one you like. Instead, always read all four answers before making your selection.

A Guessing Strategy

By simply reading the material in this book, you will immediately know how to answer many of the questions on the exam. For many others, you will have an instinctive guess. If you have studied the other chapters, you should trust that instinct. It is not there by chance. Your instinct was created by exposing yourself to this material in different ways. Your mind will begin to gravitate toward the right answer even if you are not explicitly aware of it.

Guessing on the PMP does not have to be left purely to chance. If you do not know the answer immediately, begin by eliminating wrong answers, or ones you suspect are wrong. Let's take a fairly difficult question as an example:

Q: **Organizational Process Assets are used as an input to all of the following processes EXCEPT:**

A. Define Activities.

B. Develop Project Charter.

C. Validate Scope.

D. Perform Quantitative Risk Analysis.

Unless you have memorized all of the inputs to all of the processes (the PMBOK Guide lists over 500 inputs, tools, and outputs), you are going to have to guess at this one. However, if you throw up your hands and pick one, you only have a 25% chance of getting it right. Instead, you should think about what is being asked. Organizational process assets are used as an input to processes all over the PMBOK Guide, so that doesn't offer help, but when you stop to consider that it is used primarily in initiating and planning processes, suddenly the picture becomes a little clearer. Now you can see that 'A', 'B', and 'D' are probably not the right answer. Any of these would be a good fit for historical information, which is an organizational process asset. Even if you could only narrow the choices down to 'C' and 'D', you would have a 50% chance. Look at them more carefully and ask yourself where would historical information most likely be used an input? Perform Quantitative Risk Analysis is a good guess, since you might use past results (an organizational process asset) to help you analyze and quantify risk. So now, you are left with choice 'C', Verify Scope, as the one that looks least likely to have an organizational process asset as an input. It is also the one process that takes place after execution, when historical information might not be as valuable. It may be a guess, but it is a very educated one.

The method here is simply to think about each answer and eliminate ones that are obviously wrong. Even if you only knock off one wrong answer, you have significantly increased your odds of choosing the right one. You will find that most times you can knock off at least two, evening your chances of answering the question correctly.

Spotting Tricks and Traps

The exam does have trick questions. They are designed specifically to catch people who are coming in with little formal process experience, those who have thumbed through the PMBOK Guide a few times and are now going to take the exam. These people try to rely on their work experience, which often does not line up with PMI's prescribed method for doing things. As a result, they typically don't even come close to passing the exam.

At times, however, these trick questions can also fool a seasoned pro! Listed below are some techniques you can use so that you will not fall into these traps.

Follow the Process

This is always the right answer. There will be questions on your exam that give you "common sense" scenarios that will give you a seemingly innocent way to skip the formal process and save time, or perhaps avoid some conflict by not following procedure. This is almost certainly a trap. The right answer is to follow PMI's process! Do not give in to pressure from irate customers, stakeholders, or even your boss to do otherwise.

Don't Take the Easy Way Out

There will often be choices that allow you to postpone a difficult decision, dodge a thorny issue, or ignore a problem. This is almost never the right thing to do for questions on the exam.

Act Directly and Say What You Mean

In PMI's world, project managers communicate directly. They do not dance around the issue, gossip, or imply things, and they do not communicate through a third party. If they have bad news to tell the customer, they go to the customer and tell them the facts – and the sooner, the better. If they have a problem with a team member, they confront the person, usually directly, although at times it may be appropriate to get the team member's functional manager involved.

Study the Roles

By the time you take the exam, you should be confident about the roles of stakeholders, sponsors, customers, team members, functional managers, the project office, and most importantly, the project manager (plus the other roles that are discussed in Chapter 2 – Foundational Terms and Concepts). Expect several "who should perform this activity" type questions. If you have absolutely no clue, guessing the "project manager" is a good idea.

Additionally, understand the difference between the different types of organizations (projectized, matrix, and functional). Most of your questions will pertain to matrix organizations, so focus your study on that one.

Project Manager's Role

Expanding on the previous point, project managers are the ones who make decisions and carry them out. They have the final decision on most points, can spend budget, can change schedules, and can approve or refuse scope. For the test, assume that the project manager is "large and in charge!"

Another attribute of project managers is that they are proactive in their approach to managing tasks and information. They do not wait for changes to occur. Instead, they are actively influencing the factors that contribute to change. Instead of waiting for information to come to them, they are actively communicating and making certain they have accurate and up-to-date information.

Don't Get Stuck

You should expect to find a few questions on the exam that you do not know how to answer. You will look at these and see 4 correct answers, making it impossible to pick just 1. In such cases, do not agonize. Even using every good technique, you will still have to make an educated guess at some questions. Some test-takers can get quite upset at this, and it can undermine their confidence. If a question stumps you, simply mark it for review and move on. Never spend 15 minutes staring at a single question unless you have already answered all the others. One question is only worth a fraction of a percent on the exam, so if you do not know the answer, do not obsess over it.

You may even discover that a block of questions seems especially difficult to you. This experience can be discouraging and may cause your confidence to waver. Don't be alarmed if you happen upon several difficult questions in a row. Keep marking them for review and keep moving until you come to more familiar ground. You may find that questions later in the test will offer you hints or jog your memory, helping you with those you initially found difficult.

Exam Time Management

You will have a few minutes at the beginning to go through a tutorial. You probably won't find much value in the actual tutorial; however, you absolutely should take it. After going through it, you will be given a chance to wait before taking the test. Use that time to write down essential formulas and processes on your scratch paper.

Scratch Paper

You will be given five to six sheets of scratch paper when you walk into the exam. You may not carry your own paper into the test. When you sit down to begin the exam, you should write down a few key things. Regardless of how well you know this material, at a minimum, write the following on your first sheet of scratch paper.

1. Earned Value formulas (EV, PV, AC, CPI, CPI^c, SPI, CV, SV, BAC, EAC, ETC, $TCPI_c$) from Chapter 7. You will probably need to refer to these several times during the exam, and it will save time and improve your accuracy if you have written them out.
2. The time management formulas for the three-point estimates and standard deviation.
3. The communication channels formula described in Chapter 10.

Even if you are tempted to skip this step, don't! When you come to a lengthy and confusing question that requires you to calculate several different values, you will be glad that you already have your formulas written down for review. This will free your mind to concentrate on the specific question rather than on recalling a formula.

Budgeting Your Time

Going into the exam, you may be fast or you may be a slower test-taker. Everyone should walk into the exam with a strategy for managing their time, based on their own pace. Do not underestimate how hard it is to sit for a 200 question, 4 hour exam. The test-taking process is strenuous and mentally and physically taxing.

If you have a test time management strategy that has served you well in the past, you should use that. If not, here is a generic strategy that many people have used "as is" to take and pass the PMP.

1. Sit for the tutorial and download your information to your scratch paper.
2. When the exam begins, take the first 75 questions, pacing yourself to take approximately 45 minutes.
3. Take your first break. Spend 5 minutes stretching and get a bite of food from your locker.
4. Take the next 75 questions, again pacing yourself to take 45 to 50 minutes.
5. Take your 2nd break. Spend approximately 10 minutes, go to the bathroom, and get a snack.
6. Answer the final 50 questions and then return to answer any ones you did not answer the first time. Budget approximately 45 minutes for this as well. You may not take that long, but it is normal for your pace to slow down as the test wears on.
7. Take a bigger 15 minute break (relishing the fact that you have now answered all the questions on the PMP).
8. At this point, you should be at about three hours or less into the test.
9. Perform a review of the first 100 questions. Pace yourself to finish this in about 25 minutes.
10. Take a short 5 minute stretch break if needed.
11. Review last 100 questions and any other ones in your remaining time.

Managing Your Review

When you make a review pass through the exam, you will come across questions that you missed the first time but that are apparent when you look at them again. This is normal, and you should not hesitate to change any answers that you can see you missed. Many people change as many as 10% of the answers on their review. If you catch yourself changing more than that, be careful! You may be second guessing yourself and actually do more harm than good.

When you go through your review pass on the exam, do not take the whole test over again. Instead, employ three rapid fire steps:

1. Did you read the question correctly the first time?
2. Did your selected answer match what was being asked?
3. Perform a complete check of your math where applicable.

Difficulty

Everyone wants to know what the hardest topic on the exam is. That is a difficult question to answer for two reasons:

1. The PMBOK Guide and the test are divided differently. There are ten knowledge areas in the PMBOK Guide, each given its own chapter. But all of this material also fits into one of five process groups. To make it more confusing, the PMBOK Guide is arranged by knowledge area, but the test is graded by process group. You will not be aware of this while you are taking the exam, but it can heighten the confusion when evaluating your test results!

2. The other reason that difficulty is hard to predict is that everyone's experience will differ. No two tests are alike just as no two people have identical backgrounds. If you have heavy finance and accounting experience, time and cost may be easy subjects for you. If you have a strong legal background or have worked for the government, then questions about procurement may be easy for you. If you have human resource or psychology training, human resource management may be easiest.

Based on a typical profile of someone who had earned an undergraduate degree in management and had non-industry specific experience managing projects, the material would roughly rank as shown below:

Process Framework	1	
Foundational Concepts	2	
Integration	3	Harder
Cost	4	
Time	5	
Risk	6	
Procurement	7	
Quality	8	Medium Difficulty
Scope	9	
Human Resources	10	
Communications	11	Easier
Stakeholder Management	12	

The preceding scale is relative since very little of the material on the exam is considered "easy" to everyone. Ultimately, your professional experience and study can significantly change the order of this list for you.

General Advice

Professional Responsibility is no longer a category on the exam, but there are questions that will be related to the "right thing to do," and some of these may surprise the test-taker who has not thoroughly prepared. Many of the questions may create very difficult situations that would be easier to ignore or dodge in real life; however, PMI requires that the project manager deal with these situations in a direct and open manner.

If there were one simple phrase that sums up this category of questions section of the test, it would be "Do the right thing," even (especially) if it is painful or would be tempting to avoid. If a test question offers you an easy way out, beware! You have likely spotted a trap. If the exam presents you with an option that represents a shortcut, do not take it.

There are a number of specific points you should understand in this area. International law can be a fairly tricky and sometimes ambiguous area, but you should expect questions on the exam to be generally straightforward in this regard. The rule for the exam is this: if you are asked to do something in another country that is not customarily done in your culture, you should first evaluate and investigate it, determine if it is unethical or illegal, and then act accordingly. This may be difficult for those who are not accustomed to international dealings. For instance, if you are asked to make a payment to a city council in another country in order to get a work permit, evaluate whether or not the payment is a bribe. *If it is a bribe, do not make the payment.* If it is not a bribe and it is customary, or even the law, then make the payment.

A short way of looking at it is that if it is illegal or unethical in any way then it is wrong. Otherwise, the custom in the country where the work is being performed should prevail.

There are infinite possibilities as to what may be asked here. Questions of bribery, discrimination, and illegal activity are among the favorites, but by following the thought process previously described, these questions should present no problem. Only make sure that you are not thinking so concretely that you think anything is wrong if it is different from the customary practices in your home country.

A rule to keep in mind is that your organization's policies *must be followed at all times.* If you have an interest that conflicts with a policy, the policy is to be considered first. If your organization has a policy that all travel must be booked through the company's travel agency but you find that you can get a cheaper rate through your mother's travel agency, you should adhere to the company policy and use the corporate travel agency.

Integrity may be defined as sticking to high moral principles. For the test, the important concept is that you should do what you said you would do, deal with problems openly and honestly, and do not put personal gain ahead of the project.

Company and professional politics may play a prominent role in your life or company, and many project managers learn to be quite adept at managing them, but they are relegated to a low position on the exam.

Keep in mind that carrying out the right choice may involve standing up to the company's president, refusing an order from your boss, telling the customer the whole truth, and many other things that might have unpleasant consequences.

If a choice appears sneaky, underhanded, or dishonest in any way, it is probably not the correct answer. *If the behavior is not direct, open, and straightforward, it is probably not the right behavior – even if it would ultimately appear to help the project!* This will help you eliminate wrong choices on many questions.

Questions about professionalism on the exam are testing your knowledge of how a project manager acts as a professional in the workplace. According to the code of professional conduct, a project manager is to follow the process and act with respect toward others.

One key to these questions is to take the 47 processes outlined in this book *seriously*. The process framework is not just a formality or a theoretical best-case scenario. It is a serious set of processes, inputs, tools and techniques, and outputs that will reduce risk and improve time, cost, and quality. That said, the process is not painless. For the exam, however, the process must be followed. If your customer asks you to cut corners on the process in order to save money, you should not agree.

PMI expects Project Management Professionals to stay engaged and further the profession. The PMP certification was not designed for people to earn and never use. This is reflected on the exam with questions about activities that don't necessarily relate directly to a project.

Any time a project manager has an opportunity to further the project management training or learning of someone else, such as sharing lessons learned, mentoring, teaching, or leading in best practices, there is a very good chance that is the correct choice.

General Advice

PMPs are encouraged to publish, teach, write, and disseminate the methodology and process as much as they can. Answers that offer a variant of these activities as the choice are often correct.

Project management certification is quite a milestone in one's career, but it is by no means the end. Project managers are expected to continue to study, learn, and grow professionally. As you have no doubt seen, any one of the knowledge areas could consume an entire career, so do not assume that you have learned all there is to know. Even one topic, such as quality, or risk, could provide more than a lifetime's worth of material to study and master.

Another favorite key here is that you know your own areas of weakness and continue to develop them. Do you know what your professional weaknesses are? Are you strong at planning but weak in communication? Are you good at planning tasks but poor at leading people? Everyone has strong suits as well as areas that need to be developed. It is important that the project manager knows what his or her professional growth needs are and pays attention to them.

Additionally, project managers can contribute more to the body of knowledge if they are familiar with their industries. They should study their industries, learn them well, and thus enhance their ability to apply the project management processes to their work.

You should also expect to see questions that put you in a situation of taking a hard look at your abilities, or learning where it is that you are weak. In these scenarios, the project manager should strive for continued improvement, growth, and increased proficiency.

The project manager must accurately identify the stakeholders, then understand them, and then seek to balance their interests. This can be nearly impossible at times! For the exam, keep these principles in mind:

- Be fair to everyone and respect the differences of the group.
- Resolve stakeholder conflict in favor of the customer.
- Be open and honest about the resolution. Don't hide things from one stakeholder in order to please another.
- Do the ethical thing in all decisions.

It is tempting for some people to approach questions with a sense of "fairness" about how hard someone should work, but work ethics vary from country to country, and project managers should take that into account. That does not mean that laziness or negligence should be tolerated, but it does mean that different cultures place different values upon work, and it is not the project manager's job to force them to the level of his or her home country.

As stated previously, cultural differences on the team should be respected (notice how many times the concept of "respect" is mentioned in this chapter), and multiculturalism is something PMI promotes heavily. Your dealings with your team and the many stakeholders on a project should be professional and mindful of their customs.

As in other areas, communication should be open and regular so that people are aware of what is going on with the project.

Organizations are accountable for social, environmental, and economic impacts to their projects. Project managers should factor in the interests of the community, the environment, and society when making decisions.

On the exam, you may encounter a question that poses a situation where the project would benefit but society would suffer. The project manager should avoid all such situations and scenarios. If the situation becomes untenable or unresolvable, the project manager should disclose the situation and, as a last resort, resign the project.

Sustainability is another favored answer on the exam. Answers that encourage sustainable usage of resources and sustainable team work practices are good candidates for the right answer.

Managing Anxiety

Finally, if test-taking has always been a fear-inducing activity for you, there is one simple strategy that may help you manage the physical symptoms of anxiety so that your thinking and memory are not impaired: Take a deep breath. This may sound like obvious advice, but it is based on sound research. Studies in the field of stress management have shown that feelings of anxiety (the "fight or flight" response) are linked with elevated levels of adrenaline and certain brain chemicals. One way to bring your brain chemistry back into balance is to draw a deep breath, hold it for about six seconds, and slowly release it. Repeat this breathing pattern whenever you begin to feel panicky over particular questions. It will help to slow your heart rate and clear your mind for greater concentration on the task at hand.

Another thing to remember is that many people who take the exam do not pass – especially on their first attempts. While no one wants to fail the test, you can turn around immediately and apply to take it again (at a reduced rate). You can take the exam up to three times in a year starting with the time you receive your letter of eligibility from PMI.

If you do have to take the exam again, use it as a learning experience. You will have a much higher chance for success on your next attempt, and you will have your post-exam evaluation sheet that gives you a breakdown of where you need to study. As the inspired Jerome Kern once penned to music, "Take a deep breath; pick yourself up; dust yourself off; start all over again."

PMI Code of Conduct

Carefully review the code of conduct printed on the following pages. Applicants sign this statement when applying to take the exam. While there is no longer a formal "professional responsibility" section on the PMP exam, there are still questions that relate directly back to this material. Understanding the code of conduct will give you excellent guidance in answering questions on the exam, especially when you have narrowed the correct answer down to two choices.

Code of Ethics and Professional Conduct

CHAPTER 1. VISION AND APPLICABILITY

1.1 Vision and Purpose

As practitioners of project management, we are committed to doing what is right and honorable. We set high standards for ourselves and we aspire to meet these standards in all aspects of our lives—at work, at home, and in service to our profession.

This Code of Ethics and Professional Conduct describes the expectations that we have of ourselves and our fellow practitioners in the global project management community. It articulates the ideals to which we aspire as well as the behaviors that are mandatory in our professional and volunteer roles.

The purpose of this Code is to instill confidence in the project management profession and to help an individual become a better practitioner. We do this by establishing a profession-wide understanding of appropriate behavior. We believe that the credibility and reputation of the project management profession is shaped by the collective conduct of individual practitioners.

We believe that we can advance our profession, both individually and collectively, by embracing this Code of Ethics and Professional Conduct. We also believe that this Code will assist us in making wise decisions, particularly when faced with difficult situations where we may be asked to compromise our integrity or our values.

Our hope is that this Code of Ethics and Professional Conduct will serve as a catalyst for others to study, deliberate, and write about ethics and values. Further, we hope that this Code will ultimately be used to build upon and evolve our profession.

1.2 Persons to Whom the Code Applies

The Code of Ethics and Professional Conduct applies to:

1.2.1 All PMI members

1.2.2 Individuals who are not members of PMI but meet one or more of the following criteria:

.1 Non-members who hold a PMI certification

.2 Non-members who apply to commence a PMI certification process

.3 Non-members who serve PMI in a volunteer capacity.

Comment: Those holding a Project Management Institute (PMI®) credential (whether members or not) were previously held accountable to the Project Management Professional (PMP®) or Certified Associate in Project Management (CAPM®) Code of Professional Conduct and continue to be held accountable to the PMI Code of Ethics and Professional Conduct. In the past, PMI also had separate ethics standards for members and for credentialed individuals. Stakeholders who contributed input to develop this Code concluded that having multiple codes was undesirable and that everyone should be held to one high standard. Therefore, this Code is applicable to both PMI members and individuals who have applied for or received a credential from PMI, regardless of their membership in PMI.

1.3 Structure of the Code

The Code of Ethics and Professional Conduct is divided into sections that contain standards of conduct which are aligned with the four values that were identified as most important to the project management community. Some sections of this Code include comments. Comments are not mandatory parts of the Code, but provide examples and other clarification.

1.4 Values that Support this Code

Practitioners from the global project management community were asked to identify the values that formed the basis of their decision-making and guided their actions. The values that the global project management community defined as most important were: responsibility, respect, fairness, and honesty. This Code affirms these four values as its foundation.

1.5 Aspirational and Mandatory Conduct

Each section of the Code of Ethics and Professional Conduct includes both aspirational standards and mandatory standards. The aspirational standards describe the conduct that we strive to uphold as practitioners. Although adherence to the aspirational standards is not easily measured, conducting ourselves in accordance with these is an expectation that we have of ourselves as professionals—it is not optional.

The mandatory standards establish firm requirements, and in some cases, limit or prohibit practitioner behavior. Practitioners who do not conduct themselves in accordance with these standards will be subject to disciplinary procedures before PMI's Ethics Review Committee.

Comment: The conduct covered under the aspirational standards and conduct covered under the mandatory standards are not mutually exclusive; that is, one specific act or omission could violate both aspirational and mandatory standards.

There are a few important points to note in this section. The first is that the code of conduct does not apply to everyone in the world. Instead, it applies to project managers who are affiliated with PMI. While there are many nuances to this, for the exam, use the simple rule that if someone has any real contact with PMI, even if they are not a member, then they should follow the code of conduct. You will always be safer on the exam adhering to the rule that any person in question should follow the code of conduct.

The second thing you should know about the code of conduct is that it is divided into four sub-chapters, each based on a value. The four values are: Responsibility, Respect, Fairness, and Honesty. Each of these are expanded in the following sections.

Professional Conduct

Finally, there are two more divisions for each of the four sub-chapters. They are *mandatory* and *aspirational* standards. As you might guess, mandatory conduct must be followed, while aspirational conduct is a goal.

CHAPTER 2. RESPONSIBILITY

2.1 Description of Responsibility

Responsibility is our duty to take ownership for the decisions we make or fail to make, the actions we take or fail to take, and the consequences that result.

2.2 Responsibility: Aspirational Standards

As practitioners in the global project management community:

2.2.1 We make decisions and take actions based on the best interests of society, public safety, and the environment.

2.2.2 We accept only those assignments that are consistent with our background, experience, skills, and qualifications.

Comment: Where developmental or stretch assignments are being considered, we ensure that key stakeholders receive timely and complete information regarding the gaps in our qualifications so that they may make informed decisions regarding our suitability for a particular assignment.

In the case of a contracting arrangement, we only bid on work that our organization is qualified to perform and we assign only qualified individuals to perform the work.

2.2.3 We fulfill the commitments that we undertake – we do what we say we will do.

2.2.4 When we make errors or omissions, we take ownership and make corrections promptly. When we discover errors or omissions caused by others, we communicate them to the appropriate body as soon they are discovered. We accept accountability for any issues resulting from our errors or omissions and any resulting consequences.

2.2.5 We protect proprietary or confidential information that has been entrusted to us.

2.2.6 We uphold this Code and hold each other accountable to it.

2.3 Responsibility: Mandatory Standards

As practitioners in the global project management community, we require the following of ourselves and our fellow practitioners:

Regulations and Legal Requirements

2.3.1 We inform ourselves and uphold the policies, rules, regulations and laws that govern our work, professional, and volunteer activities.

2.3.2 We report unethical or illegal conduct to appropriate management and, if necessary, to those affected by the conduct.

Comment: These provisions have several implications. Specifically, we do not engage in any illegal behavior, including but not limited to: theft, fraud, corruption, embezzlement, or bribery. Further, we do not take or abuse the property of others, including intellectual property, nor do we engage in slander or libel. In focus groups conducted with practitioners around the globe, these types of illegal behaviors were mentioned as being problematic.

As practitioners and representatives of our profession, we do not condone or assist others in engaging in illegal behavior. We report any illegal or unethical conduct. Reporting is not easy and we recognize that it may have negative consequences. Since recent corporate scandals, many organizations have adopted policies to protect employees who reveal the truth about illegal or unethical activities. Some governments have also adopted legislation to protect employees who come forward with the truth.

Ethics Complaints

2.3.3 We bring violations of this Code to the attention of the appropriate body for resolution.

Professional Conduct

2.3.4 We only file ethics complaints when they are substantiated by facts.

Comment: These provisions have several implications. We cooperate with PMI concerning ethics violations and the collection of related information whether we are a complainant or a respondent. We also abstain from accusing others of ethical misconduct when we do not have all the facts. Further, we pursue disciplinary action against individuals who knowingly make false allegations against others.

2.3.5 We pursue disciplinary action against an individual who retaliates against a person raising ethics concerns.

The value of Responsibility is an important one for the exam. In fact, most professional responsibility questions will likely touch on this value in some way.

Each of the four values is divided into mandatory and aspirational conduct, and it is important that you know the difference between them.

In this case, mandatory conduct focuses primarily on laws, regulations, policies, and ethics. The easiest way to interpret these questions is to always take the high road. For instance, if a question gives you a scenario where it appears that the right thing to do is to follow the law or a corporate policy, but it would be very difficult to you professionally, you can be confident that the right answer is to follow the law or policy.

Aspirational values generally take the mandatory ones a good step further. In the value of Responsibility, project managers aspire to not getting in over their heads, taking ownership of their actions (including mistakes), and most importantly, doing what they say they will do.

CHAPTER 3. RESPECT

3.1 Description of Respect

Respect is our duty to show a high regard for ourselves, others, and the resources entrusted to us. Resources entrusted to us may include people, money, reputation, the safety of others, and natural or environmental resources.

An environment of respect engenders trust, confidence, and performance excellence by fostering mutual cooperation — an environment where diverse perspectives and views are encouraged and valued.

3.2 Respect: Aspirational Standards

As practitioners in the global project management community:

3.2.1 We inform ourselves about the norms and customs of others and avoid engaging in behaviors they might consider disrespectful.

3.2.2 We listen to others' points of view, seeking to understand them.

3.2.3 We approach directly those persons with whom we have a conflict or disagreement.

3.2.4 We conduct ourselves in a professional manner, even when it is not reciprocated.

Comment: An implication of these provisions is that we avoid engaging in gossip and avoid making negative remarks to undermine another person's reputation. We also have a duty under this Code to confront others who engage in these types of behaviors.

3.3 Respect: Mandatory Standards

As practitioners in the global project management community, we require the following of ourselves and our fellow practitioners:

3.3.1 We negotiate in good faith.

3.3.2 We do not exercise the power of our expertise or position to influence the decisions or actions of others in order to benefit personally at their expense.

3.3.3 We do not act in an abusive manner toward others.

3.3.4 We respect the property rights of others.

This value may be challenging to implement in real life, but it should be a bit easier to navigate on the exam.

The project manager shows respect to others. This extends not only to individuals, but to cultures. PMI is a strong advocate of multiculturalism, and questions on the test will often reflect this bias. Just as PMI does not advocate forcing in other areas, the project manager is not to force or impose his culture or personal beliefs upon others. Multicultural and "politically correct" answers are usually good choices for questions related to professionalism.

Another area of respect that often appears on the test is the respect for confidentiality. This covers confidentiality of client information, trade secrets, project information, and any personal information that may be disclosed during the course of the project.

The mandatory standard is that we negotiate in good faith and do not abuse others. The respect we extend to others includes interpersonal respect and the respect of others' property, including intellectual property.

The aspirational standard here takes the mandatory standard further by valuing other people, cultures, and opinions. Keep in mind that answers that sound "politically correct" are generally considered favorable for the exam.

CHAPTER 4. FAIRNESS

4.1 Description of Fairness

Fairness is our duty to make decisions and act impartially and objectively. Our conduct must be free from competing self interest, prejudice, and favoritism.

4.2 Fairness: Aspirational Standards

As practitioners in the global project management community:

4.2.1 We demonstrate transparency in our decision-making process.

4.2.2 We constantly reexamine our impartiality and objectivity, taking corrective action as appropriate.

Comment: Research with practitioners indicated that the subject of conflicts of interest is one of the most challenging faced by our profession. One of the biggest problems practitioners report is not recognizing when we have conflicted loyalties and recognizing when we are inadvertently placing ourselves or others in a conflict-of-interest situation. We as practitioners must proactively search for potential conflicts and help each other by highlighting each other's potential conflicts of interest and insisting that they be resolved.

4.2.3 We provide equal access to information to those who are authorized to have that information.

4.2.4 We make opportunities equally available to qualified candidates.

Comment: An implication of these provisions is, in the case of a contracting arrangement, we provide equal access to information during the bidding process.

4.3 Fairness: Mandatory Standards

As practitioners in the global project management community, we require the following of ourselves and our fellow practitioners:

Conflict of Interest Situations

4.3.1 We proactively and fully disclose any real or potential conflicts of interest to the appropriate stakeholders.

4.3.2 When we realize that we have a real or potential conflict of interest, we refrain from engaging in the decision-making process or otherwise attempting to influence outcomes, unless or until: we have made full disclosure to the affected stakeholders; we have an approved mitigation plan; and we have obtained the consent of the stakeholders to proceed.

Comment: A conflict of interest occurs when we are in a position to influence decisions or other outcomes on behalf of one party when such decisions or outcomes could affect one or more other parties with which we have competing loyalties. For example, when we are acting as an employee, we have a duty of loyalty to our employer. When we are acting as a PMI volunteer, we have a duty of loyalty to the Project Management Institute. We must recognize these divergent interests and refrain from influencing decisions when we have a conflict of interest.

Further, even if we believe that we can set aside our divided loyalties and make decisions impartially, we treat the appearance of a conflict of interest as a conflict of interest and follow the provisions described in the Code.

Favoritism and Discrimination

4.3.3 We do not hire or fire, reward or punish, or award or deny contracts based on personal considerations, including but not limited to, favoritism, nepotism, or bribery.

4.3.4 We do not discriminate against others based on, but not limited to, gender, race, age, religion, disability, nationality, or sexual orientation.

4.3.5 We apply the rules of the organization (employer, Project Management Institute, or other group) without favoritism or prejudice.

The mandatory standard here is pretty clear. We must be especially careful to avoid conflicts of interest, and we never discriminate against others. The conflict of interest point is an important one. For the exam, you should choose answers that go out of their way to avoid a conflict of interest, even if it seems silly. As for discrimination, be especially attuned to situations where you might be passing over one candidate in favor of another due to age, gender, disability, etc.

The aspirational conduct for fairness can generally be summed up in The Golden Rule: "Do unto others as you would have them do unto you." Treat everyone equally, with no discrimination, nepotism, or favoritism. Further, you should make your decisions in a transparent and open way, and treat everyone equally. Finally, it is an aspirational standard for fairness that we regularly examine our own impartiality.

CHAPTER 5. HONESTY

5.1 Description of Honesty

Honesty is our duty to understand the truth and act in a truthful manner both in our communications and in our conduct.

5.2 Honesty: Aspirational Standards

As practitioners in the global project management community:

5.2.1 We earnestly seek to understand the truth.

5.2.2 We are truthful in our communications and in our conduct.

5.2.3 We provide accurate information in a timely manner.

Comment: An implication of these provisions is that we take appropriate steps to ensure that the information we are basing our decisions upon or providing to others is accurate, reliable, and timely.

This includes having the courage to share bad news even when it may be poorly received. Also, when outcomes are negative, we avoid burying information or shifting blame to others. When outcomes are positive, we avoid taking credit for the achievements of others. These provisions reinforce our commitment to be both honest and responsible.

5.2.4 We make commitments and promises, implied or explicit, in good faith.

5.2.5 We strive to create an environment in which others feel safe to tell the truth.

5.3 Honesty: Mandatory Standards

As practitioners in the global project management community, we require the following of ourselves and our fellow practitioners:

5.3.1 We do not engage in or condone behavior that is designed to deceive others, including but not limited to, making misleading or

Professional Conduct

false statements, stating half-truths, providing information out of context or withholding information that, if known, would render our statements as misleading or incomplete.

5.3.2 We do not engage in dishonest behavior with the intention of personal gain or at the expense of another.

Comment: The aspirational standards exhort us to be truthful. Half-truths and non-disclosures intended to mislead stakeholders are as unprofessional as affirmatively making misrepresentations. We develop credibility by providing complete and accurate information

Honesty is the fourth and final value in the code of conduct. The mandatory standard is short and to the point: we never deceive others. For the exam, think of the court oath to tell the truth, the whole truth, and nothing but the truth. This will serve you well on the exam.

The aspirational standard carries this further by saying that we not only try to be truthful, but we try to create an environment where it is encouraged that people tell the truth and are safe in doing so. Also, it is important that the project manager always seeks the truth in all dealings.

15 Final Exam

Instructions

This simulated PMP Exam may be used in several ways. If you take it as a final, you will get a very good idea how you would do if you walked right in to take the PMP Exam. In that way, it can be a very good readiness indicator.

Perhaps the best way to use this exam is to take it again and again, reviewing the answers that go with each question. The answers and explanations will give you insight into the formation of each question and the thought process you should follow to answer it.

Prior to taking the PMP, the best strategy is to take this exam repeatedly, reviewing the answers, until you can make a score of 90% or better.

If you are taking this as a final exam, you have 4 hours (240 minutes) to complete the following 200 questions, including any breaks you may take.

Each question has only one best answer. Mark the one best answer on your answer sheet by filling in the circle next to A, B, C, or D.

On the actual PMP Exam, only 175 of the 200 questions will be graded, but you do not know which questions count and which do not. A passing score is on the PMP Exam is 106 out of 175, which is 61%. For this practice final, you should correctly answer at least 180 out of the 200 possible questions in order to consider yourself ready for the real exam.

1. **During testing, multiple defects were identified in a product. The project manager overseeing this product's development can best use which tool to help prioritize the problems?**

    A. Pareto diagram.

    B. Control chart.

    C. Variance analysis.

    D. Order of magnitude estimate.

2. **You are the manager of an aircraft design project. A significant portion of this aircraft will be designed by a subcontracting firm. How will this affect your communications management plan?**

    A. More formal verbal communication will be required.

    B. Performance reports will be more detailed.

    C. More formal written communication will be required.

    D. Official communication channels will significantly increase.

3. **What officially creates the project?**

    A. The project initiation document.

    B. The kickoff meeting.

    C. The project charter.

    D. The statement of work.

4. **Refer to the table at right. What is the critical path?**

    A. Start-A-B-C-I-Finish.

    B. Start-A-B-H-I-Finish.

    C. Start-D-E-H-I-Finish.

    D. Start-F-G-I-Finish.

Task	Dependency	Duration
Start	None	0
A	Start	3
B	A	2
C	B	2
D	Start	4
E	D	1
F	Start	5
G	F	7
H	B, E	3
I	C, G, H	4
Finish	I	0

5. **The Delphi technique is a way to:**

   A. Analyze performance.

   B. Gather expert opinion.

   C. Resolve conflict.

   D. Estimate durations.

6. **The work authorization system makes sure that:**

   A. All the work and only the work gets performed.

   B. Work gets performed in right order and at the right time.

   C. Work is done completely and correctly.

   D. Functional managers are allowed complete control over who is assigned and when.

7. **Your team is hard at work on their assigned project tasks when one team member discovers a risk that was not identified during risk planning. What is the FIRST thing to do?**

   A. Halt work on the project.

   B. Update the risk management plan.

   C. Look for ways to mitigate the risk.

   D. Assess the risk.

8. **The activity duration estimates should be developed by:**

   A. The person or team doing the work.

   B. The project manager.

   C. Senior management.

   D. The customer.

9. **The project plan should be all of the following EXCEPT:**

   A. A formal document.

   B. Distributed to stakeholders in accordance with the communications management plan.

   C. Approved by all project stakeholders.

   D. Used to manage project execution.

10. **You have been asked to take charge of project planning for a new project, but you have very little experience in managing projects. What will be the best source of help for you?**

   A. Your education.

   B. Your on-the-job training.

   C. Historical information.

   D. Your functional manager.

11. **The majority of the project budget is expended on:**

   A. Project plan development.

   B. Project plan execution.

   C. Integrated change control.

   D. Project communication.

12. **Corrective action is:**

   A. Fixing past anomalies.

   B. Anything done to bring the project's future performance in line with the project management plan.

   C. The responsibility of the change control board.

   D. An output of project plan execution.

13. **Outputs of Direct and Manage Project Work include:**

   A. Deliverables and performance reports.

   B. Deliverables and corrective action.

   C. Deliverables and work performance data.

   D. Performance reports and change requests.

14. **Your original plan was to construct a building with six stories, with each story costing $150,000. This was to be completed in four months; however, the project has not gone as planned. Two months into the project, earned value is $400,000. What is the budgeted at completion?**

    A.   450,000

    B.   600,000

    C.   800,000

    D.   900,000

15. **Project integration is primarily the responsibility of:**

    A.   The project team.

    B.   The project manager.

    C.   Senior management.

    D.   The project sponsor.

16. **One of your team members has discovered a way to add an extra deliverable to the project that will have minimal impact on the project schedule and cost. The project cost performance index is 1.3 and the schedule performance index is 1.5. the functionality was not included in the scope. How should you proceed?**

    A.   Conform to the project scope and do not add the deliverable.

    B.   Deliver the extra work to the customer since it will not increase their costs.

    C.   Reject the deliverable because you are behind schedule.

    D.   Ask senior management for a decision.

17. **If a project manager is unsure who has the authority to approve changes in project scope, she should consult:**

    A.   The customer.

    B.   The scope statement.

    C.   The sponsor.

    D.   The scope management plan.

18. **An end user has just requested a minor change to the project that will not impact the project schedule. How should you, the project manager, respond?**

    A. Authorize the change quickly to ensure that the schedule can truly remain unaffected.

    B. Deny the change to help prevent scope creep.

    C. Evaluate the impact of the change on the other project constraints.

    D. Submit the change request to the customer for approval.

19. **Which of the following is NOT used in initiating a project?**

    A. Project statement of work.

    B. Agreements.

    C. Enterprise environmental factors.

    D. Earned value estimates.

20. **You overhear a casual conversation between two team members in which one confides to the other some problems he is having in completing his part of the project work. You realize that the work being discussed is on the project's critical path and that the information you overheard could mean a significant delay for your project. What should you do?**

    A. Let the team member know that you heard his conversation and discuss the work problems with him immediately.

    B. Begin analyzing ways to compress the project schedule in anticipation of the potential delay.

    C. Ask a third team member to get involved immediately and encourage the two other team members to come to you with the delay.

    D. Ask human resources for help in resolving the problem.

21. **In which group of processes should the project manager be assigned his or her role in the project?**

    A. Initiating.

    B. Planning.

    C. Executing.

    D. Controlling.

22. **A project charter should always include:**

    A. Historical information.

    B. The business need underlying the project.

    C. A detailed budget.

    D. The scope management plan.

23. **Your project team has just received the sponsor's approval of the scope statement. What is the NEXT step that needs to be taken?**

    A. Develop the product description.

    B. Create the scope baseline.

    C. Hold the kickoff meeting.

    D. Create the network diagram.

24. **Which of the following is NOT an input into Define Scope?**

    A. Accepted deliverables.

    B. Organizational process assets.

    C. Project charter.

    D. Requirements documentation.

25. **The key function of the project manager's job in project integration is:**

    A. Minimizing conflict to promote team unity.

    B. Making key decisions about resource allocation.

    C. Communicating with people of various backgrounds.

    D. Problem-solving and decision-making between project subsystems.

26. **In which of the following documents could the sponsor find work package descriptions?**

    A. The work breakdown structure dictionary.

    B. The project charter.

    C. The scope management plan.

    D. The project scope statement.

27. **The process in which project deliverables are reviewed and accepted is called:**

   A.   Plan scope.

   B.   Validate scope.

   C.   Initiation.

   D.   Control scope change.

28. **A procurement statement of work is:**

   A.   A type of contract.

   B.   A component of the scope baseline.

   C.   Necessary for every project.

   D.   A description of the part of a product to be obtained from an outside vendor.

29. **A commercial real-estate developer is planning to build a new office complex. He contracts with a construction firm to build one of the buildings for the actual cost of providing the materials and services plus a fixed fee for profit. What type of contract does this scenario represent?**

   A.   Independent vendor.

   B.   Fixed price.

   C.   Cost-reimbursable.

   D.   Time and materials.

30. **You and your spouse both work for large companies in different industries. However, one day you learn that your company will be soliciting bids for a project and your spouse's company intends to bid. Your spouse will not be involved in the bidding process or any of the work it might produce if won. What should you do?**

   A.   Request to be transferred off the project.

   B.   Inform management of the situation.

   C.   Say nothing and go on with the bidding process.

   D.   Say nothing but set up a system of checks and balances to ensure that your team selects the contractor impartially.

31. **Which of the following is NOT a purpose that Create WBS serves?**

    A. To increase the accuracy of estimates.

    B. To help facilitate roles and responsibilities.

    C. To document the relationship between the product and the business need.

    D. To define a baseline for project performance.

32. **You are assigned to replace a project manager on a large software project for a telecommunications company in the middle of executing the work. Portions of the software are being supplied by subcontractors working at your company's offices. You would like to know what performance metrics are going to be tracked for these contract workers. Where could you find such information?**

    A. The project charter.

    B. The procurement management plan.

    C. The work breakdown structure.

    D. The organizational chart.

33. **Which of the following is NOT a type of contract?**

    A. Cost-revisable.

    B. Fixed-price.

    C. Cost-reimbursable.

    D. Time and materials.

34. **Your team has identified a component that they need for a project. There is some concern that they have never constructed a component like this one, but there are similar components available from sellers. Which of the following procurement activities would be MOST appropriate to perform?**

    A. Solicitation.

    B. Make-or-buy analysis.

    C. Benefit/cost analysis.

    D. Conduct procurements.

35. **The activity list serves as an input to:**

    A.   Create WBS.

    B.   Define Activities.

    C.   Estimate Activity Durations.

    D.   Plan Resources.

36. **The person or group that formally accepts the project's product is:**

    A.   The quality team.

    B.   The customer.

    C.   The project team.

    D.   Senior management.

37. **The schedule activity list:**

    A.   Serves as an extension of the work breakdown structure.

    B.   Is synonymous with the work breakdown structure.

    C.   Is used to create the project scope statement.

    D.   Is included in the project charter.

38. **Float refers to:**

    A.   A method for decreasing risk on a project.

    B.   How long an activity can be delayed without affecting the critical path.

    C.   A time lapse between a project communication and the response that follows.

    D.   The difference between the budgeted cost and actual cost.

39. **If a project scope requires goods or services that must be obtained outside the project organization, what management process will be used in obtaining them?**

    A.   Project contract management.

    B.   Project solicitation management.

    C.   Project procurement management.

    D.   Project source management.

40. **You are producing a training video for your company's human resource department. After the project is underway, a member of senior management requests that you use a copyrighted piece of music as background in the video. This video will not be sold or viewed outside of your company. As the project manager, you should:**

    A. Use the song as requested by management.

    B. Investigate obtaining permission from the music publisher to use the song.

    C. Submit the request to the change control board.

    D. Produce the video without the song as specified in the project plan.

41. **What is the most important function the project manager serves?**

    A. Staffing.

    B. Motivating.

    C. Team building.

    D. Communicating.

42. **If a task has been estimated at O = 4 days, P = 9 days, and M = 7, what is the standard deviation?**

    A. 5/6 of a day.

    B. 83 days.

    C. 1/3 of a day.

    D. 1/2 of a day.

43. **Refer to the table at the right. If task H were increased from 3 to 7, what impact would this have on the project?**

Task	Dependency	Duration
Start	None	0
A	Start	3
B	A	2
C	B	2
D	Start	4
E	D	1
F	Start	5
G	F	7
H	B, E	3
I	C, G, H	4
Finish	I	0

    A. The project would finish later.

    B. The project would finish earlier.

    C. The schedule risk would decrease.

    D. The critical path would change, but the finish date would not change.

44. **All of the following are needed for creating the project budget except:**

   A.   The activity cost estimates.

   B.   The schedule.

   C.   The contract.

   D.   The cost performance baseline.

45. **Your company's CIO has requested a meeting with you and two other project managers for a status update on your various projects. What is the BEST document you can bring with you to this meeting:**

   A.   The milestone chart for this project.

   B.   The network diagram for this project.

   C.   Copies of the most recent status reports from the team members.

   D.   The project charter.

46. **Resources are estimated against which project entity:**

   A.   The work packages.

   B.   The schedule activities.

   C.   The scope baseline.

   D.   The level set by the project office.

47. **Analogous estimating uses:**

   A.   Estimates of individual activities rolled up into a project total.

   B.   Actual costs from a previous project as a basis for estimates.

   C.   Computerized estimating tools.

   D.   Parametric modeling techniques.

48. **If the optimistic estimate for an activity is 15 days and the pessimistic estimate is 25 days, what is the realistic estimate?**

   A.   19 days.

   B.   20 days.

   C.   21 days.

   D.   Unknown.

49. **What does the standard deviation tell about a data set?**

    A. How diverse the population is.

    B. The mean of the population as it relates to the median.

    C. The specification limits of the population.

    D. The range of data points within the population.

50. **Quality management theory is characterized by which of the following statements:**

    A. Inspection is the most important element for ensuring quality.

    B. Planning for quality must be emphasized.

    C. Contingency planning is a critical element of quality assurance.

    D. Quality planning quantifies efforts to exceed customer expectations.

51. **Which of the following is NOT emphasized in project quality management?**

    A. Customer satisfaction.

    B. Team responsibility.

    C. Phases within processes.

    D. Prevention over inspection.

52. **Scatter diagrams, flowcharts, statistical sampling, control charts, and inspection are all techniques of what quality process?**

    A. Plan Quality.

    B. Control Quality.

    C. Perform Quality Execution.

    D. Define Quality Metrics.

53. **Which of the following is NOT an input to Plan Quality Management?**

    A. Enterprise environmental factors.

    B. Organizational process assets.

    C. Quality metrics.

    D. Risk register.

54. **The procurement management plan provides:**

A. Templates for contracts to be used.

B. A formal description of how risks will be balanced within contracts.

C. A list of preferred sellers.

D. The types of contracts to be used for items being procured.

55. **Ultimately, responsibility for quality management lies with the:**

A. Project team.

B. Quality team.

C. Project manager.

D. Functional manager.

56. **All of the following are tools used in Control Quality EXCEPT:**

A. Benchmarking.

B. Pareto charts.

C. Histograms.

D. Statistical sampling.

57. **Control charts are:**

A. Used in product review.

B. Used to chart a project's expected value.

C. Used to determine if a process is in control.

D. Used to define a statistical sample.

58. **Which of the following statements regarding stakeholders is TRUE?**

A. They have some measurable financial interest in the project.

B. Their needs should be either qualified or quantified.

C. Key stakeholders participate in the creation of the stakeholder management plan.

D. They may either be positively or negatively affected by the outcome of the project.

59. **A probability and impact matrix is useful for:**

   A.   Identify Risks.

   B.   Perform Qualitative Risk Analysis.

   C.   Perform Quantitative Risk Analysis.

   D.   Control Risks.

60. **Your company must choose between two different projects. Project X has a net present value of $100,000. Project Y has a net present value of $75,000, What is the opportunity cost of choosing Project X?**

   A. $100,000

   B. $75,000

   C. $25,000

   D. $50,000

61. **A risk register is created during:**

   A.   Plan Risk Management.

   B.   Monitoring and Control Risks.

   C.   Assess Risks.

   D.   Identify Risks.

62. **A workaround is:**

   A.   A technique for conflict management.

   B.   An adjustment to the project budget.

   C.   A response to an unplanned risk event.

   D.   A non-critical path on the network diagram.

63. **You are managing a team developing a software product. You have contracted out a portion of the development. Midway through the project you learn that the contracting company is entering Chapter 11 bankruptcy. A manager from the subcontracting company assures you that the state of the company will not affect your project. What should you do FIRST?**

   A. Perform additional risk response planning to control the risk this situation poses.

   B. Stop all pending and future payments to the subcontractor until the threat is fully assessed.

   C. Contact your legal department to research your options.

   D. Meet with senior management to apprise them of the situation.

64. **In a functional organization:**

   A. Power primarily lies with the project manager.

   B. Power primarily lies with the functional manager.

   C. Power is blended between functional and project managers.

   D. Power primarily lies with the project office.

65. **The process of identifying, documenting, and assigning roles, responsibilities, and reporting relationships for a project is called:**

   A. Develop Project Interfaces.

   B. Align Organizational.

   C. Plan Staff Management.

   D. Plan Human Resource Management.

66. **A Responsibility Assignment Matrix (RAM) does NOT indicate:**

   A. Who does what on the project.

   B. Job roles for team members.

   C. Job roles and responsibilities for groups.

   D. Project reporting relationships.

67. **A manager who follows Theory X believes:**

    A. Employees can be trusted to direct their own efforts.

    B. Project success requires that project objectives must align with company objectives.

    C. Workers must be closely supervised because they dislike work.

    D. Effective quality management requires the use of performance measurements.

68. **Which of the following is NOT a constructive team role?**

    A. Withdrawer.

    B. Information seeker.

    C. Clarifier.

    D. Gate keeper.

69. **If a project team is experiencing conflict over a technical decision that is negatively affecting project performance, the BEST source of power the project manager could exert to bring about cooperation would be:**

    A. Legitimate.

    B. Penalty.

    C. Referent.

    D. Expert.

70. **You have asked a team member to estimate the duration for a specific activity, and she has reported back to you with three estimates. The best case scenario is that the activity could be completed in 18 days; however, her most likely estimate for the task is 30 days. She has also indicated that there is the possibility the task could take as long as 60 days. What is the three-point estimate for this task?**

    A. 4 days.

    B. 7 days.

    C. 33 days.

    D. 49 days.

71. **Which of the following types of conflict resolution provides only a temporary solution to the problem?**

   A.   Withdrawal.

   B.   Compromising.

   C.   Forcing.

   D.   Problem-solving.

72. **The communications management plan:**

   A.   Should include the performance reports.

   B.   Should always be highly detailed.

   C.   Should include the project's major milestones.

   D.   Should detail what methods should be used to gather and store information.

73. **When communication links are undefined or broken:**

   A.   The communications management plan should be rewritten.

   B.   Conflict will increase.

   C.   The project manager's power will decrease.

   D.   Project work will stop.

74. **For two days you have been asking a member of your team for a status report on one of the key deliverables of your project. You finally get the report thirty minutes before you are to meet with your manager for a project update. A quick review of the status report reveals some information that you know is incorrect. What action should you take?**

   A.   Fix what you can in the report before the meeting starts and try to steer discussion away from the areas you don't have time to fix.

   B.   Bring your team member with you to the meeting and confront her with the inaccuracies in her report.

   C.   Reschedule the meeting for a later date and have the team member rewrite the report.

   D.   Cancel the meeting, fix the report yourself, and circulate the new report to senior management in lieu of the original meeting.

75. There were 10 people on your project, and 5 more people were added last week. How many additional paths of communication were created?

    A. 10

    B. 45

    C. 60

    D. 105

76. A project manager is having difficulty getting resources from a functional manager. Which of the following would be the MOST appropriate to help resolve this problem?

    A. Senior management.

    B. The customer.

    C. Key stakeholders.

    D. The sponsor.

77. Communicating via email is considered:

    A. Formal written communication.

    B. Informal written communication.

    C. Formal electronic communication.

    D. Informal nonverbal communication.

78. Smoothing, forcing, and withdrawing are all forms of:

    A. Organizational power.

    B. Communication.

    C. Conflict resolution.

    D. Schedule compression.

79. **You have a team member who is habitually late to meetings with the customer. The customer has expressed dissatisfaction with the situation and has asked you to resolve it. Your BEST course of action is:**

   A. Issue a formal written reprimand to the team member

   B. Meet with the team member to discuss the problem and ask for solutions.

   C. Meet with the team member and the customer to promote further understanding.

   D. Email the team member to bring the situation to his attention.

80. **You are midway through managing a project with a sponsor-approved budget of $850,000. Using earned value management, you have determined that the project will run $125,000 under budget. You have also determined that if the project is delivered that far under budget you will not make your bonus since you are compensated for the hours you bill. What is your BEST course of action?**

   A. Add extra features to the project scope that take advantage of the available budget, and increase customer satisfaction.

   B. Meet with the project sponsor to inform him of your findings.

   C. Maintain current project activities, and bill for the original amount.

   D. Ask the sponsor to approve additional features, given the available budget.

81. **The most important factor in project integration is:**

   A. A clearly defined scope.

   B. Timely corrective action.

   C. Team buy-in on the project plan.

   D. Effective communication.

82. **You are a project manager for a software development firm. You are in the final stages of negotiation with a third party vendor whose product your company is considering implementing. You discover by chance that one of your employees has scheduled a product demonstration with herself, the vendor, and your boss, but you have not been notified about the meeting. What do you do?**

    A. Show up at the meeting unannounced and discuss the situation with the employee later in private.

    B. Report this employee's actions to your boss using the company's formal reporting procedure.

    C. Discuss the employee's actions with her before the meeting.

    D. Report the employee's actions to her functional manager.

83. **Your team has encountered recent unanticipated problems. After extensive earned value analysis you determine that the project has a schedule performance index of .54 and a cost performance index of 1.3. Additionally your customer has just requested a significant change. What should you do?**

    A. Alert management about the schedule delays.

    B. Alert management about the cost overruns.

    C. Alert management about the scope change.

    D. Reject the requested change.

84. **You are in the middle of bidding on a large and complex project that will produce a great deal of revenue for your company should you win the bid. The buyer has specified several conditions that accelerate some of the key dates and milestones. You have done extensive planning with your team and have determined that there is no way that your organization can perform the required scope of work under these new deadlines. Your boss, however, is not convinced that you are right and is also concerned that if you don't agree to the new dates you will lose the contract. What should you do?**

    A. Appeal to the buyer for additional time to estimate.

    B. Ask your boss to make the commitment on behalf of the team.

    C. Adhere to the estimates your team has made.

    D. Agree to the dates the customer has requested.

85. **Your company is soliciting bids from advertising firms for the marketing of the product your project will produce. A sales representative from one of the bidding firms calls to invite you to attend a sporting event with him at his expense so that he can ask you some questions about the product to help him put together his bid. How should you respond?**

  A. Attend the event and discuss the project with the representative.

  B. Accept his offer but tell him in advance that you cannot answer questions about the project.

  C. Attend the event and answer all questions, but then write a report on the questions and answers and submit the FAQ to the other bidders.

  D. Reject the offer and invite the sales representative to pose his questions at the bidders' conference.

86. **Analogous estimating is also called:**

  A. Vendor bid analysis.

  B. Bottom-up estimating.

  C. Scalable model estimating.

  D. Top-down estimating.

87. **You are beginning construction of a bridge in another country when you discover that this country requires that one of its licensed engineers sign off on the plans before you break ground. Your senior engineer on the project is licensed in your own country and is probably more qualified than anyone to sign off on this, and their engineer is not available to review the plans for another three weeks. The customer has stressed that this project must not be delayed. What do you do?**

  A. Have your engineer sign off on the plans, forward them to the other engineer and begin construction.

  B. Have your engineer sign off on the plans since he is licensed in your country and begin construction.

  C. Wait to begin construction until the country's engineer signs off on the plans.

  D. Forward the plans to the country's engineer for his signature and start construction.

88. **Which is the BEST definition for Cost of Quality?**

    A. The total cost of inspection and defect repair.

    B. All external costs related to quality plus direct overhead costs required to administer.

    C. The costs related to product quality but not related to process quality.

    D. The total cost of quality efforts throughout the product life cycle.

89. **You are managing the installation of a new oil well pump in a very productive well. Due to very efficient management and significant personal effort, the project is completed several days ahead of schedule. The customer is ecstatic and offers you a $2,500 "appreciation fee." What should you do?**

    A. Accept the fee, but notify management.

    B. Do not accept the fee and notify management.

    C. Put the gift into the project's reserve fund.

    D. Donate the gift to charity.

90. **Decomposition is a technique used in:**

    A. Define Activities.

    B. Estimate Activity Durations.

    C. Sequence Activities.

    D. Develop Schedule.

91. **A fixed-price contract offers the seller:**

    A. A higher risk than the buyer.

    B. A risk level equal to that of the buyer.

    C. A lower risk than the buyer.

    D. Reimbursement of actual costs.

92. **The individual on a project with limited authority who handles some communication and ensures that tasks are completed on time is:**

    A.   The project manager.

    B.   The project leader.

    C.   The project coordinator.

    D.   The sponsor.

93. **At what point in project planning would you decide to change the project scope in order to avoid certain high-risk activities?**

    A.   Identify Risks.

    B.   Qualify Risks.

    C.   Control Risks.

    D.   Plan Risk Responses.

94. **Which of the following techniques is used in Define Scope?**

    A.   Project selection methods.

    B.   WBS templates.

    C.   Expert judgment.

    D.   Inspection.

95. **Which of the following statements is NOT TRUE of integration management?**

    A.   Integration is primarily concerned with making sure various elements of the project are coordinated.

    B.   Integration is a discrete process.

    C.   The project management information system is used to support all aspects of the project.

    D.   The project manager must make tradeoffs between competing project objectives.

96. **Maslow's Hierarchy of Needs theory concludes that:**

   A.   Higher needs cannot be realized until the lower needs are satisfied.

   B.   Hygiene factors are those that provide physical safety and emotional security.

   C.   Psychological needs for growth and fulfillment are ineffective motivators.

   D.   The greater the financial reward, the more motivated the workers will be.

97. **A project is all of the following EXCEPT:**

   A.   Progressively elaborated.

   B.   Has never been done by this organization before.

   C.   Something that creates a product, service, or result.

   D.   Strategic to the company.

98. **Your manager has asked to review the quality management plan with you to ensure that it is being followed appropriately. In which process is your boss involved?**

   A.   Control Quality.

   B.   Perform Quality Management.

   C.   Plan Quality.

   D.   Perform Quality Assurance.

99. **Variance analysis is a tool used to:**

   A.   Measure variance between actual work and the baseline.

   B.   Measure variance between planned value and schedule variance.

   C.   Measure variance between earned value and actual cost.

   D.   Measure variance between earned value and cost variance.

100. **In a strong matrix organization:**

    A. More power is given to the functional manager.

    B. More power is given to the project manager.

    C. More power is given to the project expeditor.

    D. More power is given to the project coordinator.

101. **Team performance assessments are made during which process?**

    A. Plan Human Resource Management.

    B. Acquire Project Team.

    C. Develop Project Team.

    D. Manage Project Team.

102. **The Project Scope Statement is typically:**

    A. A definitive list of all the work and only the work to be done on the project.

    B. Issued by senior management.

    C. Progressively elaborated.

    D. Defined before the functional specifications.

103. **Which of the following is a negative team role?**

    A. Initiator.

    B. Information seeker.

    C. Devil's advocate.

    D. Gate keeper.

104. **During Manage Project Team, your project team should be:**

    A. Focused on making sure earned value is equal to planned value.

    B. Communicating work results to the stakeholders.

    C. Ensuring that all project changes are reflected in the project plan.

    D. Executing the work packages.

105. **The system that supports all aspects of the project management processes from initiating through closing is:**

    A.   Information technology.

    B.   The information distribution system.

    C.   The project management information system.

    D.   The work authorization system.

106. **In a typical project, most of the resources are utilized and expended during:**

    A.   Initiation processes.

    B.   Planning processes.

    C.   Executing processes.

    D.   Monitoring and controlling processes.

107. **A project manager is taking the product of his project to his customer for validation that it meets the scope. The customer and the project manager are working together to carefully compare the product to the project's scope to ensure that the work was done to specification. The tool that the customer and the project manager are using is:**

    A.   Inspection.

    B.   Perform Quality Assurance.

    C.   Perform Quality Control.

    D.   User acceptance testing.

108. **Which of the following is NOT a project quality management process?**

    A.   Perform Quality Assurance.

    B.   Plan Quality.

    C.   Perform Quality Audits.

    D.   Control Quality.

109. **Schedule constraints would likely include all of the following EXCEPT:**

    A.   Imposed dates.

    B.   Key events.

    C.   Major milestones.

    D.   Leads and lags.

110. **Which of the following choices fits the definition for benchmarking?**

    A.   Comparing planned results to actual results.

    B.   Comparing actual or planned results to those of other projects.

    C.   Statistical sampling of results and comparing them to the plan.

    D.   Comparing planned value with earned value.

111. **The activity list should include:**

    A.   The schedule activities on the project that are on the critical path.

    B.   A subset of all schedule activities.

    C.   All of the schedule activities defined on the project.

    D.   A superset of the schedule activities for this and related projects.

112. **Close Project or Phase should be performed:**

    A.   At the end of the project.

    B.   Before formal acceptance of the project's product.

    C.   As a safeguard against risk.

    D.   By someone other than the project manager.

113. **Release criteria for team members is defined as part of:**

    A.   The organizational management plan.

    B.   The release plan.

    C.   The staffing management plan.

    D.   The work authorization system.

114. **Which of the following is NOT an input into Define Activities?**

    A.   The scope baseline.

    B.   Organizational process assets.

    C.   The schedule management plan.

    D.   The activity list.

115. **A project to lay 10 miles of a petroleum pipeline was scheduled to be completed today, exactly 20 weeks from the start of the project. You receive a report that the project has an overall schedule performance index of 0.8. Based on this information, when would you expect the project to be completed?**

    A.   2 weeks early.

    B.   In 2 more weeks.

    C.   In 5 more weeks.

    D.   In 10 more weeks.

116. **The term "slack" is also known as:**

    A.   Lag.

    B.   Lead.

    C.   Float.

    D.   Free float.

117. **Which of the following BEST describes the project plan?**

    A.   A formal, approved document used to guide project execution, control, and closure.

    B.   The aggregate of all work performed during planning.

    C.   The work breakdown structure, schedule management plan, budget, cost management plan, and quality management plan.

    D.   The document that outlines all of the work and only the work that must be performed on a project.

118. **Which of the following is NOT a primary goal of Perform Integrated Change Control?**

    A. Influencing factors that cause change.

    B. Determining that a change has occurred.

    C. Managing change as it occurs.

    D. Denying change whenever possible.

119. **You are providing project management services in a foreign country. In an attempt to improve employment, this country has enacted a law limiting the number of hours foreigners may work per week. You are behind schedule on the project and need to work overtime. What is the BEST way to handle this situation?**

    A. Work the overtime only if your own country's laws do not prohibit this.

    B. Work the overtime if it is not constituted overtime by your country's definition.

    C. Do not work the overtime since it is prohibited by law.

    D. Speak with legal representation to find out if the law is enforceable.

120. **"The features and attributes that characterize a product" describes which of the following?**

    A. The product scope.

    B. The project scope.

    C. The work breakdown structure.

    D. The critical success factors.

121. **You have assumed responsibility for a project that has completed planning and is executing the work packages of the project. In one of your first status meetings, a member of the project team begins to question the validity of the duration estimates for a series of related tasks assigned to her. What action should you take FIRST?**

    A. Remind the team member that planning has been completed and ask her to do her best to adhere to the estimates.

    B. Temporarily suspend execution and ask the team member for updated estimates.

    C. Review the supporting detail for the estimates contained in the project plan to understand how the estimates were originally derived.

    D. Ask another team member with expertise in this area to perform a peer review on the estimates to validate or invalidate the concern.

122. **Approved budget increases should be:**

    A. Added to the schedule management plan.

    B. Added to the project's cost baseline.

    C. Added to the project's reserve fund and used only if needed.

    D. Added to the lessons learned.

123. **An organization where the project manager is in charge of the projects and has primary responsibility for the resources is:**

    A. Functional.

    B. Projectized.

    C. Matrix.

    D. Hierarchical.

Task	Dependency	Duration
Start	None	0
A	Start	3
B	A	2
C	B	2
D	Start	4
E	D	1
F	Start	5
G	F	7
H	B, E	3
I	C, G, H	4
Finish	I	0

124. **Based on the table at the right, which path listed below represents the LEAST schedule risk?**

A. Start-A-B-C-I-Finish

B. Start-A-B-H-I-Finish

C. Start-D-E-H-I-Finish

D. Start-F-G-I-Finish

125. **As part of your project, your customer needs a software module to handle credit card payments. Senior management informs you that they already own the rights to such a module and would like for you to use this piece of software on the project; however, upon investigation, you determine that your company's software is not a good match for this customer's needs. After informing your senior management, they maintain their request that you use their software. How should you resolve this conflict?**

A. Look to build or procure another solution for the customer.

B. Act in favor of the performing organization.

C. Use your company's software module as requested as long as it does not jeopardize the project.

D. Involve an objective outside party to help resolve the dispute.

126. **Leads and lags are factored into activity relationships in which process?**

A. Report Performance.

B. Estimate Costs.

C. Control Schedule.

D. Develop Schedule.

127. **You have received a report showing that your overall schedule performance index is 1.5. How should you interpret this information?**

    A.   You are earning value into your project at 1.5 times the rate you had planned.

    B.   You are spending $1.50 for every dollar you planned to spend at this point in the schedule.

    C.   You are earning $1.50 of value back into your project for every $1.00 you spend.

    D.   You are earning $0.67 of value back into your project for every $1.00 you planned to earn.

128. **The project organization chart should include which of the following:**

    A.   The performing organization's organizational structure.

    B.   A representation of all identified stakeholders.

    C.   The reporting structure for the project.

    D.   The organizational structure for all entities related to the project.

129. **Estimate Costs should be performed:**

    A.   Before the work breakdown structure is created and before the budget is developed.

    B.   Before the work breakdown structure is created and after the budget is developed.

    C.   After the work breakdown structure is created and before the budget is developed.

    D.   After the work breakdown structure is created and after the budget is developed.

130. **A list of the risks that could affect the project is developed as part of which process?**

    A.   Plan Risk Management.

    B.   Identify Risks.

    C.   Plan Risk Responses.

    D.   Control Risks.

131. **Which process focuses on producing a list of the activities needed to produce the deliverables and sub-deliverables described in the work breakdown structure?**

   A.   Define Activities.

   B.   Sequence Activities.

   C.   Identify Activities.

   D.   Estimate Activity Durations.

132. **Whose job is it to resolve competing objectives and goals between parties on the project?**

   A.   The stakeholders.

   B.   The project manager.

   C.   Senior management.

   D.   The sponsor.

133. **As project manager, you have made the decision to outsource a part of your project to an outside organization with whom you have never previously worked. You are ready to begin negotiating the contract. What should be your goal in the contract negotiations?**

   A.   Having a lawyer or the legal department review each clause in the proposed contract prior to sharing it with any outside entity.

   B.   Negotiating the best possible price for your customer or organization.

   C.   Arriving at mutually agreeable terms for the contract between your organization and the subcontracting organization.

   D.   Shifting as much of the project risk to the subcontracting organization as possible.

134. **You have been working under contract on a very large automotive project that has spanned several years. As part of this project, you have been privileged to practically all of the project information. As you are transitioning off of the project, you would like to use the extensive work breakdown structure as an input into future projects. You were never asked to sign a non-disclosure agreement with the current organization. What is the appropriate thing to do in this case?**

A. Use the work breakdown structure as you are not bound by any agreement not to.

B. Use the work breakdown structure, but do not share it with others.

C. Do not use the work breakdown structure without the organization's permission.

D. Do not use the work breakdown structure because it would still be illegal.

135. **Which of the following is NOT an output of Control Costs?**

A. Work performance information.

B. Cost forecasts.

C. Change requests.

D. Earned value alerts.

136. **If the schedule variance = $0.00, what must also be true?**

A. Earned value must be equal to planned value.

B. The cost performance index must be equal to 1.

C. The schedule performance index must be greater than 1.

D. The estimate at complete must be equal to budgeted at complete.

137. **Schedule activities are a further decomposition of which of the following:**

A. The statement of scope.

B. The work packages.

C. The project network diagram.

D. The functional specification.

138. **Which statement is TRUE regarding the human resource plan?**

    A.   It is used as an input into Control Project Team.

    B.   It is a required component of the project plan.

    C.   It should name every human and material resource who will be working on the project.

    D.   It should contain an organization chart for the performing organization.

139. **Which of the following statements is TRUE regarding risk management?**

    A.   Negative risks should be quantified, while positive risks should be qualified.

    B.   Identified risks should be added to the risk register.

    C.   All known risks should be listed in the risk management plan.

    D.   The risks that cannot be mitigated must be avoided.

140. **You have a friend in another organization who has shared with you that he is having difficulty understanding the value of doing a scope statement. Your friend's boss is not familiar with formal project management processes and does not want to waste time on the project performing unnecessary activities. What is your MOST appropriate response?**

    A.   Do not get involved since this is not within your organization.

    B.   Pay a visit to your friend's project office and educate them on the value of a scope statement.

    C.   Mentor your friend on the value of project management processes.

    D.   Encourage your friend to change organizations.

141. **You are managing a project to construct 25 miles of highway at an estimated cost of $1.2 million per mile. You have projected that you should be able to complete the project in 5 weeks. What is your planned value for the end of the 3rd week of the project?**

    A. $12,000,000

    B. $18,000,000

    C. $24,000,000

    D. $30,000,000

142. **Which term below describes the amount of time a schedule activity may be delayed before it affects the early start date of any subsequent schedule activity?**

   A.   Float.

   B.   Slack.

   C.   Free float.

   D.   Lead.

143. **When are the resource requirements estimated?**

   A.   As soon as the scope has been adequately defined.

   B.   After the schedule has been defined, but before the budget has been created.

   C.   After the work packages have been defined, but before the activities have been defined.

   D.   After the activities have been defined and before the schedule has been developed.

144. **You have an unfavorable project status to report to your customer at a weekly meeting; however, you are reasonably certain that you can correct the situation by next week's meeting. The customer will not be pleased to hear the current status and based on past history, will likely overreact. How should you handle this situation?**

   A.   Report the current status to the customer.

   B.   Report your anticipated project status for next week to the customer.

   C.   Omit the information from your meeting and cover it next week when the news improves.

   D.   Ask you project office for guidance.

145. **What type of process is Conduct Procurements?**

   A.   Planning.

   B.   Executing.

   C.   Monitoring and controlling.

   D.   Closing.

146. Who is responsible for providing funding for the project?

    A.   The qualified financial institution.

    B.   Senior management.

    C.   The sponsor.

    D.   The project manager.

147. The project has been successfully completed when:

    A.   All of the work has been completed to specification within time and budget.

    B.   The customer is happy.

    C.   The sponsor signs off on the project.

    D.   Earned value equals planned value.

148. What is the PRIMARY objective of the project manager?

    A.   To follow PMI's processes.

    B.   To deliver maximum value for the organization.

    C.   To deliver the agreed upon scope of the project within the time and budget.

    D.   To delight the customer.

149. Which of the following would NOT be an organizational process asset?

    A.   Project plan templates.

    B.   Methodology guides.

    C.   Previous activity lists from projects.

    D.   Enterprise environmental factors.

150. Change control meetings would take place in which process?

    A.   Control Scope.

    B.   Monitor and Control Risks.

    C.   Monitor and Control Project Work.

    D.   Perform Integrated Change Control.

151. **What is indicated by an activity's late finish date?**

    A. The latest the activity can finish without delaying a subsequent activity.

    B. The latest the activity can finish without delaying the project.

    C. The latest probable date that the activity will finish.

    D. The worst-case or pessimistic estimate for an activity.

152. **A speech given at a trade show is an example of which kind of communication?**

    A. Informal written.

    B. Formal written.

    C. Informal verbal.

    D. Formal verbal.

153. **Which of the following is FALSE regarding the contract change control system?**

    A. It is primarily used during the Control Procurement process.

    B. It is part of the integrated change control system.

    C. It should be defined in the contract.

    D. It should include contract dispute resolution procedures.

154. **Herzberg's theory of motivation states that:**

    A. Hygiene factors must be present for motivational factors to work.

    B. Motivation to work on the project must be related back to the individual's need.

    C. An individual's higher needs will not emerge until the lower needs are met.

    D. Individuals are motivated by a desire to reach proficiency.

155. **If there are multiple critical paths on the project, which of the following must also be true?**

    A. Only one path will ultimately emerge as the true critical path.

    B. The schedule risk will be higher with multiple critical paths than with one.

    C. The schedule should be crashed in order to resolve the conflict.

    D. The schedule should be fast-tracked in order to resolve the conflict.

156. **Which projected payback period below is the MOST desirable?**

    A. 24 months.

    B. 52 weeks.

    C. 3 years.

    D. 1000 days.

157. **Which of the following would be an output of Sequence Activities?**

    A. Mandatory dependencies.

    B. An activity on node diagram.

    C. Discretionary dependencies.

    D. External dependencies.

158. **While executing the project plan, you discover that a component was missed during planning. The project schedule is not in danger, but the component is not absolutely critical for go-live. What should you do?**

    A. Treat the component as a new project.

    B. Reject the component as it would introduce unacceptable risk.

    C. Appeal to the project sponsor for guidance.

    D. Return to planning processes for the new component.

159. **The goal of duration compression is to:**

   A.   Reduce time by reducing risk on the project.

   B.   Reduce cost on the project.

   C.   Reduce the scope by eliminating non-critical functionality from the project.

   D.   Reduce the schedule without changing the scope.

160. **You are managing two projects for two different customers. While meeting with one customer, you discover a sensitive piece of information that could help your other customer, saving them a significant percentage of their project budget. What should you do?**

   A.   Act in accordance with any legal documents you have signed.

   B.   Disclose your conflict of interest and keep the information confidential.

   C.   Share the information with the other customer if it increases project value.

   D.   Excuse yourself from both projects if possible.

161. **What is the difference between a standard and a regulation?**

   A.   A standard is issued by ANSI, and a regulation is issued by the government.

   B.   A standard is an input into quality planning, while a regulation is an input into initiation.

   C.   A standard usually should be followed, and a regulation must be followed.

   D.   There is no appreciable difference between a standard and a regulation.

162. **Evaluation techniques are used to:**

   A.   Select a qualified seller.

   B.   Measure conformance to quality.

   C.   Determine if a project should be undertaken.

   D.   Evaluate performance on the project.

163. **Richard is a project manager who is looking at the risks on his project and developing options to enhance the opportunities and reduce the threats to the project's objectives. Which process is Richard performing?**

    A. Plan Risk Management.

    B. Identify Risks.

    C. Perform Qualitative Risk Analysis.

    D. Plan Risk Responses.

164. **If you are soliciting bids for a project, which of the following would be an appropriate output from this process?**

    A. Proposals from potential sellers.

    B. Procurement statement of work.

    C. A contract award.

    D. Qualified seller lists.

165. **The work results of the project:**

    A. Are always products.

    B. Are products, services, or results.

    C. Are only considered work results if quality standards have been met.

    D. Are an output of the work authorization system.

166. **You have been directed by your customer, your sponsor, and senior management to manage a project that you believe will have a very negative impact on the economy and society. You have shared your concerns, but all parties continue to insist that you proceed. What should you do?**

    A. Manage the project because all parties agree.

    B. Refuse to manage the project.

    C. Manage the project, but document your objections.

    D. Contact PMI.

167. **The quality policy is important in quality management because:**

A. It defines the performing organization's formal position on quality.

B. It helps benchmark the project against other similar projects.

C. It provides specific quality standards that may be used to measure the output of the project.

D. It details the constraints and assumptions the project must take into consideration.

168. **During Control Costs, performance reviews are PRIMARILY used to:**

A. Discuss the project and give the team a chance to voice any concerns.

B. Evaluate new budget change requests to determine if they would have any adverse effects on the project's performance.

C. Review the status of cost information against the plan.

D. Meet with the customer to evaluate and enhance satisfaction.

169. **A project manager has a problem with a team member's attendance, but every time the project manager schedules a meeting to discuss the problem, the team member comes up with a reason he cannot attend at the last minute. Which conflict management technique is the team member exhibiting?**

A. Passive-aggressive

B. Covering up

C. Diverting

D. Withdrawing

170. **In which of the following organizations is the project manager MOST likely to be part-time?**

A. Weak matrix

B. Strong matrix

C. Functional

D. Projectized

171. **Which output would show project roles and responsibilities?**

    A.   A resource histogram.

    B.   An organization chart.

    C.   A human resource management plan.

    D.   The resource and responsibility plan.

172. **Kim is managing a multi-million dollar construction project that is scheduled to take nearly two years to complete. During one of the planning processes, she discovers a significant threat to her project's budget and schedule due to the fact that she is planning to build during the hurricane season in a high-risk area. After carefully evaluating her options, she decides to build earlier in the season when there is less of a risk of severe hurricane damage. This is an example of:**

    A.   Risk avoidance.

    B.   Risk transference.

    C.   Risk acceptance.

    D.   Risk mitigation.

173. **You are managing the development of a software product to be created under procurement. The team will span three countries and five time zones, and because of the size of the project, you are very concerned about cost. Which of the following types of contract would BEST help keep cost down?**

    A.   Time and materials.

    B.   Cost plus fixed fee.

    C.   Cost plus incentive fee.

    D.   Variable conditions.

174. **If there were 16 people on the project, and that number increases to 25, which of the following must also be true?**

    A.   The development of the communications management plan will be more difficult.

    B.   Stakeholder analysis will be more difficult.

    C.   Information distribution will be more difficult.

    D.   Controlling communication will be more difficult.

175. **You are a PMP, and PMI has contacted you regarding an investigation of your best friend who is also a PMP at your company. How should you proceed?**

    A. Cooperate fully with PMI.

    B. Protest that this is conflict of interest.

    C. Protect your friend.

    D. Find out why PMI thinks your friend should be investigated.

176. **A project is scheduled to last for 6 months and cost $300. At the end of the 1st month, the project is 20% complete. What is the Earned Value?**

    A. $50.

    B. $60.

    C. $100.

    D. $120.

177. **Which of the following roles typically has the LEAST power?**

    A. Project coordinator.

    B. Project expeditor.

    C. Project manager.

    D. Project director.

178. **Configuration management is:**

    A. A technique used in Develop Project Management Plan.

    B. Used to ensure that the product scope is complete and correct.

    C. Formally defined in initiation.

    D. A procedure to identify and document the functional and physical characteristics of an item or system.

179. **Which two processes are tightly linked when performing a project and are often performed at the same time?**

    A. Plan Scope Management and Plan Cost Management.

    B. Direct and Manage Project Execution and Acquire Project Team.

    C. Perform Quality Assurance and Manage Project Team.

    D. Control Quality and Validate Scope.

180. **A company in the middle of a new product development merges with another company in the middle of the project. The project is terminated because the new company already offers a similar product. What is the FIRST thing the project manager should do?**

    A. Make sure your lessons learned are communicated to the manager
        of the existing product.

    B. Obtain a written project termination.

    C. Perform a comparative product analysis.

    D. Perform the Close Project or Phase process.

181. **A benefit-cost ratio of 1.5 tells you that:**

    A. The payback period will be one-and-one-half years.

    B. The project cannot pay for itself.

    C. The project will yield revenue that is 1.5 times its cost.

    D. The project will cost 1.5 times the revenue it produces.

182. **The MOST important input into Estimate Activity Resources is:**

    A. The activity list.

    B. The cost estimates.

    C. The project charter.

    D. The constraints and assumptions.

183. **Life-cycle costing involves:**

    A. Determining what physical resources will be needed to complete a project.

    B. Considering the overall costs of a project during and after its completion.

    C. Assigning a value to each activity on the project.

    D. Calculating the internal rate of return.

184. **A construction company is building a new office complex and has contracted with a computer hardware firm to install computer networking cables throughout the buildings. The contract states that the construction company will buy the materials and pay an hourly rate to the computer firm to cover their time on the project. Who is assuming the primary cost risk in this contract?**

    A. The companies share the risk equally.

    B. There is not enough information given to answer the question.

    C. The seller.

    D. The buyer.

185. **Which of the following is NOT a reason to create procurement documents?**

    A. To indicate the form and structure of the desired response.

    B. To influence the factors that cause default or breach of contract.

    C. To inform prospective sellers as to whether or not they are qualified to do the work.

    D. To provide an accurate overview of the project to prospective sellers.

186. **The process where stakeholders are identified is part of which knowledge area?**

    A. Initiating

    B. Planning

    C. Project stakeholder management.

    D. Project scope management.

187. Alex is a project manager who wants to motivate his team by recognizing individual achievement, giving them control over their schedule and work environment, and building a strong sense of the team to which they belong. What theory BEST explains Alex's behavior?

   A.   Three Need theory.

   B.   Contingency theory.

   C.   Expectancy theory.

   D.   Stimulus/Response theory.

188. All of the following are needed for creating the project budget except:

   A.   Cost estimates.

   B.   Schedule.

   C.   Resource calendar.

   D.   Risk breakdown structure.

189. The fact that a software program must be written before it can be tested is an example of a(n):

   A.   Mandatory dependency.

   B.   Discretionary dependency.

   C.   External dependency.

   D.   Milestone dependency.

190. What is the difference between a Gantt chart and a milestone chart?

   A.   A Gantt chart is a project plan and a milestone chart is not.

   B.   A milestone chart is a project plan and a Gantt chart is not.

   C.   A milestone chart shows interdependencies between activities.

   D.   A milestone chart shows only major events, while a Gantt chart shows more information.

191. **Your team has created a project scope statement and a work breakdown structure. What is the NEXT step that needs to be taken?**

    A. Create a network diagram.

    B. Develop the schedule.

    C. Determine the critical path.

    D. Create the activity list.

192. **You have assumed the position of project manager for a project that is nearly 50% complete. Because this project has reportedly had many quality problems, you want to review what trends and variances have occurred over time. Which tool would be most helpful to you?**

    A. Cause and effect diagrams.

    B. Run charts.

    C. Inspection.

    D. Statistical sampling.

193. **A cable company is installing new fiber optic cables in a community. You are the project manager and you will be using subcontractors to provide some of the installations. You have completed the procurement management plan and the statement of work, and you have gathered and prepared the documents that will be distributed to the sellers. What process should happen next?**

    A. Plan Scope.

    B. Direct and Manage Project Execution.

    C. Plan Procurements..

    D. Conduct Procurements.

194. **Evaluating overall project performance on a regular basis to ensure that it meets expectations takes place in which process group of project management?**

    A. Planning.

    B. Executing.

    C. Monitoring and controlling.

    D. Closing.

195. **The MAIN use of a project network diagram is to:**

    A. Create the project plan.

    B. Show activity percentages complete.

    C. Show activity sequences and dependencies.

    D. Create paths through the network.

196. **Who issues the quality policy?**

    A. The performing organization.

    B. The stakeholders.

    C. The project manager.

    D. A standards body.

197. **You are managing a project when an unplanned risk event occurs. You meet with experts and determine a workaround to keep the project on track. In which process are you engaged?**

    A. Perform Qualitative Risk Analysis.

    B. Perform Quantitative Risk Analysis.

    C. Plan Risk Responses.

    D. Control Risks.

198. **Which definition below best describes cost aggregation?**

    A. A risk management technique to view costs and their risks by an aggregated group instead of by an individual work package.

    B. Adding the costs associated with each work package back up to the parent nodes on the WBS to ultimately get a total project cost.

    C. Multiplying the costs with each work package by a multiplier to calculate the needed reserve.

    D. Aggregating the costs associated with work packages back to a single point in time to eliminate the time value of money.

199. **A project is scheduled to last 4 months and cost $300,000. At the end of the 1st month, the project is 20% complete. What is the schedule performance index?**

    A. 0.80

    B. 1.02

    C. 1.18

    D. 2.15

200. **Bringing the entire project team and the customer on site to work together is an example of:**

    A. Communication control.

    B. Co-location.

    C. Active participation.

    D. Team integration.

Final Exam Answers

1. **A.** Pareto charts are column charts that rank defects based on the number of occurrences from highest to lowest. Because this tool is based on frequency, it prioritizes the most common causes. 'B' is used to determine whether or not a process is in control. 'C' is used to measure the difference between what was planned and what was done, and 'D' is a type of estimate used in cost management.

2. **C.** Because this is being done under contract, you will need to use more formal, written communication. Many people incorrectly guess 'D' on this one, but official channels of communication could just as easily decrease since you are using another company and will probably have a single point of contact as opposed to your own team of many people doing the work. 'B' is not correct since performance reports should be detailed regardless of who is doing the work.

3. **C.** The charter is the document that officially creates the project, names the project manager, and gives him authority on the project.

4. **D.** This problem should be solved in 3 steps. First, draw out the network diagram based on the table. Your representation should resemble the one below:

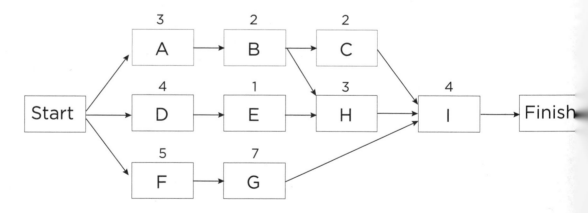

The next step is to list out all of the possible paths through the network. In this example, they are:

Start-A-B-C-I-Finish

Start-A-B-H-I-Finish

Start-D-E-H-I-Finish

Start-F-G-I-Finish

The last step is to add up the values associated with each path. Using the paths above, they are:

Start-A-B-C-I-Finish = 11 units

Start-A-B-H-I-Finish = 12 units

Start-D-E-H-I-Finish = 12 units

Start-F-G-I-Finish = 16 units

The critical path is the longest one, in this case, Start-F-G-I-Finish.

5. **B**. The Delphi technique is a way to solicit expert opinion by hiding the identities of group members from each other. This prevents the group from forming a single opinion or from letting one person dominate the group.

6. **B**. The definition of the work authorization system (WAS) is found in chapter 2 and the glossary. It is a system used to ensure that work gets done at the right time and in the right sequence.

7. **D**. Typically you should assess, investigate, understand, and evaluate before acting. There may be exceptions to this rule, but in general you probably want to select the answer that lets you get all of the information. If there is a series of answers and you are asked what to do FIRST (as in this example), selecting the answer that allows you to be fully informed is usually best. 'A' is incorrect because halting work would probably send risks skyrocketing. 'B' is a good thing to do, but not until you have fully evaluated the risk. 'C' is something you may or may not choose to do, but you should not take action until you have fully assessed the risk.

Final Exam

8.   **A**. This is frequently missed because people do not fully understand the role of the team in planning. The team should help estimate and should support those estimates. If possible, the person who will be doing the work should have a say in the estimate. 'B' is incorrect because the project manager cannot possibly estimate all of the activities on the project, nor should he even try. 'C' and 'D' are incorrect since management and the customer are probably not aware of all of the low-level details needed, and their estimates would not be accurate.

9.   **C**. The stakeholders do not have to approve the project plan. They may be very interested in the final product, but the actual plan cannot undergo approval by all stakeholders. Some stakeholders may never approve of the plan since they may be against the project! 'A' is incorrect because the project plan must be formal. 'B' is incorrect because the communications management plan will specify to whom you should communicate the plan. 'D' is incorrect since the purpose of the project plan is to guide execution and control.

10.   **C**. Your best source of help would be the information you can use from past projects. 'A' is incorrect since education may or may not be applicable to this project, and although it is good, education is principally theoretical, while historical information contains practical, hard data. 'B' is incorrect since much practical experience only reinforces bad practices. 'D' is incorrect since functional managers have expertise in domains but not necessarily in the management of projects.

11.   **B**. The majority of a project's budget is expended in the execution of the work packages. You may have guessed 'A' due to the number of processes that occur as part of planning, but most projects do not involve as many people or resources in planning as they do in execution. Choice 'D' is incorrect because, while a project manager spends 90% of his time communicating, that does not take most of the team's time or the project budget.

12.   **B**. This is a very important definition. Corrective action is making adjustments to avoid future variances. 'A' is more in line with the definition of rework. 'C' is incorrect since there may or may not be a change control board, and their job would be to approve or reject change requests that have been forwarded by the project manager.

'D' is incorrect because corrective action does not come out of execution, but out of various control processes.

13. **C.** This is the only one where both parts of the answer fit the definition. 'A' is incorrect since performance reports do not come out of the execution process. 'B' is incorrect since corrective action typically comes out of monitoring and controlling processes. 'D' is incorrect because performance reports do not come out of the Direct and Manage Project Work process.

14. **D.** This type of question often appears on the PMP. It is easier than it first appears. Did you think the question was asking for the estimate at completion (EAC)? It is the originally budgeted amount, or budgeted at completion (BAC) that the question wants. That is calculated simply by taking 6 stories and multiplying it by $150,000/story. This yields the total project amount, which is $900,000.

15. **B.** This is an important point. The project manager is the one responsible for integration. 'A' is incorrect because the team should be doing the work. 'C' is incorrect since senior management is not involved in integration management. 'D' is incorrect since the sponsor pays for the project but is not directly involved in integration.

16. **A.** You should not add the deliverable. The reason is that this represents "gold plating," or adding functionality over and above the scope. It is not a good idea since this introduces risk and a host of other potential problems on the project. 'B' is incorrect because you do not know how it will affect risk, quality, or other factors. 'C' is incorrect because you are ahead of schedule with an SPI of 1.5. 'D' is incorrect because it is the project manager's job – not the role of senior management – to deal with this kind of change request.

17. **D.** The scope management plan is the document that specifies how changes to the scope will be managed.

18. **C.** Any of the words "evaluate," "investigate," "understand," or "assess" should automatically put that answer at the top of your list to evaluate. 'D' is incorrect because the customer has hired you to evaluate and approve or reject change.

19. **D**. This question was very hard, but there was a way to reason out the answer. When initiating a project, you are essentially performing two processes: Develop Project Charter and Identify Stakeholders. During those processes, it makes sense that you might use the project's statement of work, the contract, and the enterprise environmental factors. 'D', earned value, would probably not be useful until (much) later when the work was being performed.

20. **A**. Another bias of PMI is that you should confront situations directly whenever possible. If you see a choice that represents things like confront, problem-solve, or deal with the situation directly, that is a good hint that you may be on the right answer. In this case, all of the other choices do not deal with the actual problem. Although the first choice may not be pleasant in real life, you should deal with the situation head on and solve the problem.

21. **A**. The project manager is officially named and assigned in the project charter, which is one of the outputs of Develop Project Charter, an initiating process.

22. **B**. The project charter is a document, and that document should include the business need behind the project. This is a general description of why the project was undertaken.

23. **B**. The scope statement is an output of Define Scope. The next step is the Create WBS process, and the output of that is the scope baseline, which includes the work breakdown structure (WBS).

24. **A**. Hopefully your instincts kicked in here and said "this won't happen until later." If so, then you were right. Accepted deliverables are an output of Verify Scope. During Define Scope, you are still trying to determine what the scope will include.

25. **D**. The project manager's job during integration is to solve problems and make decisions. It is not the team's job to do this! Their job should be to execute the work packages. The project manager should be fixing the problems that come up and keeping the team focused on the work.

26. **A**. Work package descriptions are contained in the WBS dictionary.

27. **B**. Validate scope is the process where the customer and sponsor verify that the deliverables match what was in the scope.

28. **D**. The procurement statement of work (SOW) describes the pieces of the project that are to be performed, by the project or by an outside vendor. 'A' is incorrect because the SOW does not meet the strict qualifications of a contract. 'B' is incorrect because the scope baseline is made of the scope statement, the WBS, and the WBS dictionary. It does not include the statement of work. 'C' is incorrect because an SOW is not needed for all projects – only those that will be procuring parts.

29. **C**. This meets the definition of a cost-reimbursable contract. 'A' is a made-up term. 'B' is incorrect since the price is not fixed. 'D' is also incorrect. If you selected this one, you should review the difference between the time and materials and cost-reimbursable contracts.

30. **B**. In the code of conduct, PMPs are instructed to avoid conflicts of interest. Your strategy in selecting answer 'B' should have been to look for the one choice that both solved the problem and avoided the conflict of interest. 'A' is incorrect because leaving the project represents avoidance and does not deal with the issue directly. 'C' is incorrect because the conflict of interest remains. 'D' is incorrect because by saying nothing, you are not dealing with the situation directly.

31. **C**. Documenting the relationship between the product and the business takes place before Create WBS. A justification of the business need is included in the project charter. 'A', 'B', and 'D' all fall under the definition of Create WBS.

32. **B**. The procurement management plan, which is created in the Plan Procurements process, includes performance reporting specifications. If one of the choices had been "the communications management plan", that might have been a better selection, but given the choices provided, 'B' was the best one.

33. **A**. Cost-revisable is not a valid choice (and from the sound of the name, it does not sound particularly safe to either party)! Choices 'B', 'C', and 'D' are all valid contract types.

34. **B**. In this case, make-or-buy analysis is the most appropriate. It is where you decide whether your organization should create the product or whether you should go through procurement. Choice 'A' would be an activity that was performed later in the process. Choice 'C' is a tool for measuring whether a project is worth pursuing and is performed in initiation. Choice 'D' is also an activity performed after the decision has been made to go through procurement.

35. **C**. With activities, the important order is define – order – estimate. The activity list is an input in Estimate Activity Durations.

36. **B**. Many people may formally accept the product, but in this list, the customer is the only one that fits the definition.

37. **A**. The activity list is a decomposition of the WBS. It takes the work packages and breaks them down into activities that can be sequenced, estimated, and assigned.

38. **B**. Float is how long an activity may be delayed without delaying the project. Choice 'B' is the only one that fits this definition.

39. **C**. Procurement management is used when you go outside of the project for components of the project.

40. **B**. This best choices here may be narrowed down to 'B' and 'D'. Think of this senior management request as a change request. Why would you simply ignore it without investigating further? 'B' is the better of the two answers since it solves the problem. If 'D' appears to be a better choice, consider that it actually represents conflict avoidance, which is almost never a good choice.

41. **D**. Communication is the most important activity because the project manager spends an estimated 90% of his time communicating.

42.   **A.** The formula for standard deviation on a PERT estimate is (P-O) ÷ 6. This equates to 5/6. If you guessed 'B', you were probably thinking of the formula for a PERT estimate.

43.   **D.** At first glance, many people think that the wording of answer 'D' is impossible, but it is the correct choice. This problem should be solved in the usual 3 steps with one additional step at the end. (Did you notice that this was the same project network diagram as shown earlier? This is not uncommon on the PMP.) First, draw out the network diagram based on the table. Your representation should resemble the one below:

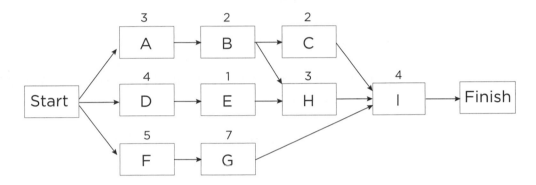

The next step is to list out all of the possible paths through the network. In this example, they are:

Start-A-B-C-I-Finish

Start-A-B-H-I-Finish

Start-D-E-H-I-Finish

Start-F-G-I-Finish

The third step is to add up the values associated with each path. Using the paths above, they are:

Start-A-B-C-I-Finish = 11

Start-A-B-H-I-Finish = 12

Start-D-E-H-I-Finish = 12

Start-F-G-I-Finish = 16

The final additional step is to increase the value of H from 3 to 7 and evaluate the impact. That would change the list to:

Start-A-B-C-I-Finish = 11

Start-A-B-H-I-Finish = 16

Start-D-E-H-I-Finish = 16

Start-F-G-I-Finish = 16

The answer, therefore, is that the critical path would change (there are now 3 critical paths), but the end date remains the same.

Moving from 1 critical path to 3 increases the schedule risk considerably, invalidating choice 'C'.

44.   **D**. The cost performance baseline is another term for the budget. 'A', 'B', and 'C' are all inputs into the process of Determine Budget, where the budget is created.

45.   **A**. Milestone charts are useful for communicating high-level status on a project. This represents the best of the 4 choices. 'B' would be far too much detail for an executive status meeting. 'C' would not be a bad thing to bring, but it would not be the best document for showing status. 'D' would not provide the status that the CIO seeks.

46.   **B**. Resource requirements should be developed against the schedule activities. This is a level below the work packages. That is why they are properly called "activity resource requirements."

47.   **B**. Analogous estimates, also called top-down estimates, use previous project costs as a guideline for estimating.

48.   **D**. You cannot calculate the three-point estimate without knowing values for optimistic, pessimistic, and realistic. In this case, you are only provided with 2 of the 3 numbers, therefore the answer is unknown.

49.   **A.** The standard deviation measures how diverse the population is. It does this by averaging all of the data points to find the mean, then calculating the average of how far each individual point is from that mean. For a very diverse population, you will have a high standard deviation. For a highly similar population, your standard deviation will be low.

50.   **B.** This is the best answer. Modern quality management stresses planning and prevention over inspection. This is based on the theory that it costs less to prevent a problem than it does to fix one. 'A' is incorrect, since prevention is stressed over inspection. 'C' is incorrect since contingency planning is part of risk management – not quality management. 'D' is incorrect since Plan Quality seeks to satisfy the quality standards. It is not focused on exceeding customer expectations.

51.   **C.** Phases within processes is a made-up term and is not stressed in quality management. Many people mistakenly select 'A' for this; however, quality management does stress that the customer's specifications should be taken into account (the implication being that if the customer's specifications are satisfied, the customer should be satisfied with the product). 'B' is incorrect because Deming's TQM philosophy stresses that the entire team has a responsibility toward quality. 'D' is incorrect because prevention over inspection is a big thrust of quality management, stressing that it costs less to prevent a problem than it does to fix one.

52.   **B.** Control Quality is the process that uses these five tools. The tool of inspection should have tipped you off.

53.   **C.** Organizational process assets, enterprise environmental factors, and the risk register are all used as inputs into Plan Quality, but the quality metrics is an output.

54.   **D.** Contract type selection is a tool used in procurement planning. The type(s) of contract(s) used are included in the procurement management plan.

55.   **C.** The project manager is ultimately responsible for the quality of the product. If you guessed 'A', you were on track because Deming said that the entire team is responsible, but the word "ultimately" is the key here. The person ultimately responsible is the PM. 'B' is

incorrect because the quality team is not a team identified by PMI. 'D' is incorrect because functional managers may be very involved in the quality management process, but they are not ultimately responsible.

56.   **A.** This one is tricky because all of these tools are used in quality management! 'B', 'C', and 'D' are all used in Control Quality, but 'A' is used in Plan Quality and Perform Quality Assurance. Benchmarking is used to establish quality standards based on the quality attributes of other projects, and it is not used in Control Quality, where the standards should already be set.

57.   **C.** The purpose of a control chart is to statistically determine if a process is in control.

58.   **D.** Stakeholders may want the project to succeed or fail! They may benefit or lose if the project succeeds. This is contrary to the way the word is used in many circles, and it is hard for many people to think of a stakeholder as potentially being hostile to the project.

59.   **B.** A probability impact matrix is the defining tool of Perform Qualitative Risk Analysis, and it is used to rank risks qualitatively, that is, based on their characteristics. It is important that you associate this tool with this process.

60.   **B.** The opportunity cost is what you missed – not the difference between them. Because you invested in Project X, you missed out on the net present value of Project Y, which equals $75,000.

61.   **D.** A risk register is created during Identify Risks, and it is used and updated in the subsequent risk processes (Perform Qualitative Risk Analysis, Perform Quantitative Risk Analysis, Plan Risk Response, and Monitor and Control Risks).

62.   **C.** When an anticipated risk event occurs, the plan for addressing that is followed; however, some risks cannot be anticipated. In that case, a workaround is needed.

63.   **A.** The first thing you should do is to plan for the new risks this situation presents. Remember that you should look for a proactive approach to almost everything. 'B' is incorrect because you cannot simply decide to withhold payment if you are in a contractual relationship. 'C' is incorrect because even though that may be

something you would do, it is not the FIRST thing you should do. 'D' is also not the FIRST thing you should do because this problem should be dealt with by the project manager. Running off to apprise senior management of the situation would not be the first thing a project manager does. It would be far better to do that after the project manager had assessed the situation and planned thoroughly for it.

64. **B**. In a functional organization, most of the power rests with the functional manager. 'A' is incorrect since that describes a projectized organization. 'C' is incorrect because that describes a matrix organization. 'D' is incorrect since there is no explicit model in which power rests with the project office.

65. **D**. Plan Human Resource Management is the process concerned with understanding and identifying the reporting relationships on a project, among other things. The organizational charts and position descriptions are tools used to create the human resource plan.

66. **D**. The responsibility assignment matrix (RAM) does not include reporting relationships. Those are included in the project's organizational chart. 'A' is incorrect because the RAM does show who is responsible for what on the project. 'B' is incorrect because it shows roles on the project for the various team members. 'C' is incorrect because the RAM can be for either individuals or for groups (e.g., engineering or information technology).

67. **C**. McGregor's Theory X manager distrusts people and believes that they must be watched every moment. 'A' is incorrect because that is more descriptive of the opposite, Theory Y manager. 'B' is incorrect because that is more descriptive of the practice of MBO (management by objectives). 'D' is incorrect because Theory X is not directly related to quality management.

68. **A**. The withdrawer is someone who does not participate in the meeting and therefore is not a constructive role. 'B' is incorrect because someone who is trying to gather more, good information is contributing in a positive way. 'C' is incorrect because a person who clarifies communication is adding to the meeting as well. 'D' is tricky, but it is incorrect. In project management terminology, a gate keeper is someone who helps others participate and draws

people out. Gate keepers would help withdrawers become active participants.

69.   **D**. In this case, the conflict is of a technical nature, so the best way the project manager could solve the problem is by using his or her technical expertise.   'A' is incorrect because legitimate power might stop the fight, but it wouldn't solve the problem. 'B' is incorrect because it also might stop the fight, but would not solve the problem. 'C' would probably be the least effective approach to solving this particular problem, since referent power is relying on personality or someone else's authority.

70.   **C**. The three-point estimate is calculated by adding the pessimistic estimate + 4 X realistic estimate + the optimistic estimate and dividing by 6. In this case, it is

$$\frac{60 + (4 \text{ X } 30) + 18}{6}$$

This reduces down to 198 ÷ 6 = 33.

71.   **C**. Forcing does do away with the conflict... but only temporarily. It is when the manager says "This is my project, and you will do things my way. Period, end of discussion." The root of the problem is not addressed by this approach, thus the solution is only temporary.

72.   **D**. Did you guess 'A' or 'B' on this one? The communication plan does not include the performance reports, and it may be either formal or informal, highly detailed or general, depending on the project and the organization. 'C' is incorrect, because it does not include the project's major milestones. 'D' is the right answer in this case because it details how you are going to gather and store information on the project.

73.   **B**. One of the main reasons conflict arises on a project is over communication, and one of the results of a project's communication lines being broken is that conflict increases.

74.   **C**. To answer this one, you should have asked "which choice solves the problem?" The problem is that an employee is giving you incorrect information, and you cannot ethically pass that

information on. The only choice that directly deals with the problem and fixes it is 'C'. The solution is not painless, but it is the best choice of the four.

75. **C**. If there were 10 people on your project, that would yield 45 communication paths. Add 5 more, and you now have 15 people, which yields 105 communication paths. The question asks how many more paths would you have, thus the answer is 105 – 45 = 60.

76. **A**. It is the role of senior management to resolve organizational conflicts and to prioritize projects, and either of those may be at the root of this problem. 'B' is incorrect since this is a matter internal to the organization, and the customer should be buffered from it. 'C' is incorrect since the stakeholders cannot always bring influence to bear inside the organization. 'D' is incorrect since the sponsor functions much like a customer internal to the organization. The sponsor does not prioritize projects and would not be the best person to go to in order to sort out an organizational conflict.

77. **B**. E-mail is informal written communication. Formal written communication involves such things as changes to the project plan, contract changes, and official communication sent through channels such as certified mail. As e-mail evolves in its usage and protocol, test takers should be aware that although they may use e-mail in a formal manner, it is not considered to be formal communication.

78. **C**. These are all considered to be forms of conflict resolution, even though none of these is considered to be an effective way to resolve conflict.

79. **B**. Again, ask yourself "what is the choice that solves the problem?" In this case, 'B' is the best choice that solves the problem. Before you do anything else, you would want to meet with the person directly and discuss the problem. 'A' may be appropriate at some point but would not be considered best in this case. 'C' is not a good choice since it is your job to resolve the problem and not the customer's job. 'D' is incorrect since it is too passive a choice and does not really deal with the problem.

Final Exam

80.   **B**. This question is not only difficult, but there is a lot of information here to distract you. In this case, you should go to the sponsor and let him know since he has approved the budget. If the project stands to deviate significantly (over or under), then the person paying for it should know as soon as possible. 'A' is incorrect because you are supposed to conform to the scope – not increase it! 'C' is also incorrect. You are working for the sponsor here, and it would not be wise to bill them more than the project costs. 'D' is incorrect since you do not want to gold plate the scope by adding more than was originally planned.

81.   **D**. Communication is important at all points in the project, but it is critical during integration. When performing integration management, the project manager's job is primarily to communicate.

82.   **C**. Focus on direct, polite confrontation over practically any other method of conflict resolution. In this case, you are the one who needs to resolve the conflict, so you should take the initiative. Discussing the employee's actions with her before the meeting should actually produce a resolution to the problem. 'A' appears direct at first, but it is not really a direct way to deal with the problem. 'B' is simply making the problem someone else's problem – in this case, your boss's. 'D' is incorrect for the same reason 'B' is. This is a problem that you, the project manager, should solve.

83.   **A**. With an SPI this far below 1, you have a significant schedule delay, and you should report this to management. 'B' is incorrect because you are doing quite well on cost, and there is no overrun. 'C' is incorrect since it is your job to deal with scope change – not management's. 'D' is incorrect because you cannot simply reject changes on the project. They must be evaluated thoroughly and fairly and sent through the change control system.

84.   **C**. The team should be involved in the estimating process, and once they have bought into those estimates, you should resist pressure to automatically slash them. 'A' is incorrect since additional estimating is not what is needed here. 'B' is incorrect since this is just delaying the inevitable and perhaps making matters much worse. 'D' is incorrect since the dates need to come from your estimates and schedule development and not from the client.

85. **D**. To answer this, you should consider two things: 1. You need to avoid all conflicts of interest. 2. The solicitation process is supposed to keep all potential sellers on a level playing field. With these facts in mind, 'D' should emerge as the only choice that makes sense.

86. **D**. Another name for analogous estimating is top-down estimating because it looks at projects as a lump sum and not broken down into pieces (which is known as bottom-up estimating).

87. **C**. This is a no-win situation, but you must obey laws in the country where you are performing the work, and 'C' is the only option that fully complies with the law. Refer to the PMI code of conduct and you will see that you cannot bend or break laws just to get the project done on time.

88. **D**. The definition of Cost of Quality is "the total cost of all efforts related to quality throughout the product life cycle." The other definitions may be true to varying degrees, but 'D' is right on the mark.

89. **B**. PMI's code of conduct states that you have a "responsibility to refrain from offering or accepting inappropriate payments, gifts, or other forms of compensation for personal gain." The best thing to do in this case is refuse the gift and let management know of the situation.

90. **A**. Define Activities uses the technique of decomposition to produce the activity list.

91. **A**. In a fixed price contact, the seller is the one who bears the risk. If the cost runs high, the seller must deliver at the original cost. The buyer's costs are set (fixed), thus offering a measure of security. 'B' is incorrect since the seller has higher risk. 'C' is incorrect since the seller's risk is higher than the buyer's. 'D' is incorrect since cost reimbursable is another form of contract separate from this.

92. **C**. A project coordinator is someone who is weaker than a project manager but may have some limited decision-making power.

'A' is incorrect since a project manager does not have "limited authority" on a project. 'B' is a made up term, and 'D' refers to the sponsor whose role on the project is to pay for the project, receive the product at the end, and give the project good visibility in the organization.

93.   **D**. Plan Risk Responses would be the point at which you determine an appropriate response to the risks that have been identified, qualified, and quantified. Only after the risks are fully understood and analyzed would you make a change to the scope.

94.   **C**. Define Scope is all about one thing: creating the project scope statement, and the tool of expert judgment is used to help create it.

95.   **B**. Integration (in addition to most of the other knowledge areas) is not discrete. In other words, it isn't performed in a vacuum, but instead it is performed with all of the other knowledge areas in mind. This is even more pertinent for integration than any of the other knowledge areas. Also keep in mind that the word "integrated" has nearly the opposite meaning of the word "discrete." 'A' is incorrect because that is exactly what integration does. 'C' is also a purpose of integration because the PMIS is the tool that the project manager uses to know what is going on with the project. 'D' is incorrect because that is also a definition of integration. The project manager is supposed to keep people focused on the work while he solves problems.

96.   **A**. Maslow's hierarchy is based on the fact that your basic needs, like food and water, must be satisfied before higher needs, such as esteem, will become important. 'B' is incorrect because Herzberg's theory of hygiene factors is a different theory of motivation. 'C' is incorrect because this is a different motivational theory. 'D' is related to another theory of scientific management not covered in PMI's materials.

97.   **D**. Definitions are very important, and this definition question is missed by many people. Understand that projects may or may not be strategic to the company. Although everyone wants his or her project to be exciting and strategic, more mundane projects also must be undertaken. 'A', 'B', and 'C' are all part of the core definition of a project.

98.   **D**. In this case, your manager is auditing the process, and audits
        are used in Perform Quality Assurance. Audits are performed
        primarily to make sure that the process is being followed. 'A' is
        incorrect because Control Quality is inspecting specific examples
        and is not focused on the overall process. 'B' is incorrect because
        quality management is too broad a term to fit the definition of this
        process. 'C' is incorrect because Plan Quality is the process where
        the quality management plan is created.

99.   **A**. Variance analysis looks at the difference between what was
        planned and what was executed. It is a tool used in four processes,
        Report Performance, Control Scope, Control Schedule, and
        Control Costs. Choice 'A' is the one that correctly identifies its
        purpose.

100.   **B**. In a matrix organization, power is shared between the project
        managers and functional managers. In a strong matrix, the project
        manager is more powerful, while in a weak matrix, the functional
        manager has more power. In no circumstances would 'D' be
        correct, as the project coordinator is, by definition, weaker than a
        project manager.

101.   **C**. Team performance assessment is a output of the Develop
        Project Team process. When creating this, the project manager
        evaluates the team's performance with the goal of understanding
        strengths and weaknesses and ultimately improving them. They
        are also used in the Manage Project Team process as an input, but
        that is not what was asked here.

102.   **C**. The project scope statement typically starts off general and
        becomes more specific as the project progresses. Progressive
        elaboration is a term that describes the way in which the details
        of the scope are discovered over time. 'A' is incorrect since it is
        more descriptive of the WBS than the project scope statement.
        'B' is incorrect since the project scope statement is created by
        the project team and not by senior management. 'D' is incorrect
        because the project scope statement is a functional specification.

103.   **C**. A devil's advocate is considered to be a negative team role.
        'D', a gate keeper, is incorrect because in project management
        terminology a gate keeper is someone that draws non-participants
        and withdrawers into the process.

104. **D**. In Manage Project Team, the team is executing the work packages and creating the product of the project. Your job as project manager is to keep them focused on this. 'A' is incorrect because that may be your focus, but it is not the team's focus. 'B' is incorrect, because that is the project manager's job and not the team's focus. 'C' incorrect for the same reason. It is the job of the project manager and not the team.

105. **C**. The project management information system (PMIS) is the one described in the question. 'A' is not a good choice because you don't have to have information technology from beginning to end in order to successfully deliver many projects. 'B' is a made up term. 'D' is not a good choice because the work authorization system (WAS) is used to make sure that the work is performed at the right time and in the right sequence.

106. **C**. On typical projects, most of the resources (both human resources and material resources) are expended during executing processes. Many people incorrectly choose 'B' because there are so many planning processes, but on the average, project planning takes less effort and resource than execution.

107. **A**. Inspection is a tool of Validate Scope, which is the process being described in the question. In inspection, the product of the project is compared with the documented scope.

108. **C**. "Perform Quality Audits" is something you may do as part of Perform Quality Assurance, but it is not a process.

109. **D**. Schedule constraints would not contain leads and lags for activities. 'A', 'B', and 'C' would all make sense to include as schedule constraints.

110. **B**. Benchmarking is a tool of quality management for both the Plan Quality and Perform Quality Assurance processes. It takes the results of previous projects and uses them to help set standards for other projects. 'A' and 'C' are incorrect because they would be more closely aligned with Control Quality. 'D' is largely unrelated to quality.

111. **C**. The activity list should include every schedule activity defined on the project. These schedule activities are then used to create the project network diagram.

112.   **A**. The Close Project or Phase process should be performed at the end of each phase or at the end of the project. Since that was not a choice, however, 'A' is closest to that. Remember that if the choice you want is not present, you should choose the best one from the list.

113.   **C**. The release criteria for team members is defined in the staffing management plan.

114.   **D**. The activity list is the output of the Define Activities process. 'A', 'B', and 'C' are all inputs into Define Activities.

115.   **C**. There are many ways to mathematically solve this problem, but perhaps the simplest is to divide the schedule performance index against the length of the project. 20 weeks ÷ 0.8 = 25 weeks. Therefore, we would expect the project to be 5 weeks late. 'A' should have been eliminated because with a schedule performance index less than 1, there is no way the project should be finished early.

116.   **C**. The term slack is synonymous with float.

117.   **A**. The project plan is a formal document. It is created during planning, and is used to guide the execution processes, monitoring and control, and closure. 'B' is incorrect because that would be closer to the definition for the product. 'C' is close to correct, although it is an incomplete list of what makes up the project plan and the question specifically asks for the BEST description. 'D' is incorrect because this is closer to the definition of the work breakdown structure than it is to the project plan.

118.   **D**. As part of Perform Integrated Change Control, the project manager will need to know when change has occurred, manage the changes, and influence the factors that cause change, but the project manager should not take on the attitude of denying change whenever possible. Some change is inevitable, and all change requests should be evaluated and not automatically rejected.

119.   **C**. Another no win situation. You cannot bend or break laws just to stay on schedule. The end does not justify the means! You have to obey laws and observe customs in the country where you are

Final Exam

performing the work. In this situation, you should look at options that do not involve working overtime.

120. **A**. There is a difference between the product scope and the project scope. The scope of the project may be much larger than the scope of the product! This question defines the product scope. 'B' would have a much broader definition than this. 'C' is the work that needs to be done to complete the project, but it does not deal with the attributes of a product. 'D' is a phrase often used in project management, but it is unrelated to this definition.

121. **C**. The supporting detail should be included with the estimates, and that supporting detail is included for situations just like this one. It will help you and the team member understand how the estimates were derived in the first place. 'A' is incorrect since the team member may well have a valid point. 'B' is incorrect because there is no reason to either stop work on the project or to send the team member scrambling for new estimates. 'D' is not a bad choice, but it isn't the FIRST thing you would do. As a starting point, go back and check the facts first. Then if it would be helpful to get another expert involved, you may elect to do that.

122. **B**. The term "baseline" causes grief for many test-takers. Memorize that the baseline (whether it is the scope baseline, schedule baseline, cost baseline, or quality baseline) includes the original plan plus all approved changes. Once the budget change was approved, it should be added to the cost baseline.

123. B. Although it is unusual in the real world, a projectized organizational structure gives the project manager near total control of the project and the resources. 'A' is a structure where the functional manager is in charge of projects and resources. 'C' is a structure where the project manager runs the projects and the functional manager manages the people, and 'D' is not a real term for organizational structures.

124. **A**. This problem should be solved in the usual 3 steps with one small bit of reasoning applied at the end. First, draw out the network diagram based on the table. Your representation should resemble the one below:

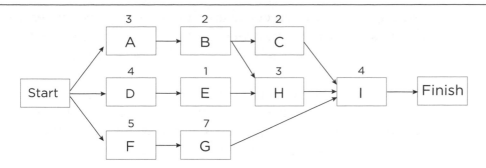

The next step is to list out all of the possible paths through the network. In this example, they are:

Start-A-B-C-I-Finish

Start-A-B-H-I-Finish

Start-D-E-H-I-Finish

Start-F-G-I-Finish

The last step is to add up the values associated with each path. Using the paths above, they are:

Start-A-B-C-I-Finish = 11 units

Start-A-B-H-I-Finish = 12 units

Start-D-E-H-I-Finish = 12 units

Start-F-G-I-Finish = 16 units

The question has asked for the path with the LEAST schedule risk, and that is represented by the shortest path (the one with the highest amount of float). The reason this path has the least risk is that tasks could slip the most here without affecting the critical path. In this case, it is Start-A-B-C-I-Finish, which corresponds to choice 'A'.

125.   **A**. When a conflict of interest arises, it should be resolved in favor of the customer. In this case, your company's module has been determined not to be a good fit, so another solution is needed. 'B' is incorrect because conflicts should be resolved in favor of the

customer. 'C' is incorrect because it has already been determined that it is not best for the project. 'D' is not correct because that is the project manager's job – not that of an outside party.

126. **D**. Leads and lags are applied as part of the Develop Schedule process. This technique is actually used first in the Sequence Activities process. That process name was not among the choices, so 'D' becomes the best answer.

127. **A**. Just as important as understanding a formula is being able to interpret it. That is what this question is calling on you to do, and it can be quite hard. The schedule performance index (SPI) = EV ÷ PV. Studying the formula, you can see that it compares how much value you actually earned (EV) and divides that by how much you planned to earn (PV). In this case, you have earned value at 1.5 times the rate you had planned.

128. **C**. The tool of Organization Charts and Position Descriptions is used to develop the human resources plan. Among other things, this tool displays the reporting structure for the project.

129. **C**. Most of the planning processes have a logical order to them, and this question relies on an understanding of that. The work breakdown structure has to be created before cost estimates are performed, and the cost estimates have to be created before the budget. This should make sense when you stop to consider it.

130. **B**. The list of risks, contained in the risk register, is an output of the Identify Risks process.

131. **A**. Define Activities is the process where the work breakdown structure is further decomposed into individual activities.

132. **B**. A good rule is that if in doubt, select the "project manager." For this question, that would be correct. It is the project manager's job to resolve competing stakeholder requests and goals.

133. **C**. Your goal is to create a win-win situation in the negotiations. A win-lose agreement will usually not let you win in the long term.

134. **C**. The project manager's professional code of conduct instructs you to keep customer information confidential. You should ask

Final Exam

permission before using or reusing any part of the project that is not owned by you or your organization.

135. **D.** Even though it may sound reasonable, there is no such thing as an output called an "Earned Value Alert." 'A', 'B', and 'C' are outputs of the Control Costs process.

136. **A.** The way to approach this question is to remember how to calculate the schedule variance. It is EV-PV. If the schedule variance = 0, then EV must be equal to PV.

137. **B.** Schedule activities are a further decomposition of the work breakdown structure, and work packages exist at the lowest levels of the work breakdown structure.

138. **B.** This one is easier than it first appears. All management plans, including the human resource management plan, become part of the project plan, and although they may be formal or informal, all of them are required (with the exception of the procurement management plan, which is only required if there are procurement activities). 'A' is incorrect because (curiously) there is no monitoring and controlling process in human resource management. 'C' is incorrect because it describes the approach to staffing and not every detail. 'D' is incorrect because the organization chart for the performing organization would not be a typical component of the human resource plan.

139. **B.** All of the identified risks should be added to the risk register. 'C' is incorrect since the risk management plan only contains the plan for how risk will be approached. It does not get down to the specifics of listing risks.

140. **C.** You have a responsibility to help mentor others in the field of project management. 'A' would be inappropriate, because your responsibility extends to the profession – not just to your organization. 'B' is incorrect because the best place to start is with your friend. 'D' is incorrect because a job change would represent withdrawal and would not solve the problem in any way.

141. **B.** Planned value is the value of the work you planned to do at a given point in time. The first step is always to calculate your budgeted at completion. It is 25 miles * 1,200,000 / mile = $30,000,000. Now you want to calculate the planned value for

3 weeks of the 5 week project. Simply multiple the budgeted at completion by 3 and divide by 5. This yields $18,000,000. The interpretation of this is that you planned to earn $18,000,000 worth of value back into your project after 3 weeks of work.

142.   **C**. Read this one carefully. It is the definition of free float. 'A' and 'B' were synonyms, which should have thrown up a red flag for you. Those terms tell you how long a task may be delayed before it changes the finish date of the project.

143.   **D**. Knowing the order in which these steps are performed is important and shows that you understand what is really taking place within the process. In this case, resources are estimated after you have defined the activities, but before you have created the schedule. This is the only answer that works, since the resources are based on activities, and you must have the resource requirements before you can create the schedule.

144.   **A**. Even when news is unpopular or unpleasant, you must deliver accurate statuses. 'B' and 'C' attempt to cover up or hide the news. Choice 'D' is unnecessary since you should report the current and accurate status to the customer.

145.   **B**. Conduct Procurements is an executing process in procurement, and yes, it is important that you know this type of information for the exam. In this process, the buyer ensures that the seller's performance is in line with the plan through inspections, audits, and reviews.

146.   **C**. Know the roles of each person or group on the project. It is the sponsor who provides funding for the project.

147.   **A**. Most importantly, the project should satisfy the scope, schedule and budget. These are the principal factors of success. 'B' is important in many organizations, but you cannot control happiness as a project manager. The best you can do is to satisfy the scope of work. 'C' may be good to have, but it does not make the project successful. 'D' is also good in that you did what you planned to do when you planned to do it, but it is only an ingredient of project success.

148. **C**. Your primary objective is to satisfy the scope of work on the project within the agreed-upon cost and schedule. 'A' is the means to your end goal of a successful project, but it is only the way you go about it. 'B' is a great goal, but there are other parties here that need to be considered – not just the performing organization. 'D' is good, but you should focus on doing so by delivering what you promised on time and on budget.

149. **D**. Organizational process assets are anything you can reuse, such as a document, a previous project deliverable, or a methodology. Enterprise environmental factors are things that influence the project due to to the climate in which it is performed. Often times both must be considered, but enterprise environmental factors are not organizational process assets.

150. **D**. Change control tools, which include change control meetings are a tool of Perform Integrated Change Control. This is a "macro" process that considers change to the whole project and not merely to the scope, schedule, or cost baseline.

151. **B**. An activity's late finish date is the latest an activity can finish without delaying the project. If it exceeds the late finish date, the critical path will change, ultimately resulting in the finish date slipping. Choice 'A' is close to the definition of free float.

152. **D**. Speeches such as this one are examples of formal verbal communication.

153. **C**. The contract change control system is defined in the procurement management plan and not in the contract itself.

154. **A**. Herzberg stated that hygiene factors must be present in order for motivational factors to work; however, hygiene factors do not motivate by themselves. They only enable the motivation factors to work.

155. **B**. The critical path represents the highest schedule risk on the project. If there is more than one critical path, schedule risk is increased. 'A' is not necessarily true. Two or more paths could be the critical path on the project all the way from beginning to end. 'C' and 'D' are ways to "resolve the conflict" when there is no conflict. There will always be at least 1 critical path, and having 2 or more critical paths by no means represents a conflict.

156. **B**. With a payback period, the shorter the time the better. The hardest thing about this problem is to reduce all of the times to a common denominator so you can see which one is the shortest! B is one year, and that is the shortest period of time of the choices.

157. **B**. A project network diagram (like activity on node) is an output of activity sequencing. The other 3 types of dependencies fall under the tool of dependency determination in Sequence Activities.

158. **D**. The processes are not set in stone so that once you have finished planning you can never return. Remember that projects are progressively elaborated, and that oftentimes you will need to revisit processes again and again. There is no reason not to return to planning in the example given here.

159. **D**. The goal of duration compression is to accelerate the due date without shortening the scope of the project.

160. **B**. Conflicts of interest should be disclosed and avoided. 'A' is not a good choice, because you are not only bound to act legally, but also ethically! 'C' is not correct because you would not be keeping information confidential. 'D' would not be a rational choice. Resigning from both projects would cause more problems and solve nothing.

161. **C**. A standard usually should be followed, while a regulation has to be followed.

162. **A**. The source selection criteria are created in the Plan Procurements process. In the Conduct Procurements process the evaluation techniques are used to select a qualified seller after responses have been received.

163. **D**. Richard is performing Plan Risk Responses. After the risks have been identified, qualified, and quantified, they should be responded to. Plan Risk Responses looks at how to make the opportunities more likely and better and the threats less likely and less severe. Remember that a risk is an uncertainty that could be good or bad.

164. **C**. In order to answer this question, you must first be able to identify in which process you solicit bids. It is the Conduct Procurements process, and the outputs include selected sellers and agreements.

165. **B**. The work results of the project may be products, services, or results. 'A' is incorrect because work results could be a product, a service, or a result. 'C' is incorrect because the work results don't have to meet quality to be considered work! 'D' is incorrect because the output of the work authorization system is not the work itself, but that a resource is authorized to do the work.

166. **B**. You have a responsibility to society, the environment, and the economy, and this comes higher than your responsibility to your boss. You are not to just follow orders, but you should think for yourself to ensure that the project does not do harm. Note that this is not merely a disagreement over the probable success of the project.

167. **A**. Some companies rest their reputations on the high quality of their product. Others do not. The quality policy defines how important quality is on this project from the performing organization's perspective. It is treated as an organizational process asset.

168. **C**. Performance reviews review the current status against the plan.

169. **D**. By not facing the problem the team member is withdrawing. 'A', 'B', and 'C' are not terms regularly used in project management circles.

170. **C**. In a functional organization, the project manager has little formal power and may even be part-time! It is the functional manager who is more powerful in this structure.

171. **C**. The human resource plan, created in Plan Human Resource Management, details roles and responsibilities on the project. 'D' may sound good, but there is no such actual plan.

172. **D**. Risk mitigation is when you try to make the risk less severe or less likely. By accelerating the construction, Kim is mitigating the likelihood of a hurricane damaging her project.

173. **C**. The answer "fixed price" would have been the best here, but it was not in the list of choices! Of the ones listed, cost plus incentive fee would provide the seller with an incentive to keep their costs down. 'A' provides no incentive at all for the seller to keep costs

down. 'B' would not provide the same incentive since the seller gets a fixed fee regardless of the project costs. 'D' is not a real contract type.

174. **D**. The more channels of communication on a project, the more difficult it is to control communications. 'A', 'B', and 'C' are probably not true because these people are internal to the project, and the creation of the plan and analysis of the stakeholders, and communication with them, would not necessarily be more difficult.

175. **A**. Here is an example where you should ignore the trigger words "find out." You have a responsibility to comply fully with PMI in an investigation. 'B', 'C', and 'D' may be tempting, but you should cooperate with PMI.

176. **B**. Earned value is what you have actually done at a point in time. In this case the budgeted at completion for the project is $300,000, and you have completed 20% of that. All of the other facts in the problem are irrelevant. The answer is $300,000 * 20% = $60,000.

177. **B**. The project expeditor is the weakest role here. This person is typically a staff assistant to an executive who is managing the project. 'C' is the most powerful, and 'A' would be next. 'D' is not a term identified within PMI's processes.

178. **D**. This is a definition of configuration management. 'A' is incorrect because it is not part of the Develop Project Management Plan process. 'B' is incorrect because that is more descriptive of inspection – a tool of scope verification. 'C' is incorrect because this is performed after initiation.

179. **D**. Control Quality and Validate Scope are very tightly linked. Control Quality is the process concerned with correctness, and Validate Scope is primarily concerned with completeness. In general, Control Quality is performed just before Validate Scope, but they can be performed at the same time.

180. **D**. When a project ends or is cancelled, the project manager should perform the Close Project or Phase process. 'A' would come out of Close Project or Phase. 'B' is not defined as part of closure. 'C' might be appropriate in some cases, but you should lean

strongly toward terms you have read in this book and not rely on experience.

181. **C**. The interpretation of this is important. A benefit-cost ratio indicates how much benefit you expect to receive for the cost expended. In this example you could get $1.50 profit for every dollar of cost.

182. **A**. The activity list is the main input into Estimate Activity Resources. None of the others listed are inputs into that process, but consider that you could not perform Estimate Activity Resources without first having the list of activities against which you will estimate.

183. **B**. Life-cycle costing takes a broad look at the project, considering such things as operational costs, scrap value, etc. It doesn't just ask how much it costs to make a product, but it looks at the total cost of ownership.

184. **D**. The buyer is primarily assuming the risk here because they are in a time and materials contract. The seller gets paid for every hour they work.

185. **B**. This answer may sound good, but 'A', 'C', and 'D' are reasons to create procurement documents. 'B' is not.

186. **C**. The process of Identify Stakeholders is a stakeholder management processes. 'A' and 'B' are process groups, and the question was asking for the knowledge area.

187. **A**. McClelland's Three Need theory is the best choice here. It states that people have needs related to achievement, power, and affiliiation. While this theory can be expressed in many different ways, it is the best of the four choices to explain Alex's motivational style.

188. **D**. The risk breakdown structure is not directly used in creating the project budget. 'A', 'B', and 'C' are all inputs to the Determine Budget process.

189. **A**. There is no way to get around that dependency, so it is a mandatory dependency.

190. **D**. A milestone chart only shows major events (milestones) on the project's timeline. 'A' and 'B' are incorrect because neither a Gantt chart nor a milestone chart are project plans. 'C' is incorrect because milestones are high level representations that do not show interdependencies between activities.

191. **D**. After the scope statement and the work breakdown structure, you should move into Define Activities. 'A' cannot be done before the activity list since the activity list is used to create the network diagram. 'B' and 'C' cannot be done until the network diagram is completed. The correct order of these choices listed would be: 'D', 'A', 'C', 'B'.

192. **B**. Run charts show trends and variances over time and are used in quality management.

193. **D**. This is not the easiest question on the exam! You must first determine what you have done and then determine what is next. Look carefully at what you have created, and you will see that you have just finished the Plan Procurements process. The next process to be performed should be Conduct Procurements.

194. **C**. Generally, any time you are looking at past performance, you are in a monitoring and controlling process.

195. **C**. The primary purpose of the project network diagram is to show the sequence of activities and their dependencies. 'A' is incorrect because the project plan is made up of all planning outputs. 'B' is incorrect because the percentage complete is not reflected on the network diagram. 'D' is incorrect because the project network shows the paths through the network, but it does not create them.

196. **A**. The quality policy is a document issued by the performing organization that describes their attitude regarding quality. As different companies place different values on quality, the quality policy will differ. For instance, a pharmaceutical company will almost certainly have a stricter quality policy than a maker of novelty toys.

197.   **D.** Did you guess 'C' for this one? The risk would have been planned in Plan Risk Responses, but if it was unforeseen and it occurred then you would have caught that in Control Risks. That is the process where workarounds are created.

198.   **B.** Cost aggregation is adding the costs associated with work packages up along the structure of the WBS to get the cost of specific branches or the entire project.

199.   **A.** The formula for the schedule performance index is earned value divided by planned value (EV÷PV). To get EV, we need to know how much we have completed to date. The budgeted at complete is $300,000, and we are 20% complete. Therefore, EV = $300,000 * 20% = $60,000. Planned value is what we had planned to complete at this point. We are 1 month into a 4 month project, or 1/4 of the way through. 1/4 = .25 (25%), and our budgeted at completion of $300,000 * 25% = $75,000. Now that we have EV ($60,000) and PV ($75,000), we can calculate the schedule performance index. It is EV÷PV, or $60,000 ÷ $75,000 = 0.80. The interpretation of this number is that the project is earning value 80% as fast as was planned, and any index that is less than 1 is a bad thing!

200.   **B.** Co-location is a tool used in the team development process where the team is brought together in a single location.

Final Exam

Acceptance: The act of approving the deliverables. Acceptance is usually performed by the project manager and the customer or sponsor at the end of the project, project phases, or at predefined milestones. Acceptance of the product, service, or result is formal.

Acquire Project Team: An executing process focused on getting the right people to work on the project at the right time. Acquire Project Team is executed according to the human resource plan.

Activity: Also called schedule activity. An activity is a task that must be performed in order to complete work on the project. Activities are created by further decomposing work packages. Under current guidelines, the primary difference between a work package and an activity is that a work package is a component of the scope and describes some aspect of the deliverable, while an activity describes the work that must be done in order to complete the work package. Schedule activities are first defined, then sequenced and estimated for duration.

Activity Attributes: The informational components that accompany each schedule activity. These may include information on dependencies, leads and lags, assignments, accountability, requirements, constraints and assumptions.

Activity List: The list of all schedule activities to be performed, derived by decomposing the work packages into their schedule components. The activity list is a primary output of the Define Activities process.

Activity on Arrow (AOA): A type of graphical project network diagram where schedule activities are represented by lines with arrows. The lines are connected by nodes, usually represented by circles. AOA diagrams are seldom used in practice today and have been replaced by AON (see next entry).

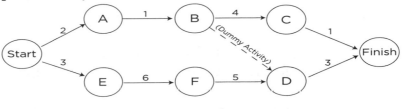

Activity on Node (AON): A type of graphical project network diagram where schedule activities are represented by nodes (usually rectangles), and their interdependencies are represented by lines with arrows.

Glossary of Terms

Activity Resource Requirements: The resources required to complete the activities in the activity list. Typically these are physical, human, and organizational resources but do not include financial resources.

Actual Cost (AC): Also know as Actual Cost of Work Performed (ACWP). A term used in earned value management. Actual cost represents the amount that has been spent by the project up to a point in time. It is often contrasted with earned value to show the difference between the amount of value earned on the project (represented by earned value) and what was spent to earn that value (represented by the actual cost).

Actual Cost of Work Performed (ACWP): See **Actual Cost**

Agreements: A document, defining intentions around the project or some component of the project, that has been accepted by both parties. It is helpful to think of agreements as contracts for purposes of the exam.

Allowable Costs: Costs that are allowed under the terms of the contract. Typically, allowable costs become relevant under certain types of cost-reimbursable contracts where the buyer reimburses the seller's allowable costs. If there are non-allowable costs in a contract, the buyer is not obligated to reimburse the seller for these.

Alternatives Generation: A tool used in the Define Scope process to identify multiple possible approaches to solving a problem.

Analogous Estimating: Also known as "Top-Down Estimating." An estimating technique that uses the historical information from previously performed activities that are similar in nature, to estimate the effort, duration, or cost needed to complete an activity.

Analytical Techniques: A logical approach that looks at the relationship between outcomes and the factors that can influence them.

Application (exam): The application for the PMP or CAPM exam which requires the applicant to document an adequate combination of education and experience in project management. The application must be received and processed by the Project Management Institute before the applicant is eligible to schedule his or her certification exam.

Arrow Diagramming Method: The method that produces activity on arrow (AOA) diagrams. See Activity On Arrow for more information.

Assumption: Anything that is considered to be true while planning. Assumptions should always be documented and validated, and they are often closely linked to constraints.

Assumptions Analysis: A review of the risks and an analysis of the factors that were treated as true for planning purposes to see if those are still valid.

Backward Pass: A technique used to calculate slack, or float, that begins with the last node of a project network diagram and logically works backward to the start. Using the backward pass technique, each schedule activity's late start and late finish dates are determined.

Bar Chart: A term in project management that equates to a Gantt chart. In a bar chart, horizontal bars represent lengths of time for schedule activities. A calendar of dates represents the horizontal (X) axis.

Activity Name	Duration	Start	Finish
Start	0 days	Thu 1/15/04	Thu 1/15/04
Activity A	7 days	Thu 1/15/04	Wed 1/21/04
Activity B	5 days	Thu 1/22/04	Mon 1/26/04
Activity C	4 days	Tue 1/27/04	Fri 1/30/04
Activity D	2 days	Thu 1/15/04	Fri 1/16/04
Activity E	9 days	Sat 1/17/04	Sun 1/25/04
Finish	0 days	Fri 1/30/04	Fri 1/30/04

Project: Sandstorm — Activity / Progress / Milestone

A bar (Gantt) chart

Baseline: The original approved scope, cost, or schedule, plus all approved changes. Baselines represent the approved plan, and they are especially useful for measuring how actual results deviate from the plan. It is important to remember that baselines can, and typically do, change throughout the life of the project as changes are approved. Baselines occasionally apply to other measured areas such as performance and quality.

Basis of Estimates: The backup detail showing how cost or schedule estimates were derived, where they came from, who was involved, what information was used, and what estimating technique was used.

Benchmarking: Using data from other projects, departments, or organizations to measure performance of the project or product.

Bottom-up Estimating: A technique for estimating overall project duration, effort, or costs by estimating the lowest levels of the schedule or work breakdown structure (WBS) and aggregating those numbers up to the summary nodes on the WBS. Bottom-up estimating is widely considered to be a relatively accurate, but often tedious, technique for estimating. This technique is the opposite of top-down or analogous estimating.

Bidder Conference: A meeting for potential sellers to come and understand the work they are considering bidding on. In a bidder conference, all bidders are given the same information and are kept on a level playing field.

Brainstorming: A technique to gather ideas that involves getting ideas from many participants in a rapid-fire and non-judgmental environment. Ideas are not evaluated until after they have all been gathered.

Budget: See **Cost Baseline**

Budgeted at Completion (BAC): The planned (budgeted) amount for the total project. The BAC represents what the project should cost at the point it is completed if everything proceeds according to plan.

Budgeted Cost of Work Performed (BCWP): See **Earned Value**

Budgeted Cost of Work Scheduled (BCWS): See **Planned Value**

Buffer: Extra time or money added to the schedule or budget to allow for unanticipated overruns. Buffers are useful since they allow for some slippage without affecting the overall schedule or budget.

Business Case: The social, economic, or business outcomes that justify undertaking this project or part of the project.

Cause-and-Effect Diagrams: Also known as an Ishikawa diagram, or a fishbone diagram. Cause and effect diagrams graphically show the relationships between causes and effects. They are primarily used in risk and quality to help uncover the causes of risks, problems, or issues.

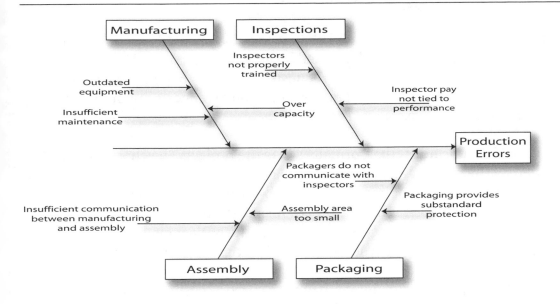

An example of a cause and effect diagram

Certified Associate in Project Management (CAPM): A project management credential created and managed by the Project Management Institute. The CAPM is for anyone who works on a project, can demonstrate the required education, and can demonstrate an adequate understanding of the PMBOK Guide.

Change Control: Deliberately managing change to a project, whether that change is to the scope, cost, schedule, or quality baseline. In change control, change requests go through a formal process before they are approved or rejected. See Perform Integrated Change Control in chapter 4 for more information on the specific process associated with change control.

Change Control Board: A group with formal responsibility for evaluating project change requests. The change control board makes up a part of the overall change control system.

Change Control System: The procedures for evaluating and managing requested changes to the project. This system varies from project to project and from organization to organization.

Change Log: The list of all changes, whether or not they were requested, made to the project. The change log is used as an input to various processes to ensure that the impacts of changes are properly reviewed and evaluated.

Change Request: Any requested change to a documented baseline. Change requests are typically only implemented once the scope, cost, schedule, or quality is "baselined." Since change requests are formal, before project baselines exist a less formal method is generally used. Change requests are processed according to the change control system.

Charter: The document that formally starts the project. The charter typically is issued by the sponsor and names the project manager. Additionally, it may list the high-level project requirements, the high-level milestones, and a summary-level preliminary budget. The charter is a formal document created in the Develop Project Charter process. It authorizes the project manager to expend organizational resources in order to accomplish the project objective.

Checklist: Any set of procedural instructions used to ensure that product or component quality is achieved. Checklists are created in the Plan Quality Management process and are used in the Perform Quality Control process.

Claim: An issue with performance against the contract brought by one party against another. Claims could be made by the buyer against the seller for non-performance, or by the seller against the buyer for untimely payment. Claims must be resolved before the contract can be properly closed out.

Close Procurements: One of two closing processes that focuses on making sure the procurement is completed, the product or service is accepted, and the contract is closed. Even if a contract is terminated early, the process of Close Procurements should be carried out.

Close Project or Phase: The closing process that administratively closes a phase or the overall project. In Close Project or Phase, all final project documentation and project files are completed, and lessons learned are documented.

Closing Processes: The group of processes that focus on closing out the project or an individual phase. Closing processes focus on closing out the contract(s), releasing resources, delivering the product, and gaining formal stakeholder approval.

Collect Requirements: A planning process in scope management that documents the stakeholders' needs for the project. The resulting requirements documentation focuses on how the requirement, once it is built, will satisfy the underlying need or meet the opportunity that drove it.

Colocation: The act of physically locating everyone on a project team in the same space or general area. Colocation is used to break down distance barriers and facilitate team-building. A war room where all project team members work together is an example of colocation.

Communication: The act of accurately encoding, sending, receiving, accurately decoding, and verifying a message. Communication between a sender and a receiver may be formal, informal, oral, or written.

Communication Channels: The number of possible formal or informal paths of communication on a project. The concept of communication channels is particularly helpful in understanding how the addition of a small number of people to a project team can complicate the project manager's job of controlling communications. The formula for calculating communication channels is:

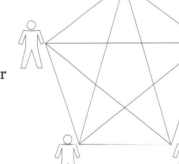

$$\frac{n\,(n\text{-}1)}{2}$$

where n = the number of people in the communication model.

Communication Model: The formal paths of communication that will be used on the project. The traditional communication model involves a sender, a receiver, and a message, and both sender and receiver have responsibilities as to how they act upon the message.

Communications Management Plan: The component of the project plan that specifies communications requirements and how those requirements will be addressed by the project. The communications management plan describes what communications will be provided, to whom, in what format, and how often.

Conduct Procurements: The executing process in procurement management, where the seller responses are gathered, a seller is selected, and the contract is awarded. Conduct Procurements will only be performed on projects that procure goods or services from outside the organization, but on those projects it may be performed multiple times as needed.

Conflict: Difference of opinion or agenda on a project among team members or stakeholders. While not all conflict can be resolved to everyone's satisfaction, it is primarily the project manager's job to drive conflict resolution so that the project is not jeopardized.

Consensus: A group decision technique where the group agrees to support an outcome, even if the individuals do not all agree with the decision.

Constraint: Any external factor that limits the ability to plan. The most common constraints are scope, time, and cost, but they could be any factor, such as the law, weather, or resource availability. Constraints and assumptions are often closely linked.

Context Diagram: A means of diagramming the scope where people and systems are shown along with how other people and systems will interact with them.

Contingency: Also known as reserve, contingency is padding time and/ or money to the project's schedule or budget to help manage overruns. Contingency may or may not be communicated to project stakeholders, and it may be added at an activity level, at any node on the WBS, or even at an overall project level.

Contract: A legal document that specifies the relationship between two parties. In project management, these two parties are most often referred to as buyer and seller.

Contract Change Control System: The formal system for managing changes to the contract so that all changes are tracked and processed, and all relevant parties are notified of the changes.

Control: See **Monitoring and Controlling**

Control Account: Also known as a "cost account," a control account is a node on the WBS where the scope, time, and cost are measured. Control accounts contain one or more work packages and are used to measure earned value. A project may have numerous control accounts placed on the WBS at nodes where it would be particularly meaningful to measure the earned value of those parts of the project.

Control Account Manager: The individual accountable for the delivery of the work contained in the Control Account to the scope, budget, and schedule.

Control Account Plan (CAP): The plan for how a given control account will be performed and measured. Since each control account is a division of the overall project, each CAP functions essentially like a mini-project plan for that division of work.

Control Chart: A specialized chart used in statistical process control to help determine whether or not a process is in control. Control charts are often associated with control limits, specification limits, means, standard deviations, and the rule of seven.

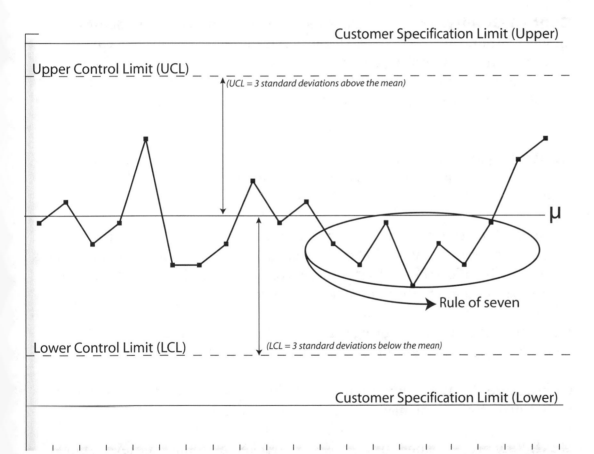

Control Costs: The process to monitor and control project costs to ensure they align with the plan. Control Costs is proactive to anticipate change and risk factors, as well as reactive to actual factors that affect project costs.

Control Limits: The upper and lower limits, used in statistical process control, that determine whether or not a process is in control. Upper and lower control limits are set at prescribed intervals and measured in standard deviations, above and below the mean. As long as the data points fall between the control limits, the process is in control.

Control Procurements: The monitoring and controlling process performed by the buyer to ensure compliance by the seller or other party. Administer Procurements compares performance against terms and conditions specified in the contract to make certain that the seller meets his or her contractual obligations. The seller's performance is typically rated or evaluated by the buyer and is communicated back to the seller.

Control Quality: The monitoring and controlling process that focuses on work product quality. Control Quality is different from Perform Quality Assurance in that Control Quality inspects actual work products and tests them against requirements, while Perform Quality Assurance looks at the overall quality process to ensure that it is being followed and that it is working effectively.

Control Risks: The process that reviews the risks that have and have not occurred on the project and evaluates how the execution of the risk management plan lines up to the plan itself.

Control Schedule: A monitoring and controlling process where the planned schedule is compared with the work performance information. If the project is ahead of schedule or behind schedule, corrective action in the form of change requests or updates to the plan may be necessary.

Control Scope: A monitoring and controlling process that ensures that changes to the scope baseline are properly controlled.

Corrective Action: Any action taken to bring future results in line with the plan. Corrective action may change the plan, or the way the plan is executed.

Cost: Any project expenditure. Costs are tracked on numerous levels, but usually tie back to a chart of accounts and nodes on the work breakdown structure.

Cost Account: See **Control Account**

Cost Aggregation: Adding activity-level costs or cost estimates to get the cost or cost estimate for a work package.

Cost-Benefit Analysis: An analysis of potential scope changes and the forecasted benefits of making these changes and the costs involved. Quality is the section on the exam where this is most relevant, and in quality management, benefits should always outweigh costs.

Cost Forecasts: Cost estimates adjusted for performance. There are several ways to do this, including using the Estimate At Complete, the Estimate To Complete, the Budgeted at Completion, the Cost Performance Index, and others.

Cost Baseline: Also known as the budget. The cost baseline is a time-phased plan for when funds will be disbursed on a project. It helps the performing organization anticipate cash flow needs for the project life-cycle. Accuracy is dependent upon a well-defined project scope and schedule, although a summary-level cost baseline is typically supplied with the project charter before the scope and schedule are fully defined.

Cost Management Plan: The plan for how project costs will be measured, monitored, and controlled. The cost management plan is created in the Develop Project Management Plan process.

Cost of Quality (COQ): The sum of all project costs expended associated with achieving quality. Cost of Quality includes a complete analysis that includes planning, execution, control, the costs of potential alternatives, and the costs of quality failure.

Cost Performance Index (CPI): Expressed as $CPI = EV \div AC$, the CPI is an earned value calculation borrowed from the discipline of cost accounting. The CPI can be useful for predicting future performance based on previous history, as well as for plotting trends over time. Conventional wisdom dictates that a CPI $>= 1$ is preferable since that indicates that the project is earning value at a cost that is better than planned, while a CPI < 1 is undesirable since it indicates that performance lags the plan.

Cost-Plus-Fee (CPF): Also known as Cost-Plus-Percentage-Of-Cost (CPPC), it is a type of contract where the buyer pays the seller's costs for performing contractual duties plus a fee that is tied to the costs. Typically this fee is calculated as a percentage of costs. This contract type places a large portion of the risk on the buyer, as the seller stands to be financially rewarded when costs run high.

Cost-Plus-Fixed-Fee (CPFF): A type of contract where the buyer pays the seller's allowable costs for performing contractual duties plus a fixed sum for performing the work. The buyer bears much of the risk by paying the seller's allowable costs; however, this contract type places some of the burden on the seller, since the seller's profit is fixed regardless of how long or expensive the contract work is.

Cost-Plus-Incentive-Fee Contract (CPIF): A type of contract where the buyer pays the seller's allowable costs for performing contractual duties plus an incentive fee tied to the seller's performance. The incentive is often calculated by the seller's performance at keeping costs down. This contract type distributes the risk between the buyer and the seller.

Cost-Reimbursable Contract (CRC): A type of contract where project costs incurred by the seller are reimbursed by the buyer. In addition, the buyer typically pays the seller an additional fee for the seller's profit. Cost-reimbursable contracts often include incentives to the seller to keep costs down, where the seller would share a percentage of the cost savings with the buyer. The share of risk distributed to the buyer and seller depends upon the specifics of the contract.

Cost Variance: Commonly abbreviated as CV, cost variance is the earned value minus the actual costs, expressed as CV = EV-AC. Cost variance is useful to represent how project spending is tracking against the plan. A positive cost variance is generally considered to be a good thing, and a negative cost variance indicates overspending and is considered to be undesirable.

Crashing: Applying additional resources to one or more activities in order to complete the work more quickly. Crashing usually increases cost more than risk and can lead to the law of diminishing returns as resource allocation passes optimal levels. Compare with Fast Tracking.

Create WBS: The planning process for creating the work breakdown structure. This process decomposes all of the work necessary to perform the project and organizes it into the work breakdown structure (WBS). The WBS dictionary, which provides expanded information on the WBS, is also an output of this process.

Criteria: Objective measures for acceptance or judging quality.

Critical Activity: Any schedule activity that appears on the project's critical path. An activity is designated as critical if its delay would delay the overall project assuming all other activities finished as planned.

Critical Chain Method: A technique for managing a project's schedule that focuses on managing the constraints caused by limited human and material resource availability. Based on the Theory of Constraints, the critical chain method manages schedule buffers and emphasizes flexibility and keeping all resources fully working.

Critical Path: One or more combinations of activities from start to finish in a project network diagram, any one of which delayed would delay the completion of the entire project.

Critical Path Method: A technique of schedule analysis, where the schedule activities are evaluated to determine the float (or slack) for each activity and the overall schedule. The critical path method uses forward pass, backward pass, and float analysis to identify all network paths, including the critical path. The reason this technique is known as the critical path method is that the path of least flexibility and highest risk (i.e., the critical path) is identified so that it may be managed appropriately.

Customer: The individual or organization who will accept the project's deliverable. The role of customer should not be confused with the sponsor even if the same person fills both roles.

Decision Tree: A tool used in risk management to analyze risk and the expected monetary value of a decision or event to evaluate the outcome of certain scenarios. Decision trees are used to evaluate uncertainty.

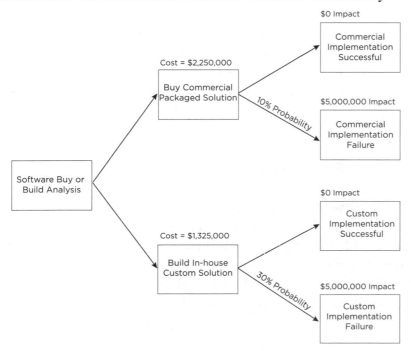

Glossary of Terms

Decomposition: A technique for progressively breaking down the scope into smaller and smaller components. Decomposition is performed on nodes of the work breakdown structure and typically stops when the decomposed pieces are small enough to be assigned and estimated for time and cost. These smaller nodes (work packages) are later decomposed further into schedule activities.

Defect: An issue when the project's product, service, or result does not match the documented scope. Defects are often costly and require rework.

Define Activities: The planning process that takes work packages from the work breakdown structure (WBS) and further decomposes them into schedule activities.

Define Scope: The planning process that results in the project scope statement. The goal of this process is to develop a detailed understanding of the scope and to document that understanding.

Deliverable: A part of the product, or the product itself, that is presented to the customer or stakeholders for acceptance.

Delphi Technique: A form of expert judgment where a group of stakeholders is asked a question or opinion in a way that prevents the people being polled from knowing who the others are. Named after the blind oracle at Delphi in ancient Greece, the Delphi Technique is often used to prevent highly-opinionated stakeholders from influencing the rest of the group.

Dependency: A relationship between two or more activities where one activity must be started or completed before another related activity may be started or completed. Considering two activities of "Purchase Laptops" and "Configure Laptops," the start of activity "Configure Laptops" might be said to be dependent upon the finish of activity "Purchase Laptops." A Dependency may be mandatory, discretionary, or external to the organization. It is also known as a logical relationship between nodes. See entries on **Start-Finish, Start-Start, Finish-Finish, and Finish-Start**.

Design Of Experiments (DOE): A technique using data analysis to determine optimal condition. It is most often used when there are multiple variables to be considered, and this technique analyzes how factors influence and change these variables. An engineer might use DOE to evaluate and determine the right combination of transmission gearing, wheel size, and tires for a new automobile within the cost constraints he or she has been given.

Determine Budget: The planning process where the individual cost estimates are compiled into the cost baseline. The cost baseline is a time-phased representation of costs so that stakeholders can see what funds will be needed and when they will be needed.

Develop Project Charter: An initiating process where the project charter is produced. This process typically occurs very early in the project, but also may take place at the beginning of each project phase. The output of this process formally authorizes the project to begin, names the project manager, and provides resources for the project.

Develop Project Management Plan: The planning process in which all subsidiary components of the project plan are integrated into a single plan that will drive the rest of the project. The subsidiary components include: the Requirements Management Plan, the Scope Management Plan, the Schedule Management Plan, the Cost Management Plan, the Quality Management Plan, the Process Improvement Plan, the Human Resource Management Plan, the Communications Management Plan, the Risk Management Plan, the Procurement Management Plan, the Stakeholder Management Plan, the Schedule Baseline, the Cost Baseline, the Scope Baseline, the Change Management Plan, and the Configuration Management Plan.

Develop Project Team: The executing process of enhancing the project team. Develop Project Team focuses on improving the overall sense of teamwork and the individual skills and abilities of the project team members.

Develop Schedule: The planning process where the activities are arranged on a calendar to create a schedule. The project schedule may take several forms and have varying degrees of detail.

Diagramming Techniques: Various means of depicting a system or a virtual concept such as a business or system process flow using drawings to show entities, relationships, and interactions.

Dictatorship: A group decision technique where one person makes the decisions for the entire group. This technique is generally not viewed favorably when it comes to the exam.

Direct and Manage Project Work: A high-level executing process as part of integration management that focuses on carrying out the project plan. Direct and Manage Project Work is closely tied to the process Monitor and Control Project Work, where the performance and quality of the execution is measured against the plan.

Direct Cost: A cost, usually measured and reported in Control Procurements, that is a direct project expense. Direct costs may include salaries of project workers, materials, and other expenses that are solely for the project. They do not include overhead or shared expenses. Generally, direct cost data is collected and reported as part of the Direct and Manage Project Execution process and becomes part of the Work Performance Information.

Distribute Information: The executing process where information is distributed to the stakeholders according to the communications management plan.

Document Analysis: A technique used in the Collect Requirements process to review existing documentation in order to gather requirements for a new product. An organization's marketing literature developed for a product that does not yet exist would be a good example of a document that would be used for analysis.

Dummy Activity: A part of Activity On Arrow (AOA) project network diagrams where a "false" schedule activity is assigned a duration of 0. A dummy activity, represented as a dashed line between two circular nodes, is used to create logical relationships.

Duration: The amount of time needed to complete a schedule activity or work package. Duration is different from effort, since duration is concerned with calendar time, while effort is concerned with work hours. For example, a schedule activity that takes 8 workers 5 days, would require 40 days of effort, but may be possible to complete in the duration of only one workweek. Durations are estimated during the Estimate Activity Durations process.

Early Finish Date (EF): Used for schedule activities on project network diagrams, the early finish date is the earliest date possible that an activity could be completed given all of the constraints, durations, and logical relationships that exist within the schedule.

Early Start Date (ES): Used for schedule activities on project network diagrams, the early start is the earliest date possible that an activity could start given all of the constraints, durations, and logical relationships that exist within the schedule.

Earned Value (EV): Also known as Budgeted Cost of Work Performed (BCWP), Earned Value is a cost accounting term representing the value of the work that has actually been completed up to a point in time. Earned Value (EV) is different from Actual Cost (AC) because EV measures what was actually done and how much that is worth, which is different from what has been spent. For instance, if the project spent $100,000 but got $200,000 of value out of that, the EV would be $200,000, while the AC would only be $100,000.

Earned Value Management (EVM): The cost accounting technique of measuring work completed (earned value) against the plan (planned value). There are various calculations to show past performance and to predict future performance.

Effort: The amount of work needed to complete an activity. Effort is different from duration, as duration measures how long something will take on a calendar. For example, 3 people working on an activity for 2 weeks might expend approximately 240 man hours of effort, but might require only 80 schedule hours (duration) to complete. Effort is determined or estimated during the Estimate Activity Durations process.

Enterprise Environmental Factors: Any factor outside of the project's control that influences the project. This could include organizational attitudes, culture, reporting relationships, government, the economy, laws, etc.

Estimate: A numerical representation of cost or time. Estimates should always specify the confidence and expected margin of error. For example, an early estimate for the design of a software database might be represented as follows: Database Design, Preliminary Estimate = 92 hours +/- 50%.

Estimate Activity Durations: The planning process that estimates how long a schedule activity should take. These estimates may be expressed as a specific number (e.g., 2 weeks) or as a range (e.g., 1 to 3 weeks). Activity durations are derived through a variety of methods, but are generally a function of the amount of work to be done, the resources applied to the task, expert judgment, and historical information.

Estimate Activity Resources: The planning process that estimates the material and human resources needed to perform a schedule activity to completion. This process may be performed before, after, or in parallel with the process of Sequence Activities.

Estimate at Complete (EAC): The forecasted amount a project should cost at its end, factoring in all of the performance metrics that have occurred at this point in the project. At a project's beginning, the Estimate at Complete (EAC) should be equal to Budgeted at Complete (BAC); however, if the project performs better than expected, or if risk occurrence is lower than expected,

EAC could be lower than BAC. Conversely, if there are performance or risk problems with the project, the EAC may well trend higher than the BAC. There are numerous methods for calculating EAC and the closely related ETC. For the purposes of exam preparation, use the formula of EAC = BAC ÷ CPI.

Estimate Costs: The planning process of estimating the costs of activities which have not been performed. Estimate Costs is performed after the scope has been defined, the activities have been decomposed, and the duration and resources for each activity have been estimated. The cost estimates are later mapped back to the work breakdown structure and are used to create the budget.

Estimate To Complete (ETC): The forecasted amount it will take to finish a project from a point in time going forward. The Estimate To Complete (ETC) factors in known performance metrics. The ETC answers the question "how much more will it cost us to complete the project at this point?" There are numerous methods for calculating the ETC and the closely related EAC. For the purposes of exam preparation, use the formula ETC = EAC - AC.

Executing Process Group: One of the five process groups. All of the 47 project processes and activities are organized into one of five process groups, Initiating, Planning, Executing, Monitoring and Controlling, or Closing. Eight of the 47 processes are executing. All executing processes and activities focus on carrying out some aspect of the project plan, and on most projects, the majority of project costs are expended during executing processes.

Exit Gate: A logical point at the end of a project phase, where an independent party reviews that phase's deliverables to determine whether or not they were completed successfully and the subsequent project phase should be initiated. Exit gates are also commonly referred to as stage gates, phase gates, or kill points.

Expected Monetary Value (EMV): A method to calculate the value of potential future outcomes, factoring in the possible costs and probability of events. Decision tree analysis is one method that uses expected monetary value.

Expert Judgment: Using knowledgeable groups or individuals to assist in project decisions. Expert judgment is a highly favored technique within project management.

Facilitated Workshops: A meeting or series of meetings where a facilitator works with project stakeholders from various disciplines to determine requirements. Joint Application Design (JAD) is an example of a specific type of facilitated workshop.

Facilitation Techniques: A technique used in integration management to move early stakeholders toward consensus on the broad goals of the project.

Fast Tracking: Performing project activities in parallel that would have been performed in sequence. It is most often the discretionary dependencies that are discarded in order to fast track activities. Fast tracking usually results in the project schedule being completed in a shorter time frame, but it typically increases risk.

Finish Date: The date that an activity is predicted (or permitted) to finish, based on the analysis of the schedule. The early finish date of a schedule activity is calculated by performing a forward pass on the project network diagram, and the late finish date is calculated by performing a backward pass.

Finish-to-Finish (FF): The logical relationship between nodes in a project network diagram. A finish-to-finish relationship between two schedule activities (e.g., activities T and W) indicates that regardless of when activity W starts, it cannot finish before activity T does.

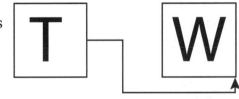

Depiction of a finish-to-finish relationship

Finish-to-Start (FS): The most common logical relationship between nodes in a project network diagram. A finish-to-start relationship between two schedule activities (e.g., activities D and E) indicates that the successor activity (activity E) cannot be started until the preceding activity (activity D) has finished.

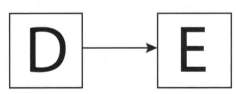

Depiction of a finish-to-start relationship

Firm-Fixed-Price Contract: See **Fixed-Price Contract**

Fishbone diagram: See **Cause-and-Effect diagram**

Fixed-Price-Incentive-Fee Contract: A type of contract where the seller is paid a fixed price for the contract but can also earn an incentive fee, paid by the buyer, for achieving predefined targets related to the seller's contract performance.

Fixed-Price Contract (AKA Lump Sum): A contract that specifies a fixed price for the deliverable paid by the buyer to the seller. Firm-fixed-price contracts transfer primary risk to the seller, since the seller is paid one price regardless of costs, efforts, or any other potential uncertainty. Firm-fixed-price contracts are also referred to simply as fixed price contracts. A purchase order is one example of a fixed-price contract.

Float (slack): The amount of time a schedule activity could be delayed without impacting the finish date of the project.

Flowcharting: A graphical, logical representation of a sequence. In project management, flowcharts are most often used in the area of quality to determine how one set of inputs may lead to one or more outcomes.

Forward Pass: A technique for calculating the early start and early finish dates of schedule activities. The forward pass is part of the critical path method and is paired with a backward pass to determine activity and schedule float and the critical path.

Free Float: The amount of time a schedule activity may slip without impacting the start of any other activities. Free float is often confused with float, but it is different in that float is concerned with disrupting the finish date of the project and the critical path, while free float is concerned with disrupting the planned start or finish date of any successor schedule activity.

Functional Manager: A manager of a department or functional group within an organization. Functional managers are vital to most companies since they have deep expertise within a given area and perform the human resource management duties for the employees of their departments. Project managers experience most of their conflict with functional managers.

Functional Organization: A very common type of organization that has strong (vertical) departments, organized around function or expertise. In a functional organization, the functional manager generally has more organizational power than the project manager, and project management may struggle to receive significant support, recognition, or authority.

Gantt Chart: See **Bar Chart**

Gatekeeper: The person responsible for evaluating the project deliverables between phases at the phase exit gates. The gatekeeper is preferably an impartial person from senior management who does not work directly on the project.

The term "gatekeeper" also has a usage in human resource management to describe a constructive team role where a person works to ensure that others are involved in a discussion or a process.

Grade: A way of evaluating the product's suitability for use. In project management low grade may be acceptable, depending on the application; however, low quality is never acceptable. For example, a project may call for producing a consumer-grade refrigerator. Producing a higher grade refrigerator would not only be uncalled for but would likely incur unjustified higher expense. While grade traditionally applies to physical items (e.g., steel, foodstuffs, video monitors), it may also apply to non-physical items (e.g., software encryption or communication signals).

Ground Rules: Rules of conduct that apply to the entire project team. Ground rules are adopted by the team to establish behavioral norms among the members.

Group Creativity Techniques: Techniques used in meetings and workshops such as brainstorming, mind mapping, and the nominal group technique to generate creative thinking and potential solutions.

Group Decision-Making Techniques: Techniques used by the project manager to move the group toward consensus or decision. The four popular group decision-making techniques for the exam are **Unanimity**, **Majority**, **Plurality**, and **Dictatorship**.

Hammock Activity: An activity that summarizes other schedule activities. While the project execution occurs at the lower (sub) activity level, hammock activities are used for tracking and reporting purposes. Most times, a hammock activity groups activities that would not be related through the work breakdown structure.

Histogram: A statistical tool that uses a column chart to show frequency of occurrence of a particular item. For instance, a histogram showing the ages of a group of people might show the number of people from 0 up to 10 years of age as the first bar, the number of people 10 up to 20 as the second bar, and so on. Histograms are widely used in quality management to determine statistical trends and identify issues or problems. See Resource Histogram.

Historical Information: Any information from previous projects that has been archived by the performing organization. Historical information can be used to help evaluate future project decisions.

Historical Relationships: A tool used in the Determine Budget process. When using historical relationships, past data or project results are considered to estimate or forecast budgets for the current project. For example, a project to build a road might be estimated at a certain amount of money per kilometer based on similar projects.

Identify Risks: The planning process of anticipating all of the risks that could happen on the project. Common tools used to facilitate risk identification include checklist analysis, diagramming techniques, SWOT analysis, and expert judgment.

Identify Stakeholders: The initiating process where all of the groups or people who will be considered on this project are identified. The resulting stakeholder register documents their names, their interests, and their involvement on the project.

Imposed Date: A date that is provided to the project and may not be moved. An imposed date may come from internal sources, such as senior management, or external sources, such as a government entity. Imposed dates are treated as constraints during Estimate Activity Durations and Develop Schedule.

Independent Estimates: Estimates generated by experts outside of the project for the purposes of comparing with those from the team. When used as part of procurement, independent estimates involve parties that do not intend to bid on the project, therefore presumably making them less likely to be biased.

Indirect Cost: A cost, usually tracked as part of a contract, that is not expended directly for the project's benefit. Indirect costs include such things as overhead and management expense that may be shared by things other than a single project. How indirect costs are tracked and accounted for varies depending on the organization or the contract.

Influence Diagram: A chart showing how a set of influencers may affect outcomes. The diagrams depict the components that go into the decision-making process. Influence diagrams are used as a tool in the Identify Risks process, along with flowcharting and cause and effect diagrams.

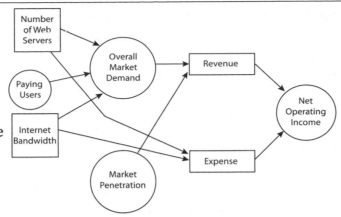

Influencer: Stakeholders who can positively or negatively affect the project due to their ability to influence the customer, the performing organization, or the project team.

Information Management Systems: A way to collect, manage, and distribute project information. A project portal or collaboration site could be examples of information management systems.

Interpersonal Skills: The ability to build trust and to relate to others.

Initiating Process Group: The processes that take place early in a project or project phase. Initiating processes are involved with starting (chartering) the project or phase and the identification of stakeholders. Only two of the 47 processes are initiating processes.

Input: Something needed or used by a process to create the outputs for that process.

Inspection: Reviewing the functionality or suitability of a product, service, or result against the requirements. The desired result of inspection is acceptance.

Interviews: A meeting between a business analyst and a user, key stakeholder, or expert to gather and document requirements.

Invitation for Bid (IFB): See **Request for Proposal**

Ishikawa Diagram: See **Cause-and-Effect Diagram**

Issue: An unresolved threat or problem on the project, or a point of disagreement.

Issue Log: A document where all stakeholder issues can be recorded. The issue log is an important tool for tracking, communicating, and managing issues.

Kill Point: See **Exit Gate**

Knowledge Area: One of the competency domains within project management. The 47 processes of project management are grouped into ten knowledge areas.

Lag: Changing the finish-to-start relationship between two schedule activities so that the dependent activity cannot start until a given amount of time after its preceding activity finishes. Given that activity B (erecting a building frame) cannot start until Activity A (pouring concrete) has finished, if 3 days of lag time were applied to activity A (e.g., to allow the concrete to cure), then activity B could not start until 3 days after activity A finishes. Lags are used to represent calendar time that must elapse when no actual work is taking place by project resources. (Contrast with "lead" below.)

Late Finish Date (LF): The latest possible date a schedule activity can finish without impacting the critical path, assuming all estimated durations are accurate. The late finish (LF) is calculated as follows: LF = EF + Float, or by performing a backward pass on the project network diagram.

Late Start Date (LS): The latest possible date a schedule activity can start without impacting the critical path, assuming all estimated durations are accurate. The late start is calculated as follows: LS = LF − DURATION + 1, or LS = ES + Float, or by performing a backward pass on the project network diagram.

Lead: Changing the finish-to-start relationship between two schedule activities so that the dependent activity can start before preceding activity finishes. Given that activity B cannot start until Activity A has finished, if 2 days of lead time were applied to activity B, then activity B could start 2 days before activity A finishes. Leads are used to efficiently manage the schedule and get a head start on certain activities where possible.

Lessons Learned: The formally documented information the team has acquired during execution of the project. Lessons learned specifically focus on variances in the project and document how the team would plan or execute differently if they had a specific component of the project to perform again.

Level of Effort (LOE): Supporting work that does not produce an actual deliverable such as support or follow-up activities. Level of effort is often difficult to measure effectively and to relate back to a product or service. It is tracked and reported at a high level.

Logical Relationship: See **Dependency**

Majority: A group decision-making technique where a simple majority of votes is enough to make a decision. Many political elections are examples of the majority technique, where anything over 50% is sufficient to decide the outcome.

Make-or-Buy Analysis: A technique used in Plan Procurement Management. Make-or-buy analysis looks at the component of the project to determine whether it is rational to make it internally or to buy it from an outside vendor. Several factors go into this decision; however, *all other things being equal, buying is favored over making*.

Manage Project Team: The executing process of directing the project team to complete the work of the project plan, monitoring their performance, and working to improve performance and resolve issues where necessary.

Manage Stakeholder Engagement: The executing process where the project team communicates and works with stakeholders to ensure their needs are addressed and their issues are resolved.

Market Research: Looking outside of the performing organization to gather information about current trends and capabilities in the industry. Market research is a tool used in the Plan Procurement Management process.

Matrix Organization: An increasingly popular organization that is a hybrid between a functional and a projectized organization. A matrix organization provides a project manager with control over the projects, while preserving the functional manager's control over departments. The project manager "borrows" resources from one or more departments for a temporary project, while the functional manager performs administrative and human resource duties for the resources.

Meetings: Live or online sessions where the participants exchange information and collaborate in real time. A meeting is a common tool used frequently in the processes.

Methodology:A set of steps to manage a project. Methodologies are an organization's specific implementation of the processes of project management. They typically include checklists, procedures, and document templates.

Milestone:A notable event in the project. A milestone may be a date, a project deliverable, or any significant point of interest.

Milestone Schedule: A high-level schedule that shows only significant schedule points. A milestone schedule is often supplied along with the project charter, where the milestones become schedule constraints.

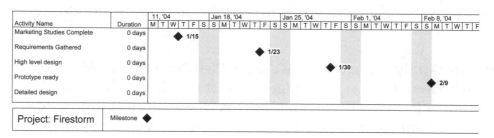

A Milestone Schedule, With Four Milestones Represented

Modeling: A tool used in time management and risk management. Modeling and simulation can help identify problems or areas of risk with the project before they actually occur. What-if scenario analysis and Monte Carlo analysis are examples of modeling techniques.

Monitor and Control Project Work: A high-level integration process used to ensure that the project work being performed matches the plan. If the results do not line up with the plan, either the way the work is being performed is altered, or the plan is changed to reflect a more realistic scenario.

Monitoring and Controlling Processes: One of the five process groups. Monitoring and controlling processes constitute 11 of the overall 47 processes which generally measure the work results against the plan and make adjustments or take corrective action where variances exist.

Monte Carlo Analysis: The risk management technique used to compute large numbers of possible scenarios and identify areas of high risk. Monte Carlo analysis is almost always performed by computer due to the high numbers of scenarios considered. The output is a range of possible schedule due dates and costs.

Multi-Criteria Decision Analysis: A tool used during interviewing to score and rank candidates.

Networking: The tool used to build or leverage existing relationships to help complete the project work.

Node: A point on a project network diagram. In activity on node diagrams, a node represents a schedule activity, while in activity on arrow diagrams, a node is simply a connecting point.

Observations (Job Shadowing): Watching project users or subject matter experts work as a way to gather scope and requirements.

Operations: Ongoing activities needed to continue business. Operations are not considered part of a project, but they often are considered part of a program.

Opportunity: Anything that could have a positive impact on the project's scope, schedule, or cost. Opportunities are also considered as risks to the project, as they represent uncertainty.

Opportunity Cost: The value of a project that was not performed so that another one could be. Opportunity cost is typically calculated by taking the value of the best alternative that was passed up.

Organization Chart: A chart that shows the reporting relationships among a group of people working for an organization or for a project.

Organizational Breakdown Structure (OBS):A chart that relates work packages to the parties in the organization responsible for their completion.

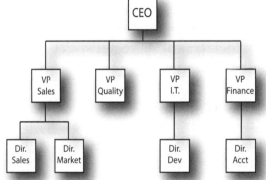

An organizational chart

Organizational Process Assets: All historical information or knowledge that an organization has at its disposal, which may be used to help future projects. Examples of organizational process assets would include templates, forms, research results, work breakdown structures, quality standards, benchmarks, previous plans, contracts, etc.

Output: Something coming out of a process. For example, in the process Create WBS, the work breakdown structure is part of the scope baseline, which is the output.

Parametric Estimating: Using organizational process assets such as historical data to formulate estimates based on past performance or results. Parametric estimating is considered to work best on highly linear and scalable components with adequate historical information. The better the parametric model and the information coming in, the more reliable the parametric estimate will be.

Pareto Chart: A column chart, or histogram, used in quality management to show problems and help the team to know where to focus their efforts based on frequency of the problem.

Material Defects by Overseas Suppliers

Path: A series of schedule activities that have a relationship that carries through from the project's start to the finish.

Path Convergence: A point at which two or more network paths converge.

Percent Complete: An estimated or actual value showing how much of the activity's work has been completed. Percent complete is sometimes used to report on various levels of the work breakdown structure as well.

Perform Integrated Change Control: The monitoring and controlling process where requested and unrequested changes are reviewed according to the change control system. Perform Integrated Change Control focuses on changes to the product, service, or result as well as the organizational process assets that endure past the project.

Perform Qualitative Risk Analysis: A planning process to look at non-quantifiable aspects of each risk. Perform Qualitative Risk Analysis prioritizes the risks using the probability impact matrix, according to which risks have the highest factors of likelihood and potential impact.

Perform Quality Assurance: The executing process that focuses on the overall quality activities to ensure that all of the plans are being followed and that the project meets the quality requirements. Contrast with **Control Quality**.

Perform Quantitative Risk Analysis: The planning process where all risks are analyzed and assigned a value as it relates to the risk's impact on the project. Risks are typically quantified in terms of potential impact on budget or schedule so they may be weighed against the risk tolerance of the key stakeholders.

Performing Organization: The organization responsible for executing the project. A project manager typically works for the performing organization to manage planning, execution, monitoring and controlling, and closing activities. While the project sponsor typically works for the performing organization, the customer may or may not.

Personnel Assessment Tools: Surveys and assessments to give the project manager and the team greater insight into team member working styles and preferences. A personality assessment would be one example of a personnel assessment tool.

Phase: A grouping of project activities. Many projects are divided into two or more phases in order to provide a point where the deliverables can be evaluated. Phases are separated by exit gates or kill points where someone who does not directly work with the project (the gatekeeper) evaluates the deliverables to determine whether or not the next phase is initiated. Phases should not be confused with process groups.

Plan Communications Management: The planning process that analyzes the project, the stakeholders, and the communications needs of the project and creates the communications management plan.

Plan Human Resource Management: The planning process that determines how the project will be organized in terms of the personnel. Plan Human Resource Management determines the project roles, the project organizational chart, and the responsibility assignment matrix. The most significant output of this process is the human resource plan, which is a primary component of the project management plan.

Plan Procurement Management: The planning process where the project team performs make-or-buy analysis and decides what goods and services will be created or performed internally and what will be procured from external sources.

Additionally, the procurement documents are created, and potential sellers are identified.

Plan Quality Management: The planning process where quality targets are identified. Plan Quality Management also determines how these targets will be met and spells out how the other two quality processes (Perform Quality Assurance and Control Quality) will be carried out.

Plan Risk Management: The process that creates the risk management plan. Plan Risk Management focuses on planning for the five subsequent risk processes.

Plan Risk Responses: The planning process that determines how each identified risk will be mitigated, avoided, transferred, shared, exploited, enhanced, or accepted.

Plan Scope Management: The process in the scope knowledge area that plans how the other five scope management processes will be carried out. The two major outputs of this process are the scope management plan and the requirements management plan.

Planned Finish Date: The date a schedule activity should be finished if that activity's work begins on time and is completed according to plan.

Planned Start Date: The date work on a schedule activity should begin according to the plan.

Planned Value (PV): Also known as the Budgeted Cost of Work Scheduled (BCWS). An earned value management term representing the value that should have been realized on the project at a given point in the schedule. Planned Value (PV) is contrasted with Earned Value (EV). See Earned Value for more information.

Planning Processes: The process group containing all of the processes associated with planning or creating a plan. 24 of the 47 processes of project management are planning processes, which accounts for more than any other process group.

Plurality: A group decision-making technique where the largest block of individuals decides the outcome. Plurality differs from **Majority** in that plurality does not require more than 50% to be in agreement. For example, if 30% vote in favor of outcome A, and 30% in favor of outcome B, and 40% in favor of outcome C, outcome C would carry the group because it represents the largest block. It is not uncommon for the plurality technique to employ a run-off between the two options that received the highest votes until one option receives a true majority.

PMBOK: Different from the PMBOK Guide, the PMBOK is an acronym for the project management body of knowledge, which includes the sum of all knowledge in the profession of project management.

PMBOK Guide: The ANSI Standard for project management. PMBOK Guide is an abbreviation for the full title of the standard, which is "A Guide to the Project Management Body of Knowledge." The standard is defined as being applicable to most projects, most of the time.

Portfolio: A group of projects intended to achieve a business result. A portfolio usually refers to all of the projects in an organization.

Position Description: A document describing the responsibilities of a specific project team role. For most positions, the position description should be created in advance of filling the position. This document can be a useful tool for recruiting.

Precedence Diagramming Method (PDM): The technique that uses the analysis of logical relationships to create Activity on Node diagrams. See entry for Activity on Node for more information.

Preventive Action: Action taken proactively in order to prevent or avoid anticipated future problems. Preventive action is tied to risk management.

Probability and Impact Matrix: A graphical risk analysis tool that plots the likelihood (probability) of each risk event on the Y (vertical) axis, and the risk event's potential impact on the X (horizontal) axis. The X and Y values are multiplied together to give a risk score. Risks with the highest scores are prioritized higher for analysis and response.

Procedure: A set of rules to be followed in order to achieve a desired result.

Process: A set of inputs, tools, and techniques, used together to produce one or more specific outputs for the project. There are 47 processes of project management which make up the core of the PMBOK Guide. Each process is organized so that it belongs to one knowledge area and one process group.

Process Group: An organization of the 47 processes of project management by overall function. Every process is assigned to a single process group according to whether its purpose is initiating, planning, executing, monitoring and controlling, or closing the project.

Process Improvement Plan: The quality management plan for how activities will be reviewed and analyzed so that efficiency improves as the project progresses.

Procurement Management Plan: The component of the project plan that is used to manage one or more contracts that exist on the project. The procurement management plan details the types of contracts to be used and governs how changes to the contract will be managed, how claims will be processed, and how contract-related communication will be handled. Any information known about the procurement process will be detailed in this plan, and it should specify the process by which any contract(s) may be updated.

Product: The primary deliverable of the project. Projects may produce products, services, or results, and these must be accepted by the customer or sponsor.

Product Life Cycle: The different market phases of a product. Not to be confused with project life cycle.

Product Scope: All of the requirements and functionality necessary to create an acceptable product, service, or result.

Product Scope Description: A document that describes the characteristic of the project's product. The product scope description is progressively elaborated. Its main purpose is to help create a common understanding of the product among stakeholders.

Program: A group of related projects, managed together, usually to realize some common efficiencies. Programs may also include ongoing operations, which individual projects do not have.

Program Management: Coordinated management of two or more projects in order to realize common efficiency.

Program Management Office: The group within the performing organization responsible for establishing project standards, supporting with expert knowledge, and providing templates and a repository for organizational process assets and other historical information. The actual authority of program management offices varies according to organization and industry.

Progressive Elaboration: An iterative approach where planning occurs in cycles rather than up front. Projects which use progressive elaboration typically do some planning, some execution, some monitoring and controlling, and then repeat that cycle.

Project:A time-limited undertaking to deliver a unique product, service, or outcome. In this definition, "unique" means that it has never been performed by this organization before. Projects do not include ongoing operations, although they do need to consider them up front.

Project Calendar:A calendar that is specific to this project, factoring in the constraints of all participating organizations and geographical and demographic regions. Project calendars show which days will be working days and which ones will be non-working.

Project Charter: The document that creates the project. Although it may be created by the project manager, it is signed by the sponsor, and it names the project manager and gives him or her the authority to manage the project.

Project Coordinator: The project role that is weaker than a project manager in terms of authority. A project coordinator can typically assign project resources but is not authorized to spend project funds. When the role of project coordinator exists on a project, it is in the place of a project manager. Project coordinators report to someone from senior management who has ultimate responsibility for the project.

Project Expeditor: The project role that has some project responsibility but little organizational authority. Project expeditors ensure that tasks are completed on time and that the project is progressing as planned; however, they cannot assign project resources or spend project funds. Project expeditors report to someone from senior management who has ultimate responsibility for the project.

Project Life Cycle:A group of project phases specified by an organization's project management methodology. The project life cycle is made up of all of the project phases, viewed as a whole. Projects are divided into phases in order to create logical management and decision points. See Phase for more information.

Project Management Information System (PMIS): The system used to support management of the project. It serves as a repository for information and a tool to help with communication and tracking. The PMIS supports the project from beginning to end.

Project Management Office (PMO): A group within the performing organization responsible for providing standards and guidance to projects and project managers. The role and responsibility of the PMO varies from organization to organization, with some PMOs directly accountable for project success.

Project Management Plan: The plan for how the project will be managed. The project management plan is a formal, approved document composed of the other planning documents. Once approved, the project management plan is placed under control. The project management plan is also known, more succinctly, as the project plan.

Scope Baseline	Schedule Baseline	Cost Baseline	Scope Management Plan	Requirements Management Plan	Schedule Management Plan	Cost Management Plan	Quality Management Plan	Process Improvement Plan	Human Resource Plan	Communications Management Plan	Risk Management Plan	Procurement Management Plan	Stakeholder Management Plan	Change Management Plan	Configuration Management Plan

Project Management Professional (PMP): A project management certification managed by the Project Management Institute.

Project Management Software: Software to automate and assist the processes of project management, including the gathering, storing, updating, and reporting of information and the calculating of schedules and budgets.

Project Management System: All of the processes, people, tools and techniques, and methodologies used to manage the project. The project management system should be described in the project plan.

Project Manager: The role of the person ultimately responsible for the project. The project manager has the authority to spend project budget and to assign project resources in order to realize the project's goals.

Project Organization Chart: A graphical chart depicting reporting relationships of all team members, specifically for this project. A project organization chart may differ from the standard organization chart in that it is not unusual for a project manager to have someone who ranks higher than him in the organization reporting to him on the project.

Project Plan: See **Project Management Plan Project Schedule:** A central component of the project plan that prescribes when activities should take place and in what order.

Project Scope: All of the work to be performed on the project. The project scope is documented in the project scope statement and the work breakdown structure.

Project Scope Statement: The document that states the project requirements by describing objectives, deliverables, boundaries, and acceptance criteria.

Projectized Organization: An organizational structure that is arranged around projects. In a projectized organization, the project manager also fills the role of functional manager for the project team, meaning that the human resources report directly to the project manager. Projectized organizations give the project manager a great degree of control and authority; however, that control comes with more administrative responsibility that can reduce the project manager's ability to focus on the actual project.

Prototypes: Functional or non-functional incomplete models of a product to allow stakeholders to interact with it and refine design before it is constructed.

Quality: Conformance to specifications.

Quality Control Measurements: The results after the tools and techniques of Control Quality have been applied.

Quality Management Plan: The plan which specifies how the quality policy will be implemented on a project. The quality management plan is a component of the project plan.

Questionnaires and Surveys: A tool used in Collect Requirements to gather scope from a large group of stakeholders.

Regulation: A requirement that must be followed, issued by an authority.

Request for Information (RFI): Also known as an RFI, a request for information is issued by a buyer to potential sellers to supply information relevant to the procurement process.

Request for Proposal (RFP): A formal document, issued by the buyer to potential sellers. Potential sellers respond to the request for proposal with a proposal for how they would satisfy the buyer's request. The response should answer all of the questions asked by the buyer in the RFP.

Request for Quotation (RFQ): A formal document, issued by the buyer to potential sellers. An RFQ typically requests pricing on pre-existing products or offerings. Potential sellers respond to the request for quotation with pricing.

Requirement: Something the product or service must do or satisfy in order to satisfy an underlying need.

Requirements Documentation: A document that ties each deliverable back to the underlying need it will address.

Requirements Management Plan: The plan, produced in Plan Scope Management, that specifies how the requirements will be collected, documented, and updated.

Requirements Traceability Matrix: A table showing the stakeholder or origin that produced each requirement and the functionality that will address that requirement. This is a useful document since projects may have difficulty remembering how and why a particular requirement came to be.

Reserve: Time or funding that is added to the schedule or budget to protect against overrun. Reserve is used so that the project manager can deal with routine overruns without having to reformulate the cost or schedule baselines after each individual slippage.

Reserve Analysis: A technique used to determine how much cost or schedule reserve is appropriate for a given activity, work breakdown structure node, or time or funding category.

Residual Risk: Risks that remain after planning has been completed. All projects carry some residual risks.

Resources: People, organizations, or materials that can be used on a project.

Resource Breakdown Structure (RBS): A graphical organizational chart that groups resources together by their function. For example, an RBS might show all of the database designers grouped together, and all of the programmers. Within the programmers node, they may be further subdivided by the software language in which they program. This is useful for resource leveling. The RBS is most often used for human resources but may also include material resources. See Resource Leveling for more information.

Resource Calendar: A calendar that shows the dates project resources will be in use on the project and days when they will not be used. This facilitates making these resources available to other projects or needs within the organization.

Resource Histogram: A column chart that graphically represents when a resource will be in use on the project. Resource histograms provide a good visual representation of how project resources will be used over time.

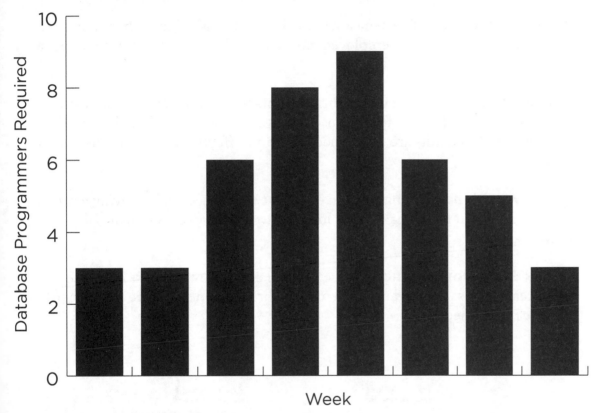

Resource Leveling: The technique of making the resource requirements match up with the organizational realities. Resource leveling effectively means adjusting the requirements to meet what the organization can supply, and negotiating with the organization to make sure it can supply the project's resource needs. All of this takes place within the cost and time constraints imposed upon the project. One application of resource leveling would be to try to ensure that all resources work a 40 hour week and that no overtime is incurred.

Resource Optimization Techniques: Using optimization techniques such as resource leveling to match the schedule for when a task needs to be completed to a resource's availability.

Glossary of Terms

Responsibility Assignment Matrix:A grid where the work packages are represented in the rows, and the resources are represented in the columns. Each cell shows what responsibility (if any) a particular group of resources will have in relation to a work package.

Rework: Anything done to make a product or service conform to specifications.

Risk: Any unknown on the project. Risks may be positive or negative.

Risk Acceptance: The decision to deal with the risk if and when it occurs. When risk acceptance is employed, no additional planning or steps will be taken before the risk event occurs.

Risk Audits: Periodic reviews of risk events to see if the events that were anticipated are the ones that are occurring and if new risks have become apparent. Risk audits are concerned with how effective the overall risk process is.

Risk Avoidance: Taking steps to eliminate the project risk. Moving a project site from a potentially hazardous location would be an example of risk avoidance.

Risk Breakdown Structure:A graphical chart showing risks organized into categories. The organization of a risk breakdown structure will vary from project to project.

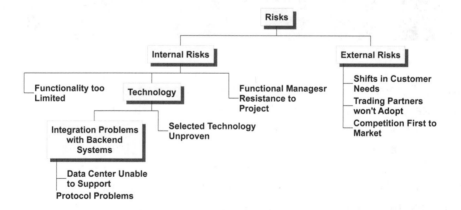

Risk Database: The risk database contains all information on identified risks throughout the life of the project. The risk database will be used by future projects to assist in risk analysis.

Risk Enhancement:A risk management strategy for making a positive uncertainty even better for the project. For example, if labor rates for work in another country came in at 75% of what was expected, a risk enhancement strategy might be to move even more work to that location to capitalize on the resource.

Risk Exploitation:A risk management strategy for making a positive uncertainty more likely to occur.

Risk Management Plan: The component of the project plan that shows how subsequent risk processes and activities will be performed.

Risk Mitigation: Looking to decrease either the likelihood of an identified risk's occurrence, or its impact on the project if it does occur.

Risk Reassessment: Cleaning up the risk register by removing risks that are no longer relevant and adding any new risks that have been identified.

Risk Register: The document containing all identified risks relevant to the project. The risk register, which is a component of the project plan, contains information about each risk and is updated throughout the project.

Risk Transference: The risk response technique of shifting the risk to another entity, usually a subcontractor or a vendor specializing in that type of risk. Firm fixed price contracts would be one type of risk transference, as would be purchasing an insurance policy that protected the project.

Risk Urgency Assessment:A tool of Perform Qualitative Risk Analysis to prioritize the risks by the order in which they would be expected to occur to help determine which ones get the most prompt attention and resources.

Role: The part a person will play on the project. For example, a senior person in the organization may play a junior role on a given project.

Rolling Wave Planning:A planning technique that does not seek to answer all questions or plan all project activities at the beginning. Instead, only imminent project activities are planned in detail, while activities further in the future are planned at a higher level.

Root Cause Analysis:A technique that places a premium on understanding the underlying reasons behind a problem rather than focusing on the problem or symptom. Root cause analysis is used in quality management as a tool to prevent future defects.

Scatter Diagram:A chart that plots events against a dependent and an independent variable to identify correlation and spot trends. Scatter diagrams are most often used in quality management, specifically in the Perform Quality Control process.

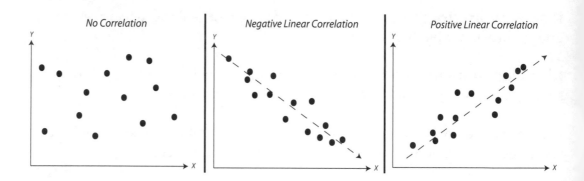

Three different scatter diagrams

Schedule Activity: See **Activity**

Schedule Data: Supporting information related to the schedule that would not appear on the schedule network diagram.

Schedule Network Analysis: The techniques of performing a forward pass or a backward pass through the schedule to determine early start, early finish, late start, and late finish dates along with float and free float.

Schedule Compression: Work to reduce the overall calendar time for a project. Crashing and fast-tracking are examples of schedule compression techniques.

Schedule Forecasts: Updated projections for the activities and overall schedule based on performance and actual data.

Schedule Management Plan: The plan for how the project schedule will be measured, monitored, and controlled. The schedule management plan is created in the Develop Project Management Plan process.

Schedule Tool:A software tool that uses schedule data and manual adjustments to automatically calculate and update the schedule.

Scope Baseline: The combination of the scope statement, the WBS and the WBS dictionary. When these documents are put under control they become the scope baseline.

Scope Management Plan: The plan, created in Plan Scope Management, that describes how the other five scope management processes will be carried out.

Sequence Activities: The planning process of Sequence Activities takes the schedule activities from the activity list and sequences them according to the order in which they must be performed. This is accomplished by determining which activities are dependent upon other activities. This process produces project network diagrams as its primary output, and these are used later to create the schedule.

Seven Basic Quality Tools: Seven tools used frequently in quality management. They are: cause-and-effect diagrams, flowcharts, check sheets, Pareto diagrams, histograms, control charts, and scatter diagrams.

Sponsor: The person responsible for funding the project. The sponsor is typically someone from senior management and may or may not be the same person as the customer.

Stage Gate: See **Exit Gate**

Stakeholder Register: A table that documents all of the project stakeholders, their interest on the project, and often their importance on this project.

Start-to-Finish: A logical relationship between nodes in a project network diagram. A start-to-finish relationship between two scheduled activities (e.g., activities A and B) indicates that regardless of when activity B starts, it cannot finish until Activity A begins.

Start-to-Start: A logical relationship between nodes in a project network diagram. A start-to-start relationship between two scheduled activities (e.g., activities Q and R) indicates that activity R cannot start until activity Q starts.

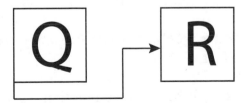

Statement of Work (SOW): The narrative description of the project's product, service, or result. The statement of work is intended to foster a common understanding among stakeholders.

Statistical Sampling: Using a representative sample to draw statistical inferences about a larger population.

SWOT Analysis: An technique used to gather and categorize strengths, weaknesses, opportunities, and threats about a population. Strengths and weaknesses are internal, while opportunities and threats are external to the organization.

System: The rules, processes, procedures, people, and other elements that support an outcome or process. Several systems are defined in project management, including the project management information system, the change control system, and the work authorization system.

Task: A schedule activity. Some project management resources treat a task as a sub-activity, or a further decomposition of a schedule activity; however, for the purposes of the exam, you should think of the two terms as being equivalent.

To-Complete Performance Index (TCPI$_C$): The performance the project would need to achieve to end on target. In this case, a lower index is good, since it means that you could underperform and still meet your target, while an index of greater than one is bad since you are essentially saying that you would need to overperform against the plan in order to meet your goals or targets.

Team: The entire group responsible for planning, executing, and monitoring and controlling the project. The project team typically involves the sponsor as well.

Team-Building Activities: Exercises designed to strengthen the sense of team. Team building works best when the activities are begun early, and the focus should last throughout the project.

Team Performance Assessments: Evaluations conducted to gauge a team's effectiveness.

Template: A document that serves as a starting point for a particular output. Examples of templates include documents with mandatory headers and placeholders, complete examples from previous projects, or commercially available documents. Templates are often provided by the project management office, and they may be generic or specific.

Threat: Anything that potentially jeopardizes the project's planned scope, time, or cost. Due to their uncertainty, threats are considered to be risks. Also see Opportunity.

Three-Point Estimate: A technique for estimating duration or cost. The three-point estimate uses a pessimistic, optimistic, and realistic estimate to calculate. The formula most often associated with the three-point estimate is a weighted average expressed as follows: Estimate = (Pessimistic + (4 × Realistic) + Optimistic) ÷ 6. This formula is also commonly referred to as a PERT estimate.

Time and Materials Contract (T&M): A type of contract where the buyer reimburses the seller for the seller's time at a predefined rate, and for material expenses the seller incurs on the project. A pure time and materials contract shifts the primary risk to the buyer, as there are no direct financial incentives for the seller to control labor or material costs.

Top-Down Estimate: See **Analogous Estimate**

Tornado Diagram: A graphical chart used in Perform Quantitative Risk Analysis. Tornado diagrams show how sensitive the project is to risk by depicting the effect of a single variable change, while holding all other variables steady.

Change in project cost due to a 10% change in labor costs with all other project costs held constant.

Change in Project Costs

Total Float: The sum of all time that an individual activity can slip from its early start date without affecting the finish date of the project.

Total Quality Management (TQM): A philosophy of quality management that focuses on bringing quality into the entire organization. TQM became popular in the second half of the twentieth century by expanding the view of quality beyond the product to include all people and processes within an organization. Feigenbaum, Deming, Juran, Crosby, and Ishikawa are considered to be the primary architects of TQM.

Training: Efforts to build the capabilities of the individuals and the team. Non-project-specific training should generally be paid for by the functional manager or the department.

Trend Analysis: A statistical forecasting technique to predict results related to scope, time, or cost by plotting a trend line based on previous performance. Run charts are often used in trend analysis to create trend lines.

Trigger: A warning sign that a risk has occurred, is occurring, or is about to occur.

Triple Constraint: The intersection of scope, time, and cost on a project. The triple constraint emphasizes that one of these cannot change without affecting at least one of the other two.

Unanimity: A group decision technique where everyone on the team must agree with the decision before a decision is made. A jury is a common example where unanimity is used.

Validate Scope: The monitoring and controlling process of inspecting project deliverables and gaining their formal acceptance from the appropriate stakeholders.

Value Engineering: The practice of trying to get more out of the project in every way. The goal of value engineering is to decrease costs, increase the bottom line, improve quality, and shorten the schedule, without negatively affecting the scope.

Variance: A difference between the plan and the executed results.

Variance Analysis: A tool used frequently in controlling processes to look at the difference between the plan and the results and to understand the contributing factors.

Variance at Complete (VAC): The difference between what was budgeted and what is forecasted to have been spent. The VAC is calculated by subtracting the estimate at complete from the budgeted at completion, or VAC = BAC - EAC.

Vendor Bid Analysis: An analysis of what the project should cost performed by aggregating individual vendor bids.

Verification: Inspecting the product, service, or result to ensure that the processes and deliverables meet quality requirements.

Verified Deliverables: The primary output of Control Quality. Verified deliverables are deliverables that have been reviewed to determine that they are correct.

Virtual Team: A team that is not colocated. Virtual teams are connected by electronic means to enhance collaboration.

War Room: A centralized room for project planning that may also be used for execution and other project activities. A common use of the war room is to co-locate the team for a period of time.

Work Authorization System: Part of the overall project management information system (PMIS), the work authorization system is used to ensure that work gets performed at the right time and in the right sequence. It may be an informal e-mail sent by the project manager to a functional manager, or a formal system to get an assigned resource released to complete scheduled work.

Work Breakdown Structure (WBS): A graphical, hierarchical chart composed of nodes that are logically organized from top to bottom. The WBS represents all of the work and only the work to be performed on the project. Each node on the WBS has a unique number used to locate and identify it.

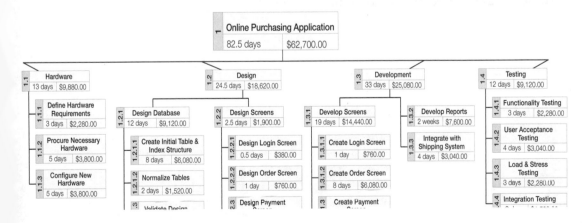

Example WBS

Work Breakdown Structure (WBS) Dictionary: The WBS dictionary is a companion document to the work breakdown structure (WBS). Since the WBS is a graphical chart, there is not room for all of the supporting information and attribute information that accompanies each node. Therefore, the WBS dictionary provides a place for this information and is organized so that it corresponds back to each node on the WBS. Supporting information found in the WBS dictionary may include the following: time and cost estimates, the person or group responsible for the deliverable, due dates, further descriptions, etc.

Work Package: The lowest hierarchical level of the work breakdown structure. Work packages represent deliverables on the project and should be small enough to estimate for cost and duration. Work packages are further decomposed into activities for further estimating and scheduling purposes.

Work Performance Data: Raw, unprocessed data about how the team has executed the work. Compare with work performance information.

Work Performance Information: Processed information on how the work is being performed, gathered during the executing processes. Work performance information begins to flow as soon as the work is executed. Among other things, it includes the status of deliverables, how things are performing against cost and schedule goals, and how the product measures up against quality standards.

Work Performance Reports: Useful and often actionable formats of work performance information.

Workaround: A response to an unplanned risk event.

Index

Index

Index

Index

Index

Use the key inside the back cover flap to access:

http://insite.velociteach. com/book_key/keynote.htm

PMP Exam content, additional questions, and study aids

If your book did not come with a Key to InSite on the inside back cover, it may not be authentic. If you do not have a Key to InSite, you may purchase one at http://insite.velociteach.com.